GU00793188

Proceeds of Crime Act 2002

CHAPTER 29

CONTENTS

PART 3

CONFISCATION: SCOTLAND

Enforcement abroad

Interpretation

General

PART 4

CONFISCATION: NORTHERN IRELAND

Confiscation orders

Procedural matters

Reconsideration

General

PART 5

CIVIL RECOVERY OF THE PROCEEDS ETC. OF UNLAWFUL CONDUCT

CHAPTER 1

INTRODUCTORY

CHAPTER 2

CIVIL RECOVERY IN THE HIGH COURT OR COURT OF SESSION

Proceedings for recovery orders

Interim receiving orders (England and Wales and Northern Ireland)

Interim administration orders (Scotland)

CHAPTER 3

RECOVERY OF CASH IN SUMMARY PROCEEDINGS

Searches

PART 7

MONEY LAUNDERING

Offences

Consent

Disclosures

Interpretation

PART 8

INVESTIGATIONS

CHAPTER 1

INTRODUCTION

CHAPTER 2

ENGLAND AND WALES AND NORTHERN IRELAND

Judges and courts

Production orders

Search and seizure warrants

Disclosure orders

Customer information orders

CHAPTER 3

SCOTLAND

CHAPTER 4

INTERPRETATION

PART 9

INSOLVENCY ETC.

Part 10

Information

Part 11

Co-operation

PART 12

MISCELLANEOUS AND GENERAL

Miscellaneous

General

Proceeds of Crime Act 2002

2002 CHAPTER 29

An Act to establish the Assets Recovery Agency and make provision about the appointment of its Director and his functions (including Revenue functions), to provide for confiscation orders in relation to persons who benefit from criminal conduct and for restraint orders to prohibit dealing with property, to allow the recovery of property which is or represents property obtained through unlawful conduct or which is intended to be used in unlawful conduct, to make provision about money laundering, to make provision about investigations relating to benefit from criminal conduct or to property which is or represents property obtained through unlawful conduct or to money laundering, to make provision to give effect to overseas requests and orders made where property is found or believed to be obtained through criminal conduct, and for connected purposes.   [24th July 2002]

B E IT ENACTED by the Queen's most Excellent Majesty, by and with the advice and consent of the Lords Spiritual and Temporal, and Commons, in this present Parliament assembled, and by the authority of the same, as follows:—

PART 1

ASSETS RECOVERY AGENCY

1   **The Agency and its Director**

(1)   There shall be an Assets Recovery Agency (referred to in this Act as the Agency).

(2)   The Secretary of State must appoint a Director of the Agency (referred to in this Act as the Director).

(3)   The Director is a corporation sole.

(4)   The Director may—
        (a)   appoint such persons as members of staff of the Agency, and

(b)   make such arrangements for the provision of services,

as he considers appropriate for or in connection with the exercise of his functions.

(5)   But the Director must obtain the approval of the Minister for the Civil Service as to the number of staff appointed under subsection (4)(a).

(6)   Anything which the Director is authorised or required to do may be done by –

    (a)   a member of staff of the Agency, or

    (b)   a person providing services under arrangements made by the Director,

if authorised by the Director (generally or specifically) for that purpose.

(7)   Schedule 1 contains further provisions about the Agency and the Director.

2   Director's functions: general

(1)   The Director must exercise his functions in the way which he considers is best calculated to contribute to the reduction of crime.

(2)   In exercising his functions as required by subsection (1) the Director must –

    (a)   act efficiently and effectively;

    (b)   have regard to his current annual plan (as approved by the Secretary of State in accordance with Schedule 1).

(3)   The Director may do anything (including the carrying out of investigations) which he considers is –

    (a)   appropriate for facilitating, or

    (b)   incidental or conducive to,

the exercise of his functions.

(4)   But subsection (3) does not allow the Director to borrow money.

(5)   In considering under subsection (1) the way which is best calculated to contribute to the reduction of crime the Director must have regard to any guidance given to him by the Secretary of State.

(6)   The guidance must indicate that the reduction of crime is in general best secured by means of criminal investigations and criminal proceedings.

3   Accreditation and training

(1)   The Director must establish a system for the accreditation of financial investigators.

(2)   The system of accreditation must include provision for –

    (a)   the monitoring of the performance of accredited financial investigators, and

    (b)   the withdrawal of accreditation from any person who contravenes or fails to comply with any condition subject to which he was accredited.

(3)   A person may be accredited –

    (a)   in relation to this Act;

    (b)   in relation to particular provisions of this Act.

(4)   But the accreditation may be limited to specified purposes.

(5) A reference in this Act to an accredited financial investigator is to be construed accordingly.

(6) The Director may charge a person —
   (a) for being accredited as a financial investigator, and
   (b) for the monitoring of his performance as an accredited financial investigator.

(7) The Director must make provision for the training of persons in —
   (a) financial investigation, and
   (b) the operation of this Act.

(8) The Director may charge the persons who receive the training.

4   Co-operation

(1) Persons who have functions relating to the investigation or prosecution of offences must co-operate with the Director in the exercise of his functions.

(2) The Director must co-operate with those persons in the exercise of functions they have under this Act.

5   Advice and assistance

The Director must give the Secretary of State advice and assistance which he reasonably requires and which —
   (a) relate to matters connected with the operation of this Act, and
   (b) are designed to help the Secretary of State to exercise his functions so as to reduce crime.

PART 2

CONFISCATION: ENGLAND AND WALES

Confiscation orders

6   Making of order

(1) The Crown Court must proceed under this section if the following two conditions are satisfied.

(2) The first condition is that a defendant falls within any of the following paragraphs —
   (a) he is convicted of an offence or offences in proceedings before the Crown Court;
   (b) he is committed to the Crown Court for sentence in respect of an offence or offences under section 3, 4 or 6 of the Sentencing Act;
   (c) he is committed to the Crown Court in respect of an offence or offences under section 70 below (committal with a view to a confiscation order being considered).

(3) The second condition is that —
   (a) the prosecutor or the Director asks the court to proceed under this section, or

(b) the court believes it is appropriate for it to do so.

(4) The court must proceed as follows—

    (a) it must decide whether the defendant has a criminal lifestyle;

    (b) if it decides that he has a criminal lifestyle it must decide whether he has benefited from his general criminal conduct;

    (c) if it decides that he does not have a criminal lifestyle it must decide whether he has benefited from his particular criminal conduct.

(5) If the court decides under subsection (4)(b) or (c) that the defendant has benefited from the conduct referred to it must—

    (a) decide the recoverable amount, and

    (b) make an order (a confiscation order) requiring him to pay that amount.

(6) But the court must treat the duty in subsection (5) as a power if it believes that any victim of the conduct has at any time started or intends to start proceedings against the defendant in respect of loss, injury or damage sustained in connection with the conduct.

(7) The court must decide any question arising under subsection (4) or (5) on a balance of probabilities.

(8) The first condition is not satisfied if the defendant absconds (but section 27 may apply).

(9) References in this Part to the offence (or offences) concerned are to the offence (or offences) mentioned in subsection (2).

7 Recoverable amount

(1) The recoverable amount for the purposes of section 6 is an amount equal to the defendant's benefit from the conduct concerned.

(2) But if the defendant shows that the available amount is less than that benefit the recoverable amount is—

    (a) the available amount, or

    (b) a nominal amount, if the available amount is nil.

(3) But if section 6(6) applies the recoverable amount is such amount as—

    (a) the court believes is just, but

    (b) does not exceed the amount found under subsection (1) or (2) (as the case may be).

(4) In calculating the defendant's benefit from the conduct concerned for the purposes of subsection (1), any property in respect of which—

    (a) a recovery order is in force under section 266, or

    (b) a forfeiture order is in force under section 298(2),

must be ignored.

(5) If the court decides the available amount, it must include in the confiscation order a statement of its findings as to the matters relevant for deciding that amount.

8   Defendant's benefit

(1)   If the court is proceeding under section 6 this section applies for the purpose of –

     (a)   deciding whether the defendant has benefited from conduct, and

     (b)   deciding his benefit from the conduct.

(2)   The court must –

     (a)   take account of conduct occurring up to the time it makes its decision;

     (b)   take account of property obtained up to that time.

(3)   Subsection (4) applies if –

     (a)   the conduct concerned is general criminal conduct,

     (b)   a confiscation order mentioned in subsection (5) has at an earlier time been made against the defendant, and

     (c)   his benefit for the purposes of that order was benefit from his general criminal conduct.

(4)   His benefit found at the time the last confiscation order mentioned in subsection (3)(c) was made against him must be taken for the purposes of this section to be his benefit from his general criminal conduct at that time.

(5)   If the conduct concerned is general criminal conduct the court must deduct the aggregate of the following amounts –

     (a)   the amount ordered to be paid under each confiscation order previously made against the defendant;

     (b)   the amount ordered to be paid under each confiscation order previously made against him under any of the provisions listed in subsection (7).

(6)   But subsection (5) does not apply to an amount which has been taken into account for the purposes of a deduction under that subsection on any earlier occasion.

(7)   These are the provisions –

     (a)   the Drug Trafficking Offences Act 1986 (c. 32);

     (b)   Part 1 of the Criminal Justice (Scotland) Act 1987 (c. 41);

     (c)   Part 6 of the Criminal Justice Act 1988 (c. 33);

     (d)   the Criminal Justice (Confiscation) (Northern Ireland) Order 1990 (S.I. 1990/2588 (N.I. 17));

     (e)   Part 1 of the Drug Trafficking Act 1994 (c. 37);

     (f)   Part 1 of the Proceeds of Crime (Scotland) Act 1995 (c. 43);

     (g)   the Proceeds of Crime (Northern Ireland) Order 1996 (S.I. 1996/1299 (N.I. 9));

     (h)   Part 3 or 4 of this Act.

(8)   The reference to general criminal conduct in the case of a confiscation order made under any of the provisions listed in subsection (7) is a reference to conduct in respect of which a court is required or entitled to make one or more assumptions for the purpose of assessing a person's benefit from the conduct.

9   Available amount

(1)   For the purposes of deciding the recoverable amount, the available amount is the aggregate of –

> (a) the total of the values (at the time the confiscation order is made) of all the free property then held by the defendant minus the total amount payable in pursuance of obligations which then have priority, and
>
> (b) the total of the values (at that time) of all tainted gifts.

(2) An obligation has priority if it is an obligation of the defendant—

> (a) to pay an amount due in respect of a fine or other order of a court which was imposed or made on conviction of an offence and at any time before the time the confiscation order is made, or
>
> (b) to pay a sum which would be included among the preferential debts if the defendant's bankruptcy had commenced on the date of the confiscation order or his winding up had been ordered on that date.

(3) "Preferential debts" has the meaning given by section 386 of the Insolvency Act 1986 (c. 45).

10 Assumptions to be made in case of criminal lifestyle

(1) If the court decides under section 6 that the defendant has a criminal lifestyle it must make the following four assumptions for the purpose of—

> (a) deciding whether he has benefited from his general criminal conduct, and
>
> (b) deciding his benefit from the conduct.

(2) The first assumption is that any property transferred to the defendant at any time after the relevant day was obtained by him—

> (a) as a result of his general criminal conduct, and
>
> (b) at the earliest time he appears to have held it.

(3) The second assumption is that any property held by the defendant at any time after the date of conviction was obtained by him—

> (a) as a result of his general criminal conduct, and
>
> (b) at the earliest time he appears to have held it.

(4) The third assumption is that any expenditure incurred by the defendant at any time after the relevant day was met from property obtained by him as a result of his general criminal conduct.

(5) The fourth assumption is that, for the purpose of valuing any property obtained (or assumed to have been obtained) by the defendant, he obtained it free of any other interests in it.

(6) But the court must not make a required assumption in relation to particular property or expenditure if—

> (a) the assumption is shown to be incorrect, or
>
> (b) there would be a serious risk of injustice if the assumption were made.

(7) If the court does not make one or more of the required assumptions it must state its reasons.

(8) The relevant day is the first day of the period of six years ending with—

> (a) the day when proceedings for the offence concerned were started against the defendant, or
>
> (b) if there are two or more offences and proceedings for them were started on different days, the earliest of those days.

(9)   But if a confiscation order mentioned in section 8(3)(c) has been made against the defendant at any time during the period mentioned in subsection (8) –

    (a)   the relevant day is the day when the defendant's benefit was calculated for the purposes of the last such confiscation order;

    (b)   the second assumption does not apply to any property which was held by him on or before the relevant day.

(10)   The date of conviction is –

    (a)   the date on which the defendant was convicted of the offence concerned, or

    (b)   if there are two or more offences and the convictions were on different dates, the date of the latest.

11   Time for payment

(1)   The amount ordered to be paid under a confiscation order must be paid on the making of the order; but this is subject to the following provisions of this section.

(2)   If the defendant shows that he needs time to pay the amount ordered to be paid, the court making the confiscation order may make an order allowing payment to be made in a specified period.

(3)   The specified period –

    (a)   must start with the day on which the confiscation order is made, and

    (b)   must not exceed six months.

(4)   If within the specified period the defendant applies to the Crown Court for the period to be extended and the court believes there are exceptional circumstances, it may make an order extending the period.

(5)   The extended period –

    (a)   must start with the day on which the confiscation order is made, and

    (b)   must not exceed 12 months.

(6)   An order under subsection (4) –

    (a)   may be made after the end of the specified period, but

    (b)   must not be made after the end of the period of 12 months starting with the day on which the confiscation order is made.

(7)   The court must not make an order under subsection (2) or (4) unless it gives –

    (a)   the prosecutor, or

    (b)   if the Director was appointed as the enforcement authority for the order under section 34, the Director,

an opportunity to make representations.

12   Interest on unpaid sums

(1)   If the amount required to be paid by a person under a confiscation order is not paid when it is required to be paid, he must pay interest on the amount for the period for which it remains unpaid.

(2)   The rate of interest is the same rate as that for the time being specified in section 17 of the Judgments Act 1838 (c. 110) (interest on civil judgment debts).

(3) For the purposes of this section no amount is required to be paid under a confiscation order if—

    (a) an application has been made under section 11(4),

    (b) the application has not been determined by the court, and

    (c) the period of 12 months starting with the day on which the confiscation order was made has not ended.

(4) In applying this Part the amount of the interest must be treated as part of the amount to be paid under the confiscation order.

13 Effect of order on court's other powers

(1) If the court makes a confiscation order it must proceed as mentioned in subsections (2) and (4) in respect of the offence or offences concerned.

(2) The court must take account of the confiscation order before—

    (a) it imposes a fine on the defendant, or

    (b) it makes an order falling within subsection (3).

(3) These orders fall within this subsection—

    (a) an order involving payment by the defendant, other than an order under section 130 of the Sentencing Act (compensation orders);

    (b) an order under section 27 of the Misuse of Drugs Act 1971 (c. 38) (forfeiture orders);

    (c) an order under section 143 of the Sentencing Act (deprivation orders);

    (d) an order under section 23 of the Terrorism Act 2000 (c. 11) (forfeiture orders).

(4) Subject to subsection (2), the court must leave the confiscation order out of account in deciding the appropriate sentence for the defendant.

(5) Subsection (6) applies if—

    (a) the Crown Court makes both a confiscation order and an order for the payment of compensation under section 130 of the Sentencing Act against the same person in the same proceedings, and

    (b) the court believes he will not have sufficient means to satisfy both the orders in full.

(6) In such a case the court must direct that so much of the compensation as it specifies is to be paid out of any sums recovered under the confiscation order; and the amount it specifies must be the amount it believes will not be recoverable because of the insufficiency of the person's means.

Procedural matters

14 Postponement

(1) The court may—

    (a) proceed under section 6 before it sentences the defendant for the offence (or any of the offences) concerned, or

    (b) postpone proceedings under section 6 for a specified period.

(2) A period of postponement may be extended.

(3) A period of postponement (including one as extended) must not end after the permitted period ends.

(4) But subsection (3) does not apply if there are exceptional circumstances.

(5) The permitted period is the period of two years starting with the date of conviction.

(6) But if—
(a) the defendant appeals against his conviction for the offence (or any of the offences) concerned, and
(b) the period of three months (starting with the day when the appeal is determined or otherwise disposed of) ends after the period found under subsection (5),
the permitted period is that period of three months.

(7) A postponement or extension may be made—
(a) on application by the defendant;
(b) on application by the prosecutor or the Director (as the case may be);
(c) by the court of its own motion.

(8) If—
(a) proceedings are postponed for a period, and
(b) an application to extend the period is made before it ends,
the application may be granted even after the period ends.

(9) The date of conviction is—
(a) the date on which the defendant was convicted of the offence concerned, or
(b) if there are two or more offences and the convictions were on different dates, the date of the latest.

(10) References to appealing include references to applying under section 111 of the Magistrates' Courts Act 1980 (c. 43) (statement of case).

(11) A confiscation order must not be quashed only on the ground that there was a defect or omission in the procedure connected with the application for or the granting of a postponement.

(12) But subsection (11) does not apply if before it made the confiscation order the court—
(a) imposed a fine on the defendant;
(b) made an order falling within section 13(3);
(c) made an order under section 130 of the Sentencing Act (compensation orders).

15 Effect of postponement

(1) If the court postpones proceedings under section 6 it may proceed to sentence the defendant for the offence (or any of the offences) concerned.

(2) In sentencing the defendant for the offence (or any of the offences) concerned in the postponement period the court must not—
(a) impose a fine on him,
(b) make an order falling within section 13(3), or

> (c)   make an order for the payment of compensation under section 130 of the Sentencing Act.

(3)   If the court sentences the defendant for the offence (or any of the offences) concerned in the postponement period, after that period ends it may vary the sentence by –

> (a)   imposing a fine on him,
>
> (b)   making an order falling within section 13(3), or
>
> (c)   making an order for the payment of compensation under section 130 of the Sentencing Act.

(4)   But the court may proceed under subsection (3) only within the period of 28 days which starts with the last day of the postponement period.

(5)   For the purposes of –

> (a)   section 18(2) of the Criminal Appeal Act 1968 (c. 19) (time limit for notice of appeal or of application for leave to appeal), and
>
> (b)   paragraph 1 of Schedule 3 to the Criminal Justice Act 1988 (c. 33) (time limit for notice of application for leave to refer a case under section 36 of that Act),

the sentence must be regarded as imposed or made on the day on which it is varied under subsection (3).

(6)   If the court proceeds to sentence the defendant under subsection (1), section 6 has effect as if the defendant's particular criminal conduct included conduct which constitutes offences which the court has taken into consideration in deciding his sentence for the offence or offences concerned.

(7)   The postponement period is the period for which proceedings under section 6 are postponed.

16   Statement of information

(1)   If the court is proceeding under section 6 in a case where section 6(3)(a) applies, the prosecutor or the Director (as the case may be) must give the court a statement of information within the period the court orders.

(2)   If the court is proceeding under section 6 in a case where section 6(3)(b) applies and it orders the prosecutor to give it a statement of information, the prosecutor must give it such a statement within the period the court orders.

(3)   If the prosecutor or the Director (as the case may be) believes the defendant has a criminal lifestyle the statement of information is a statement of matters the prosecutor or the Director believes are relevant in connection with deciding these issues –

> (a)   whether the defendant has a criminal lifestyle;
>
> (b)   whether he has benefited from his general criminal conduct;
>
> (c)   his benefit from the conduct.

(4)   A statement under subsection (3) must include information the prosecutor or Director believes is relevant –

> (a)   in connection with the making by the court of a required assumption under section 10;
>
> (b)   for the purpose of enabling the court to decide if the circumstances are such that it must not make such an assumption.

(5) If the prosecutor or the Director (as the case may be) does not believe the defendant has a criminal lifestyle the statement of information is a statement of matters the prosecutor or the Director believes are relevant in connection with deciding these issues –

    (a) whether the defendant has benefited from his particular criminal conduct;

    (b) his benefit from the conduct.

(6) If the prosecutor or the Director gives the court a statement of information –

    (a) he may at any time give the court a further statement of information;

    (b) he must give the court a further statement of information if it orders him to do so, and he must give it within the period the court orders.

(7) If the court makes an order under this section it may at any time vary it by making another one.

17 Defendant's response to statement of information

(1) If the prosecutor or the Director gives the court a statement of information and a copy is served on the defendant, the court may order the defendant –

    (a) to indicate (within the period it orders) the extent to which he accepts each allegation in the statement, and

    (b) so far as he does not accept such an allegation, to give particulars of any matters he proposes to rely on.

(2) If the defendant accepts to any extent an allegation in a statement of information the court may treat his acceptance as conclusive of the matters to which it relates for the purpose of deciding the issues referred to in section 16(3) or (5) (as the case may be).

(3) If the defendant fails in any respect to comply with an order under subsection (1) he may be treated for the purposes of subsection (2) as accepting every allegation in the statement of information apart from –

    (a) any allegation in respect of which he has complied with the requirement;

    (b) any allegation that he has benefited from his general or particular criminal conduct.

(4) For the purposes of this section an allegation may be accepted or particulars may be given in a manner ordered by the court.

(5) If the court makes an order under this section it may at any time vary it by making another one.

(6) No acceptance under this section that the defendant has benefited from conduct is admissible in evidence in proceedings for an offence.

18 Provision of information by defendant

(1) This section applies if –

    (a) the court is proceeding under section 6 in a case where section 6(3)(a) applies, or

    (b) it is proceeding under section 6 in a case where section 6(3)(b) applies or it is considering whether to proceed.

(2)   For the purpose of obtaining information to help it in carrying out its functions the court may at any time order the defendant to give it information specified in the order.

(3)   An order under this section may require all or a specified part of the information to be given in a specified manner and before a specified date.

(4)   If the defendant fails without reasonable excuse to comply with an order under this section the court may draw such inference as it believes is appropriate.

(5)   Subsection (4) does not affect any power of the court to deal with the defendant in respect of a failure to comply with an order under this section.

(6)   If the prosecutor or the Director (as the case may be) accepts to any extent an allegation made by the defendant—

      (a)   in giving information required by an order under this section, or

      (b)   in any other statement given to the court in relation to any matter relevant to deciding the available amount under section 9,

the court may treat the acceptance as conclusive of the matters to which it relates.

(7)   For the purposes of this section an allegation may be accepted in a manner ordered by the court.

(8)   If the court makes an order under this section it may at any time vary it by making another one.

(9)   No information given under this section which amounts to an admission by the defendant that he has benefited from criminal conduct is admissible in evidence in proceedings for an offence.

Reconsideration

19   No order made: reconsideration of case

(1)   This section applies if—

      (a)   the first condition in section 6 is satisfied but no court has proceeded under that section,

      (b)   there is evidence which was not available to the prosecutor on the relevant date,

      (c)   before the end of the period of six years starting with the date of conviction the prosecutor or the Director applies to the Crown Court to consider the evidence, and

      (d)   after considering the evidence the court believes it is appropriate for it to proceed under section 6.

(2)   If this section applies the court must proceed under section 6, and when it does so subsections (3) to (8) below apply.

(3)   If the court has already sentenced the defendant for the offence (or any of the offences) concerned, section 6 has effect as if his particular criminal conduct included conduct which constitutes offences which the court has taken into consideration in deciding his sentence for the offence or offences concerned.

(4)   Section 8(2) does not apply, and the rules applying instead are that the court must—

    (a)   take account of conduct occurring before the relevant date;

    (b)   take account of property obtained before that date;

    (c)   take account of property obtained on or after that date if it was obtained as a result of or in connection with conduct occurring before that date.

(5)   In section 10—

    (a)   the first and second assumptions do not apply with regard to property first held by the defendant on or after the relevant date;

    (b)   the third assumption does not apply with regard to expenditure incurred by him on or after that date;

    (c)   the fourth assumption does not apply with regard to property obtained (or assumed to have been obtained) by him on or after that date.

(6)   The recoverable amount for the purposes of section 6 is such amount as—

    (a)   the court believes is just, but

    (b)   does not exceed the amount found under section 7.

(7)   In arriving at the just amount the court must have regard in particular to—

    (a)   the amount found under section 7;

    (b)   any fine imposed on the defendant in respect of the offence (or any of the offences) concerned;

    (c)   any order which falls within section 13(3) and has been made against him in respect of the offence (or any of the offences) concerned and has not already been taken into account by the court in deciding what is the free property held by him for the purposes of section 9;

    (d)   any order which has been made against him in respect of the offence (or any of the offences) concerned under section 130 of the Sentencing Act (compensation orders).

(8)   If an order for the payment of compensation under section 130 of the Sentencing Act has been made against the defendant in respect of the offence or offences concerned, section 13(5) and (6) above do not apply.

(9)   The relevant date is—

    (a)   if the court made a decision not to proceed under section 6, the date of the decision;

    (b)   if the court did not make such a decision, the date of conviction.

(10)   The date of conviction is—

    (a)   the date on which the defendant was convicted of the offence concerned, or

    (b)   if there are two or more offences and the convictions were on different dates, the date of the latest.

20   No order made: reconsideration of benefit

(1)   This section applies if the following two conditions are satisfied.

(2)   The first condition is that in proceeding under section 6 the court has decided that—

    (a)   the defendant has a criminal lifestyle but has not benefited from his general criminal conduct, or

    (b)   the defendant does not have a criminal lifestyle and has not benefited from his particular criminal conduct.

(3)   If the court proceeded under section 6 because the Director asked it to, the
      second condition is that —
      (a)   the Director has evidence which was not available to him when the
            court decided that the defendant had not benefited from his general or
            particular criminal conduct,
      (b)   before the end of the period of six years starting with the date of
            conviction the Director applies to the Crown Court to consider the
            evidence, and
      (c)   after considering the evidence the court concludes that it would have
            decided that the defendant had benefited from his general or particular
            criminal conduct (as the case may be) if the evidence had been available
            to it.

(4)   If the court proceeded under section 6 because the prosecutor asked it to or
      because it believed it was appropriate for it to do so, the second condition is
      that —
      (a)   there is evidence which was not available to the prosecutor when the
            court decided that the defendant had not benefited from his general or
            particular criminal conduct,
      (b)   before the end of the period of six years starting with the date of
            conviction the prosecutor or the Director applies to the Crown Court to
            consider the evidence, and
      (c)   after considering the evidence the court concludes that it would have
            decided that the defendant had benefited from his general or particular
            criminal conduct (as the case may be) if the evidence had been available
            to it.

(5)   If this section applies the court —
      (a)   must make a fresh decision under section 6(4)(b) or (c) whether the
            defendant has benefited from his general or particular criminal conduct
            (as the case may be);
      (b)   may make a confiscation order under that section.

(6)   Subsections (7) to (12) below apply if the court proceeds under section 6 in
      pursuance of this section.

(7)   If the court has already sentenced the defendant for the offence (or any of the
      offences) concerned, section 6 has effect as if his particular criminal conduct
      included conduct which constitutes offences which the court has taken into
      consideration in deciding his sentence for the offence or offences concerned.

(8)   Section 8(2) does not apply, and the rules applying instead are that the court
      must —
      (a)   take account of conduct occurring before the date of the original
            decision that the defendant had not benefited from his general or
            particular criminal conduct;
      (b)   take account of property obtained before that date;
      (c)   take account of property obtained on or after that date if it was obtained
            as a result of or in connection with conduct occurring before that date.

(9)   In section 10 —
      (a)   the first and second assumptions do not apply with regard to property
            first held by the defendant on or after the date of the original decision
            that the defendant had not benefited from his general or particular
            criminal conduct;

     (b)   the third assumption does not apply with regard to expenditure incurred by him on or after that date;

     (c)   the fourth assumption does not apply with regard to property obtained (or assumed to have been obtained) by him on or after that date.

(10)   The recoverable amount for the purposes of section 6 is such amount as –

     (a)   the court believes is just, but

     (b)   does not exceed the amount found under section 7.

(11)   In arriving at the just amount the court must have regard in particular to –

     (a)   the amount found under section 7;

     (b)   any fine imposed on the defendant in respect of the offence (or any of the offences) concerned;

     (c)   any order which falls within section 13(3) and has been made against him in respect of the offence (or any of the offences) concerned and has not already been taken into account by the court in deciding what is the free property held by him for the purposes of section 9;

     (d)   any order which has been made against him in respect of the offence (or any of the offences) concerned under section 130 of the Sentencing Act (compensation orders).

(12)   If an order for the payment of compensation under section 130 of the Sentencing Act has been made against the defendant in respect of the offence or offences concerned, section 13(5) and (6) above do not apply.

(13)   The date of conviction is the date found by applying section 19(10).

21   Order made: reconsideration of benefit

(1)   This section applies if –

     (a)   a court has made a confiscation order,

     (b)   there is evidence which was not available to the prosecutor or the Director at the relevant time,

     (c)   the prosecutor or the Director believes that if the court were to find the amount of the defendant's benefit in pursuance of this section it would exceed the relevant amount,

     (d)   before the end of the period of six years starting with the date of conviction the prosecutor or the Director applies to the Crown Court to consider the evidence, and

     (e)   after considering the evidence the court believes it is appropriate for it to proceed under this section.

(2)   The court must make a new calculation of the defendant's benefit from the conduct concerned, and when it does so subsections (3) to (6) below apply.

(3)   If a court has already sentenced the defendant for the offence (or any of the offences) concerned section 6 has effect as if his particular criminal conduct included conduct which constitutes offences which the court has taken into consideration in deciding his sentence for the offence or offences concerned.

(4)   Section 8(2) does not apply, and the rules applying instead are that the court must –

     (a)   take account of conduct occurring up to the time it decided the defendant's benefit for the purposes of the confiscation order;

     (b)   take account of property obtained up to that time;

(c)   take account of property obtained after that time if it was obtained as a result of or in connection with conduct occurring before that time.

(5)   In applying section 8(5) the confiscation order must be ignored.

(6)   In section 10–

    (a)   the first and second assumptions do not apply with regard to property first held by the defendant after the time the court decided his benefit for the purposes of the confiscation order;

    (b)   the third assumption does not apply with regard to expenditure incurred by him after that time;

    (c)   the fourth assumption does not apply with regard to property obtained (or assumed to have been obtained) by him after that time.

(7)   If the amount found under the new calculation of the defendant's benefit exceeds the relevant amount the court–

    (a)   must make a new calculation of the recoverable amount for the purposes of section 6, and

    (b)   if it exceeds the amount required to be paid under the confiscation order, may vary the order by substituting for the amount required to be paid such amount as it believes is just.

(8)   In applying subsection (7)(a) the court must–

    (a)   take the new calculation of the defendant's benefit;

    (b)   apply section 9 as if references to the time the confiscation order is made were to the time of the new calculation of the recoverable amount and as if references to the date of the confiscation order were to the date of that new calculation.

(9)   In applying subsection (7)(b) the court must have regard in particular to–

    (a)   any fine imposed on the defendant for the offence (or any of the offences) concerned;

    (b)   any order which falls within section 13(3) and has been made against him in respect of the offence (or any of the offences) concerned and has not already been taken into account by the court in deciding what is the free property held by him for the purposes of section 9;

    (c)   any order which has been made against him in respect of the offence (or any of the offences) concerned under section 130 of the Sentencing Act (compensation orders).

(10)   But in applying subsection (7)(b) the court must not have regard to an order falling within subsection (9)(c) if a court has made a direction under section 13(6).

(11)   In deciding under this section whether one amount exceeds another the court must take account of any change in the value of money.

(12)   The relevant time is–

    (a)   when the court calculated the defendant's benefit for the purposes of the confiscation order, if this section has not applied previously;

    (b)   when the court last calculated the defendant's benefit in pursuance of this section, if this section has applied previously.

(13)   The relevant amount is–

    (a)   the amount found as the defendant's benefit for the purposes of the confiscation order, if this section has not applied previously;

      (b)   the amount last found as the defendant's benefit in pursuance of this section, if this section has applied previously.

(14)   The date of conviction is the date found by applying section 19(10).

22   Order made: reconsideration of available amount

(1)   This section applies if –
      (a)   a court has made a confiscation order,
      (b)   the amount required to be paid was the amount found under section 7(2), and
      (c)   an applicant falling within subsection (2) applies to the Crown Court to make a new calculation of the available amount.

(2)   These applicants fall within this subsection –
      (a)   the prosecutor;
      (b)   the Director;
      (c)   a receiver appointed under section 50 or 52.

(3)   In a case where this section applies the court must make the new calculation, and in doing so it must apply section 9 as if references to the time the confiscation order is made were to the time of the new calculation and as if references to the date of the confiscation order were to the date of the new calculation.

(4)   If the amount found under the new calculation exceeds the relevant amount the court may vary the order by substituting for the amount required to be paid such amount as –
      (a)   it believes is just, but
      (b)   does not exceed the amount found as the defendant's benefit from the conduct concerned.

(5)   In deciding what is just the court must have regard in particular to –
      (a)   any fine imposed on the defendant for the offence (or any of the offences) concerned;
      (b)   any order which falls within section 13(3) and has been made against him in respect of the offence (or any of the offences) concerned and has not already been taken into account by the court in deciding what is the free property held by him for the purposes of section 9;
      (c)   any order which has been made against him in respect of the offence (or any of the offences) concerned under section 130 of the Sentencing Act (compensation orders).

(6)   But in deciding what is just the court must not have regard to an order falling within subsection (5)(c) if a court has made a direction under section 13(6).

(7)   In deciding under this section whether one amount exceeds another the court must take account of any change in the value of money.

(8)   The relevant amount is –
      (a)   the amount found as the available amount for the purposes of the confiscation order, if this section has not applied previously;
      (b)   the amount last found as the available amount in pursuance of this section, if this section has applied previously.

(9)   The amount found as the defendant's benefit from the conduct concerned is –

(a) the amount so found when the confiscation order was made, or

(b) if one or more new calculations of the defendant's benefit have been made under section 21 the amount found on the occasion of the last such calculation.

23 Inadequacy of available amount: variation of order

(1) This section applies if –

(a) a court has made a confiscation order, and

(b) the defendant, or a receiver appointed under section 50 or 52, applies to the Crown Court to vary the order under this section.

(2) In such a case the court must calculate the available amount, and in doing so it must apply section 9 as if references to the time the confiscation order is made were to the time of the calculation and as if references to the date of the confiscation order were to the date of the calculation.

(3) If the court finds that the available amount (as so calculated) is inadequate for the payment of any amount remaining to be paid under the confiscation order it may vary the order by substituting for the amount required to be paid such smaller amount as the court believes is just.

(4) If a person has been adjudged bankrupt or his estate has been sequestrated, or if an order for the winding up of a company has been made, the court must take into account the extent to which realisable property held by that person or that company may be distributed among creditors.

(5) The court may disregard any inadequacy which it believes is attributable (wholly or partly) to anything done by the defendant for the purpose of preserving property held by the recipient of a tainted gift from any risk of realisation under this Part.

(6) In subsection (4) "company" means any company which may be wound up under the Insolvency Act 1986 (c. 45) or the Insolvency (Northern Ireland) Order 1989 (S.I. 1989/2405 (N.I. 19)).

24 Inadequacy of available amount: discharge of order

(1) This section applies if –

(a) a court has made a confiscation order,

(b) a justices' chief executive applies to the Crown Court for the discharge of the order, and

(c) the amount remaining to be paid under the order is less than £1,000.

(2) In such a case the court must calculate the available amount, and in doing so it must apply section 9 as if references to the time the confiscation order is made were to the time of the calculation and as if references to the date of the confiscation order were to the date of the calculation.

(3) If the court –

(a) finds that the available amount (as so calculated) is inadequate to meet the amount remaining to be paid, and

(b) is satisfied that the inadequacy is due wholly to a specified reason or a combination of specified reasons,

it may discharge the confiscation order.

(4)   The specified reasons are—

     (a)   in a case where any of the realisable property consists of money in a currency other than sterling, that fluctuations in currency exchange rates have occurred;

     (b)   any reason specified by the Secretary of State by order.

(5)   The Secretary of State may by order vary the amount for the time being specified in subsection (1)(c).

25   Small amount outstanding: discharge of order

(1)   This section applies if—

     (a)   a court has made a confiscation order,

     (b)   a justices' chief executive applies to the Crown Court for the discharge of the order, and

     (c)   the amount remaining to be paid under the order is £50 or less.

(2)   In such a case the court may discharge the order.

(3)   The Secretary of State may by order vary the amount for the time being specified in subsection (1)(c).

26   Information

(1)   This section applies if—

     (a)   the court proceeds under section 6 in pursuance of section 19 or 20, or

     (b)   the prosecutor or the Director applies under section 21.

(2)   In such a case—

     (a)   the prosecutor or the Director (as the case may be) must give the court a statement of information within the period the court orders;

     (b)   section 16 applies accordingly (with appropriate modifications where the prosecutor or the Director applies under section 21);

     (c)   section 17 applies accordingly;

     (d)   section 18 applies as it applies in the circumstances mentioned in section 18(1).

Defendant absconds

27   Defendant convicted or committed

(1)   This section applies if the following two conditions are satisfied.

(2)   The first condition is that a defendant absconds after—

     (a)   he is convicted of an offence or offences in proceedings before the Crown Court,

     (b)   he is committed to the Crown Court for sentence in respect of an offence or offences under section 3, 4 or 6 of the Sentencing Act, or

     (c)   he is committed to the Crown Court in respect of an offence or offences under section 70 below (committal with a view to a confiscation order being considered).

(3)   The second condition is that—

> (a) the prosecutor or the Director applies to the Crown Court to proceed under this section, and
>
> (b) the court believes it is appropriate for it to do so.

(4) If this section applies the court must proceed under section 6 in the same way as it must proceed if the two conditions there mentioned are satisfied; but this is subject to subsection (5).

(5) If the court proceeds under section 6 as applied by this section, this Part has effect with these modifications—

> (a) any person the court believes is likely to be affected by an order under section 6 is entitled to appear before the court and make representations;
>
> (b) the court must not make an order under section 6 unless the prosecutor or the Director (as the case may be) has taken reasonable steps to contact the defendant;
>
> (c) section 6(9) applies as if the reference to subsection (2) were to subsection (2) of this section;
>
> (d) sections 10, 16(4), 17 and 18 must be ignored;
>
> (e) sections 19, 20 and 21 must be ignored while the defendant is still an absconder.

(6) Once the defendant ceases to be an absconder section 19 has effect as if subsection (1)(a) read—

> "(a) at a time when the first condition in section 27 was satisfied the court did not proceed under section 6,".

(7) If the court does not believe it is appropriate for it to proceed under this section, once the defendant ceases to be an absconder section 19 has effect as if subsection (1)(b) read—

> "(b) there is evidence which was not available to the prosecutor or the Director on the relevant date,".

28   Defendant neither convicted nor acquitted

(1) This section applies if the following two conditions are satisfied.

(2) The first condition is that—

> (a) proceedings for an offence or offences are started against a defendant but are not concluded,
>
> (b) he absconds, and
>
> (c) the period of two years (starting with the day the court believes he absconded) has ended.

(3) The second condition is that—

> (a) the prosecutor or the Director applies to the Crown Court to proceed under this section, and
>
> (b) the court believes it is appropriate for it to do so.

(4) If this section applies the court must proceed under section 6 in the same way as it must proceed if the two conditions there mentioned are satisfied; but this is subject to subsection (5).

(5) If the court proceeds under section 6 as applied by this section, this Part has effect with these modifications—

    (a)   any person the court believes is likely to be affected by an order under section 6 is entitled to appear before the court and make representations;

    (b)   the court must not make an order under section 6 unless the prosecutor or the Director (as the case may be) has taken reasonable steps to contact the defendant;

    (c)   section 6(9) applies as if the reference to subsection (2) were to subsection (2) of this section;

    (d)   sections 10, 16(4) and 17 to 20 must be ignored;

    (e)   section 21 must be ignored while the defendant is still an absconder.

(6)   Once the defendant has ceased to be an absconder section 21 has effect as if references to the date of conviction were to –

    (a)   the day when proceedings for the offence concerned were started against the defendant, or

    (b)   if there are two or more offences and proceedings for them were started on different days, the earliest of those days.

(7)   If –

    (a)   the court makes an order under section 6 as applied by this section, and

    (b)   the defendant is later convicted in proceedings before the Crown Court of the offence (or any of the offences) concerned,

section 6 does not apply so far as that conviction is concerned.

29   Variation of order

(1)   This section applies if –

    (a)   the court makes a confiscation order under section 6 as applied by section 28,

    (b)   the defendant ceases to be an absconder,

    (c)   he is convicted of an offence (or any of the offences) mentioned in section 28(2)(a),

    (d)   he believes that the amount required to be paid was too large (taking the circumstances prevailing when the amount was found for the purposes of the order), and

    (e)   before the end of the relevant period he applies to the Crown Court to consider the evidence on which his belief is based.

(2)   If (after considering the evidence) the court concludes that the defendant's belief is well founded –

    (a)   it must find the amount which should have been the amount required to be paid (taking the circumstances prevailing when the amount was found for the purposes of the order), and

    (b)   it may vary the order by substituting for the amount required to be paid such amount as it believes is just.

(3)   The relevant period is the period of 28 days starting with –

    (a)   the date on which the defendant was convicted of the offence mentioned in section 28(2)(a), or

    (b)   if there are two or more offences and the convictions were on different dates, the date of the latest.

(4)   But in a case where section 28(2)(a) applies to more than one offence the court must not make an order under this section unless it is satisfied that there is no

possibility of any further proceedings being taken or continued in relation to any such offence in respect of which the defendant has not been convicted.

30   Discharge of order

(1)   Subsection (2) applies if —

    (a)   the court makes a confiscation order under section 6 as applied by section 28,

    (b)   the defendant is later tried for the offence or offences concerned and acquitted on all counts, and

    (c)   he applies to the Crown Court to discharge the order.

(2)   In such a case the court must discharge the order.

(3)   Subsection (4) applies if —

    (a)   the court makes a confiscation order under section 6 as applied by section 28,

    (b)   the defendant ceases to be an absconder,

    (c)   subsection (1)(b) does not apply, and

    (d)   he applies to the Crown Court to discharge the order.

(4)   In such a case the court may discharge the order if it finds that —

    (a)   there has been undue delay in continuing the proceedings mentioned in section 28(2), or

    (b)   the prosecutor does not intend to proceed with the prosecution.

(5)   If the court discharges a confiscation order under this section it may make such a consequential or incidental order as it believes is appropriate.

Appeals

31   Appeal by prosecutor or Director

(1)   If the Crown Court makes a confiscation order the prosecutor or the Director may appeal to the Court of Appeal in respect of the order.

(2)   If the Crown Court decides not to make a confiscation order the prosecutor or the Director may appeal to the Court of Appeal against the decision.

(3)   Subsections (1) and (2) do not apply to an order or decision made by virtue of section 19, 20, 27 or 28.

32   Court's powers on appeal

(1)   On an appeal under section 31(1) the Court of Appeal may confirm, quash or vary the confiscation order.

(2)   On an appeal under section 31(2) the Court of Appeal may confirm the decision, or if it believes the decision was wrong it may —

    (a)   itself proceed under section 6 (ignoring subsections (1) to (3)), or

    (b)   direct the Crown Court to proceed afresh under section 6.

(3)   In proceeding afresh in pursuance of this section the Crown Court must comply with any directions the Court of Appeal may make.

(4) If a court makes or varies a confiscation order under this section or in pursuance of a direction under this section it must—

    (a) have regard to any fine imposed on the defendant in respect of the offence (or any of the offences) concerned;

    (b) have regard to any order which falls within section 13(3) and has been made against him in respect of the offence (or any of the offences) concerned, unless the order has already been taken into account by a court in deciding what is the free property held by the defendant for the purposes of section 9.

(5) If the Court of Appeal proceeds under section 6 or the Crown Court proceeds afresh under that section in pursuance of a direction under this section subsections (6) to (10) apply.

(6) If a court has already sentenced the defendant for the offence (or any of the offences) concerned, section 6 has effect as if his particular criminal conduct included conduct which constitutes offences which the court has taken into consideration in deciding his sentence for the offence or offences concerned.

(7) If an order has been made against the defendant in respect of the offence (or any of the offences) concerned under section 130 of the Sentencing Act (compensation orders)—

    (a) the court must have regard to it, and

    (b) section 13(5) and (6) above do not apply.

(8) Section 8(2) does not apply, and the rules applying instead are that the court must—

    (a) take account of conduct occurring before the relevant date;

    (b) take account of property obtained before that date;

    (c) take account of property obtained on or after that date if it was obtained as a result of or in connection with conduct occurring before that date.

(9) In section 10—

    (a) the first and second assumptions do not apply with regard to property first held by the defendant on or after the relevant date;

    (b) the third assumption does not apply with regard to expenditure incurred by him on or after that date;

    (c) the fourth assumption does not apply with regard to property obtained (or assumed to have been obtained) by him on or after that date.

(10) Section 26 applies as it applies in the circumstances mentioned in subsection (1) of that section.

(11) The relevant date is the date on which the Crown Court decided not to make a confiscation order.

33 Appeal to House of Lords

(1) An appeal lies to the House of Lords from a decision of the Court of Appeal on an appeal under section 31.

(2) An appeal under this section lies at the instance of—

    (a) the defendant or the prosecutor (if the prosecutor appealed under section 31);

    (b) the defendant or the Director (if the Director appealed under section 31).

(3)   On an appeal from a decision of the Court of Appeal to confirm, vary or make a confiscation order the House of Lords may confirm, quash or vary the order.

(4)   On an appeal from a decision of the Court of Appeal to confirm the decision of the Crown Court not to make a confiscation order or from a decision of the Court of Appeal to quash a confiscation order the House of Lords may—

    (a)   confirm the decision, or

    (b)   direct the Crown Court to proceed afresh under section 6 if it believes the decision was wrong.

(5)   In proceeding afresh in pursuance of this section the Crown Court must comply with any directions the House of Lords may make.

(6)   If a court varies a confiscation order under this section or makes a confiscation order in pursuance of a direction under this section it must—

    (a)   have regard to any fine imposed on the defendant in respect of the offence (or any of the offences) concerned;

    (b)   have regard to any order which falls within section 13(3) and has been made against him in respect of the offence (or any of the offences) concerned, unless the order has already been taken into account by a court in deciding what is the free property held by the defendant for the purposes of section 9.

(7)   If the Crown Court proceeds afresh under section 6 in pursuance of a direction under this section subsections (8) to (12) apply.

(8)   If a court has already sentenced the defendant for the offence (or any of the offences) concerned, section 6 has effect as if his particular criminal conduct included conduct which constitutes offences which the court has taken into consideration in deciding his sentence for the offence or offences concerned.

(9)   If an order has been made against the defendant in respect of the offence (or any of the offences) concerned under section 130 of the Sentencing Act (compensation orders)—

    (a)   the Crown Court must have regard to it, and

    (b)   section 13(5) and (6) above do not apply.

(10)   Section 8(2) does not apply, and the rules applying instead are that the Crown Court must—

    (a)   take account of conduct occurring before the relevant date;

    (b)   take account of property obtained before that date;

    (c)   take account of property obtained on or after that date if it was obtained as a result of or in connection with conduct occurring before that date.

(11)   In section 10—

    (a)   the first and second assumptions do not apply with regard to property first held by the defendant on or after the relevant date;

    (b)   the third assumption does not apply with regard to expenditure incurred by him on or after that date;

    (c)   the fourth assumption does not apply with regard to property obtained (or assumed to have been obtained) by him on or after that date.

(12)   Section 26 applies as it applies in the circumstances mentioned in subsection (1) of that section.

(13)   The relevant date is—

(a) in a case where the Crown Court made a confiscation order which was quashed by the Court of Appeal, the date on which the Crown Court made the order;

(b) in any other case, the date on which the Crown Court decided not to make a confiscation order.

Enforcement authority

34 Enforcement authority

(1) Subsection (2) applies if a court makes a confiscation order and any of the following paragraphs applies —

(a) the court proceeded under section 6 after being asked to do so by the Director;

(b) the court proceeded under section 6 by virtue of an application by the Director under section 19, 20, 27 or 28;

(c) the court proceeded under section 6 as a result of an appeal by the Director under section 31(2) or 33;

(d) before the court made the order the Director applied to the court to appoint him as the enforcement authority for the order.

(2) In any such case the court must appoint the Director as the enforcement authority for the order.

Enforcement as fines etc

35 Director not appointed as enforcement authority

(1) This section applies if a court —

(a) makes a confiscation order, and

(b) does not appoint the Director as the enforcement authority for the order.

(2) Sections 139(2) to (4) and (9) and 140(1) to (4) of the Sentencing Act (functions of court as to fines and enforcing fines) apply as if the amount ordered to be paid were a fine imposed on the defendant by the court making the confiscation order.

(3) In the application of Part 3 of the Magistrates' Courts Act 1980 (c. 43) to an amount payable under a confiscation order —

(a) ignore section 75 of that Act (power to dispense with immediate payment);

(b) such an amount is not a sum adjudged to be paid by a conviction for the purposes of section 81 (enforcement of fines imposed on young offenders) or a fine for the purposes of section 85 (remission of fines) of that Act;

(c) in section 87 of that Act ignore subsection (3) (inquiry into means).

36 Director appointed as enforcement authority

(1) This section applies if a court —

(a) makes a confiscation order, and

(b) appoints the Director as the enforcement authority for the order.

(2) Section 139(2) to (4) and (9) of the Sentencing Act (functions of court as to fines) applies as if the amount ordered to be paid were a fine imposed on the defendant by the court making the confiscation order.

37   Director's application for enforcement

(1) If the Director believes that the conditions set out in subsection (2) are satisfied he may make an ex parte application to the Crown Court for the issue of a summons against the defendant.

(2) The conditions are that—

    (a)   a confiscation order has been made;

    (b)   the Director has been appointed as the enforcement authority for the order;

    (c)   because of the defendant's wilful refusal or culpable neglect the order is not satisfied;

    (d)   the order is not subject to appeal;

    (e)   the Director has done all that is practicable (apart from this section) to enforce the order.

(3) If it appears to the Crown Court that the conditions are satisfied it may issue a summons ordering the defendant to appear before the court at the time and place specified in the summons.

(4) If the defendant fails to appear before the Crown Court in pursuance of the summons the court may issue a warrant for his arrest.

(5) If—

    (a)   the defendant appears before the Crown Court in pursuance of the summons or of a warrant issued under subsection (4), and

    (b)   the court is satisfied that the conditions set out in subsection (2) are satisfied,

it may issue a warrant committing the defendant to prison or detention for default in payment of the amount ordered to be paid by the confiscation order.

(6) Subsection (7) applies if the amount remaining to be paid under the confiscation order when the warrant under subsection (5) is issued is less than the amount ordered to be paid.

(7) In such a case the court must substitute for the term of imprisonment or detention fixed in respect of the order under section 139(2) of the Sentencing Act such term as bears to the original term the same proportion as the amount remaining to be paid bears to the amount ordered to be paid.

(8) Subsections (9) and (10) apply if—

    (a)   the defendant has been committed to prison or detention in pursuance of a warrant issued under subsection (5), and

    (b)   a payment is made in respect of some or all of the amount remaining to be paid under the confiscation order.

(9) If the payment is for the whole amount remaining to be paid the defendant must be released unless he is in custody for another reason.

(10) If the payment is for less than that amount, the period of commitment is reduced so that it bears to the term fixed under section 139(2) of the Sentencing

Act the same proportion as the amount remaining to be paid bears to the amount ordered to be paid.

38 Provisions about imprisonment or detention

(1) Subsection (2) applies if—

    (a) a warrant committing the defendant to prison or detention is issued for a default in payment of an amount ordered to be paid under a confiscation order in respect of an offence or offences, and

    (b) at the time the warrant is issued the defendant is liable to serve a term of custody in respect of the offence (or any of the offences).

(2) In such a case the term of imprisonment or of detention under section 108 of the Sentencing Act (detention of persons aged 18 to 20 for default) to be served in default of payment of the amount does not begin to run until after the term mentioned in subsection (1)(b) above.

(3) The reference in subsection (1)(b) to the term of custody the defendant is liable to serve in respect of the offence (or any of the offences) is a reference to the term of imprisonment, or detention in a young offender institution, which he is liable to serve in respect of the offence (or any of the offences).

(4) For the purposes of subsection (3) consecutive terms and terms which are wholly or partly concurrent must be treated as a single term and the following must be ignored—

    (a) any sentence suspended under section 118(1) of the Sentencing Act which has not taken effect at the time the warrant is issued;

    (b) in the case of a sentence of imprisonment passed with an order under section 47(1) of the Criminal Law Act 1977 (c. 45) (sentences of imprisonment partly served and partly suspended) any part of the sentence which the defendant has not at that time been required to serve in prison;

    (c) any term of imprisonment or detention fixed under section 139(2) of the Sentencing Act (term to be served in default of payment of fine etc) for which a warrant committing the defendant to prison or detention has not been issued at that time.

(5) If the defendant serves a term of imprisonment or detention in default of paying any amount due under a confiscation order, his serving that term does not prevent the confiscation order from continuing to have effect so far as any other method of enforcement is concerned.

39 Reconsideration etc: variation of prison term

(1) Subsection (2) applies if—

    (a) a court varies a confiscation order under section 21, 22, 23, 29, 32 or 33,

    (b) the effect of the variation is to vary the maximum period applicable in relation to the order under section 139(4) of the Sentencing Act, and

    (c) the result is that that maximum period is less than the term of imprisonment or detention fixed in respect of the order under section 139(2) of the Sentencing Act.

(2) In such a case the court must fix a reduced term of imprisonment or detention in respect of the confiscation order under section 139(2) of the Sentencing Act in place of the term previously fixed.

(3) Subsection (4) applies if paragraphs (a) and (b) of subsection (1) apply but paragraph (c) does not.

(4) In such a case the court may amend the term of imprisonment or detention fixed in respect of the confiscation order under section 139(2) of the Sentencing Act.

(5) If the effect of section 12 is to increase the maximum period applicable in relation to a confiscation order under section 139(4) of the Sentencing Act, on the application of the appropriate person the Crown Court may amend the term of imprisonment or detention fixed in respect of the order under section 139(2) of that Act.

(6) The appropriate person is —

    (a) the Director, if he was appointed as the enforcement authority for the order under section 34;

    (b) the prosecutor, in any other case.

Restraint orders

40 Conditions for exercise of powers

(1) The Crown Court may exercise the powers conferred by section 41 if any of the following conditions is satisfied.

(2) The first condition is that —

    (a) a criminal investigation has been started in England and Wales with regard to an offence, and

    (b) there is reasonable cause to believe that the alleged offender has benefited from his criminal conduct.

(3) The second condition is that —

    (a) proceedings for an offence have been started in England and Wales and not concluded, and

    (b) there is reasonable cause to believe that the defendant has benefited from his criminal conduct.

(4) The third condition is that —

    (a) an application by the prosecutor or the Director has been made under section 19, 20, 27 or 28 and not concluded, or the court believes that such an application is to be made, and

    (b) there is reasonable cause to believe that the defendant has benefited from his criminal conduct.

(5) The fourth condition is that —

    (a) an application by the prosecutor or the Director has been made under section 21 and not concluded, or the court believes that such an application is to be made, and

    (b) there is reasonable cause to believe that the court will decide under that section that the amount found under the new calculation of the defendant's benefit exceeds the relevant amount (as defined in that section).

(6) The fifth condition is that —

(a) an application by the prosecutor or the Director has been made under section 22 and not concluded, or the court believes that such an application is to be made, and

(b) there is reasonable cause to believe that the court will decide under that section that the amount found under the new calculation of the available amount exceeds the relevant amount (as defined in that section).

(7) The second condition is not satisfied if the court believes that—

(a) there has been undue delay in continuing the proceedings, or

(b) the prosecutor does not intend to proceed.

(8) If an application mentioned in the third, fourth or fifth condition has been made the condition is not satisfied if the court believes that—

(a) there has been undue delay in continuing the application, or

(b) the prosecutor or the Director (as the case may be) does not intend to proceed.

(9) If the first condition is satisfied—

(a) references in this Part to the defendant are to the alleged offender;

(b) references in this Part to the prosecutor are to the person the court believes is to have conduct of any proceedings for the offence;

(c) section 77(9) has effect as if proceedings for the offence had been started against the defendant when the investigation was started.

41   Restraint orders

(1) If any condition set out in section 40 is satisfied the Crown Court may make an order (a restraint order) prohibiting any specified person from dealing with any realisable property held by him.

(2) A restraint order may provide that it applies—

(a) to all realisable property held by the specified person whether or not the property is described in the order;

(b) to realisable property transferred to the specified person after the order is made.

(3) A restraint order may be made subject to exceptions, and an exception may in particular—

(a) make provision for reasonable living expenses and reasonable legal expenses;

(b) make provision for the purpose of enabling any person to carry on any trade, business, profession or occupation;

(c) be made subject to conditions.

(4) But an exception to a restraint order must not make provision for any legal expenses which—

(a) relate to an offence which falls within subsection (5), and

(b) are incurred by the defendant or by a recipient of a tainted gift.

(5) These offences fall within this subsection—

(a) the offence mentioned in section 40(2) or (3), if the first or second condition (as the case may be) is satisfied;

    (b)   the offence (or any of the offences) concerned, if the third, fourth or fifth condition is satisfied.

(6)   Subsection (7) applies if —

    (a)   a court makes a restraint order, and

    (b)   the applicant for the order applies to the court to proceed under subsection (7) (whether as part of the application for the restraint order or at any time afterwards).

(7)   The court may make such order as it believes is appropriate for the purpose of ensuring that the restraint order is effective.

(8)   A restraint order does not affect property for the time being subject to a charge under any of these provisions —

    (a)   section 9 of the Drug Trafficking Offences Act 1986 (c. 32);

    (b)   section 78 of the Criminal Justice Act 1988 (c. 33);

    (c)   Article 14 of the Criminal Justice (Confiscation) (Northern Ireland) Order 1990 (S.I. 1990/2588 (N.I. 17));

    (d)   section 27 of the Drug Trafficking Act 1994 (c. 37);

    (e)   Article 32 of the Proceeds of Crime (Northern Ireland) Order 1996 (S.I. 1996/1299 (N.I. 9)).

(9)   Dealing with property includes removing it from England and Wales.

42   Application, discharge and variation

(1)   A restraint order —

    (a)   may be made only on an application by an applicant falling within subsection (2);

    (b)   may be made on an ex parte application to a judge in chambers.

(2)   These applicants fall within this subsection —

    (a)   the prosecutor;

    (b)   the Director;

    (c)   an accredited financial investigator.

(3)   An application to discharge or vary a restraint order or an order under section 41(7) may be made to the Crown Court by —

    (a)   the person who applied for the order;

    (b)   any person affected by the order.

(4)   Subsections (5) to (7) apply to an application under subsection (3).

(5)   The court —

    (a)   may discharge the order;

    (b)   may vary the order.

(6)   If the condition in section 40 which was satisfied was that proceedings were started or an application was made, the court must discharge the order on the conclusion of the proceedings or of the application (as the case may be).

(7)   If the condition in section 40 which was satisfied was that an investigation was started or an application was to be made, the court must discharge the order if within a reasonable time proceedings for the offence are not started or the application is not made (as the case may be).

43   Appeal to Court of Appeal

(1)   If on an application for a restraint order the court decides not to make one, the person who applied for the order may appeal to the Court of Appeal against the decision.

(2)   If an application is made under section 42(3) in relation to a restraint order or an order under section 41(7) the following persons may appeal to the Court of Appeal in respect of the Crown Court's decision on the application –
    (a)   the person who applied for the order;
    (b)   any person affected by the order.

(3)   On an appeal under subsection (1) or (2) the Court of Appeal may –
    (a)   confirm the decision, or
    (b)   make such order as it believes is appropriate.

44   Appeal to House of Lords

(1)   An appeal lies to the House of Lords from a decision of the Court of Appeal on an appeal under section 43.

(2)   An appeal under this section lies at the instance of any person who was a party to the proceedings before the Court of Appeal.

(3)   On an appeal under this section the House of Lords may –
    (a)   confirm the decision of the Court of Appeal, or
    (b)   make such order as it believes is appropriate.

45   Seizure

(1)   If a restraint order is in force a constable or a customs officer may seize any realisable property to which it applies to prevent its removal from England and Wales.

(2)   Property seized under subsection (1) must be dealt with in accordance with the directions of the court which made the order.

46   Hearsay evidence

(1)   Evidence must not be excluded in restraint proceedings on the ground that it is hearsay (of whatever degree).

(2)   Sections 2 to 4 of the Civil Evidence Act 1995 (c. 38) apply in relation to restraint proceedings as those sections apply in relation to civil proceedings.

(3)   Restraint proceedings are proceedings –
    (a)   for a restraint order;
    (b)   for the discharge or variation of a restraint order;
    (c)   on an appeal under section 43 or 44.

(4)   Hearsay is a statement which is made otherwise than by a person while giving oral evidence in the proceedings and which is tendered as evidence of the matters stated.

(5)   Nothing in this section affects the admissibility of evidence which is admissible apart from this section.

47   Supplementary

(1)   The registration Acts —

    (a)   apply in relation to restraint orders as they apply in relation to orders which affect land and are made by the court for the purpose of enforcing judgments or recognisances;

    (b)   apply in relation to applications for restraint orders as they apply in relation to other pending land actions.

(2)   The registration Acts are —

    (a)   the Land Registration Act 1925 (c. 21);

    (b)   the Land Charges Act 1972 (c. 61);

    (c)   the Land Registration Act 2002 (c. 9).

(3)   But no notice may be entered in the register of title under the Land Registration Act 2002 in respect of a restraint order.

(4)   The person applying for a restraint order must be treated for the purposes of section 57 of the Land Registration Act 1925 (inhibitions) as a person interested in relation to any registered land to which —

    (a)   the application relates, or

    (b)   a restraint order made in pursuance of the application relates.

Management receivers

48   Appointment

(1)   Subsection (2) applies if —

    (a)   the Crown Court makes a restraint order, and

    (b)   the applicant for the restraint order applies to the court to proceed under subsection (2) (whether as part of the application for the restraint order or at any time afterwards).

(2)   The Crown Court may by order appoint a receiver in respect of any realisable property to which the restraint order applies.

49   Powers

(1)   If the court appoints a receiver under section 48 it may act under this section on the application of the person who applied for the restraint order.

(2)   The court may by order confer on the receiver the following powers in relation to any realisable property to which the restraint order applies —

    (a)   power to take possession of the property;

    (b)   power to manage or otherwise deal with the property;

    (c)   power to start, carry on or defend any legal proceedings in respect of the property;

    (d)   power to realise so much of the property as is necessary to meet the receiver's remuneration and expenses.

(3)   The court may by order confer on the receiver power to enter any premises in England and Wales and to do any of the following —

    (a)   search for or inspect anything authorised by the court;

    (b)   make or obtain a copy, photograph or other record of anything so authorised;

    (c)   remove anything which the receiver is required or authorised to take possession of in pursuance of an order of the court.

(4)   The court may by order authorise the receiver to do any of the following for the purpose of the exercise of his functions –

    (a)   hold property;

    (b)   enter into contracts;

    (c)   sue and be sued;

    (d)   employ agents;

    (e)   execute powers of attorney, deeds or other instruments;

    (f)   take any other steps the court thinks appropriate.

(5)   The court may order any person who has possession of realisable property to which the restraint order applies to give possession of it to the receiver.

(6)   The court –

    (a)   may order a person holding an interest in realisable property to which the restraint order applies to make to the receiver such payment as the court specifies in respect of a beneficial interest held by the defendant or the recipient of a tainted gift;

    (b)   may (on the payment being made) by order transfer, grant or extinguish any interest in the property.

(7)   Subsections (2), (5) and (6) do not apply to property for the time being subject to a charge under any of these provisions –

    (a)   section 9 of the Drug Trafficking Offences Act 1986 (c. 32);

    (b)   section 78 of the Criminal Justice Act 1988 (c. 33);

    (c)   Article 14 of the Criminal Justice (Confiscation) (Northern Ireland) Order 1990 (S.I. 1990/2588 (N.I. 17));

    (d)   section 27 of the Drug Trafficking Act 1994 (c. 37);

    (e)   Article 32 of the Proceeds of Crime (Northern Ireland) Order 1996 (S.I. 1996/1299 (N.I. 9)).

(8)   The court must not –

    (a)   confer the power mentioned in subsection (2)(b) or (d) in respect of property, or

    (b)   exercise the power conferred on it by subsection (6) in respect of property,

unless it gives persons holding interests in the property a reasonable opportunity to make representations to it.

(9)   The court may order that a power conferred by an order under this section is subject to such conditions and exceptions as it specifies.

(10)   Managing or otherwise dealing with property includes –

    (a)   selling the property or any part of it or interest in it;

    (b)   carrying on or arranging for another person to carry on any trade or business the assets of which are or are part of the property;

    (c)   incurring capital expenditure in respect of the property.

Enforcement receivers

50   Appointment

(1)   This section applies if —

   (a)   a confiscation order is made,

   (b)   it is not satisfied, and

   (c)   it is not subject to appeal.

(2)   On the application of the prosecutor the Crown Court may by order appoint a receiver in respect of realisable property.

51   Powers

(1)   If the court appoints a receiver under section 50 it may act under this section on the application of the prosecutor.

(2)   The court may by order confer on the receiver the following powers in relation to the realisable property —

   (a)   power to take possession of the property;

   (b)   power to manage or otherwise deal with the property;

   (c)   power to realise the property, in such manner as the court may specify;

   (d)   power to start, carry on or defend any legal proceedings in respect of the property.

(3)   The court may by order confer on the receiver power to enter any premises in England and Wales and to do any of the following —

   (a)   search for or inspect anything authorised by the court;

   (b)   make or obtain a copy, photograph or other record of anything so authorised;

   (c)   remove anything which the receiver is required or authorised to take possession of in pursuance of an order of the court.

(4)   The court may by order authorise the receiver to do any of the following for the purpose of the exercise of his functions —

   (a)   hold property;

   (b)   enter into contracts;

   (c)   sue and be sued;

   (d)   employ agents;

   (e)   execute powers of attorney, deeds or other instruments;

   (f)   take any other steps the court thinks appropriate.

(5)   The court may order any person who has possession of realisable property to give possession of it to the receiver.

(6)   The court —

   (a)   may order a person holding an interest in realisable property to make to the receiver such payment as the court specifies in respect of a beneficial interest held by the defendant or the recipient of a tainted gift;

   (b)   may (on the payment being made) by order transfer, grant or extinguish any interest in the property.

(7) Subsections (2), (5) and (6) do not apply to property for the time being subject to a charge under any of these provisions —
   (a) section 9 of the Drug Trafficking Offences Act 1986 (c. 32);
   (b) section 78 of the Criminal Justice Act 1988 (c. 33);
   (c) Article 14 of the Criminal Justice (Confiscation) (Northern Ireland) Order 1990 (S.I. 1990/2588 (N.I. 17));
   (d) section 27 of the Drug Trafficking Act 1994 (c. 37);
   (e) Article 32 of the Proceeds of Crime (Northern Ireland) Order 1996 (S.I. 1996/1299 (N.I. 9)).

(8) The court must not —
   (a) confer the power mentioned in subsection (2)(b) or (c) in respect of property, or
   (b) exercise the power conferred on it by subsection (6) in respect of property,
   unless it gives persons holding interests in the property a reasonable opportunity to make representations to it.

(9) The court may order that a power conferred by an order under this section is subject to such conditions and exceptions as it specifies.

(10) Managing or otherwise dealing with property includes —
   (a) selling the property or any part of it or interest in it;
   (b) carrying on or arranging for another person to carry on any trade or business the assets of which are or are part of the property;
   (c) incurring capital expenditure in respect of the property.

Director's receivers

52   Appointment

(1) This section applies if —
   (a) a confiscation order is made, and
   (b) the Director is appointed as the enforcement authority for the order under section 34.

(2) But this section does not apply if —
   (a) the confiscation order was made by the Court of Appeal, and
   (b) when the Crown Court comes to proceed under this section the confiscation order has been satisfied.

(3) If this section applies the Crown Court must make an order for the appointment of a receiver in respect of realisable property.

(4) An order under subsection (3) —
   (a) must confer power on the Director to nominate the person who is to be the receiver, and
   (b) takes effect when the Director nominates that person.

(5) The Director must not nominate a person under subsection (4) unless at the time he does so the confiscation order —
   (a) is not satisfied, and
   (b) is not subject to appeal.

(6)   A person nominated to be the receiver under subsection (4) may be —

   (a)   a member of the staff of the Agency;

   (b)   a person providing services under arrangements made by the Director.

(7)   If this section applies section 50 does not apply.

53   Powers

(1)   If the court makes an order for the appointment of a receiver under section 52 it may act under this section on the application of the Director.

(2)   The court may by order confer on the receiver the following powers in relation to the realisable property —

   (a)   power to take possession of the property;

   (b)   power to manage or otherwise deal with the property;

   (c)   power to realise the property, in such manner as the court may specify;

   (d)   power to start, carry on or defend any legal proceedings in respect of the property.

(3)   The court may by order confer on the receiver power to enter any premises in England and Wales and to do any of the following —

   (a)   search for or inspect anything authorised by the court;

   (b)   make or obtain a copy, photograph or other record of anything so authorised;

   (c)   remove anything which the receiver is required or authorised to take possession of in pursuance of an order of the court.

(4)   The court may by order authorise the receiver to do any of the following for the purpose of the exercise of his functions —

   (a)   hold property;

   (b)   enter into contracts;

   (c)   sue and be sued;

   (d)   employ agents;

   (e)   execute powers of attorney, deeds or other instruments;

   (f)   take any other steps the court thinks appropriate.

(5)   The court may order any person who has possession of realisable property to give possession of it to the receiver.

(6)   The court —

   (a)   may order a person holding an interest in realisable property to make to the receiver such payment as the court specifies in respect of a beneficial interest held by the defendant or the recipient of a tainted gift;

   (b)   may (on the payment being made) by order transfer, grant or extinguish any interest in the property.

(7)   Subsections (2), (5) and (6) do not apply to property for the time being subject to a charge under any of these provisions —

   (a)   section 9 of the Drug Trafficking Offences Act 1986 (c. 32);

   (b)   section 78 of the Criminal Justice Act 1988 (c. 33);

   (c)   Article 14 of the Criminal Justice (Confiscation) (Northern Ireland) Order 1990 (S.I. 1990/2588 (N.I. 17));

   (d)   section 27 of the Drug Trafficking Act 1994 (c. 37);

(e)   Article 32 of the Proceeds of Crime (Northern Ireland) Order 1996 (S.I. 1996/1299 (N.I. 9)).

(8)   The court must not—

    (a)   confer the power mentioned in subsection (2)(b) or (c) in respect of property, or

    (b)   exercise the power conferred on it by subsection (6) in respect of property,

unless it gives persons holding interests in the property a reasonable opportunity to make representations to it.

(9)   The court may order that a power conferred by an order under this section is subject to such conditions and exceptions as it specifies.

(10)   Managing or otherwise dealing with property includes—

    (a)   selling the property or any part of it or interest in it;

    (b)   carrying on or arranging for another person to carry on any trade or business the assets of which are or are part of the property;

    (c)   incurring capital expenditure in respect of the property.

Application of sums

54   Enforcement receivers

(1)   This section applies to sums which are in the hands of a receiver appointed under section 50 if they are—

    (a)   the proceeds of the realisation of property under section 51;

    (b)   sums (other than those mentioned in paragraph (a)) in which the defendant holds an interest.

(2)   The sums must be applied as follows—

    (a)   first, they must be applied in payment of such expenses incurred by a person acting as an insolvency practitioner as are payable under this subsection by virtue of section 432;

    (b)   second, they must be applied in making any payments directed by the Crown Court;

    (c)   third, they must be applied on the defendant's behalf towards satisfaction of the confiscation order.

(3)   If the amount payable under the confiscation order has been fully paid and any sums remain in the receiver's hands he must distribute them—

    (a)   among such persons who held (or hold) interests in the property concerned as the Crown Court directs, and

    (b)   in such proportions as it directs.

(4)   Before making a direction under subsection (3) the court must give persons who held (or hold) interests in the property concerned a reasonable opportunity to make representations to it.

(5)   For the purposes of subsections (3) and (4) the property concerned is—

    (a)   the property represented by the proceeds mentioned in subsection (1)(a);

    (b)   the sums mentioned in subsection (1)(b).

(6) The receiver applies sums as mentioned in subsection (2)(c) by paying them to the appropriate justices' chief executive on account of the amount payable under the order.

(7) The appropriate justices' chief executive is the one for the magistrates' court responsible for enforcing the confiscation order as if the amount ordered to be paid were a fine.

55 Sums received by justices' chief executive

(1) This section applies if a justices' chief executive receives sums on account of the amount payable under a confiscation order (whether the sums are received under section 54 or otherwise).

(2) The chief executive's receipt of the sums reduces the amount payable under the order, but he must apply the sums received as follows.

(3) First he must apply them in payment of such expenses incurred by a person acting as an insolvency practitioner as –
   (a) are payable under this subsection by virtue of section 432, but
   (b) are not already paid under section 54(2)(a).

(4) If the justices' chief executive received the sums under section 54 he must next apply them –
   (a) first, in payment of the remuneration and expenses of a receiver appointed under section 48, to the extent that they have not been met by virtue of the exercise by that receiver of a power conferred under section 49(2)(d);
   (b) second, in payment of the remuneration and expenses of the receiver appointed under section 50.

(5) If a direction was made under section 13(6) for an amount of compensation to be paid out of sums recovered under the confiscation order, the justices' chief executive must next apply the sums in payment of that amount.

(6) If any amount remains after the justices' chief executive makes any payments required by the preceding provisions of this section, the amount must be treated for the purposes of section 60 of the Justices of the Peace Act 1997 (c. 25) (application of fines etc) as if it were a fine imposed by a magistrates' court.

(7) Subsection (4) does not apply if the receiver is a member of the staff of the Crown Prosecution Service or of the Commissioners of Customs and Excise; and it is immaterial whether he is a permanent or temporary member or he is on secondment from elsewhere.

56 Director's receivers

(1) This section applies to sums which are in the hands of a receiver appointed under section 52 if they are –
   (a) the proceeds of the realisation of property under section 53;
   (b) sums (other than those mentioned in paragraph (a)) in which the defendant holds an interest.

(2) The sums must be applied as follows –

(a) first, they must be applied in payment of such expenses incurred by a person acting as an insolvency practitioner as are payable under this subsection by virtue of section 432;

(b) second, they must be applied in making any payments directed by the Crown Court;

(c) third, they must be applied on the defendant's behalf towards satisfaction of the confiscation order by being paid to the Director on account of the amount payable under it.

(3) If the amount payable under the confiscation order has been fully paid and any sums remain in the receiver's hands he must distribute them —

(a) among such persons who held (or hold) interests in the property concerned as the Crown Court directs, and

(b) in such proportions as it directs.

(4) Before making a direction under subsection (3) the court must give persons who held (or hold) interests in the property concerned a reasonable opportunity to make representations to it.

(5) For the purposes of subsections (3) and (4) the property concerned is —

(a) the property represented by the proceeds mentioned in subsection (1)(a);

(b) the sums mentioned in subsection (1)(b).

57 Sums received by Director

(1) This section applies if the Director receives sums on account of the amount payable under a confiscation order (whether the sums are received under section 56 or otherwise).

(2) The Director's receipt of the sums reduces the amount payable under the order, but he must apply the sums received as follows.

(3) First he must apply them in payment of such expenses incurred by a person acting as an insolvency practitioner as —

(a) are payable under this subsection by virtue of section 432, but

(b) are not already paid under section 56(2)(a).

(4) If the Director received the sums under section 56 he must next apply them —

(a) first, in payment of the remuneration and expenses of a receiver appointed under section 48, to the extent that they have not been met by virtue of the exercise by that receiver of a power conferred under section 49(2)(d);

(b) second, in payment of the remuneration and expenses of the receiver appointed under section 52.

(5) If a direction was made under section 13(6) for an amount of compensation to be paid out of sums recovered under the confiscation order, the Director must next apply the sums in payment of that amount.

(6) Subsection (4) does not apply if the receiver is a member of the staff of the Agency or a person providing services under arrangements made by the Director.

Restrictions

58   Restraint orders

(1)   Subsections (2) to (4) apply if a court makes a restraint order.

(2)   No distress may be levied against any realisable property to which the order applies except with the leave of the Crown Court and subject to any terms the Crown Court may impose.

(3)   If the order applies to a tenancy of any premises, no landlord or other person to whom rent is payable may exercise a right within subsection (4) except with the leave of the Crown Court and subject to any terms the Crown Court may impose.

(4)   A right is within this subsection if it is a right of forfeiture by peaceable re-entry in relation to the premises in respect of any failure by the tenant to comply with any term or condition of the tenancy.

(5)   If a court in which proceedings are pending in respect of any property is satisfied that a restraint order has been applied for or made in respect of the property, the court may either stay the proceedings or allow them to continue on any terms it thinks fit.

(6)   Before exercising any power conferred by subsection (5), the court must give an opportunity to be heard to —

   (a)   the applicant for the restraint order, and

   (b)   any receiver appointed in respect of the property under section 48, 50 or 52.

59   Enforcement receivers

(1)   Subsections (2) to (4) apply if a court makes an order under section 50 appointing a receiver in respect of any realisable property.

(2)   No distress may be levied against the property except with the leave of the Crown Court and subject to any terms the Crown Court may impose.

(3)   If the receiver is appointed in respect of a tenancy of any premises, no landlord or other person to whom rent is payable may exercise a right within subsection (4) except with the leave of the Crown Court and subject to any terms the Crown Court may impose.

(4)   A right is within this subsection if it is a right of forfeiture by peaceable re-entry in relation to the premises in respect of any failure by the tenant to comply with any term or condition of the tenancy.

(5)   If a court in which proceedings are pending in respect of any property is satisfied that an order under section 50 appointing a receiver in respect of the property has been applied for or made, the court may either stay the proceedings or allow them to continue on any terms it thinks fit.

(6)   Before exercising any power conferred by subsection (5), the court must give an opportunity to be heard to —

   (a)   the prosecutor, and

   (b)   the receiver (if the order under section 50 has been made).

60   Director's receivers

(1)   Subsections (2) to (4) apply if—

(a)   the Crown Court has made an order under section 52 for the appointment of a receiver in respect of any realisable property, and

(b)   the order has taken effect.

(2)   No distress may be levied against the property except with the leave of the Crown Court and subject to any terms the Crown Court may impose.

(3)   If the order is for the appointment of a receiver in respect of a tenancy of any premises, no landlord or other person to whom rent is payable may exercise a right within subsection (4) except with the leave of the Crown Court and subject to any terms the Crown Court may impose.

(4)   A right is within this subsection if it is a right of forfeiture by peaceable re-entry in relation to the premises in respect of any failure by the tenant to comply with any term or condition of the tenancy.

(5)   If a court (whether the Crown Court or any other court) in which proceedings are pending in respect of any property is satisfied that an order under section 52 for the appointment of a receiver in respect of the property has taken effect, the court may either stay the proceedings or allow them to continue on any terms it thinks fit.

(6)   Before exercising any power conferred by subsection (5), the court must give an opportunity to be heard to—

(a)   the Director, and

(b)   the receiver.

Receivers: further provisions

61   Protection

If a receiver appointed under section 48, 50 or 52—

(a)   takes action in relation to property which is not realisable property,

(b)   would be entitled to take the action if it were realisable property, and

(c)   believes on reasonable grounds that he is entitled to take the action,

he is not liable to any person in respect of any loss or damage resulting from the action, except so far as the loss or damage is caused by his negligence.

62   Further applications

(1)   This section applies to a receiver appointed under section 48, 50 or 52.

(2)   The receiver may apply to the Crown Court for an order giving directions as to the exercise of his powers.

(3)   The following persons may apply to the Crown Court—

(a)   any person affected by action taken by the receiver;

(b)   any person who may be affected by action the receiver proposes to take.

(4)   On an application under this section the court may make such order as it believes is appropriate.

63   Discharge and variation

(1)   The following persons may apply to the Crown Court to vary or discharge an order made under any of sections 48 to 53 —

     (a)   the receiver;

     (b)   the person who applied for the order or (if the order was made under section 52 or 53) the Director;

     (c)   any person affected by the order.

(2)   On an application under this section the court —

     (a)   may discharge the order;

     (b)   may vary the order.

(3)   But in the case of an order under section 48 or 49 —

     (a)   if the condition in section 40 which was satisfied was that proceedings were started or an application was made, the court must discharge the order on the conclusion of the proceedings or of the application (as the case may be);

     (b)   if the condition which was satisfied was that an investigation was started or an application was to be made, the court must discharge the order if within a reasonable time proceedings for the offence are not started or the application is not made (as the case may be).

64   Management receivers: discharge

(1)   This section applies if —

     (a)   a receiver stands appointed under section 48 in respect of realisable property (the management receiver), and

     (b)   the court appoints a receiver under section 50 or makes an order for the appointment of a receiver under section 52.

(2)   The court must order the management receiver to transfer to the other receiver all property held by the management receiver by virtue of the powers conferred on him by section 49.

(3)   But in a case where the court makes an order under section 52 its order under subsection (2) above does not take effect until the order under section 52 takes effect.

(4)   Subsection (2) does not apply to property which the management receiver holds by virtue of the exercise by him of his power under section 49(2)(d).

(5)   If the management receiver complies with an order under subsection (2) he is discharged —

     (a)   from his appointment under section 48;

     (b)   from any obligation under this Act arising from his appointment.

(6)   If this section applies the court may make such a consequential or incidental order as it believes is appropriate.

65   Appeal to Court of Appeal

(1)   If on an application for an order under any of sections 48 to 51 or section 53 the court decides not to make one, the person who applied for the order may appeal to the Court of Appeal against the decision.

(2) If the court makes an order under any of sections 48 to 51 or section 53, the following persons may appeal to the Court of Appeal in respect of the court's decision —

    (a) the person who applied for the order;

    (b) any person affected by the order.

(3) If on an application for an order under section 62 the court decides not to make one, the person who applied for the order may appeal to the Court of Appeal against the decision.

(4) If the court makes an order under section 62, the following persons may appeal to the Court of Appeal in respect of the court's decision —

    (a) the person who applied for the order;

    (b) any person affected by the order;

    (c) the receiver.

(5) The following persons may appeal to the Court of Appeal against a decision of the court on an application under section 63 —

    (a) the person who applied for the order in respect of which the application was made or (if the order was made under section 52 or 53) the Director;

    (b) any person affected by the court's decision;

    (c) the receiver.

(6) On an appeal under this section the Court of Appeal may —

    (a) confirm the decision, or

    (b) make such order as it believes is appropriate.

66   Appeal to House of Lords

(1) An appeal lies to the House of Lords from a decision of the Court of Appeal on an appeal under section 65.

(2) An appeal under this section lies at the instance of any person who was a party to the proceedings before the Court of Appeal.

(3) On an appeal under this section the House of Lords may —

    (a) confirm the decision of the Court of Appeal, or

    (b) make such order as it believes is appropriate.

Seized money

67   Seized money

(1) This section applies to money which —

    (a) is held by a person, and

    (b) is held in an account maintained by him with a bank or a building society.

(2) This section also applies to money which is held by a person and which —

    (a) has been seized by a constable under section 19 of the Police and Criminal Evidence Act 1984 (c. 60) (general power of seizure etc), and

    (b) is held in an account maintained by a police force with a bank or a building society.

(3) This section also applies to money which is held by a person and which—

    (a) has been seized by a customs officer under section 19 of the 1984 Act as applied by order made under section 114(2) of that Act, and

    (b) is held in an account maintained by the Commissioners of Customs and Excise with a bank or a building society.

(4) This section applies if the following conditions are satisfied—

    (a) a restraint order has effect in relation to money to which this section applies;

    (b) a confiscation order is made against the person by whom the money is held;

    (c) the Director has not been appointed as the enforcement authority for the confiscation order;

    (d) a receiver has not been appointed under section 50 in relation to the money;

    (e) any period allowed under section 11 for payment of the amount ordered to be paid under the confiscation order has ended.

(5) In such a case a magistrates' court may order the bank or building society to pay the money to the justices' chief executive for the court on account of the amount payable under the confiscation order.

(6) If a bank or building society fails to comply with an order under subsection (5)—

    (a) the magistrates' court may order it to pay an amount not exceeding £5,000, and

    (b) for the purposes of the Magistrates' Courts Act 1980 (c. 43) the sum is to be treated as adjudged to be paid by a conviction of the court.

(7) In order to take account of changes in the value of money the Secretary of State may by order substitute another sum for the sum for the time being specified in subsection (6)(a).

(8) For the purposes of this section—

    (a) a bank is a deposit-taking business within the meaning of the Banking Act 1987 (c. 22);

    (b) "building society" has the same meaning as in the Building Societies Act 1986 (c. 53).

Financial investigators

68 Applications and appeals

(1) Subsections (2) and (3) apply to—

    (a) an application under section 41, 42, 48, 49 or 63;

    (b) an appeal under section 43, 44, 65 or 66.

(2) An accredited financial investigator must not make such an application or bring such an appeal unless he falls within subsection (3).

(3) An accredited financial investigator falls within this subsection if he is one of the following or is authorised for the purposes of this section by one of the following—

    (a) a police officer who is not below the rank of superintendent,

    (b)   a customs officer who is not below such grade as is designated by the Commissioners of Customs and Excise as equivalent to that rank,

    (c)   an accredited financial investigator who falls within a description specified in an order made for the purposes of this paragraph by the Secretary of State under section 453.

(4)   If such an application is made or appeal brought by an accredited financial investigator any subsequent step in the application or appeal or any further application or appeal relating to the same matter may be taken, made or brought by a different accredited financial investigator who falls within subsection (3).

(5)   If —

    (a)   an application for a restraint order is made by an accredited financial investigator, and

    (b)   a court is required under section 58(6) to give the applicant for the order an opportunity to be heard,

the court may give the opportunity to a different accredited financial investigator who falls within subsection (3).

Exercise of powers

69   Powers of court and receiver

(1)   This section applies to —

    (a)   the powers conferred on a court by sections 41 to 60 and sections 62 to 67;

    (b)   the powers of a receiver appointed under section 48, 50 or 52.

(2)   The powers —

    (a)   must be exercised with a view to the value for the time being of realisable property being made available (by the property's realisation) for satisfying any confiscation order that has been or may be made against the defendant;

    (b)   must be exercised, in a case where a confiscation order has not been made, with a view to securing that there is no diminution in the value of realisable property;

    (c)   must be exercised without taking account of any obligation of the defendant or a recipient of a tainted gift if the obligation conflicts with the object of satisfying any confiscation order that has been or may be made against the defendant;

    (d)   may be exercised in respect of a debt owed by the Crown.

(3)   Subsection (2) has effect subject to the following rules —

    (a)   the powers must be exercised with a view to allowing a person other than the defendant or a recipient of a tainted gift to retain or recover the value of any interest held by him;

    (b)   in the case of realisable property held by a recipient of a tainted gift, the powers must be exercised with a view to realising no more than the value for the time being of the gift;

    (c)   in a case where a confiscation order has not been made against the defendant, property must not be sold if the court so orders under subsection (4).

(4)   If on an application by the defendant, or by the recipient of a tainted gift, the court decides that property cannot be replaced it may order that it must not be sold.

(5)   An order under subsection (4) may be revoked or varied.

Committal

70   Committal by magistrates' court

(1)   This section applies if—

      (a)   a defendant is convicted of an offence by a magistrates' court, and

      (b)   the prosecutor asks the court to commit the defendant to the Crown Court with a view to a confiscation order being considered under section 6.

(2)   In such a case the magistrates' court—

      (a)   must commit the defendant to the Crown Court in respect of the offence, and

      (b)   may commit him to the Crown Court in respect of any other offence falling within subsection (3).

(3)   An offence falls within this subsection if—

      (a)   the defendant has been convicted of it by the magistrates' court or any other court, and

      (b)   the magistrates' court has power to deal with him in respect of it.

(4)   If a committal is made under this section in respect of an offence or offences—

      (a)   section 6 applies accordingly, and

      (b)   the committal operates as a committal of the defendant to be dealt with by the Crown Court in accordance with section 71.

(5)   If a committal is made under this section in respect of an offence for which (apart from this section) the magistrates' court could have committed the defendant for sentence under section 3(2) of the Sentencing Act (offences triable either way) the court must state whether it would have done so.

(6)   A committal under this section may be in custody or on bail.

71   Sentencing by Crown Court

(1)   If a defendant is committed to the Crown Court under section 70 in respect of an offence or offences, this section applies (whether or not the court proceeds under section 6).

(2)   In the case of an offence in respect of which the magistrates' court has stated under section 70(5) that it would have committed the defendant for sentence, the Crown Court—

      (a)   must inquire into the circumstances of the case, and

      (b)   may deal with the defendant in any way in which it could deal with him if he had just been convicted of the offence on indictment before it.

(3)   In the case of any other offence the Crown Court—

      (a)   must inquire into the circumstances of the case, and

(b)   may deal with the defendant in any way in which the magistrates' court could deal with him if it had just convicted him of the offence.

Compensation

72   Serious default

(1)   If the following three conditions are satisfied the Crown Court may order the payment of such compensation as it believes is just.

(2)   The first condition is satisfied if a criminal investigation has been started with regard to an offence and proceedings are not started for the offence.

(3)   The first condition is also satisfied if proceedings for an offence are started against a person and—
  (a)   they do not result in his conviction for the offence, or
  (b)   he is convicted of the offence but the conviction is quashed or he is pardoned in respect of it.

(4)   If subsection (2) applies the second condition is that—
  (a)   in the criminal investigation there has been a serious default by a person mentioned in subsection (9), and
  (b)   the investigation would not have continued if the default had not occurred.

(5)   If subsection (3) applies the second condition is that—
  (a)   in the criminal investigation with regard to the offence or in its prosecution there has been a serious default by a person who is mentioned in subsection (9), and
  (b)   the proceedings would not have been started or continued if the default had not occurred.

(6)   The third condition is that an application is made under this section by a person who held realisable property and has suffered loss in consequence of anything done in relation to it by or in pursuance of an order under this Part.

(7)   The offence referred to in subsection (2) may be one of a number of offences with regard to which the investigation is started.

(8)   The offence referred to in subsection (3) may be one of a number of offences for which the proceedings are started.

(9)   Compensation under this section is payable to the applicant and—
  (a)   if the person in default was or was acting as a member of a police force, the compensation is payable out of the police fund from which the expenses of that force are met;
  (b)   if the person in default was a member of the Crown Prosecution Service or was acting on its behalf, the compensation is payable by the Director of Public Prosecutions;
  (c)   if the person in default was a member of the Serious Fraud Office, the compensation is payable by the Director of that Office;
  (d)   if the person in default was a customs officer, the compensation is payable by the Commissioners of Customs and Excise;
  (e)   if the person in default was an officer of the Commissioners of Inland Revenue, the compensation is payable by those Commissioners.

73   Order varied or discharged

(1)   This section applies if –

   (a)   the court varies a confiscation order under section 29 or discharges one under section 30, and

   (b)   an application is made to the Crown Court by a person who held realisable property and has suffered loss as a result of the making of the order.

(2)   The court may order the payment of such compensation as it believes is just.

(3)   Compensation under this section is payable –

   (a)   to the applicant;

   (b)   by the Lord Chancellor.

Enforcement abroad

74   Enforcement abroad

(1)   This section applies if –

   (a)   any of the conditions in section 40 is satisfied,

   (b)   the prosecutor or the Director believes that realisable property is situated in a country or territory outside the United Kingdom (the receiving country), and

   (c)   the prosecutor or the Director (as the case may be) sends a request for assistance to the Secretary of State with a view to it being forwarded under this section.

(2)   In a case where no confiscation order has been made, a request for assistance is a request to the government of the receiving country to secure that any person is prohibited from dealing with realisable property.

(3)   In a case where a confiscation order has been made and has not been satisfied, discharged or quashed, a request for assistance is a request to the government of the receiving country to secure that –

   (a)   any person is prohibited from dealing with realisable property;

   (b)   realisable property is realised and the proceeds are applied in accordance with the law of the receiving country.

(4)   No request for assistance may be made for the purposes of this section in a case where a confiscation order has been made and has been satisfied, discharged or quashed.

(5)   If the Secretary of State believes it is appropriate to do so he may forward the request for assistance to the government of the receiving country.

(6)   If property is realised in pursuance of a request under subsection (3) the amount ordered to be paid under the confiscation order must be taken to be reduced by an amount equal to the proceeds of realisation.

(7)   A certificate purporting to be issued by or on behalf of the requested government is admissible as evidence of the facts it states if it states –

   (a)   that property has been realised in pursuance of a request under subsection (3),

   (b)   the date of realisation, and

(c)   the proceeds of realisation.

(8)   If the proceeds of realisation made in pursuance of a request under subsection (3) are expressed in a currency other than sterling, they must be taken to be the sterling equivalent calculated in accordance with the rate of exchange prevailing at the end of the day of realisation.

Interpretation

75   Criminal lifestyle

(1)   A defendant has a criminal lifestyle if (and only if) the following condition is satisfied.

(2)   The condition is that the offence (or any of the offences) concerned satisfies any of these tests —
    (a)   it is specified in Schedule 2;
    (b)   it constitutes conduct forming part of a course of criminal activity;
    (c)   it is an offence committed over a period of at least six months and the defendant has benefited from the conduct which constitutes the offence.

(3)   Conduct forms part of a course of criminal activity if the defendant has benefited from the conduct and —
    (a)   in the proceedings in which he was convicted he was convicted of three or more other offences, each of three or more of them constituting conduct from which he has benefited, or
    (b)   in the period of six years ending with the day when those proceedings were started (or, if there is more than one such day, the earliest day) he was convicted on at least two separate occasions of an offence constituting conduct from which he has benefited.

(4)   But an offence does not satisfy the test in subsection (2)(b) or (c) unless the defendant obtains relevant benefit of not less than £5000.

(5)   Relevant benefit for the purposes of subsection (2)(b) is —
    (a)   benefit from conduct which constitutes the offence;
    (b)   benefit from any other conduct which forms part of the course of criminal activity and which constitutes an offence of which the defendant has been convicted;
    (c)   benefit from conduct which constitutes an offence which has been or will be taken into consideration by the court in sentencing the defendant for an offence mentioned in paragraph (a) or (b).

(6)   Relevant benefit for the purposes of subsection (2)(c) is —
    (a)   benefit from conduct which constitutes the offence;
    (b)   benefit from conduct which constitutes an offence which has been or will be taken into consideration by the court in sentencing the defendant for the offence mentioned in paragraph (a).

(7)   The Secretary of State may by order amend Schedule 2.

(8)   The Secretary of State may by order vary the amount for the time being specified in subsection (4).

76   Conduct and benefit

(1)   Criminal conduct is conduct which—

    (a)   constitutes an offence in England and Wales, or

    (b)   would constitute such an offence if it occurred in England and Wales.

(2)   General criminal conduct of the defendant is all his criminal conduct, and it is immaterial—

    (a)   whether conduct occurred before or after the passing of this Act;

    (b)   whether property constituting a benefit from conduct was obtained before or after the passing of this Act.

(3)   Particular criminal conduct of the defendant is all his criminal conduct which falls within the following paragraphs—

    (a)   conduct which constitutes the offence or offences concerned;

    (b)   conduct which constitutes offences of which he was convicted in the same proceedings as those in which he was convicted of the offence or offences concerned;

    (c)   conduct which constitutes offences which the court will be taking into consideration in deciding his sentence for the offence or offences concerned.

(4)   A person benefits from conduct if he obtains property as a result of or in connection with the conduct.

(5)   If a person obtains a pecuniary advantage as a result of or in connection with conduct, he is to be taken to obtain as a result of or in connection with the conduct a sum of money equal to the value of the pecuniary advantage.

(6)   References to property or a pecuniary advantage obtained in connection with conduct include references to property or a pecuniary advantage obtained both in that connection and some other.

(7)   If a person benefits from conduct his benefit is the value of the property obtained.

77   Tainted gifts

(1)   Subsections (2) and (3) apply if—

    (a)   no court has made a decision as to whether the defendant has a criminal lifestyle, or

    (b)   a court has decided that the defendant has a criminal lifestyle.

(2)   A gift is tainted if it was made by the defendant at any time after the relevant day.

(3)   A gift is also tainted if it was made by the defendant at any time and was of property—

    (a)   which was obtained by the defendant as a result of or in connection with his general criminal conduct, or

    (b)   which (in whole or part and whether directly or indirectly) represented in the defendant's hands property obtained by him as a result of or in connection with his general criminal conduct.

(4)   Subsection (5) applies if a court has decided that the defendant does not have a criminal lifestyle.

(5)   A gift is tainted if it was made by the defendant at any time after—

(a)   the date on which the offence concerned was committed, or

(b)   if his particular criminal conduct consists of two or more offences and they were committed on different dates, the date of the earliest.

(6)   For the purposes of subsection (5) an offence which is a continuing offence is committed on the first occasion when it is committed.

(7)   For the purposes of subsection (5) the defendant's particular criminal conduct includes any conduct which constitutes offences which the court has taken into consideration in deciding his sentence for the offence or offences concerned.

(8)   A gift may be a tainted gift whether it was made before or after the passing of this Act.

(9)   The relevant day is the first day of the period of six years ending with—

(a)   the day when proceedings for the offence concerned were started against the defendant, or

(b)   if there are two or more offences and proceedings for them were started on different days, the earliest of those days.

78   Gifts and their recipients

(1)   If the defendant transfers property to another person for a consideration whose value is significantly less than the value of the property at the time of the transfer, he is to be treated as making a gift.

(2)   If subsection (1) applies the property given is to be treated as such share in the property transferred as is represented by the fraction—

(a)   whose numerator is the difference between the two values mentioned in subsection (1), and

(b)   whose denominator is the value of the property at the time of the transfer.

(3)   References to a recipient of a tainted gift are to a person to whom the defendant has made the gift.

79   Value: the basic rule

(1)   This section applies for the purpose of deciding the value at any time of property then held by a person.

(2)   Its value is the market value of the property at that time.

(3)   But if at that time another person holds an interest in the property its value, in relation to the person mentioned in subsection (1), is the market value of his interest at that time, ignoring any charging order under a provision listed in subsection (4).

(4)   The provisions are—

(a)   section 9 of the Drug Trafficking Offences Act 1986 (c. 32);

(b)   section 78 of the Criminal Justice Act 1988 (c. 33);

(c)   Article 14 of the Criminal Justice (Confiscation) (Northern Ireland) Order 1990 (S.I. 1990/2588 (N.I. 17));

(d)   section 27 of the Drug Trafficking Act 1994 (c. 37);

(e) Article 32 of the Proceeds of Crime (Northern Ireland) Order 1996 (S.I. 1996/1299 (N.I. 9)).

(5) This section has effect subject to sections 80 and 81.

80 Value of property obtained from conduct

(1) This section applies for the purpose of deciding the value of property obtained by a person as a result of or in connection with his criminal conduct; and the material time is the time the court makes its decision.

(2) The value of the property at the material time is the greater of the following—

    (a) the value of the property (at the time the person obtained it) adjusted to take account of later changes in the value of money;

    (b) the value (at the material time) of the property found under subsection (3).

(3) The property found under this subsection is as follows—

    (a) if the person holds the property obtained, the property found under this subsection is that property;

    (b) if he holds no part of the property obtained, the property found under this subsection is any property which directly or indirectly represents it in his hands;

    (c) if he holds part of the property obtained, the property found under this subsection is that part and any property which directly or indirectly represents the other part in his hands.

(4) The references in subsection (2)(a) and (b) to the value are to the value found in accordance with section 79.

81 Value of tainted gifts

(1) The value at any time (the material time) of a tainted gift is the greater of the following—

    (a) the value (at the time of the gift) of the property given, adjusted to take account of later changes in the value of money;

    (b) the value (at the material time) of the property found under subsection (2).

(2) The property found under this subsection is as follows—

    (a) if the recipient holds the property given, the property found under this subsection is that property;

    (b) if the recipient holds no part of the property given, the property found under this subsection is any property which directly or indirectly represents it in his hands;

    (c) if the recipient holds part of the property given, the property found under this subsection is that part and any property which directly or indirectly represents the other part in his hands.

(3) The references in subsection (1)(a) and (b) to the value are to the value found in accordance with section 79.

82   Free property

Property is free unless an order is in force in respect of it under any of these provisions —

(a)   section 27 of the Misuse of Drugs Act 1971 (c. 38) (forfeiture orders);

(b)   Article 11 of the Criminal Justice (Northern Ireland) Order 1994 (S.I. 1994/2795 (N.I. 15)) (deprivation orders);

(c)   Part 2 of the Proceeds of Crime (Scotland) Act 1995 (c. 43) (forfeiture of property used in crime);

(d)   section 143 of the Sentencing Act (deprivation orders);

(e)   section 23 or 111 of the Terrorism Act 2000 (c. 11) (forfeiture orders);

(f)   section 246, 266, 295(2) or 298(2) of this Act.

83   Realisable property

Realisable property is —

(a)   any free property held by the defendant;

(b)   any free property held by the recipient of a tainted gift.

84   Property: general provisions

(1)   Property is all property wherever situated and includes —

(a)   money;

(b)   all forms of real or personal property;

(c)   things in action and other intangible or incorporeal property.

(2)   The following rules apply in relation to property —

(a)   property is held by a person if he holds an interest in it;

(b)   property is obtained by a person if he obtains an interest in it;

(c)   property is transferred by one person to another if the first one transfers or grants an interest in it to the second;

(d)   references to property held by a person include references to property vested in his trustee in bankruptcy, permanent or interim trustee (within the meaning of the Bankruptcy (Scotland) Act 1985 (c. 66)) or liquidator;

(e)   references to an interest held by a person beneficially in property include references to an interest which would be held by him beneficially if the property were not so vested;

(f)   references to an interest, in relation to land in England and Wales or Northern Ireland, are to any legal estate or equitable interest or power;

(g)   references to an interest, in relation to land in Scotland, are to any estate, interest, servitude or other heritable right in or over land, including a heritable security;

(h)   references to an interest, in relation to property other than land, include references to a right (including a right to possession).

85   Proceedings

(1)   Proceedings for an offence are started —

(a)   when a justice of the peace issues a summons or warrant under section 1 of the Magistrates' Courts Act 1980 (c. 43) in respect of the offence;

(b) when a person is charged with the offence after being taken into custody without a warrant;

(c) when a bill of indictment is preferred under section 2 of the Administration of Justice (Miscellaneous Provisions) Act 1933 (c. 36) in a case falling within subsection (2)(b) of that section (preferment by Court of Appeal or High Court judge).

(2) If more than one time is found under subsection (1) in relation to proceedings they are started at the earliest of them.

(3) If the defendant is acquitted on all counts in proceedings for an offence, the proceedings are concluded when he is acquitted.

(4) If the defendant is convicted in proceedings for an offence and the conviction is quashed or the defendant is pardoned before a confiscation order is made, the proceedings are concluded when the conviction is quashed or the defendant is pardoned.

(5) If a confiscation order is made against the defendant in proceedings for an offence (whether the order is made by the Crown Court or the Court of Appeal) the proceedings are concluded —

(a) when the order is satisfied or discharged, or

(b) when the order is quashed and there is no further possibility of an appeal against the decision to quash the order.

(6) If the defendant is convicted in proceedings for an offence but the Crown Court decides not to make a confiscation order against him, the following rules apply —

(a) if an application for leave to appeal under section 31(2) is refused, the proceedings are concluded when the decision to refuse is made;

(b) if the time for applying for leave to appeal under section 31(2) expires without an application being made, the proceedings are concluded when the time expires;

(c) if on appeal under section 31(2) the Court of Appeal confirms the Crown Court's decision, and an application for leave to appeal under section 33 is refused, the proceedings are concluded when the decision to refuse is made;

(d) if on appeal under section 31(2) the Court of Appeal confirms the Crown Court's decision, and the time for applying for leave to appeal under section 33 expires without an application being made, the proceedings are concluded when the time expires;

(e) if on appeal under section 31(2) the Court of Appeal confirms the Crown Court's decision, and on appeal under section 33 the House of Lords confirms the Court of Appeal's decision, the proceedings are concluded when the House of Lords confirms the decision;

(f) if on appeal under section 31(2) the Court of Appeal directs the Crown Court to reconsider the case, and on reconsideration the Crown Court decides not to make a confiscation order against the defendant, the proceedings are concluded when the Crown Court makes that decision;

(g) if on appeal under section 33 the House of Lords directs the Crown Court to reconsider the case, and on reconsideration the Crown Court decides not to make a confiscation order against the defendant, the proceedings are concluded when the Crown Court makes that decision.

(7) In applying subsection (6) any power to extend the time for making an application for leave to appeal must be ignored.

(8) In applying subsection (6) the fact that a court may decide on a later occasion to make a confiscation order against the defendant must be ignored.

86 Applications

(1) An application under section 19, 20, 27 or 28 is concluded –
 (a) in a case where the court decides not to make a confiscation order against the defendant, when it makes the decision;
 (b) in a case where a confiscation order is made against him as a result of the application, when the order is satisfied or discharged, or when the order is quashed and there is no further possibility of an appeal against the decision to quash the order;
 (c) in a case where the application is withdrawn, when the person who made the application notifies the withdrawal to the court to which the application was made.

(2) An application under section 21 or 22 is concluded –
 (a) in a case where the court decides not to vary the confiscation order concerned, when it makes the decision;
 (b) in a case where the court varies the confiscation order as a result of the application, when the order is satisfied or discharged, or when the order is quashed and there is no further possibility of an appeal against the decision to quash the order;
 (c) in a case where the application is withdrawn, when the person who made the application notifies the withdrawal to the court to which the application was made.

87 Confiscation orders

(1) A confiscation order is satisfied when no amount is due under it.

(2) A confiscation order is subject to appeal until there is no further possibility of an appeal on which the order could be varied or quashed; and for this purpose any power to grant leave to appeal out of time must be ignored.

88 Other interpretative provisions

(1) A reference to the offence (or offences) concerned must be construed in accordance with section 6(9).

(2) A criminal investigation is an investigation which police officers or other persons have a duty to conduct with a view to it being ascertained whether a person should be charged with an offence.

(3) A defendant is a person against whom proceedings for an offence have been started (whether or not he has been convicted).

(4) A reference to sentencing the defendant for an offence includes a reference to dealing with him otherwise in respect of the offence.

(5) The Sentencing Act is the Powers of Criminal Courts (Sentencing) Act 2000 (c. 6).

(6)   The following paragraphs apply to references to orders –
       (a)   a confiscation order is an order under section 6;
       (b)   a restraint order is an order under section 41.

(7)   Sections 75 to 87 and this section apply for the purposes of this Part.

General

89   Procedure on appeal to the Court of Appeal

(1)   An appeal to the Court of Appeal under this Part lies only with the leave of that
       Court.

(2)   Subject to rules of court made under section 53(1) of the Supreme Court Act
       1981 (c. 54) (distribution of business between civil and criminal divisions) the
       criminal division of the Court of Appeal is the division –
       (a)   to which an appeal to that Court under this Part is to lie, and
       (b)   which is to exercise that Court's jurisdiction under this Part.

(3)   In relation to appeals to the Court of Appeal under this Part, the Secretary of
       State may make an order containing provision corresponding to any provision
       in the Criminal Appeal Act 1968 (c. 19) (subject to any specified modifications).

90   Procedure on appeal to the House of Lords

(1)   Section 33(3) of the Criminal Appeal Act 1968 (limitation on appeal from
       criminal division of the Court of Appeal) does not prevent an appeal to the
       House of Lords under this Part.

(2)   In relation to appeals to the House of Lords under this Part, the Secretary of
       State may make an order containing provision corresponding to any provision
       in the Criminal Appeal Act 1968 (subject to any specified modifications).

91   Crown Court Rules

In relation to –
       (a)   proceedings under this Part, or
       (b)   receivers appointed under this Part,
Crown Court Rules may make provision corresponding to provision in Civil
Procedure Rules.

PART 3

CONFISCATION: SCOTLAND

Confiscation orders

92   Making of order

(1)   The court must act under this section where the following three conditions are
       satisfied.

(2)   The first condition is that an accused falls within either of the following
       paragraphs –

  (a) he is convicted of an offence or offences, whether in solemn or summary proceedings, or

  (b) in the case of summary proceedings in respect of an offence (without proceeding to conviction) an order is made discharging him absolutely.

(3) The second condition is that the prosecutor asks the court to act under this section.

(4) The third condition is that the court decides to order some disposal in respect of the accused; and an absolute discharge is a disposal for the purpose of this subsection.

(5) If the court acts under this section it must proceed as follows —

  (a) it must decide whether the accused has a criminal lifestyle;

  (b) if it decides that he has a criminal lifestyle it must decide whether he has benefited from his general criminal conduct;

  (c) if it decides that he does not have a criminal lifestyle it must decide whether he has benefited from his particular criminal conduct.

(6) If the court decides under subsection (5)(b) or (c) that the accused has benefited from the conduct referred to —

  (a) it must decide the recoverable amount, and

  (b) it must make an order (a confiscation order) requiring him to pay that amount.

(7) But the court must treat the duty in subsection (6) as a power if it believes that any victim of the conduct has at any time started or intends to start proceedings against the accused in respect of loss, injury or damage sustained in connection with the conduct.

(8) Before making an order under this section the court must take into account any representations made to it by any person whom the court thinks is likely to be affected by the order.

(9) The standard of proof required to decide any question arising under subsection (5) or (6) is the balance of probabilities.

(10) The first condition is not satisfied if the accused is unlawfully at large (but section 111 may apply).

(11) For the purposes of any appeal or review, an order under this section is a sentence.

(12) References in this Part to the offence (or offences) concerned are to the offence (or offences) mentioned in subsection (2).

(13) In this section and sections 93 to 118 "the court" means the High Court of Justiciary or the sheriff.

93 Recoverable amount

(1) The recoverable amount for the purposes of section 92 is an amount equal to the accused's benefit from the conduct concerned.

(2) But if the accused shows that the available amount is less than that benefit the recoverable amount is —

  (a) the available amount, or

  (b) a nominal amount, if the available amount is nil.

(3) But if section 92(7) applies the recoverable amount is such amount as—

    (a) the court believes is just, but

    (b) does not exceed the amount found under subsection (1) or (2) (as the case may be).

(4) In calculating the accused's benefit from the conduct concerned for the purposes of subsection (1), any property in respect of which—

    (a) a recovery order is in force under section 266, or

    (b) a forfeiture order is in force under section 298(2),

must be ignored.

(5) If the court decides the available amount, it must include in the confiscation order a statement of its findings as to the matters relevant for deciding that amount.

94 Accused's benefit

(1) If the court is acting under section 92 this section applies for the purpose of—

    (a) deciding whether the accused has benefited from conduct, and

    (b) deciding his benefit from the conduct.

(2) The court must take account of—

    (a) conduct occurring up to the time it makes its decision;

    (b) property obtained up to that time.

(3) Subsection (4) applies if—

    (a) the conduct concerned is general criminal conduct,

    (b) a confiscation order mentioned in subsection (5) has at an earlier time been made against the accused, and

    (c) his benefit for the purposes of that order was benefit from his general criminal conduct.

(4) His benefit found at the time the last confiscation order mentioned in subsection (3)(c) was made against him must be taken for the purposes of this section to be his benefit from his general criminal conduct at that time.

(5) If the conduct concerned is general criminal conduct the court must deduct the aggregate of the following amounts—

    (a) the amount ordered to be paid under each confiscation order previously made against the accused;

    (b) the amount ordered to be paid under each confiscation order previously made against him under—

      (i) the Drug Trafficking Offences Act 1986 (c. 32);

      (ii) Part 1 of the Criminal Justice (Scotland) Act 1987 (c. 41);

      (iii) Part 6 of the Criminal Justice Act 1988 (c. 33);

      (iv) the Criminal Justice (Confiscation) (Northern Ireland) Order 1990 (S.I. 1990/2588 (N.I.17));

      (v) Part 1 of the Drug Trafficking Act 1994 (c. 37);

      (vi) Part 1 of the Proceeds of Crime (Scotland) Act 1995 (c. 43);

      (vii) the Proceeds of Crime (Northern Ireland) Order 1996 (S.I. 1996/1299 (N.I.9)); or

      (viii) Part 2 or 4 of this Act.

(6)   But subsection (5) does not apply to an amount which has been taken into account for the purposes of a deduction under that subsection on any earlier occasion.

(7)   The reference to general criminal conduct in the case of a confiscation order made under any of the provisions listed in subsection (5)(b) is a reference to conduct in respect of which a court is required or entitled to make one or more assumptions for the purpose of assessing a person's benefit from the conduct.

95   Available amount

(1)   For the purposes of deciding the recoverable amount, the available amount is the aggregate of—
   (a)   the total of the values (at the time the confiscation order is made) of all the free property then held by the accused minus the total amount payable in pursuance of obligations which then have priority, and
   (b)   the total of the values (at that time) of all tainted gifts.

(2)   An obligation has priority if—
   (a)   it is an obligation of the accused to pay an amount due in respect of a fine or other order of a court which was imposed or made on conviction for an offence and at any time before the confiscation order is made, or
   (b)   it is an obligation of the accused to pay a sum which would be—
      (i)   a preferred debt if the accused's estate were sequestrated on the date of the confiscation order, or
      (ii)   a preferential debt if his winding up were ordered on that date.

(3)   In subsection (2)—
   "preferred debt" has the meaning given by section 51(2) of the Bankruptcy (Scotland) Act 1985 (c. 66);
   "preferential debt" has the meaning given by section 386 of the Insolvency Act 1986 (c. 45).

96   Assumptions to be made in case of criminal lifestyle

(1)   Where the court decides under section 92 that the accused has a criminal lifestyle it must make the following four assumptions for the purpose of—
   (a)   deciding whether he has benefited from his general criminal conduct, and
   (b)   deciding his benefit from the conduct.

(2)   The first assumption is that any property transferred to the accused at any time after the relevant day was obtained by him—
   (a)   as a result of his general criminal conduct, and
   (b)   at the earliest time he appears to have held it.

(3)   The second assumption is that any property held by the accused at any time after the date of conviction was obtained by him—
   (a)   as a result of his general criminal conduct, and
   (b)   at the earliest time he appears to have held it.

(4)   The third assumption is that any expenditure incurred by the accused at any time after the relevant day was met from property obtained by him as a result of his general criminal conduct.

(5) The fourth assumption is that, for the purpose of valuing any property obtained (or assumed to have been obtained) by the accused, he obtained it free of any other interests in it.

(6) But the court must not make any of those assumptions in relation to particular property or expenditure if —

    (a) the assumption is shown to be incorrect, or

    (b) there would be a serious risk of injustice if the assumption were made.

(7) If the court does not make one or more of those assumptions it must state its reasons.

(8) The relevant day is the first day of the period of six years ending with —

    (a) the day when proceedings for the offence concerned were instituted against the accused, or

    (b) if there are two or more offences and proceedings for them were instituted on different days, the earliest of those days.

(9) But if a confiscation order mentioned in section 94(3)(c) has been made against the accused at any time during the period mentioned in subsection (8) —

    (a) the relevant day is the day when the accused's benefit was calculated for the purposes of the last such confiscation order;

    (b) the second assumption does not apply to any property which was held by him on or before the relevant day.

(10) The date of conviction is —

    (a) the date on which the accused was convicted of the offence concerned, or

    (b) if there are two or more offences and the convictions are on different dates, the date of the latest.

97 Effect of order on court's other powers

(1) If the court decides to make a confiscation order it must act as mentioned in subsections (2) and (4) in respect of the offence or offences concerned.

(2) The court must take account of the confiscation order before —

    (a) it imposes a fine on the accused, or

    (b) it makes an order falling within subsection (3).

(3) These orders fall within this subsection —

    (a) an order involving payment by the accused, other than a compensation order under section 249 of the Procedure Act (compensation orders);

    (b) an order under section 27 of the Misuse of Drugs Act 1971 (c. 38) (forfeiture orders);

    (c) an order under Part 2 of the Proceeds of Crime (Scotland) Act 1995 (c. 43) (forfeiture orders);

    (d) an order under section 23 of the Terrorism Act 2000 (c. 11) (forfeiture orders).

(4) Subject to subsection (2), the court must leave the confiscation order out of account in deciding the appropriate sentence for the accused.

(5) Subsection (6) applies if —

> (a) a court makes both a confiscation order and a compensation order under section 249 of the Procedure Act against the same person in the same proceedings, and
>
> (b) the court believes he will not have sufficient means to satisfy both the orders in full.

(6) In such a case the court must direct that so much of the compensation as it specifies is to be paid out of any sums recovered under the confiscation order; and the amount it specifies must be the amount it believes will not be recoverable because of the insufficiency of the person's means.

98 Disposal of family home

(1) This section applies where a confiscation order has been made in relation to any person and the prosecutor has not satisfied the court that the person's interest in his family home has been acquired as a benefit from his criminal conduct.

(2) Where this section applies, then, before the administrator disposes of any right or interest in the person's family home he shall—

> (a) obtain the relevant consent; or
>
> (b) where he is unable to do so, apply to the court for authority to carry out the disposal.

(3) On an application being made to it under subsection (2)(b), the court, after having regard to all the circumstances of the case including—

> (a) the needs and financial resources of the spouse or former spouse of the person concerned;
>
> (b) the needs and financial resources of any child of the family;
>
> (c) the length of the period during which the family home has been used as a residence by any of the persons referred to in paragraph (a) or (b),

may refuse to grant the application or may postpone the granting of the application for such period (not exceeding 12 months) as it may consider reasonable in the circumstances or may grant the application subject to such conditions as it may prescribe.

(4) Subsection (3) shall apply—

> (a) to an action for division and sale of the family home of the person concerned; or
>
> (b) to an action for the purpose of obtaining vacant possession of that home,

brought by the administrator as it applies to an application under subsection (2)(b) and, for the purposes of this subsection, any reference in subsection (3) to the granting of the application shall be construed as a reference to the granting of decree in the action.

(5) In this section—

> "family home", in relation to any person (in this subsection referred to as "the relevant person") means any property in which the relevant person has or had (whether alone or in common with any other person) a right or interest, being property which is occupied as a residence by the relevant person and his or her spouse or by the relevant person's spouse or former spouse (in any case with or without a child of the family) or by the relevant person with a child of the family;

"child of the family" includes any child or grandchild of either the relevant person or his or her spouse or former spouse, and any person who has been treated by either the relevant person or his or her spouse or former spouse as if he or she were a child of the relevant person, spouse or former spouse, whatever the age of such a child, grandchild or person may be; and

"relevant consent" means in relation to the disposal of any right or interest in a family home—

(a)   in a case where the family home is occupied by the spouse or former spouse of the relevant person, the consent of the spouse or, as the case may be, of the former spouse, whether or not the family home is also occupied by the relevant person;

(b)   where paragraph (a) does not apply, in a case where the family home is occupied by the relevant person with a child of the family, the consent of the relevant person.

Procedural matters

99   Postponement

(1)   The court may—

(a)   proceed under section 92 before it sentences the accused for the offence (or any of the offences concerned), or

(b)   postpone proceedings under section 92 for a specified period.

(2)   A period of postponement may be extended.

(3)   A period of postponement (including one as extended) must not end after the permitted period ends.

(4)   But subsection (3) does not apply if there are exceptional circumstances or if the accused has failed to comply with an order under section 102(1).

(5)   The permitted period is the period of two years starting with the date of conviction.

(6)   But if—

(a)   the accused appeals against his conviction for the offence (or any of the offences) concerned, and

(b)   the period of three months (starting with the day when the appeal is determined or otherwise disposed of) ends after the period found under subsection (5),

the permitted period is that period of three months.

(7)   A postponement or extension may be made—

(a)   on application by the accused;

(b)   on application by the prosecutor;

(c)   by the court of its own motion.

(8)   If—

(a)   proceedings are postponed for a period, and

(b)   an application to extend the period is made before it ends,

the application may be granted even after the period ends.

(9)   The date of conviction is—

   (a) the date on which the accused was convicted of the offence concerned, or

   (b) if there are two or more offences and the convictions were on different dates, the date of the latest.

(10) A confiscation order must not be quashed only on the ground that there was a defect or omission in the procedure connected with the application for or the granting of a postponement.

(11) But subsection (10) does not apply if before it made the confiscation order the court has —

   (a) imposed a fine on the accused;

   (b) made an order falling within section 97(3);

   (c) made an order under section 249 of the Procedure Act.

100 Effect of postponement

(1) If the court postpones proceedings under section 92 it may proceed to sentence the accused for the offence (or any of the offences) concerned.

(2) Subsection (1) is without prejudice to sections 201 and 202 of the Procedure Act.

(3) In sentencing the accused for the offence (or any of the offences) concerned in the postponement period the court must not —

   (a) impose a fine on him,

   (b) make an order falling within section 97(3), or

   (c) make an order for the payment of compensation under section 249 of the Procedure Act.

(4) If the court sentences the accused for the offence (or any of the offences) concerned in the postponement period, after that period ends it may vary the sentence by —

   (a) imposing a fine on him,

   (b) making an order falling within section 97(3), or

   (c) making an order for the payment of compensation under section 249 of the Procedure Act.

(5) But the court may proceed under subsection (4) only within the period of 28 days which starts with the last day of the postponement period.

(6) Where the court postpones proceedings under section 92 following conviction on indictment, section 109(1) of the Procedure Act (intimation of intention to appeal against conviction or conviction and sentence) has effect as if the reference to the final determination of the proceedings were a reference to the relevant day.

(7) Despite subsection (6), the accused may appeal under section 106 of the Procedure Act against any confiscation order made, or any other sentence passed, after the end of the postponement period, in respect of the conviction.

(8) Where the court postpones proceedings under section 92 following conviction on complaint —

   (a) section 176(1) of the Procedure Act (stated case: manner and time of appeal) has effect in relation to an appeal under section 175(2)(a) or (d) as if the reference to the final determination of the proceedings were a reference to the relevant day, and

(b) the draft stated case in such an appeal must be prepared and issued within 3 weeks of the relevant day.

(9) Despite subsection (8), the accused may appeal under section 175(2)(b), and the prosecutor may appeal under section 175(3)(b), of the Procedure Act against any confiscation order made, or any other sentence passed, after the end of the postponement period, in respect of the conviction.

(10) The relevant day is—

(a) in the case of an appeal against conviction where the court has sentenced the accused under subsection (1), the day on which the postponement period commenced;

(b) in any other case, the day on which sentence is passed in open court.

(11) The postponement period is the period for which proceedings under section 92 are postponed.

101 Statement of information

(1) When the court is proceeding under section 92 the prosecutor must, within such period as the court may order, give the court a statement of information.

(2) If the prosecutor believes the accused has a criminal lifestyle the statement of information is a statement of matters the prosecutor believes are relevant in connection with deciding these issues—

(a) whether the accused has a criminal lifestyle;

(b) whether he has benefited from his general criminal conduct;

(c) his benefit from the conduct.

(3) A statement under subsection (2) must include information the prosecutor believes is relevant—

(a) in connection with the making by the court of a required assumption under section 96;

(b) for the purpose of enabling the court to decide if the circumstances are such that it must not make such an assumption.

(4) If the prosecutor does not believe the accused has a criminal lifestyle the statement of information is a statement of matters the prosecutor believes are relevant in connection with deciding these issues—

(a) whether the accused has benefited from his particular criminal conduct;

(b) his benefit from the conduct.

(5) If the prosecutor gives the court a statement of information—

(a) he may at any time give the court a further statement of information;

(b) he must give the court a further statement of information if it orders him to do so, and he must give it within the period the court orders.

(6) If the court makes an order under this section it may at any time vary it by making another one.

102   Accused's response to statement of information

(1)   When the prosecutor gives the court a statement of information and the court is satisfied that he has served a copy on the accused, the court shall order the accused –

   (a)   to indicate the extent to which he accepts each allegation in the statement, and

   (b)   so far as he does not accept such an allegation, to give particulars of any matters he proposes to rely on,

within the period it orders.

(2)   Where by virtue of section 99 the court postpones proceedings under section 92, the period ordered by the court under subsection (1) shall be a period ending not less than six months before the end of the permitted period mentioned in section 99.

(3)   If the accused accepts to any extent an allegation in a statement of information the court may treat his acceptance as conclusive of the matters to which it relates for the purpose of deciding the issues referred to in section 101(2) or (4) (as the case may be).

(4)   If the accused fails in any respect to comply with an order under subsection (1) he may be treated for the purposes of subsection (3) as accepting every allegation in the statement of information apart from –

   (a)   any allegation in respect of which he has complied with the requirement;

   (b)   any allegation that he has benefited from his general or particular criminal conduct.

(5)   Where –

   (a)   an allegation in a statement of information is challenged by the accused, or

   (b)   the matters referred to in subsection (1)(b) are challenged by the prosecutor,

the court must consider the matters being challenged at a hearing.

(6)   The judge presiding at the hearing may, if he is not the trial judge and he considers it in the interests of justice to do so, adjourn the hearing to a date when the trial judge is available.

(7)   If the court makes an order under this section it may at any time vary it by making another one.

(8)   No acceptance under this section that the accused has benefited from conduct is admissible in evidence in proceedings for an offence.

103   Provision of information by accused

(1)   For the purpose of obtaining information to help it in carrying out its functions under section 92 the court may at any time order the accused to give it information specified in the order.

(2)   An order under this section may require all or a specified part of the information to be given in a specified manner and before a specified date.

(3)   If the accused fails without reasonable excuse to comply with an order under this section the court may draw such inference as it thinks appropriate.

(4)   Subsection (3) does not affect any power of the court to deal with the accused in respect of a failure to comply with an order under this section.

(5)   If the prosecutor accepts to any extent an allegation made by the accused –

    (a)   in giving information required by an order under this section, or

    (b)   in any other statement given to the court in relation to any matter relevant to deciding the available amount under section 95,

the court may treat the acceptance as conclusive of the matters to which it relates.

(6)   For the purposes of this section an allegation may be accepted in a manner ordered by the court.

(7)   If the court makes an order under this section it may at any time vary it by making another order.

(8)   No information given under this section which amounts to an admission by the accused that he has benefited from criminal conduct is admissible in evidence in proceedings for an offence.

Reconsideration

104   No order made: reconsideration of case

(1)   This section applies if –

    (a)   the first condition in section 92 is satisfied but no court has proceeded under that section,

    (b)   the prosecutor has evidence which was not available to him on the relevant date,

    (c)   before the end of the period of six years starting with the date of conviction the prosecutor applies to the court to consider the evidence, and

    (d)   after considering the evidence the court thinks it is appropriate for it to proceed under section 92.

(2)   The court must proceed under section 92, and when it does so subsections (3) to (8) below apply.

(3)   If the court has already sentenced the accused for the offence (or any of the offences) concerned section 92(4) does not apply.

(4)   Section 94(2) does not apply, and the rules applying instead are that the court must take account of –

    (a)   conduct occurring before the relevant date;

    (b)   property obtained before that date;

    (c)   property obtained on or after that date if it was obtained as a result of or in connection with conduct occurring before that date.

(5)   In relation to the assumptions that the court must make under section 96 –

    (a)   the first and second assumptions do not apply with regard to property first held by the accused on or after the relevant date;

    (b)   the third assumption does not apply with regard to expenditure incurred by him on or after that date;

    (c)   the fourth assumption does not apply with regard to property obtained (or assumed to have been obtained) by him on or after that date.

(6) The recoverable amount for the purposes of section 92 is such amount as—
    (a) the court believes is just, but
    (b) does not exceed the amount found under section 93.

(7) In arriving at the just amount the court must have regard in particular to—
    (a) the amount found under section 93;
    (b) any fine imposed on the accused in respect of the offence (or any of the offences) concerned;
    (c) any order which falls within section 97(3) and has been made against him in respect of the offence (or any of the offences) concerned and has not already been taken into account by a court in deciding what is the free property held by the accused for the purposes of section 95;
    (d) any compensation order which has been made against him in respect of the offence (or any of the offences) concerned under section 249 of the Procedure Act.

(8) If an order for payment of compensation under section 249 of the Procedure Act has been made against the accused in respect of the offence or offences concerned, section 97(5) and (6) do not apply.

(9) The relevant date is—
    (a) if the court made a decision not to proceed under section 92, the date of the decision;
    (b) if the court did not make such a decision, the date of the conviction.

(10) The date of conviction is—
    (a) the date on which the accused was convicted of the offence concerned, or
    (b) if there are two or more offences and the convictions were on different dates, the date of the latest.

(11) In this section references to the court are to the court which had jurisdiction in respect of the offence or offences concerned to make a confiscation order.

105 No order made: reconsideration of benefit

(1) This section applies if the following two conditions are satisfied.

(2) The first condition is that in proceeding under section 92 the court has decided that—
    (a) the accused has a criminal lifestyle but has not benefited from his general criminal conduct, or
    (b) the accused does not have a criminal lifestyle and has not benefited from his particular criminal conduct.

(3) The second condition is that—
    (a) the prosecutor has evidence which was not available to him when the court decided that the accused had not benefited from his general or particular criminal conduct,
    (b) before the end of the period of six years starting with the date of conviction the prosecutor applies to the court to consider the evidence, and
    (c) after considering the evidence the court concludes that it would have decided that the accused had benefited from his general or particular

criminal conduct (as the case may be) if the evidence had been available to it.

(4) If this section applies the court—

    (a) must make a fresh decision under section 92(5)(b) or (c) as to whether the accused has benefited from his general or particular criminal conduct (as the case may be);

    (b) may make a confiscation order under that section.

(5) Subsections (6) to (11) below apply if the court proceeds under section 92 in pursuance of this section.

(6) If the court has already sentenced the accused for the offence (or any of the offences) concerned section 92(4) does not apply.

(7) Section 94(2) does not apply, and the rules applying instead are that the court must take account of—

    (a) conduct occurring before the date of the original decision that the accused had not benefited from his general or particular criminal conduct;

    (b) property obtained before that date;

    (c) property obtained on or after that date if it was obtained as a result of or in connection with conduct occurring before that date.

(8) In relation to the assumptions that the court must make under section 96—

    (a) the first and second assumptions do not apply with regard to property first held by the accused on or after the date of the original decision that the accused had not benefited from his general or particular criminal conduct;

    (b) the third assumption does not apply with regard to expenditure incurred by him on or after that date;

    (c) the fourth assumption does not apply with regard to property obtained (or assumed to have been obtained) by him on or after that date.

(9) The recoverable amount for the purposes of section 92 is such amount as—

    (a) the court believes is just, but

    (b) does not exceed the amount found under section 93.

(10) In arriving at the just amount the court must have regard in particular to—

    (a) the amount found under section 93;

    (b) any fine imposed on the accused in respect of the offence (or any of the offences) concerned;

    (c) any order which falls within section 97(3) and has been made against him in respect of the offence (or any of the offences) concerned and has not already been taken into account by a court in deciding what is the free property held by the accused for the purposes of section 95;

    (d) any compensation order which has been made against him in respect of the offence (or any of the offences) concerned under section 249 of the Procedure Act.

(11) If an order for the payment of compensation under section 249 of the Procedure Act has been made against the accused in respect of the offence or offences concerned, section 97(5) and (6) do not apply.

(12) The date of conviction is the date found by applying section 104(10).

(13)   In this section references to the court are to the court which had jurisdiction in respect of the offence or offences concerned to make a confiscation order.

106   Order made: reconsideration of benefit

(1)   This section applies if –
    (a)   a court has made a confiscation order,
    (b)   there is evidence which was not available to the prosecutor at the relevant time,
    (c)   the prosecutor believes that if the court were to find the amount of the accused's benefit in pursuance of this section it would exceed the relevant amount,
    (d)   before the end of the period of six years starting with the date of conviction the prosecutor applies to the court to consider the evidence, and
    (e)   after considering the evidence the court thinks it is appropriate for it to proceed under this section.

(2)   The court must make a new calculation of the accused's benefit from the conduct concerned, and when it does so subsections (3) to (5) below apply.

(3)   Section 94(2) does not apply, and the rules applying instead are that the court must take account of –
    (a)   conduct occurring up to the time it decided the accused's benefit for the purposes of the confiscation order;
    (b)   property obtained up to that time;
    (c)   property obtained after that time if it was obtained as a result of or in connection with conduct occurring before that time.

(4)   In applying section 94(3) the confiscation order must be ignored.

(5)   In relation to the assumptions that the court must make under section 96 –
    (a)   the first and second assumptions do not apply with regard to property first held by the accused after the time the court decided his benefit for the purposes of the confiscation order;
    (b)   the third assumption does not apply with regard to expenditure incurred by him after that time;
    (c)   the fourth assumption does not apply with regard to property obtained (or assumed to have been obtained) by him after that time.

(6)   If the amount found under the new calculation of the accused's benefit exceeds the relevant amount the court –
    (a)   must make a new calculation of the recoverable amount for the purposes of section 92, and
    (b)   if it exceeds the amount required to be paid under the confiscation order, may vary the order by substituting for the amount required to be paid such amount as it believes just.

(7)   In applying subsection (6)(a) the court must –
    (a)   take the new calculation of the accused's benefit;
    (b)   apply section 95 as if references to the time the confiscation order is made were to the time of the new calculation of the recoverable amount and as if references to the date of the confiscation order were to the date of that new calculation.

(8) In applying subsection (6)(b) the court must have regard in particular to—

(a) any fine imposed on the accused for the offence (or any of the offences) concerned;

(b) any order which falls within section 97(3) and has been made against him in respect of the offence (or any of the offences) concerned and has not already been taken into account by a court in deciding what is the free property held by the accused for the purposes of section 95;

(c) any order which has been made against him in respect of the offence (or any of the offences) concerned under section 249 of the Procedure Act.

(9) But in applying subsection (6)(b) the court must not have regard to an order falling within subsection (8)(c) if a court has made a direction under section 97(6).

(10) In deciding under this section whether one amount exceeds another the court must take account of any change in the value of money.

(11) The relevant time is—

(a) when the court calculated the accused's benefit for the purposes of the confiscation order, if this section has not applied previously;

(b) when the court last calculated the accused's benefit in pursuance of this section, if this section has applied previously.

(12) The relevant amount is—

(a) the amount found as the accused's benefit for the purposes of the confiscation order, if this section has not applied previously;

(b) the amount last found as the accused's benefit in pursuance of this section, if this section has applied previously.

(13) The date of conviction is the date found by applying section 104(10).

107 Order made: reconsideration of available amount

(1) This section applies if—

(a) a court has made a confiscation order,

(b) the amount required to be paid was the amount found under section 93(2), and

(c) the prosecutor applies to the court to make a new calculation of the available amount.

(2) In a case where this section applies the court must make the new calculation, and in doing so it must apply section 95 as if references to the time the confiscation order is made were to the time of the new calculation and as if references to the date of the confiscation order were to the date of the new calculation.

(3) If the amount found under the new calculation exceeds the relevant amount the court may vary the order by substituting for the amount required to be paid such amount as—

(a) it thinks is just, but

(b) does not exceed the amount found as the accused's benefit from the conduct concerned.

(4) In arriving at the just amount the court must have regard in particular to—

(a)   any fine imposed on the accused for the offence (or any of the offences) concerned;

(b)   any order which falls within section 97(3) and has been made against him in respect of the offence (or any of the offences) concerned and has not already been taken into account by a court in deciding what is the free property held by the accused for the purposes of section 95;

(c)   any order which has been made against him in respect of the offence (or any of the offences) concerned under section 249 of the Procedure Act.

(5)   But in deciding what is just the court must not have regard to an order falling within subsection (4)(c) if a court has made a direction under section 97(6).

(6)   In deciding under this section whether one amount exceeds another the court must take account of any change in the value of money.

(7)   The relevant amount is —
(a)   the amount found as the available amount for the purposes of the confiscation order, if this section has not applied previously;
(b)   the amount last found as the available amount in pursuance of this section, if this section has applied previously.

(8)   The amount found as the accused's benefit from the conduct concerned is —
(a)   the amount so found when the confiscation order was made, or
(b)   if one or more new calculations of the accused's benefit have been made under section 106 the amount found on the occasion of the last such calculation.

108   Inadequacy of available amount: variation of order

(1)   This section applies if —
(a)   a court has made a confiscation order, and
(b)   the accused or the prosecutor applies to the court to vary the order under this section.

(2)   In such a case the court must calculate the available amount and in doing so it must apply section 95 as if references to the time the confiscation order is made were to the time of the calculation and as if references to the date of the confiscation order were to the date of the calculation.

(3)   If the court finds that the available amount (as so calculated) is inadequate to meet the amount remaining to be paid it may vary the order by substituting for the amount required to be paid such smaller amount as the court believes is just.

(4)   If a person's estate has been sequestrated or he has been adjudged bankrupt, or if an order for the winding up of a company has been made, the court must take into account the extent to which realisable property held by him or by the company may be distributed among creditors.

(5)   The court may disregard any inadequacy which it thinks is attributable (wholly or partly) to anything done by the accused for the purpose of preserving property held by the recipient of a tainted gift from any risk of realisation under this Part.

(6)   In subsection (4) "company" means any company which may be wound up under the Insolvency Act 1986 (c. 45) or the Insolvency (Northern Ireland) Order 1989 (S.I. 1989/2405 (N.I. 19)).

109 Inadequacy of available amount: discharge of order

(1) This section applies if —

    (a) a court has made a confiscation order,

    (b) the prosecutor applies to the court to discharge the order under this section, and

    (c) the amount remaining to be paid under the order is less than £1,000.

(2) In such a case the court must calculate the available amount, and in doing so it must apply section 95 as if references to the time the confiscation order is made were to the time of the calculation and as if references to the date of the confiscation order were to the date of the calculation.

(3) If the court —

    (a) finds that the available amount (as so calculated) is inadequate to meet the amount remaining to be paid, and

    (b) is satisfied that the inadequacy is due wholly to a specified reason or a combination of specified reasons,

it may discharge the confiscation order.

(4) The specified reasons are —

    (a) in a case where any of the realisable property consists of money in a currency other than sterling, that fluctuations in currency exchange rates have occurred;

    (b) any reason specified by the Scottish Ministers.

(5) The Scottish Ministers may by order vary the amount for the time being specified in subsection (1)(c).

110 Information

(1) This section applies if —

    (a) the court proceeds under section 92 in pursuance of section 104 or 105, or

    (b) the prosecutor applies under section 106.

(2) In such a case —

    (a) the prosecutor must give the court a statement of information within such period as the court may specify;

    (b) section 101 applies accordingly (with appropriate modifications where the prosecutor applies under section 106);

    (c) sections 102 and 103 apply accordingly.

Accused unlawfully at large

111 Conviction or other disposal of accused

(1) This section applies if an accused is unlawfully at large after —

    (a) he is convicted of an offence or offences, whether in solemn or summary proceedings, or

    (b) in the case of summary proceedings in respect of an offence (without proceeding to conviction) an order is made discharging him absolutely.

(2) If this section applies the court may, on the application of the prosecutor and if it believes it is appropriate for it to do so, proceed under section 92 in the same way as it must proceed if the conditions there mentioned are satisfied; but this is subject to subsection (3).

(3) If the court proceeds under section 92 as applied by this section, this Part has effect with these modifications –

    (a) any person the court believes is likely to be affected by an order under section 92 is entitled to appear before the court and make representations;

    (b) the court must not make an order under section 92 unless the prosecutor has taken reasonable steps to contact the accused;

    (c) section 92(12) applies as if the reference to subsection (2) were to subsection (1) of this section;

    (d) sections 96, 101(3), 102 and 103 do not apply;

    (e) sections 104, 105 and 106 do not apply while the accused is still unlawfully at large.

(4) Once the accused has ceased to be unlawfully at large, section 104 has effect as if subsection (1)(a) read –

    "(a) in a case where section 111 applies the court did not proceed under section 92,".

112 Accused neither convicted nor acquitted

(1) This section applies if –

    (a) proceedings for an offence or offences are instituted against an accused but are not concluded,

    (b) he is unlawfully at large, and

    (c) the period of two years (starting with the day the court believes he first became unlawfully at large) has ended.

(2) If this section applies the court may, on an application by the prosecutor and if it believes it is appropriate for it to do so, proceed under section 92 in the same way as it must proceed if the conditions there mentioned are satisfied; but this is subject to subsection (3).

(3) If the court proceeds under section 92 as applied by this section, this Part has effect with these modifications –

    (a) any person the court believes is likely to be affected by an order under section 92 is entitled to appear before the court and make representations;

    (b) the court must not make an order under section 92 unless the prosecutor has taken reasonable steps to contact the accused;

    (c) section 92(12) applies as if the reference to subsection (2) were to subsection (1) of this section;

    (d) sections 96, 101(3), 102, 103, 104 and 105 do not apply;

    (e) section 106 does not apply while the accused is still unlawfully at large.

(4) Once the accused has ceased to be unlawfully at large, section 106 has effect as if references to the date of conviction were to –

    (a) the day when proceedings for the offence were instituted against the accused, or

    (b)   if there are two or more offences and proceedings for them were instituted on different days, the earliest of those days.

  (5)   If—

    (a)   the court makes an order under section 92 as applied by this section, and

    (b)   the accused is later convicted of the offence (or any of the offences) concerned,

section 92 does not apply so far as that conviction is concerned.

113   Variation of order

  (1)   This section applies if—

    (a)   the court makes a confiscation order under section 92 as applied by section 112,

    (b)   the accused ceases to be unlawfully at large,

    (c)   he is convicted of an offence (or any of the offences) mentioned in section 112(1)(a),

    (d)   he believes that the amount required to be paid was too large (taking the circumstances prevailing when the amount was found for the purposes of the order), and

    (e)   before the end of the relevant period he applies to the court to consider the evidence on which his belief is based.

  (2)   If (after considering the evidence) the court concludes that the accused's belief is well founded—

    (a)   it must find the amount which should have been the amount required to be paid (taking the circumstances prevailing when the amount was found for the purposes of the order), and

    (b)   it may vary the order by substituting for the amount required to be paid such amount as it believes is just.

  (3)   The relevant period is the period of 28 days starting with—

    (a)   the date on which the accused was convicted of the offence mentioned in section 112(1)(a), or

    (b)   if there are two or more offences and the convictions were on different dates, the date of the latest.

  (4)   But in a case where section 112(1)(a) applies to more than one offence the court must not make an order under this section unless it is satisfied that there is no possibility of any further proceedings being taken or continued in relation to any such offence in respect of which the accused has not been convicted.

114   Discharge of order

  (1)   Subsection (2) applies if—

    (a)   the court makes a confiscation order under section 92 as applied by section 112,

    (b)   the accused is later tried for the offence or offences concerned and acquitted of the offence or offences, and

    (c)   he applies to the court to discharge the order.

  (2)   In such a case the court must discharge the order.

(3) Subsection (4) applies if—

    (a) the court makes a confiscation order under section 92 as applied by section 112,

    (b) the accused ceases to be unlawfully at large,

    (c) subsection (1)(b) does not apply, and

    (d) he applies to the court to discharge the order.

(4) In such a case the court may discharge the order if it finds that—

    (a) there has been undue delay in continuing the proceedings mentioned in section 112(1), or

    (b) the prosecutor does not intend to proceed with the prosecution.

(5) If the court discharges a confiscation order under this section it may make such a consequential or incidental order as it thinks is appropriate.

Appeals

115 Appeal by prosecutor

(1) Section 108 of the Procedure Act (Lord Advocate's right of appeal in solemn proceedings) is amended as provided in subsections (2) to (4).

(2) In subsection (1), after paragraph (c) insert—

    "(ca) a decision under section 92 of the Proceeds of Crime Act 2002 not to make a confiscation order;".

(3) In subsection (2)(b)(ii), for the words "or (c)" substitute ", (c) or (ca)".

(4) After subsection (2) insert—

    "(3) For the purposes of subsection (2)(b)(i) above in its application to a confiscation order by virtue of section 92(11) of the Proceeds of Crime Act 2002, the reference to the disposal being unduly lenient is a reference to the amount required to be paid by the order being unduly low."

(5) Section 175 of the Procedure Act (right of appeal in summary proceedings) is amended as provided in subsections (6) to (8).

(6) In subsection (4), after paragraph (c) insert—

    "(ca) a decision under section 92 of the Proceeds of Crime Act 2002 not to make a confiscation order;".

(7) In subsection (4A)(b)(ii), for the words "or (c)" substitute ", (c) or (ca)".

(8) After subsection (4A) insert—

    "(4B) For the purposes of subsection (4A)(b)(i) above in its application to a confiscation order by virtue of section 92(11) of the Proceeds of Crime Act 2002, the reference to the disposal being unduly lenient is a reference to the amount required to be paid by the order being unduly low."

Payment and enforcement

116   Time for payment

(1)   The amount ordered to be paid under a confiscation order must be paid on the making of the order; but this is subject to the following provisions of this section.

(2)   If the accused shows that he needs time to pay the amount ordered to be paid, the court making the confiscation order may make an order allowing payment to be made in a specified period.

(3)   The specified period –
(a)   must start with the day on which the confiscation order is made, and
(b)   must not exceed six months.

(4)   If within the specified period the accused applies to the sheriff court for the period to be extended and the court, after giving the prosecutor an opportunity of being heard, believes there are exceptional circumstances, it may make an order extending the period.

(5)   The extended period –
(a)   must start with the day on which the confiscation order is made, and
(b)   must not exceed 12 months.

(6)   An order under subsection (4) –
(a)   may be made after the end of the specified period, but
(b)   must not be made after the end of the period of twelve months starting with the day on which the confiscation order is made.

(7)   The court must not make an order under subsection (2) or (4) unless it gives the prosecutor an opportunity to make representations.

117   Interest on unpaid sums

(1)   If the amount required to be paid by a person under a confiscation order is not paid when it is required to be paid (whether when the order is made or within a period specified under section 116), he must pay interest on the amount for the period for which it remains unpaid.

(2)   The rate of interest is the rate payable under a decree of the Court of Session.

(3)   For the purposes of this section no amount is required to be paid under a confiscation order if –
(a)   an application has been made under section 116(4),
(b)   the application has not been determined by the court, and
(c)   the period of 12 months starting with the day on which the confiscation order was made has not ended.

(4)   In applying this Part the amount of the interest must be treated as part of the amount to be paid under the confiscation order.

118   Application of provisions about fine enforcement

(1)   The provisions of the Procedure Act specified in subsection (2) apply, with the qualifications mentioned in that subsection, in relation to a confiscation order

as if the amount ordered to be paid were a fine imposed on the accused by the court making the confiscation order.

(2) Those provisions are—

(a) section 211(3) to (6);

(b) section 214(4) to (6), but as if the references in subsection (4) to payment by instalments were omitted;

(c) section 216, but as if subsection (1)—

(i) gave the prosecutor an opportunity to be heard at any enquiry under that subsection; and

(ii) applied whether the offender was in prison or not;

(d) section 217;

(e) section 218(2) and (3);

(f) section 219, provided that—

(i) where a court imposes a period of imprisonment in respect of both a fine and a confiscation order the amounts in respect of which the period is imposed must, for the purposes of subsection (2), be aggregated;

(ii) before imposing a period of imprisonment by virtue of that section the court must require a report from any administrator appointed in relation to the confiscation order as to whether and how he is likely to exercise his powers and duties under this Part and must take that report into account; and the court may, pending such exercise, postpone any decision as to such imposition; and

(iii) where an administrator has not been appointed in relation to the confiscation order, or where the accused does not ask under section 116 for time for payment of any confiscation order imposed by the court, the prosecutor may apply to the court to postpone the imposition of any period of imprisonment for a period not exceeding 3 months to enable the prosecutor to apply to the court for the appointment of an administrator;

(g) section 220, but as if the reference in subsection (1) to payment of a sum by the person included a reference to payment of the sum in respect of the person by an administrator appointed in relation to the confiscation order;

(h) section 221, except where an administrator is appointed in relation to the confiscation order;

(i) section 222, except that for the purposes of that section "confiscation order" in subsection (1) above must be construed as including such an order within the meaning of the Drug Trafficking Act 1994 (c. 37), the Criminal Justice (Confiscation) (Northern Ireland) Order 1990 (S.I. 1990/2588 (N.I. 17)), the Proceeds of Crime (Northern Ireland) Order 1996 (S.I. 1996/1299 (N.I. 9)) or of Part 2 or 4 of this Act;

(j) section 223;

(k) section 224.

(3) Where a court, by virtue of subsection (1), orders the amount ordered to be paid under a confiscation order to be recovered by civil diligence under section 221 of the Procedure Act, any arrestment executed by a prosecutor under subsection (3) of section 124 of this Act is to be treated as having been executed by the court as if that subsection authorised such execution.

(4)   Subsection (5) applies where—

    (a)   a warrant for apprehension of the accused is issued for a default in payment of the amount ordered to be paid under a confiscation order in respect of an offence or offences, and

    (b)   at the time the warrant is issued the accused is liable to serve a period of imprisonment or detention (other than one of life imprisonment or detention for life) in respect of the offence (or any of the offences).

(5)   In such a case any period of imprisonment or detention to which the accused is liable by virtue of section 219 of the Procedure Act runs from the expiry of the period of imprisonment or detention mentioned in subsection (4)(b).

Restraint orders etc

119   Conditions for exercise of powers

(1)   The court may exercise the powers conferred by section 120 if any of the following conditions is satisfied.

(2)   The first condition is that—

    (a)   a criminal investigation has been instituted in Scotland with regard to an offence, and

    (b)   there is reasonable cause to believe that the alleged offender has benefited from his criminal conduct.

(3)   The second condition is that—

    (a)   proceedings for an offence have been instituted in Scotland and not concluded, and

    (b)   there is reasonable cause to believe that the accused has benefited from his criminal conduct.

(4)   The third condition is that—

    (a)   an application by the prosecutor has been made under section 104, 105, 111 or 112 and not concluded, or the court believes that such an application is to be made, and

    (b)   there is reasonable cause to believe that the accused has benefited from his criminal conduct.

(5)   The fourth condition is that—

    (a)   an application by the prosecutor has been made under section 106 and not concluded, or the court believes that such an application is to be made, and

    (b)   there is reasonable cause to believe that the court will decide under that section that the amount found under the new calculation of the accused's benefit exceeds the relevant amount (as defined in that section).

(6)   The fifth condition is that—

    (a)   an application by the prosecutor has been made under section 107 and not concluded, or the court believes that such an application is to be made, and

    (b)   there is reasonable cause to believe that the court will decide under that section that the amount found under the new calculation of the available amount exceeds the relevant amount (as defined in that section).

(7) The second condition is not satisfied if the court believes that—

    (a) there has been undue delay in continuing the proceedings, or

    (b) the prosecutor does not intend to proceed.

(8) If an application mentioned in the third, fourth or fifth condition has been made the condition is not satisfied if the court believes that—

    (a) there has been undue delay in continuing the application, or

    (b) the prosecutor does not intend to proceed.

(9) If the first condition is satisfied—

    (a) references in this Part to the accused are to the alleged offender;

    (b) references in this Part to the prosecutor are to the person the court believes is to have conduct of any proceedings for the offence;

    (c) section 144(8) has effect as if proceedings for the offence had been instituted against the accused when the investigation was instituted.

(10) In this section, sections 120 to 140 and Schedule 3 "the court" means—

    (a) the Court of Session, where a trial diet or a diet fixed for the purposes of section 76 of the Procedure Act in proceedings for the offence or offences concerned is to be, is being or has been held in the High Court of Justiciary;

    (b) the sheriff exercising his civil jurisdiction, where a diet referred to in paragraph (a) is to be, is being or has been held in the sheriff court.

120 Restraint orders etc

(1) If any condition set out in section 119 is satisfied the court may make an order (a restraint order) interdicting any specified person from dealing with any realisable property held by him.

(2) A restraint order may provide that it applies—

    (a) to all realisable property held by the specified person whether or not the property is described in the order;

    (b) to realisable property transferred to the specified person after the order is made.

(3) A restraint order may be made subject to exceptions, and an exception may in particular—

    (a) make provision for reasonable living expenses and reasonable legal expenses;

    (b) make provision for the purpose of enabling any person to carry on any trade, business, profession or occupation;

    (c) be made subject to conditions.

(4) But an exception to a restraint order may not make provision for any legal expenses which—

    (a) relate to an offence which falls within subsection (5), and

    (b) are incurred by a person against whom proceedings for the offence have been instituted or by a recipient of a tainted gift.

(5) These offences fall within this subsection—

    (a)   the offence mentioned in section 119(2) or (3), if the first or second condition (as the case may be) is satisfied;

    (b)   the offence (or any of the offences) concerned, if the third, fourth or fifth condition is satisfied.

(6)   The court may make such order as it believes is appropriate for the purpose of ensuring that the restraint order is effective.

(7)   A restraint order does not affect property subject to a charge under—

    (a)   section 9 of the Drug Trafficking Offences Act 1986 (c. 32),

    (b)   Part 6 of the Criminal Justice Act 1988 (c. 33),

    (c)   Article 14 of the Criminal Justice (Confiscation) (Northern Ireland) Order 1990 (S.I. 1990/2588 (N.I. 17)),

    (d)   section 27 of the Drug Trafficking Act 1994 (c. 37), or

    (e)   Article 32 of the Proceeds of Crime (Northern Ireland) Order 1996 (S.I. 1996/1299 (N.I. 9)).

(8)   Dealing with property includes removing the property from Scotland.

121 Application, recall and variation

(1)   This section applies to a restraint order.

(2)   An order may be made on an ex parte application by the prosecutor, which may be heard in chambers.

(3)   The prosecutor must intimate an order to every person affected by it.

(4)   Subsection (3) does not affect the time when the order becomes effective.

(5)   The prosecutor and any other person affected by the order may apply to the court to recall an order or to vary it; and subsections (6) to (9) apply in such a case.

(6)   If an application under subsection (5) in relation to an order has been made but not determined, realisable property to which the order applies must not be realised.

(7)   The court may—

    (a)   recall the order;

    (b)   vary the order.

(8)   In the case of a restraint order, if the condition in section 119 which was satisfied was that proceedings were instituted or an application was made, the court must recall the order on the conclusion of the proceedings or of the application (as the case may be).

(9)   In the case of a restraint order, if the condition in section 119 which was satisfied was that an investigation was instituted or an application was to be made, the court must recall the order if within a reasonable time proceedings for the offence are not instituted or the application is not made (as the case may be).

122 Appeals

(1)   If on an application for a restraint order the court decides not to make one, the prosecutor may reclaim or appeal to the Court of Session against the decision.

(2) The prosecutor and any person affected by the order may reclaim or appeal to the Court of Session against the decision of the court on an application under section 121(5).

123 Inhibition of property affected by order

(1) On the application of the Lord Advocate, the Court of Session may, in relation to the property mentioned in subsection (2), grant warrant for inhibition against any person specified in a restraint order.

(2) That property is the heritable realisable property to which the restraint order applies (whether generally or such of it as is specified in the application).

(3) The warrant for inhibition—
  (a) has effect as if granted on the dependence of an action for debt by the Lord Advocate against the person and may be executed, recalled, loosed or restricted accordingly, and
  (b) has the effect of letters of inhibition and must forthwith be registered by the Lord Advocate in the Register of Inhibitions and Adjudications.

(4) Section 155 of the Titles to Land Consolidation (Scotland) Act 1868 (c. 101) (effective date of inhibition) applies in relation to an inhibition for which warrant is granted under subsection (1) as it applies to an inhibition by separate letters or contained in a summons.

(5) The execution of an inhibition under this section in respect of property does not prejudice the exercise of an administrator's powers under or for the purposes of this Part in respect of that property.

(6) An inhibition executed under this section ceases to have effect when, or in so far as, the restraint order ceases to apply in respect of the property in relation to which the warrant for inhibition was granted.

(7) If an inhibition ceases to have effect to any extent by virtue of subsection (6) the Lord Advocate must—
  (a) apply for the recall or, as the case may be, the restriction of the inhibition, and
  (b) ensure that the recall or restriction is reflected in the Register of Inhibitions and Adjudications.

124 Arrestment of property affected by order

(1) On the application of the prosecutor the court may, in relation to moveable realisable property to which a restraint order applies (whether generally or such of it as is specified in the application), grant warrant for arrestment.

(2) Such a warrant for arrestment may be granted only if the property would be arrestable if the person entitled to it were a debtor.

(3) A warrant under subsection (1) has effect as if granted on the dependence of an action for debt at the instance of the prosecutor against the person and may be executed, recalled, loosed or restricted accordingly.

(4) The execution of an arrestment under this section in respect of property does not prejudice the exercise of an administrator's powers under or for the purposes of this Part in respect of that property.

(5) An arrestment executed under this section ceases to have effect when, or in so far as, the restraint order ceases to apply in respect of the property in relation to which the warrant for arrestment was granted.

(6) If an arrestment ceases to have effect to any extent by virtue of subsection (5) the prosecutor must apply to the court for an order recalling, or as the case may be, restricting the arrestment.

125 Management administrators

(1) If the court makes a restraint order it may at any time, on the application of the prosecutor –

    (a) appoint an administrator to take possession of any realisable property to which the order applies and (in accordance with the court's directions) to manage or otherwise deal with the property;

    (b) order a person who has possession of property in respect of which an administrator is appointed to give him possession of it.

(2) An appointment of an administrator may be made subject to conditions or exceptions.

(3) Where the court makes an order under subsection (1)(b), the clerk of court must notify the accused and any person subject to the order of the making of the order.

(4) Any dealing of the accused or any such person in relation to property to which the order applies is of no effect in a question with the administrator unless the accused or, as the case may be, that person had no knowledge of the administrator's appointment.

(5) The court –

    (a) may order a person holding an interest in realisable property to which the restraint order applies to make to the administrator such payment as the court specifies in respect of a beneficial interest held by the accused or the recipient of a tainted gift;

    (b) may (on the payment being made) by order transfer, grant or extinguish any interest in the property.

(6) The court must not –

    (a) confer the power mentioned in subsection (1) to manage or otherwise deal with the property, or

    (b) exercise the power conferred on it by subsection (5),

unless it gives persons holding interests in the property a reasonable opportunity to make representations to it.

(7) The court may order that a power conferred by an order under this section is subject to such conditions and exceptions as it specifies.

(8) Managing or otherwise dealing with property includes –

    (a) selling the property or any part of it or interest in it;

    (b) carrying on or arranging for another person to carry on any trade or business the assets of which are or are part of the property;

    (c) incurring capital expenditure in respect of the property.

(9) Subsections (1)(b) and (5) do not apply to property for the time being subject to a charge under –

    (a)   section (9) of the Drug Trafficking Offences Act 1986 (c. 32);

    (b)   section 78 of the Criminal Justice Act 1988 (c. 33);

    (c)   Article 14 of the Criminal Justice (Confiscation) (Northern Ireland) Order 1990 (S.I. 1990/2588 (N.I. 17));

    (d)   section 27 of the Drug Trafficking Act 1994 (c. 37);

    (e)   Article 32 of the Proceeds of Crime (Northern Ireland) Order 1996 (S.I. 1996/1299 (N.I. 9)).

126 Seizure

(1)   If a restraint order is in force a constable or a customs officer may seize any realisable property to which it applies to prevent its removal from Scotland.

(2)   Property seized under subsection (1) must be dealt with in accordance with the directions of the court which made the order.

127 Restraint orders: restriction on proceedings and remedies

(1)   While a restraint order has effect, the court may sist any action, execution or any legal process in respect of the property to which the order applies.

(2)   If a court (whether the Court of Session or any other court) in which proceedings are pending in respect of any property is satisfied that a restraint order has been made or applied for or made in respect of the property, the court may either sist the proceedings or allow them to continue on any terms it thinks fit.

(3)   Before exercising any power conferred by subsection (2), the court must give an opportunity to be heard to—

    (a)   the applicant for the restraint order;

    (b)   any administrator appointed under section 125.

Realisation of property: general

128 Enforcement administrators

(1)   This section applies if—

    (a)   a confiscation order is made,

    (b)   it is not satisfied, and

    (c)   it is not subject to appeal.

(2)   In such a case the court may on the application of the prosecutor exercise the powers conferred on it by this section.

(3)   The court may appoint an administrator in respect of realisable property.

(4)   An appointment of an administrator may be made subject to conditions or exceptions.

(5)   The court may confer the powers mentioned in subsection (6) on an administrator appointed under subsection (3) above.

(6)   Those powers are—

    (a)   power to take possession of any realisable property;

    (b)   power to manage or otherwise deal with the property;

    (c)   power to realise any realisable property, in such manner as the court may specify.

(7)   The court may order any person who has possession of realisable property to give possession of it to an administrator referred to in subsection (5).

(8)   The clerk of court must notify the accused and any person subject to an order under subsection (7) of the making of the order.

(9)   Any dealing of the accused or any such person in relation to property to which the order applies is of no effect in a question with the administrator unless the accused or, as the case may be, that person had no knowledge of the administrator's appointment.

(10)   The court—

    (a)   may order a person holding an interest in realisable property to make to the administrator such payment as the court specifies in respect of a beneficial interest held by the accused or the recipient of a tainted gift;

    (b)   may (on the payment being made) by order transfer, grant or extinguish any interest in the property.

(11)   The court must not—

    (a)   confer the power mentioned in subsection (6)(b) or (c) in respect of property, or

    (b)   exercise the power conferred on it by subsection (10) in respect of property,

unless it gives persons holding interests in the property a reasonable opportunity to make representations to it.

(12)   Managing or otherwise dealing with property includes—

    (a)   selling the property or any part of it or interest in it;

    (b)   carrying on or arranging for another person to carry on any trade or business the assets of which are or are part of the property;

    (c)   incurring capital expenditure in respect of the property.

(13)   The court may order that a power conferred by an order under this section is subject to such conditions and exceptions as it specifies.

(14)   Subsection (6) does not apply to property for the time being subject to a charge under—

    (a)   section 9 of the Drug Trafficking Offences Act 1986 (c. 32);

    (b)   section 78 of the Criminal Justice Act 1988 (c. 33);

    (c)   Article 14 of the Criminal Justice (Confiscation) (Northern Ireland) Order 1990 (S.I. 199/2588 (N.I. 17));

    (d)   section 27 of the Drug Trafficking Act 1994 (c. 37);

    (e)   Article 32 of the Proceeds of Crime (Northern Ireland) Order 1996 (S.I. 1996/1299 (N.I. 9)).

129 Management administrators: discharge

(1)   This section applies if—

    (a)   an administrator stands appointed under section 125 in respect of realisable property (the management administrator), and

    (b)   the court appoints an administrator under section 128.

(2)   The court must order the management administrator to transfer to the other administrator all property held by him by virtue of the powers conferred on him by section 125.

(3)   If the management administrator complies with an order under subsection (2) he is discharged –

    (a)   from his appointment under that section,

    (b)   from any obligation under this Act arising from his appointment.

130   Application of sums by enforcement administrator

(1)   This section applies to sums which –

    (a)   are in the hands of an administrator appointed under section 128(3), and

    (b)   fall within subsection (2).

(2)   These sums fall within this subsection –

    (a)   the proceeds of the realisation of property under section 128(6)(c);

    (b)   any sums (other than those mentioned in paragraph (a)) in which the accused holds an interest.

(3)   The sums must be applied as follows –

    (a)   first, they must be applied in payment of such expenses incurred by a person acting as an insolvency practitioner as are payable under this subsection by virtue of section 432;

    (b)   second, they must be applied in making any payments as directed by the court;

    (c)   third, they must be applied on the accused's behalf towards satisfaction of the confiscation order.

(4)   If the amount payable under any confiscation order has been fully paid and any sums remain in the administrator's hands he must distribute them –

    (a)   among such persons who held (or hold) interests in the property concerned as the court directs, and

    (b)   in such proportions as it directs.

(5)   Before making a direction under subsection (4) the court must give persons who held (or hold) interests in the property concerned a reasonable opportunity to make representations to it.

(6)   For the purposes of subsections (4) and (5) the property concerned is –

    (a)   the property represented by the proceeds mentioned in subsection (2)(a);

    (b)   the sums mentioned in subsection (2)(b).

(7)   The administrator applies sums as mentioned in subsection (3)(c) by paying them to the appropriate clerk of court on account of the amount payable under the order.

(8)   The appropriate clerk of court is the sheriff clerk of the sheriff court responsible for enforcing the confiscation order under section 211 of the Procedure Act as applied by section 118(1) of this Act.

131 Sums received by clerk of court

(1) This section applies if a clerk of court receives sums on account of the amount payable under a confiscation order (whether the sums are received under section 130 or otherwise).

(2) The clerk of court's receipt of the sums reduces the amount payable under the order, but he must apply the sums received as follows.

(3) First he must apply them in payment of such expenses incurred by a person acting as an insolvency practitioner as –
   (a) are payable under this subsection by virtue of section 432, but
   (b) are not already paid under section 130(3)(a).

(4) If the Lord Advocate has reimbursed the administrator in respect of remuneration or expenses under section 133 the clerk of court must next apply the sums in reimbursing the Lord Advocate.

(5) If the clerk of court received the sums under section 130 he must next apply them in payment of the administrator's remuneration and expenses.

(6) If a direction was made under section 97(6) for an amount of compensation to be paid out of sums recovered under the confiscation order, the clerk of court must next apply the sums in payment of that amount.

(7) If any amount remains after the clerk of court makes any payments required by the preceding provisions of this section, the amount must be disposed of in accordance with section 211(5) or (6) of the Procedure Act as applied by section 118(1) of this Act.

Exercise of powers

132 Powers of court and administrator

(1) This section applies to –
   (a) the powers conferred on a court by sections 119 to 131, 134 to 136 and Schedule 3;
   (b) the powers of an administrator appointed under section 125 or 128(3).

(2) The powers –
   (a) must be exercised with a view to the value for the time being of realisable property being made available (by the property's realisation) for satisfying any confiscation order that has been or may be made against the accused;
   (b) must be exercised, in a case where a confiscation order has not been made, with a view to securing that there is no diminution in the value of realisable property or of the proceeds of realisation;
   (c) must be exercised without taking account of any obligation of the accused or a recipient of a tainted gift if the obligation conflicts with the object of satisfying any confiscation order that has been or may be made against the accused;
   (d) may be exercised in respect of a debt owed by the Crown.

(3) Subsection (2) has effect subject to the following rules –

(a) the powers must be exercised with a view to allowing a person other than the accused or a recipient of a tainted gift to retain or recover the value of any interest held by him;

(b) in the case of realisable property held by a recipient of a tainted gift, the powers must be exercised with a view to realising no more than the value for the time being of the gift;

(c) in a case where a confiscation order has not been made against the accused, property must not be realised if the court so orders under subsection (4).

(4) If on an application by the accused or by the recipient of a tainted gift the court decides that property cannot be replaced it may order that it must not be sold.

(5) An order under subsection (4) may be revoked or varied.

Administrators: general

133 Protection of administrators

(1) If an administrator appointed under section 125 or 128(3) –
    (a) takes action in relation to property which is not realisable property,
    (b) would be entitled to take the action if it were realisable property, and
    (c) believes on reasonable grounds that he is entitled to take the action,
he is not liable to any person in respect of any loss or damage resulting from the action, except so far as the loss or damage is caused by his negligence.

(2) Subsection (3) applies if an administrator incurs expenses in the exercise of his functions at a time when –
    (a) a confiscation order has not been made, or
    (b) a confiscation order has been made but the administrator has recovered no money.

(3) As soon as is practicable after they have been incurred the expenses must be reimbursed by the Lord Advocate.

(4) Subsection (5) applies if –
    (a) an amount is due in respect of the administrator's remuneration and expenses, but
    (b) nothing (or not enough) is available to be applied in payment of them under section 131(4).

(5) The remuneration and expenses must be paid (or must be paid to the extent of the shortfall) by the Lord Advocate.

134 Protection of persons affected

(1) This section applies where an administrator is appointed under section 125 or 128(3).

(2) The following persons may apply to the court –
    (a) any person affected by action taken by the administrator;
    (b) any person who may be affected by action the administrator proposes to take.

(3)   On an application under this section the court may make such order as it thinks appropriate.

135   Recall and variation of order

(1)   The prosecutor, an administrator and any other person affected by an order made under section 125 or 128 may apply to the court to vary or recall the order.

(2)   On an application under this section the court —

     (a)   may vary the order;

     (b)   may recall the order.

(3)   But in the case of an order under section 125 —

     (a)   if the condition in section 119 which was satisfied was that proceedings were started or an application was made, the court must recall the order on the conclusion of the proceedings or of the application (as the case may be);

     (b)   if the condition which was satisfied was that an investigation was started or an application was to be made, the court must recall the order if within a reasonable time proceedings for the offence are not started or the application is not made (as the case may be).

136   Appeals

(1)   If on an application for an order under section 125 or 128 the court decides not to make one, the prosecutor may appeal to the Court of Session against the decision.

(2)   If the court makes an order under section 125 or 128 the following persons may appeal to the Court of Session in respect of the court's decision —

     (a)   the prosecutor;

     (b)   any person affected by the order.

(3)   If on an application for an order under section 134 the court decides not to make one, the person who applied for the order may appeal to the Court of Session against the decision.

(4)   If the court makes an order under section 134, the following persons may appeal to the Court of Session in respect of the court's decision —

     (a)   the person who applied for the order;

     (b)   any person affected by the order;

     (c)   the administrator.

(5)   The following persons may appeal to the Court of Session against a decision of the court on an application under section 135 —

     (a)   the person who applied for the order in respect of which the application was made;

     (b)   any person affected by the court's decision;

     (c)   the administrator.

(6)   On an appeal under this section the Court of Session may —

     (a)   confirm the decision, or

     (b)   make such order as it believes is appropriate.

137 Administrators: further provision

Schedule 3, which makes further provision about administrators appointed under section 125 and 128(3), has effect.

138 Administrators: restriction on proceedings and remedies

(1) Where an administrator is appointed under section 128, the court may sist any action, execution or other legal process in respect of the property to which the order appointing the administrator relates.

(2) If a court (whether the Court of Session or any other court) in which proceedings are pending in respect of any property is satisfied that an application has been made for the appointment of an administrator or that an administrator has been appointed in relation to that property, the court may either sist the proceedings or allow them to continue on any terms it thinks fit.

(3) Before exercising any power conferred by subsection (2) the court must give an opportunity to be heard to—
    (a) the prosecutor;
    (b) if appointed, the administrator.

Compensation

139 Serious default

(1) If the following three conditions are satisfied the court may order the payment of such compensation as it thinks is just.

(2) The first condition is satisfied if a criminal investigation has been instituted with regard to an offence and proceedings are not instituted for the offence.

(3) The first condition is also satisfied if proceedings for an offence are instituted against a person and—
    (a) they do not result in his conviction for the offence, or
    (b) he is convicted of the offence but the conviction is quashed or he is pardoned in respect of it.

(4) If subsection (2) applies the second condition is that—
    (a) in the criminal investigation there has been a serious default by a person mentioned in subsection (9), and
    (b) the investigation would not have continued if the default had not occurred.

(5) If subsection (3) applies the second condition is that—
    (a) in the criminal investigation with regard to the offence or in its prosecution there has been a serious default by a person mentioned in subsection (9), and
    (b) the proceedings would not have been instituted or continued if the default had not occurred.

(6) The third condition is that an application is made under this section by a person who held realisable property and has suffered loss in consequence of anything done in relation to it by or in pursuance of an order under this Part.

(7) The offence referred to in subsection (2) may be one of a number of offences with regard to which the investigation is instituted.

(8) The offence referred to in subsection (3) may be one of a number of offences for which the proceedings are instituted.

(9) Compensation under this section is payable to the applicant and –

    (a) if the person in default was a constable of a police force (within the meaning of the Police (Scotland) Act 1967 (c. 77)), the compensation is payable by the police authority or joint police board for the police area for which that force is maintained;

    (b) if the person in default was a constable not falling within paragraph (a), the compensation is payable by the body under whose authority he acts;

    (c) if the person in default was a procurator fiscal or was acting on behalf of the Lord Advocate, the compensation is payable by the Lord Advocate;

    (d) if the person in default was a customs officer, the compensation is payable by the Commissioners of Customs and Excise;

    (e) if the person in default was an officer of the Commissioners of Inland Revenue, the compensation is payable by those Commissioners.

(10) Nothing in this section affects any delictual liability in relation to a serious default.

140 Confiscation order varied or discharged

(1) This section applies if –

    (a) the court varies a confiscation order under section 113 or discharges one under section 114, and

    (b) an application is made to the court by a person who held realisable property and has suffered loss as a result of the making of the order.

(2) The court may order the payment to the applicant of such compensation as it believes is just.

(3) Compensation payable under this section is payable by the Lord Advocate.

Enforcement abroad

141 Enforcement abroad

(1) This section applies if –

    (a) any of the conditions in section 119 are satisfied,

    (b) the prosecutor believes that realisable property is situated in a country or territory outside the United Kingdom (the receiving country), and

    (c) the prosecutor sends a request for assistance to the Secretary of State with a view to it being forwarded under this section.

(2) In a case where no confiscation order has been made, a request for assistance is a request to the government of the receiving country to secure that any person is prohibited from dealing with realisable property.

(3)   In a case where a confiscation order has been made and has not been satisfied, discharged or quashed, a request for assistance is a request to the government of the receiving country to secure that—

    (a)   any person is prohibited from dealing with realisable property,

    (b)   realisable property is realised and the proceeds are applied in accordance with the law of the receiving country.

(4)   No request for assistance may be made for the purposes of this section in a case where a confiscation order has been made and has been satisfied, discharged or quashed.

(5)   If the Secretary of State believes it is appropriate to do so he may forward the request for assistance to the government of the receiving country.

(6)   If property is realised in pursuance of a request under subsection (3) the amount ordered to be paid under the confiscation order must be taken to be reduced by an amount equal to the proceeds of the realisation.

(7)   A certificate purporting to be issued by or on behalf of the requested government is sufficient evidence of the facts it states if it states—

    (a)   that the property has been realised in pursuance of a request under subsection (3),

    (b)   the date of realisation, and

    (c)   the proceeds of realisation.

(8)   If the proceeds of realisation made in pursuance of a request under subsection (3) are expressed in a currency other than sterling, they must be taken to be the sterling equivalent calculated in accordance with the rate of exchange prevailing at the end of the day of realisation.

Interpretation

142   Criminal lifestyle

(1)   An accused has a criminal lifestyle if (and only if) the offence (or any of the offences) concerned satisfies any of these tests—

    (a)   it is specified in Schedule 4;

    (b)   it constitutes conduct forming part of a course of criminal activity;

    (c)   it is an offence committed over a period of at least six months and the accused has benefited from the conduct which constitutes the offence.

(2)   Conduct forms part of a course of criminal activity if the accused has benefited from the conduct and—

    (a)   in the proceedings in which he was convicted he was convicted of three or more other offences, each of three or more of them constituting conduct from which he has benefited, or

    (b)   in the period of six years ending with the day when those proceedings were instituted (or, if there is more than one such day, the earliest day) he was convicted on at least two separate occasions of an offence constituting conduct from which he has benefited.

(3)   But an offence does not satisfy the test in subsection (1)(b) or (c) unless the accused obtains relevant benefit of not less than £5000.

(4)   Relevant benefit for the purposes of subsection (1)(b) is—

    (a)   benefit from conduct which constitutes the offence;

    (b)   benefit from any other conduct which forms part of the course of criminal activity and which constitutes an offence of which the accused has been convicted.

(5)   Relevant benefit for the purposes of subsection (1)(c) is benefit from conduct which constitutes the offence.

(6)   The Scottish Ministers may by order amend Schedule 4.

(7)   The Scottish Ministers may by order vary the amount for the time being specified in subsection (3).

143   Conduct and benefit

(1)   Criminal conduct is conduct which—

    (a)   constitutes an offence in Scotland, or

    (b)   would constitute such an offence if it had occurred in Scotland.

(2)   General criminal conduct of the accused is all his criminal conduct, and it is immaterial—

    (a)   whether conduct occurred before or after the passing of this Act;

    (b)   whether property constituting a benefit from conduct was obtained before or after the passing of this Act.

(3)   Particular criminal conduct of the accused is all his criminal conduct which falls within the following paragraphs—

    (a)   conduct which constitutes the offence or offences concerned;

    (b)   conduct which constitutes offences of which he was convicted in the same proceedings as those in which he was convicted of the offence or offences concerned.

(4)   A person benefits from conduct if he obtains property as a result of or in connection with the conduct.

(5)   If a person obtains a pecuniary advantage as a result of or in connection with conduct, he is to be taken to obtain as a result of or in connection with the conduct a sum of money equal to the value of the pecuniary advantage.

(6)   References to property or a pecuniary advantage obtained in connection with conduct include references to property or a pecuniary advantage obtained both in that connection and in some other.

(7)   If a person benefits from conduct his benefit is the value of the property obtained.

144   Tainted gifts and their recipients

(1)   Subsections (2) and (3) apply if—

    (a)   no court has made a decision as to whether the accused has a criminal lifestyle, or

    (b)   a court has decided that the accused has a criminal lifestyle.

(2)   A gift is tainted if it was made by the accused at any time after the relevant day.

(3)   A gift is also tainted if it was made by the accused at any time and was of property—

(a) which was obtained by the accused as a result of or in connection with his general criminal conduct, or

(b) which (in whole or part and whether directly or indirectly) represented in the accused's hands property obtained by him as a result of or in connection with his general criminal conduct.

(4) Subsection (5) applies if a court has decided that an accused does not have a criminal lifestyle.

(5) A gift is tainted if it was made by the accused at any time after—

(a) the date on which the offence concerned was committed, or

(b) if his particular criminal conduct consists of two or more offences and they were committed on different dates, the earliest of those dates.

(6) For the purposes of subsection (5) an offence which is a continuing offence is committed on the first occasion when it is committed.

(7) A gift may be a tainted gift whether it was made before or after the passing of this Act.

(8) The relevant day is the first day of the period of six years ending with—

(a) the day when proceedings for the offence concerned were instituted against the accused, or

(b) if there are two or more offences and proceedings for them were instituted on different days, the earliest of those days.

(9) If the accused transfers property to another person (whether directly or indirectly) for a consideration whose value is significantly less than the value of the property at the time of the transfer, he is to be treated as making a gift.

(10) If subsection (9) applies the property given is to be treated as such share in the property transferred as is represented by the fraction—

(a) whose numerator is the difference between the two values mentioned in subsection (9), and

(b) whose denominator is the value of the property at the time of the transfer.

(11) References to a recipient of a tainted gift are to a person to whom the accused has (whether directly or indirectly) made the gift.

145 Value: the basic rule

(1) This section applies for the purpose of deciding the value at any time of property then held by a person.

(2) Its value is the market value of the property at that time.

(3) But if at that time another person holds an interest in the property its value, in relation to the person mentioned in subsection (1), is the market value of his interest at that time ignoring any charging order under a provision listed in subsection (4).

(4) The provisions are—

(a) section 9 of the Drug Trafficking Offences Act 1986 (c. 32);

(b) section 78 of the Criminal Justice Act 1988 (c. 33);

(c) Article 14 of the Criminal Justice (Confiscation) (Northern Ireland) Order 1990 (S.I. 199/2588 (N.I. 17));

     (d)   section 27 of the Drug Trafficking Act 1994 (c. 37);

     (e)   Article 32 of the Proceeds of Crime (Northern Ireland) Order 1996 (S.I. 1996/1299 (N.I. 9)).

    (5)   This section has effect subject to sections 146 and 147.

146 Value of property obtained from conduct

(1)   This section applies for the purpose of deciding the value of property obtained by a person as a result of or in connection with his criminal conduct; and the material time is the time the court makes its decision.

(2)   The value of the property at the material time is the greater of the following –

     (a)   the value of the property (at the time the person obtained it) adjusted to take account of later changes in the value of money;

     (b)   the value (at the material time) of the property found under subsection (3).

(3)   The property found under this subsection is –

     (a)   if the person holds the property obtained, that property;

     (b)   if he holds no part of the property obtained, any property which directly or indirectly represents it in his hands;

     (c)   if he holds part of the property obtained, that part and any property which directly or indirectly represents the other part in his hands.

(4)   The references in subsection (2)(a) and (b) to the value are to the value found in accordance with section 145.

147 Value of tainted gifts

(1)   The value at any time (the material time) of a tainted gift is the greater of the following –

     (a)   the value (at the time of the gift) of the property given, adjusted to take account of later changes in the value of money;

     (b)   the value (at the material time) of the property found under subsection (2).

(2)   The property found under this subsection is –

     (a)   if the recipient holds the property given, that property;

     (b)   if the recipient holds no part of the property given, any property which directly or indirectly represents it in his hands;

     (c)   if the recipient holds part of the property given, that part and any property which directly or indirectly represents the other part in his hands.

(3)   The references in subsection (1)(a) and (b) to the value are to the value found in accordance with section 145.

148 Free property

    Property is free unless an order is in force in respect of it under –

     (a)   section 27 of the Misuse of Drugs Act 1971 (c. 38) (forfeiture orders),

     (b)   Article 11 of the Criminal Justice (Northern Ireland) Order 1994 (S.I. 1994/2795 (N.I. 15) (deprivation orders),

   (c)   Part 2 of the Proceeds of Crime (Scotland) Act 1995 (c. 43) (forfeiture of property used in crime),
   (d)   section 143 of the Powers of Criminal Courts (Sentencing) Act 2000 (c. 6) (deprivation orders),
   (e)   section 23 or 111 of the Terrorism Act 2000 (c. 11) (forfeiture orders), or
   (f)   section 246, 266, 295(2) or 298(2) of this Act.

149   Realisable property

Realisable property is —
   (a)   any free property held by the accused;
   (b)   any free property held by the recipient of a tainted gift.

150   Property: general provisions

(1)   Property is all property wherever situated and includes —
   (a)   money;
   (b)   all forms of property whether heritable or moveable and whether corporeal or incorporeal.

(2)   The following rules apply in relation to property —
   (a)   property is held by a person if he holds an interest in it;
   (b)   property is obtained by a person if he obtains an interest in it;
   (c)   property is transferred by one person to another if the first one transfers or grants an interest in it to the second;
   (d)   references to property held by a person include references to his property vested in his permanent or interim trustee (within the meaning of the Bankruptcy (Scotland) Act 1985 (c. 66)), trustee in bankruptcy or liquidator;
   (e)   references to an interest held by a person beneficially in property include references to an interest which would be held by him beneficially if the property were not so vested;
   (f)   references to an interest, in relation to land in England, Wales or Northern Ireland, are to any legal estate or equitable interest or power;
   (g)   references to an interest, in relation to land in Scotland, are to any estate, interest, servitude or other heritable right in or over land, including a heritable security;
   (h)   references to an interest, in relation to property other than land, include references to a right (including a right to possession).

151   Proceedings

(1)   Proceedings for an offence are instituted against a person —
   (a)   on his arrest without warrant;
   (b)   when he is charged with the offence without being arrested;
   (c)   when a warrant to arrest him is granted;
   (d)   when a warrant to cite him is granted;
   (e)   when he first appears on petition or when an indictment or complaint is served on him.

(2)   If more than one time is found under subsection (1) in relation to proceedings they are instituted at the earliest of those times.

(3) Proceedings for an offence are concluded when —
    (a) the trial diet is deserted simpliciter,
    (b) the accused is acquitted or, under section 65 or 147 of the Procedure Act, discharged or liberated,
    (c) the court sentences the accused without making a confiscation order and without postponing a decision as regards making such an order,
    (d) the court decides, after such a postponement, not to make a confiscation order,
    (e) the accused's conviction is quashed, or
    (f) the accused is pardoned.

(4) If a confiscation order is made against the accused in proceedings for an offence, the proceedings are concluded —
    (a) when the order is satisfied or discharged, or
    (b) when the order is quashed and there is no further possibility of an appeal against the decision to quash the order.

(5) If —
    (a) the accused is convicted in proceedings for an offence but the court decides not to make a confiscation order against him, and
    (b) on appeal under section 108(1)(ca) or 175(4)(ca) of the Procedure Act, the High Court of Justiciary refuses the appeal,
    the proceedings are concluded on the determination of the appeal.

152 Applications

(1) An application under section 104, 105, 111 or 112 is concluded —
    (a) in a case where the court decides not to make a confiscation order against the accused, when it makes the decision;
    (b) in a case where a confiscation order is made against him as a result of the application, when the order is satisfied or discharged, or when the order is quashed and there is no further possibility of an appeal against the decision to quash the order;
    (c) in a case where the application is withdrawn, when the prosecutor notifies the withdrawal to the court to which the application was made.

(2) An application under section 106 or 107 is concluded —
    (a) in a case where the court decides not to vary the confiscation order concerned, when it makes the decision;
    (b) in a case where the court varies the confiscation order as a result of the application, when the order is satisfied or discharged, or when the order is quashed and there is no further possibility of an appeal against the decision to quash the order;
    (c) in a case where the application is withdrawn, when the prosecutor notifies the withdrawal to the court to which the application was made.

153 Satisfaction of confiscation orders

(1) A confiscation order is satisfied —
    (a) when no amount is due under it;
    (b) where the accused against whom it was made serves a term of imprisonment or detention in default of payment of the amount due

under the order, on the completion of that term of imprisonment or detention.

(2) A confiscation order is subject to appeal until there is no further possibility of an appeal on which the order could be varied or quashed; and for this purpose any power to grant leave to appeal out of time must be ignored.

154 Other interpretative provisions

(1) In this Part—

"accused" means a person against whom proceedings for an offence have been instituted (whether or not he has been convicted);

"clerk of court" includes the sheriff clerk;

"confiscation order" means an order under section 92;

"conviction", in relation to an offence, includes a finding that the offence has been committed;

"court" must be construed in accordance with sections 92(13) and 119(10);

"criminal investigation" means an investigation which police officers or other persons have a duty to conduct with a view to it being ascertained whether a person should be charged with an offence;

"the Procedure Act" means the Criminal Procedure (Scotland) Act 1995 (c. 46);

"restraint order" means an order under section 120.

(2) A reference to the offence (or offences) concerned must be construed in accordance with section 92(12).

(3) A reference to sentencing the accused for an offence includes a reference to dealing with him otherwise in respect of the offence.

General

155 Rules of court

(1) Provision may be made by act of sederunt as to—

(a) giving notice or serving any document for the purposes of this Part;

(b) the accountant of court's functions under Schedule 3;

(c) the accounts to be kept by the administrator in relation to the exercise of his functions.

(2) Subsection (1) is without prejudice to section 32 of the Sheriff Courts (Scotland) Act 1971 (c. 58) or section 5 of the Court of Session Act 1988 (c. 36).

PART 4

CONFISCATION: NORTHERN IRELAND

Confiscation orders

156 Making of order

(1) The Crown Court must proceed under this section if the following two conditions are satisfied.

(2)   The first condition is that a defendant falls within either of the following paragraphs—

   (a)   he is convicted of an offence or offences in proceedings before the Crown Court;

   (b)   he is committed to the Crown Court in respect of an offence or offences under section 218 below (committal with a view to a confiscation order being considered).

(3)   The second condition is that—

   (a)   the prosecutor or the Director asks the court to proceed under this section, or

   (b)   the court believes it is appropriate for it to do so.

(4)   The court must proceed as follows—

   (a)   it must decide whether the defendant has a criminal lifestyle;

   (b)   if it decides that he has a criminal lifestyle it must decide whether he has benefited from his general criminal conduct;

   (c)   if it decides that he does not have a criminal lifestyle it must decide whether he has benefited from his particular criminal conduct.

(5)   If the court decides under subsection (4)(b) or (c) that the defendant has benefited from the conduct referred to it must—

   (a)   decide the recoverable amount, and

   (b)   make an order (a confiscation order) requiring him to pay that amount.

(6)   But the court must treat the duty in subsection (5) as a power if it believes that any victim of the conduct has at any time started or intends to start proceedings against the defendant in respect of loss, injury or damage sustained in connection with the conduct.

(7)   The court must decide any question arising under subsection (4) or (5) on a balance of probabilities.

(8)   The first condition is not satisfied if the defendant absconds (but section 177 may apply).

(9)   References in this Part to the offence (or offences) concerned are to the offence (or offences) mentioned in subsection (2).

157   Recoverable amount

(1)   The recoverable amount for the purposes of section 156 is an amount equal to the defendant's benefit from the conduct concerned.

(2)   But if the defendant shows that the available amount is less than that benefit the recoverable amount is—

   (a)   the available amount, or

   (b)   a nominal amount, if the available amount is nil.

(3)   But if section 156(6) applies the recoverable amount is such amount as—

   (a)   the court believes is just, but

   (b)   does not exceed the amount found under subsection (1) or (2) (as the case may be).

(4)   In calculating the defendant's benefit from the conduct concerned for the purposes of subsection (1), any property in respect of which—

    (a)   a recovery order is in force under section 266, or

    (b)   a forfeiture order is in force under section 298(2),

must be ignored.

(5)   If the court decides the available amount, it must include in the confiscation order a statement of its findings as to the matters relevant for deciding that amount.

158   Defendant's benefit

(1)   If the court is proceeding under section 156 this section applies for the purpose of —

    (a)   deciding whether the defendant has benefited from conduct, and

    (b)   deciding his benefit from the conduct.

(2)   The court must —

    (a)   take account of conduct occurring up to the time it makes its decision;

    (b)   take account of property obtained up to that time.

(3)   Subsection (4) applies if —

    (a)   the conduct concerned is general criminal conduct,

    (b)   a confiscation order mentioned in subsection (5) has at an earlier time been made against the defendant, and

    (c)   his benefit for the purposes of that order was benefit from his general criminal conduct.

(4)   His benefit found at the time the last confiscation order mentioned in subsection (3)(c) was made against him must be taken for the purposes of this section to be his benefit from his general criminal conduct at that time.

(5)   If the conduct concerned is general criminal conduct the court must deduct the aggregate of the following amounts —

    (a)   the amount ordered to be paid under each confiscation order previously made against the defendant;

    (b)   the amount ordered to be paid under each confiscation order previously made against him under any of the provisions listed in subsection (7).

(6)   But subsection (5) does not apply to an amount which has been taken into account for the purposes of a deduction under that subsection on any earlier occasion.

(7)   These are the provisions —

    (a)   the Drug Trafficking Offences Act 1986 (c. 32);

    (b)   Part 1 of the Criminal Justice (Scotland) Act 1987 (c. 41);

    (c)   Part 6 of the Criminal Justice Act 1988 (c. 33);

    (d)   the Criminal Justice (Confiscation) (Northern Ireland) Order 1990 (S.I. 1990/2588 (N.I. 17));

    (e)   Part 1 of the Drug Trafficking Act 1994 (c. 37);

    (f)   Part 1 of the Proceeds of Crime (Scotland) Act 1995 (c. 43);

    (g)   the Proceeds of Crime (Northern Ireland) Order 1996 (S.I. 1996/1299 (N.I. 9));

    (h)   Part 2 or 3 of this Act.

(8)   The reference to general criminal conduct in the case of a confiscation order made under any of the provisions listed in subsection (7) is a reference to conduct in respect of which a court is required or entitled to make one or more assumptions for the purpose of assessing a person's benefit from the conduct.

159   Available amount

(1)   For the purposes of deciding the recoverable amount, the available amount is the aggregate of —

    (a)   the total of the values (at the time the confiscation order is made) of all the free property then held by the defendant minus the total amount payable in pursuance of obligations which then have priority, and

    (b)   the total of the values (at that time) of all tainted gifts.

(2)   An obligation has priority if it is an obligation of the defendant —

    (a)   to pay an amount due in respect of a fine or other order of a court which was imposed or made on conviction of an offence and at any time before the time the confiscation order is made, or

    (b)   to pay a sum which would be included among the preferential debts if the defendant's bankruptcy had commenced on the date of the confiscation order or his winding up had been ordered on that date.

(3)   "Preferential debts" has the meaning given by Article 346 of the Insolvency (Northern Ireland) Order 1989 (S.I. 1989/2405 (N.I. 19)).

160   Assumptions to be made in case of criminal lifestyle

(1)   If the court decides under section 156 that the defendant has a criminal lifestyle it must make the following four assumptions for the purpose of —

    (a)   deciding whether he has benefited from his general criminal conduct, and

    (b)   deciding his benefit from the conduct.

(2)   The first assumption is that any property transferred to the defendant at any time after the relevant day was obtained by him —

    (a)   as a result of his general criminal conduct, and

    (b)   at the earliest time he appears to have held it.

(3)   The second assumption is that any property held by the defendant at any time after the date of conviction was obtained by him —

    (a)   as a result of his general criminal conduct, and

    (b)   at the earliest time he appears to have held it.

(4)   The third assumption is that any expenditure incurred by the defendant at any time after the relevant day was met from property obtained by him as a result of his general criminal conduct.

(5)   The fourth assumption is that, for the purpose of valuing any property obtained (or assumed to have been obtained) by the defendant, he obtained it free of any other interests in it.

(6)   But the court must not make a required assumption in relation to particular property or expenditure if —

    (a)   the assumption is shown to be incorrect, or

    (b)   there would be a serious risk of injustice if the assumption were made.

(7)   If the court does not make one or more of the required assumptions it must state its reasons.

(8)   The relevant day is the first day of the period of six years ending with –
   (a)   the day when proceedings for the offence concerned were started against the defendant, or
   (b)   if there are two or more offences and proceedings for them were started on different days, the earliest of those days.

(9)   But if a confiscation order mentioned in section 158(3)(c) has been made against the defendant at any time during the period mentioned in subsection (8) –
   (a)   the relevant day is the day when the defendant's benefit was calculated for the purposes of the last such confiscation order;
   (b)   the second assumption does not apply to any property which was held by him on or before the relevant day.

(10)   The date of conviction is –
   (a)   the date on which the defendant was convicted of the offence concerned, or
   (b)   if there are two or more offences and the convictions were on different dates, the date of the latest.

161   Time for payment

(1)   The amount ordered to be paid under a confiscation order must be paid on the making of the order; but this is subject to the following provisions of this section.

(2)   If the defendant shows that he needs time to pay the amount ordered to be paid, the court making the confiscation order may make an order allowing payment to be made in a specified period.

(3)   The specified period –
   (a)   must start with the day on which the confiscation order is made, and
   (b)   must not exceed six months.

(4)   If within the specified period the defendant applies to the Crown Court for the period to be extended and the court believes there are exceptional circumstances, it may make an order extending the period.

(5)   The extended period –
   (a)   must start with the day on which the confiscation order is made, and
   (b)   must not exceed 12 months.

(6)   An order under subsection (4) –
   (a)   may be made after the end of the specified period, but
   (b)   must not be made after the end of the period of 12 months starting with the day on which the confiscation order is made.

(7)   The court must not make an order under subsection (2) or (4) unless it gives –
   (a)   the prosecutor, or
   (b)   if the Director was appointed as the enforcement authority for the order under section 184, the Director,
an opportunity to make representations.

162   Interest on unpaid sums

(1)   If the amount required to be paid by a person under a confiscation order is not
paid when it is required to be paid, he must pay interest on the amount for the
period for which it remains unpaid.

(2)   The rate of interest is the same rate as that for the time being applying to a
money judgment of the High Court.

(3)   For the purposes of this section no amount is required to be paid under a
confiscation order if—

    (a)   an application has been made under section 161(4),

    (b)   the application has not been determined by the court, and

    (c)   the period of 12 months starting with the day on which the confiscation
order was made has not ended.

(4)   In applying this Part the amount of the interest must be treated as part of the
amount to be paid under the confiscation order.

163   Effect of order on court's other powers

(1)   If the court makes a confiscation order it must proceed as mentioned in
subsections (2) and (4) in respect of the offence or offences concerned.

(2)   The court must take account of the confiscation order before—

    (a)   it imposes a fine on the defendant, or

    (b)   it makes an order falling within subsection (3).

(3)   These orders fall within this subsection—

    (a)   an order involving payment by the defendant, other than an order
under Article 14 of the Criminal Justice (Northern Ireland) Order 1994
(S.I. 1994/2795 (N.I. 15)) (compensation orders);

    (b)   an order under section 27 of the Misuse of Drugs Act 1971 (c. 38)
(forfeiture orders);

    (c)   an order under Article 11 of the Criminal Justice (Northern Ireland)
Order 1994 (S.I. 1994/2795 (N.I. 15)) (deprivation orders);

    (d)   an order under section 23 or 111 of the Terrorism Act 2000 (c. 11)
(forfeiture orders).

(4)   Subject to subsection (2), the court must leave the confiscation order out of
account in deciding the appropriate sentence for the defendant.

(5)   Subsection (6) applies if—

    (a)   a court makes both a confiscation order and an order for the payment
of compensation under Article 14 of the Criminal Justice (Northern
Ireland) Order 1994 (S.I. 1994/2795 (N.I. 15)) against the same person in
the same proceedings, and

    (b)   the court believes he will not have sufficient means to satisfy both the
orders in full.

(6)   In such a case the court must direct that so much of the compensation as it
specifies is to be paid out of any sums recovered under the confiscation order;
and the amount it specifies must be the amount it believes will not be
recoverable because of the insufficiency of the person's means.

Procedural matters

164 Postponement

(1) The court may —
- (a) proceed under section 161 before it sentences the defendant for the offence (or any of the offences) concerned, or
- (b) postpone proceedings under section 161 for a specified period.

(2) A period of postponement may be extended.

(3) A period of postponement (including one as extended) must not end after the permitted period ends.

(4) But subsection (3) does not apply if there are exceptional circumstances.

(5) The permitted period is the period of two years starting with the date of conviction.

(6) But if —
- (a) the defendant appeals against his conviction for the offence (or any of the offences) concerned, and
- (b) the period of three months (starting with the day when the appeal is determined or otherwise disposed of) ends after the period found under subsection (5),

the permitted period is that period of three months.

(7) A postponement or extension may be made —
- (a) on application by the defendant;
- (b) on application by the prosecutor or the Director (as the case may be);
- (c) by the court of its own motion.

(8) If —
- (a) proceedings are postponed for a period, and
- (b) an application to extend the period is made before it ends,

the application may be granted even after the period ends.

(9) The date of conviction is —
- (a) the date on which the defendant was convicted of the offence concerned, or
- (b) if there are two or more offences and the convictions were on different dates, the date of the latest.

(10) References to appealing include references to applying under Article 146 of the Magistrates' Courts (Northern Ireland) Order 1981 (S.I. 1981/1675 (N.I. 26)) (statement of case).

(11) A confiscation order must not be quashed only on the ground that there was a defect or omission in the procedure connected with the application for or the granting of a postponement.

(12) But subsection (11) does not apply if before it made the confiscation order the court —
- (a) imposed a fine on the defendant;
- (b) made an order falling within section 163(3);

    (c)   made an order under Article 14 of the Criminal Justice (Northern Ireland) Order 1994 (S.I. 1994/2795 (N.I. 15)) (compensation orders).

165   Effect of postponement

(1)   If the court postpones proceedings under section 156 it may proceed to sentence the defendant for the offence (or any of the offences) concerned.

(2)   In sentencing the defendant for the offence (or any of the offences) concerned in the postponement period the court must not—

    (a)   impose a fine on him,

    (b)   make an order falling within section 163(3), or

    (c)   make an order for the payment of compensation under Article 14 of the Criminal Justice (Northern Ireland) Order 1994 (S.I. 1994/2795 (N.I. 15)).

(3)   If the court sentences the defendant for the offence (or any of the offences) concerned in the postponement period, after that period ends it may vary the sentence by—

    (a)   imposing a fine on him,

    (b)   making an order falling within section 163(3), or

    (c)   making an order for the payment of compensation under Article 14 of the Criminal Justice (Northern Ireland) Order 1994.

(4)   But the court may proceed under subsection (3) only within the period of 28 days which starts with the last day of the postponement period.

(5)   For the purposes of—

    (a)   section 16(1) of the Criminal Appeal (Northern Ireland) Act 1980 (c. 47) (time limit for notice of appeal or of application for leave to appeal), and

    (b)   paragraph 1 of Schedule 3 to the Criminal Justice Act 1988 (c. 33) (time limit for notice of application for leave to refer a case under section 36 of that Act),

the sentence must be regarded as imposed or made on the day on which it is varied under subsection (3).

(6)   If the court proceeds to sentence the defendant under subsection (1), section 156 has effect as if the defendant's particular criminal conduct included conduct which constitutes offences which the court has taken into consideration in deciding his sentence for the offence or offences concerned.

(7)   The postponement period is the period for which proceedings under section 156 are postponed.

166   Statement of information

(1)   If the court is proceeding under section 156 in a case where section 156(3)(a) applies, the prosecutor or the Director (as the case may be) must give the court a statement of information within the period the court orders.

(2)   If the court is proceeding under section 156 in a case where section 156(3)(b) applies and it orders the prosecutor to give it a statement of information, the prosecutor must give it such a statement within the period the court orders.

(3)   If the prosecutor or the Director (as the case may be) believes the defendant has a criminal lifestyle the statement of information is a statement of matters the

prosecutor or the Director believes are relevant in connection with deciding these issues —

    (a)   whether the defendant has a criminal lifestyle;

    (b)   whether he has benefited from his general criminal conduct;

    (c)   his benefit from the conduct.

(4)   A statement under subsection (3) must include information the prosecutor or Director believes is relevant —

    (a)   in connection with the making by the court of a required assumption under section 160;

    (b)   for the purpose of enabling the court to decide if the circumstances are such that it must not make such an assumption.

(5)   If the prosecutor or the Director (as the case may be) does not believe the defendant has a criminal lifestyle the statement of information is a statement of matters the prosecutor or the Director believes are relevant in connection with deciding these issues —

    (a)   whether the defendant has benefited from his particular criminal conduct;

    (b)   his benefit from the conduct.

(6)   If the prosecutor or the Director gives the court a statement of information —

    (a)   he may at any time give the court a further statement of information;

    (b)   he must give the court a further statement of information if it orders him to do so, and he must give it within the period the court orders.

(7)   If the court makes an order under this section it may at any time vary it by making another one.

167   Defendant's response to statement of information

(1)   If the prosecutor or the Director gives the court a statement of information and a copy is served on the defendant, the court may order the defendant —

    (a)   to indicate (within the period it orders) the extent to which he accepts each allegation in the statement, and

    (b)   so far as he does not accept such an allegation, to give particulars of any matters he proposes to rely on.

(2)   If the defendant accepts to any extent an allegation in a statement of information the court may treat his acceptance as conclusive of the matters to which it relates for the purpose of deciding the issues referred to in section 166(3) or (5) (as the case may be).

(3)   If the defendant fails in any respect to comply with an order under subsection (1) he may be treated for the purposes of subsection (2) as accepting every allegation in the statement of information apart from —

    (a)   any allegation in respect of which he has complied with the requirement;

    (b)   any allegation that he has benefited from his general or particular criminal conduct.

(4)   For the purposes of this section an allegation may be accepted or particulars may be given in a manner ordered by the court.

(5)   If the court makes an order under this section it may at any time vary it by making another one.

(6)   No acceptance under this section that the defendant has benefited from conduct is admissible in evidence in proceedings for an offence.

168   Provision of information by defendant

(1)   This section applies if —
    (a)   the court is proceeding under section 156 in a case where section 156(3)(a) applies, or
    (b)   it is proceeding under section 156 in a case where section 156(3)(b) applies or it is considering whether to proceed.

(2)   For the purpose of obtaining information to help it in carrying out its functions the court may at any time order the defendant to give it information specified in the order.

(3)   An order under this section may require all or a specified part of the information to be given in a specified manner and before a specified date.

(4)   If the defendant fails without reasonable excuse to comply with an order under this section the court may draw such inference as it believes is appropriate.

(5)   Subsection (4) does not affect any power of the court to deal with the defendant in respect of a failure to comply with an order under this section.

(6)   If the prosecutor or the Director (as the case may be) accepts to any extent an allegation made by the defendant —
    (a)   in giving information required by an order under this section, or
    (b)   in any other statement given to the court in relation to any matter relevant to deciding the available amount under section 159,
the court may treat the acceptance as conclusive of the matters to which it relates.

(7)   For the purposes of this section an allegation may be accepted in a manner ordered by the court.

(8)   If the court makes an order under this section it may at any time vary it by making another one.

(9)   No information given under this section which amounts to an admission by the defendant that he has benefited from criminal conduct is admissible in evidence in proceedings for an offence.

Reconsideration

169   No order made: reconsideration of case

(1)   This section applies if —
    (a)   the first condition in section 156 is satisfied but no court has proceeded under that section,
    (b)   there is evidence which was not available to the prosecutor on the relevant date,

> (c) before the end of the period of six years starting with the date of conviction the prosecutor or the Director applies to the Crown Court to consider the evidence, and
>
> (d) after considering the evidence the court believes it is appropriate for it to proceed under section 156.

(2) If this section applies the court must proceed under section 156, and when it does so subsections (3) to (8) below apply.

(3) If the court has already sentenced the defendant for the offence (or any of the offences) concerned, section 156 has effect as if his particular criminal conduct included conduct which constitutes offences which the court has taken into consideration in deciding his sentence for the offence or offences concerned.

(4) Section 158(2) does not apply, and the rules applying instead are that the court must —

> (a) take account of conduct occurring before the relevant date;
>
> (b) take account of property obtained before that date;
>
> (c) take account of property obtained on or after that date if it was obtained as a result of or in connection with conduct occurring before that date.

(5) In section 160 —

> (a) the first and second assumptions do not apply with regard to property first held by the defendant on or after the relevant date;
>
> (b) the third assumption does not apply with regard to expenditure incurred by him on or after that date;
>
> (c) the fourth assumption does not apply with regard to property obtained (or assumed to have been obtained) by him on or after that date.

(6) The recoverable amount for the purposes of section 156 is such amount as —

> (a) the court believes is just, but
>
> (b) does not exceed the amount found under section 157.

(7) In arriving at the just amount the court must have regard in particular to —

> (a) the amount found under section 157;
>
> (b) any fine imposed on the defendant in respect of the offence (or any of the offences) concerned;
>
> (c) any order which falls within section 163(3) and has been made against him in respect of the offence (or any of the offences) concerned and has not already been taken into account by the court in deciding what is the free property held by him for the purposes of section 159;
>
> (d) any order which has been made against him in respect of the offence (or any of the offences) concerned under Article 14 of the Criminal Justice (Northern Ireland) Order 1994 (S.I. 1994/2795 (N.I. 15)) (compensation orders).

(8) If an order for the payment of compensation under Article 14 of the Criminal Justice (Northern Ireland) Order 1994 has been made against the defendant in respect of the offence or offences concerned, section 163(5) and (6) above do not apply.

(9) The relevant date is —

> (a) if the court made a decision not to proceed under section 156, the date of the decision;
>
> (b) if the court did not make such a decision, the date of conviction.

(10) The date of conviction is—

(a) the date on which the defendant was convicted of the offence concerned, or

(b) if there are two or more offences and the convictions were on different dates, the date of the latest.

170 No order made: reconsideration of benefit

(1) This section applies if the following two conditions are satisfied.

(2) The first condition is that in proceeding under section 156 the court has decided that—

(a) the defendant has a criminal lifestyle but has not benefited from his general criminal conduct, or

(b) the defendant does not have a criminal lifestyle and has not benefited from his particular criminal conduct.

(3) If the court proceeded under section 156 because the Director asked it to, the second condition is that—

(a) the Director has evidence which was not available to him when the court decided that the defendant had not benefited from his general or particular criminal conduct,

(b) before the end of the period of six years starting with the date of conviction the Director applies to the Crown Court to consider the evidence, and

(c) after considering the evidence the court concludes that it would have decided that the defendant had benefited from his general or particular criminal conduct (as the case may be) if the evidence had been available to it.

(4) If the court proceeded under section 156 because the prosecutor asked it to or because it believed it was appropriate for it to do so, the second condition is that—

(a) there is evidence which was not available to the prosecutor when the court decided that the defendant had not benefited from his general or particular criminal conduct,

(b) before the end of the period of six years starting with the date of conviction the prosecutor or the Director applies to the Crown Court to consider the evidence, and

(c) after considering the evidence the court concludes that it would have decided that the defendant had benefited from his general or particular criminal conduct (as the case may be) if the evidence had been available to it.

(5) If this section applies the court—

(a) must make a fresh decision under section 156(4)(b) or (c) whether the defendant has benefited from his general or particular criminal conduct (as the case may be);

(b) may make a confiscation order under that section.

(6) Subsections (7) to (12) below apply if the court proceeds under section 156 in pursuance of this section.

(7) If the court has already sentenced the defendant for the offence (or any of the offences) concerned, section 156 has effect as if his particular criminal conduct

included conduct which constitutes offences which the court has taken into consideration in deciding his sentence for the offence or offences concerned.

(8) Section 158(2) does not apply, and the rules applying instead are that the court must—

    (a) take account of conduct occurring before the date of the original decision that the defendant had not benefited from his general or particular criminal conduct;

    (b) take account of property obtained before that date;

    (c) take account of property obtained on or after that date if it was obtained as a result of or in connection with conduct occurring before that date.

(9) In section 160—

    (a) the first and second assumptions do not apply with regard to property first held by the defendant on or after the date of the original decision that the defendant had not benefited from his general or particular criminal conduct;

    (b) the third assumption does not apply with regard to expenditure incurred by him on or after that date;

    (c) the fourth assumption does not apply with regard to property obtained (or assumed to have been obtained) by him on or after that date.

(10) The recoverable amount for the purposes of section 156 is such amount as—

    (a) the court believes is just, but

    (b) does not exceed the amount found under section 157.

(11) In arriving at the just amount the court must have regard in particular to—

    (a) the amount found under section 157;

    (b) any fine imposed on the defendant in respect of the offence (or any of the offences) concerned;

    (c) any order which falls within section 163(3) and has been made against him in respect of the offence (or any of the offences) concerned and has not already been taken into account by the court in deciding what is the free property held by him for the purposes of section 159;

    (d) any order which has been made against him in respect of the offence (or any of the offences) concerned under Article 14 of the Criminal Justice (Northern Ireland) Order 1994 (S.I. 1994/2795 (N.I. 15)) (compensation orders).

(12) If an order for the payment of compensation under Article 14 of the Criminal Justice (Northern Ireland) Order 1994 has been made against the defendant in respect of the offence or offences concerned, section 163(5) and (6) above do not apply.

(13) The date of conviction is the date found by applying section 169(10).

171 Order made: reconsideration of benefit

(1) This section applies if—

    (a) a court has made a confiscation order,

    (b) there is evidence which was not available to the prosecutor or the Director at the relevant time,

(c) the prosecutor or the Director believes that if the court were to find the amount of the defendant's benefit in pursuance of this section it would exceed the relevant amount,

(d) before the end of the period of six years starting with the date of conviction the prosecutor or the Director applies to the Crown Court to consider the evidence, and

(e) after considering the evidence the court believes it is appropriate for it to proceed under this section.

(2) The court must make a new calculation of the defendant's benefit from the conduct concerned, and when it does so subsections (3) to (6) below apply.

(3) If a court has already sentenced the defendant for the offence (or any of the offences) concerned section 156 has effect as if his particular criminal conduct included conduct which constitutes offences which the court has taken into consideration in deciding his sentence for the offence or offences concerned.

(4) Section 158(2) does not apply, and the rules applying instead are that the court must —

(a) take account of conduct occurring up to the time it decided the defendant's benefit for the purposes of the confiscation order;

(b) take account of property obtained up to that time;

(c) take account of property obtained after that time if it was obtained as a result of or in connection with conduct occurring before that time.

(5) In applying section 158(5) the confiscation order must be ignored.

(6) In section 160 —

(a) the first and second assumptions do not apply with regard to property first held by the defendant after the time the court decided his benefit for the purposes of the confiscation order;

(b) the third assumption does not apply with regard to expenditure incurred by him after that time;

(c) the fourth assumption does not apply with regard to property obtained (or assumed to have been obtained) by him after that time.

(7) If the amount found under the new calculation of the defendant's benefit exceeds the relevant amount the court —

(a) must make a new calculation of the recoverable amount for the purposes of section 156, and

(b) if it exceeds the amount required to be paid under the confiscation order, may vary the order by substituting for the amount required to be paid such amount as it believes is just.

(8) In applying subsection (7)(a) the court must —

(a) take the new calculation of the defendant's benefit;

(b) apply section 159 as if references to the time the confiscation order is made were to the time of the new calculation of the recoverable amount and as if references to the date of the confiscation order were to the date of that new calculation.

(9) In applying subsection (7)(b) the court must have regard in particular to —

(a) any fine imposed on the defendant for the offence (or any of the offences) concerned;

(b)   any order which falls within section 163(3) and has been made against him in respect of the offence (or any of the offences) concerned and has not already been taken into account by the court in deciding what is the free property held by him for the purposes of section 159;

(c)   any order which has been made against him in respect of the offence (or any of the offences) concerned under Article 14 of the Criminal Justice (Northern Ireland) Order 1994 (S.I. 1994/2795 (N.I. 15)) (compensation orders).

(10)   But in applying subsection (7)(b) the court must not have regard to an order falling within subsection (9)(c) if a court has made a direction under section 163(6).

(11)   In deciding under this section whether one amount exceeds another the court must take account of any change in the value of money.

(12)   The relevant time is —

(a)   when the court calculated the defendant's benefit for the purposes of the confiscation order, if this section has not applied previously;

(b)   when the court last calculated the defendant's benefit in pursuance of this section, if this section has applied previously.

(13)   The relevant amount is —

(a)   the amount found as the defendant's benefit for the purposes of the confiscation order, if this section has not applied previously;

(b)   the amount last found as the defendant's benefit in pursuance of this section, if this section has applied previously.

(14)   The date of conviction is the date found by applying section 169(10).

172   Order made: reconsideration of available amount

(1)   This section applies if —

(a)   a court has made a confiscation order,

(b)   the amount required to be paid was the amount found under section 157(2), and

(c)   an applicant falling within subsection (2) applies to the Crown Court to make a new calculation of the available amount.

(2)   These applicants fall within this subsection —

(a)   the prosecutor;

(b)   the Director;

(c)   a receiver appointed under section 198 or 200.

(3)   In a case where this section applies the court must make the new calculation, and in doing so it must apply section 159 as if references to the time the confiscation order is made were to the time of the new calculation and as if references to the date of the confiscation order were to the date of the new calculation.

(4)   If the amount found under the new calculation exceeds the relevant amount the court may vary the order by substituting for the amount required to be paid such amount as —

(a)   it believes is just, but

(b)   does not exceed the amount found as the defendant's benefit from the conduct concerned.

(5)   In deciding what is just the court must have regard in particular to −

(a)   any fine imposed on the defendant for the offence (or any of the offences) concerned;

(b)   any order which falls within section 163(3) and has been made against him in respect of the offence (or any of the offences) concerned and has not already been taken into account by the court in deciding what is the free property held by him for the purposes of section 159;

(c)   any order which has been made against him in respect of the offence (or any of the offences) concerned under Article 14 of the Criminal Justice (Northern Ireland) Order 1994 (S.I. 1994/2795 (N.I. 15)) (compensation orders).

(6)   But in deciding what is just the court must not have regard to an order falling within subsection (5)(c) if a court has made a direction under section 163(6).

(7)   In deciding under this section whether one amount exceeds another the court must take account of any change in the value of money.

(8)   The relevant amount is −

(a)   the amount found as the available amount for the purposes of the confiscation order, if this section has not applied previously;

(b)   the amount last found as the available amount in pursuance of this section, if this section has applied previously.

(9)   The amount found as the defendant's benefit from the conduct concerned is −

(a)   the amount so found when the confiscation order was made, or

(b)   if one or more new calculations of the defendant's benefit have been made under section 171 the amount found on the occasion of the last such calculation.

173   Inadequacy of available amount: variation of order

(1)   This section applies if −

(a)   a court has made a confiscation order, and

(b)   the defendant, or a receiver appointed under section 198 or 200, applies to the Crown Court to vary the order under this section.

(2)   In such a case the court must calculate the available amount, and in doing so it must apply section 159 as if references to the time the confiscation order is made were to the time of the calculation and as if references to the date of the confiscation order were to the date of the calculation.

(3)   If the court finds that the available amount (as so calculated) is inadequate for the payment of any amount remaining to be paid under the confiscation order it may vary the order by substituting for the amount required to be paid such smaller amount as the court believes is just.

(4)   If a person has been adjudged bankrupt or his estate has been sequestrated, or if an order for the winding up of a company has been made, the court must take into account the extent to which realisable property held by that person or that company may be distributed among creditors.

(5) The court may disregard any inadequacy which it believes is attributable (wholly or partly) to anything done by the defendant for the purpose of preserving property held by the recipient of a tainted gift from any risk of realisation under this Part.

(6) In subsection (4) "company" means any company which may be wound up under the Insolvency (Northern Ireland) Order 1989 (S.I. 1989/2405 (N.I. 19)) or the Insolvency Act 1986 (c. 45).

174 Inadequacy of available amount: discharge of order

(1) This section applies if—
   (a) a court has made a confiscation order,
   (b) the prosecutor applies to the Crown Court for the discharge of the order, and
   (c) the amount remaining to be paid under the order is less than £1,000.

(2) In such a case the court must calculate the available amount, and in doing so it must apply section 159 as if references to the time the confiscation order is made were to the time of the calculation and as if references to the date of the confiscation order were to the date of the calculation.

(3) If the court—
   (a) finds that the available amount (as so calculated) is inadequate to meet the amount remaining to be paid, and
   (b) is satisfied that the inadequacy is due wholly to a specified reason or a combination of specified reasons,
   it may discharge the confiscation order.

(4) The specified reasons are—
   (a) in a case where any of the realisable property consists of money in a currency other than sterling, that fluctuations in currency exchange rates have occurred;
   (b) any reason specified by the Secretary of State by order.

(5) The Secretary of State may by order vary the amount for the time being specified in subsection (1)(c).

175 Small amount outstanding: discharge of order

(1) This section applies if—
   (a) a court has made a confiscation order,
   (b) a chief clerk applies to the Crown Court for the discharge of the order, and
   (c) the amount remaining to be paid under the order is £50 or less.

(2) In such a case the court may discharge the order.

(3) The Secretary of State may by order vary the amount for the time being specified in subsection (1)(c).

176 Information

(1) This section applies if—

(a) the court proceeds under section 156 in pursuance of section 169 or 170, or

(b) the prosecutor or the Director applies under section 171.

(2) In such a case—

(a) the prosecutor or the Director (as the case may be) must give the court a statement of information within the period the court orders;

(b) section 166 applies accordingly (with appropriate modifications where the prosecutor or the Director applies under section 171);

(c) section 167 applies accordingly;

(d) section 168 applies as it applies in the circumstances mentioned in section 168(1).

Defendant absconds

177 Defendant convicted or committed

(1) This section applies if the following two conditions are satisfied.

(2) The first condition is that a defendant absconds after—

(a) he is convicted of an offence or offences in proceedings before the Crown Court, or

(b) he is committed to the Crown Court in respect of an offence or offences under section 218 below (committal with a view to a confiscation order being considered).

(3) The second condition is that—

(a) the prosecutor or the Director applies to the Crown Court to proceed under this section, and

(b) the court believes it is appropriate for it to do so.

(4) If this section applies the court must proceed under section 156 in the same way as it must proceed if the two conditions there mentioned are satisfied; but this is subject to subsection (5).

(5) If the court proceeds under section 156 as applied by this section, this Part has effect with these modifications—

(a) any person the court believes is likely to be affected by an order under section 156 is entitled to appear before the court and make representations;

(b) the court must not make an order under section 156 unless the prosecutor or the Director (as the case may be) has taken reasonable steps to contact the defendant;

(c) section 156(9) applies as if the reference to subsection (2) were to subsection (2) of this section;

(d) sections 160, 166(4), 167 and 168 must be ignored;

(e) sections 169, 170 and 171 must be ignored while the defendant is still an absconder.

(6) Once the defendant has ceased to be an absconder section 169 has effect as if subsection (1)(a) read—

"(a) at a time when the first condition in section 177 was satisfied the court did not proceed under section 156,".

(7)   If the court does not believe it is appropriate for it to proceed under this section, once the defendant ceases to be an absconder section 169 has effect as if subsection (1)(b) read —

>   "(b)   there is evidence which was not available to the prosecutor or the Director on the relevant date,".

178   Defendant neither convicted nor acquitted

(1)   This section applies if the following two conditions are satisfied.

(2)   The first condition is that —

(a)   proceedings for an offence or offences are started against a defendant but are not concluded,

(b)   he absconds, and

(c)   the period of two years (starting with the day the court believes he absconded) has ended.

(3)   The second condition is that —

(a)   the prosecutor or the Director applies to the Crown Court to proceed under this section, and

(b)   the court believes it is appropriate for it to do so.

(4)   If this section applies the court must proceed under section 156 in the same way as it must proceed if the two conditions there mentioned are satisfied; but this is subject to subsection (5).

(5)   If the court proceeds under section 156 as applied by this section, this Part has effect with these modifications —

(a)   any person the court believes is likely to be affected by an order under section 156 is entitled to appear before the court and make representations;

(b)   the court must not make an order under section 156 unless the prosecutor or the Director (as the case may be) has taken reasonable steps to contact the defendant;

(c)   section 156(9) applies as if the reference to subsection (2) were to subsection (2) of this section;

(d)   sections 160, 166(4) and 167 to 170 must be ignored;

(e)   section 171 must be ignored while the defendant is still an absconder.

(6)   Once the defendant has ceased to be an absconder section 171 has effect as if references to the date of conviction were to —

(a)   the day when proceedings for the offence concerned were started against the defendant, or

(b)   if there are two or more offences and proceedings for them were started on different days, the earliest of those days.

(7)   If —

(a)   the court makes an order under section 156 as applied by this section, and

(b)   the defendant is later convicted in proceedings before the Crown Court of the offence (or any of the offences) concerned,

section 156 does not apply so far as that conviction is concerned.

179   Variation of order

(1)   This section applies if —

    (a)   the court makes a confiscation order under section 156 as applied by section 178,

    (b)   the defendant ceases to be an absconder,

    (c)   he is convicted of an offence (or any of the offences) mentioned in section 178(2)(a),

    (d)   he believes that the amount required to be paid was too large (taking the circumstances prevailing when the amount was found for the purposes of the order), and

    (e)   before the end of the relevant period he applies to the Crown Court to consider the evidence on which his belief is based.

(2)   If (after considering the evidence) the court concludes that the defendant's belief is well founded —

    (a)   it must find the amount which should have been the amount required to be paid (taking the circumstances prevailing when the amount was found for the purposes of the order), and

    (b)   it may vary the order by substituting for the amount required to be paid such amount as it believes is just.

(3)   The relevant period is the period of 28 days starting with —

    (a)   the date on which the defendant was convicted of the offence mentioned in section 178(2)(a), or

    (b)   if there are two or more offences and the the the convictions were on different dates, the date of the latest.

(4)   But in a case where section 178(2)(a) applies to more than one offence the court must not make an order under this section unless it is satisfied that there is no possibility of any further proceedings being taken or continued in relation to any such offence in respect of which the defendant has not been convicted.

180   Discharge of order

(1)   Subsection (2) applies if —

    (a)   the court makes a confiscation order under section 156 as applied by section 178,

    (b)   the defendant is later tried for the offence or offences concerned and acquitted on all counts, and

    (c)   he applies to the Crown Court to discharge the order.

(2)   In such a case the court must discharge the order.

(3)   Subsection (4) applies if —

    (a)   the court makes a confiscation order under section 156 as applied by section 178,

    (b)   the defendant ceases to be an absconder,

    (c)   subsection (1)(b) does not apply, and

    (d)   he applies to the Crown Court to discharge the order.

(4)   In such a case the court may discharge the order if it finds that —

    (a)   there has been undue delay in continuing the proceedings mentioned in section 178(2), or

(b)   the prosecutor does not intend to proceed with the prosecution.

(5)   If the court discharges a confiscation order under this section it may make such a consequential or incidental order as it believes is appropriate.

Appeals

181   Appeal by prosecutor or Director

(1)   If the Crown Court makes a confiscation order the prosecutor or the Director may appeal to the Court of Appeal in respect of the order.

(2)   If the Crown Court decides not to make a confiscation order the prosecutor or the Director may appeal to the Court of Appeal against the decision.

(3)   Subsections (1) and (2) do not apply to an order or decision made by virtue of section 169, 170, 177 or 178.

182   Court's powers on appeal

(1)   On an appeal under section 181(1) the Court of Appeal may confirm, quash or vary the confiscation order.

(2)   On an appeal under section 181(2) the Court of Appeal may confirm the decision, or if it believes the decision was wrong it may—
   (a)   itself proceed under section 156 (ignoring subsections (1) to (3)), or
   (b)   direct the Crown Court to proceed afresh under section 156.

(3)   In proceeding afresh in pursuance of this section the Crown Court must comply with any directions the Court of Appeal may make.

(4)   If a court makes or varies a confiscation order under this section or in pursuance of a direction under this section it must—
   (a)   have regard to any fine imposed on the defendant in respect of the offence (or any of the offences) concerned;
   (b)   have regard to any order which falls within section 163(3) and has been made against him in respect of the offence (or any of the offences) concerned, unless the order has already been taken into account by a court in deciding what is the free property held by the defendant for the purposes of section 159.

(5)   If the Court of Appeal proceeds under section 156 or the Crown Court proceeds afresh under that section in pursuance of a direction under this section subsections (6) to (10) apply.

(6)   If a court has already sentenced the defendant for the offence (or any of the offences) concerned, section 156 has effect as if his particular criminal conduct included conduct which constitutes offences which the court has taken into consideration in deciding his sentence for the offence or offences concerned.

(7)   If an order has been made against the defendant in respect of the offence (or any of the offences) concerned under Article 14 of the Criminal Justice (Northern Ireland) Order 1994 (S.I. 1994/2795 (N.I. 15)) (compensation orders)—
   (a)   the court must have regard to it, and
   (b)   section 163(5) and (6) above do not apply.

(8)   Section 158(2) does not apply, and the rules applying instead are that the court must—

    (a)   take account of conduct occurring before the relevant date;

    (b)   take account of property obtained before that date;

    (c)   take account of property obtained on or after that date if it was obtained as a result of or in connection with conduct occurring before that date.

(9)   In section 160—

    (a)   the first and second assumptions do not apply with regard to property first held by the defendant on or after the relevant date;

    (b)   the third assumption does not apply with regard to expenditure incurred by him on or after that date;

    (c)   the fourth assumption does not apply with regard to property obtained (or assumed to have been obtained) by him on or after that date.

(10)   Section 176 applies as it applies in the circumstances mentioned in subsection (1) of that section.

(11)   The relevant date is the date on which the Crown Court decided not to make a confiscation order.

183   Appeal to House of Lords

(1)   An appeal lies to the House of Lords from a decision of the Court of Appeal on an appeal under section 181.

(2)   An appeal under this section lies at the instance of—

    (a)   the defendant or the prosecutor (if the prosecutor appealed under section 181);

    (b)   the defendant or the Director (if the Director appealed under section 181).

(3)   On an appeal from a decision of the Court of Appeal to confirm, vary or make a confiscation order the House of Lords may confirm, quash or vary the order.

(4)   On an appeal from a decision of the Court of Appeal to confirm the decision of the Crown Court not to make a confiscation order or from a decision of the Court of Appeal to quash a confiscation order the House of Lords may—

    (a)   confirm the decision, or

    (b)   direct the Crown Court to proceed afresh under section 156 if it believes the decision was wrong.

(5)   In proceeding afresh in pursuance of this section the Crown Court must comply with any directions the House of Lords may make.

(6)   If a court varies a confiscation order under this section or makes a confiscation order in pursuance of a direction under this section it must—

    (a)   have regard to any fine imposed on the defendant in respect of the offence (or any of the offences) concerned;

    (b)   have regard to any order which falls within section 163(3) and has been made against him in respect of the offence (or any of the offences) concerned, unless the order has already been taken into account by a court in deciding what is the free property held by the defendant for the purposes of section 159.

(7) If the Crown Court proceeds afresh under section 156 in pursuance of a direction under this section subsections (8) to (12) apply.

(8) If a court has already sentenced the defendant for the offence (or any of the offences) concerned, section 156 has effect as if his particular criminal conduct included conduct which constitutes offences which the court has taken into consideration in deciding his sentence for the offence or offences concerned.

(9) If an order has been made against the defendant in respect of the offence (or any of the offences) concerned under Article 14 of the Criminal Justice (Northern Ireland) Order 1994 (S.I. 1994/2795 (N.I. 15)) (compensation orders)—

    (a) the Crown Court must have regard to it, and

    (b) section 163(5) and (6) above do not apply.

(10) Section 158(2) does not apply, and the rules applying instead are that the Crown Court must—

    (a) take account of conduct occurring before the relevant date;

    (b) take account of property obtained before that date;

    (c) take account of property obtained on or after that date if it was obtained as a result of or in connection with conduct occurring before that date.

(11) In section 160—

    (a) the first and second assumptions do not apply with regard to property first held by the defendant on or after the relevant date;

    (b) the third assumption does not apply with regard to expenditure incurred by him on or after that date;

    (c) the fourth assumption does not apply with regard to property obtained (or assumed to have been obtained) by him on or after that date.

(12) Section 176 applies as it applies in the circumstances mentioned in subsection (1) of that section.

(13) The relevant date is—

    (a) in a case where the Crown Court made a confiscation order which was quashed by the Court of Appeal, the date on which the Crown Court made the order;

    (b) in any other case, the date on which the Crown Court decided not to make a confiscation order.

Enforcement authority

184 Enforcement authority

(1) Subsection (2) applies if a court makes a confiscation order and any of the following paragraphs applies—

    (a) the court proceeded under section 156 after being asked to do so by the Director;

    (b) the court proceeded under section 156 by virtue of an application by the Director under section 169, 170, 177 or 178;

    (c) the court proceeded under section 156 as a result of an appeal by the Director under section 181(2) or 183;

    (d) before the court made the order the Director applied to the court to appoint him as the enforcement authority for the order.

(2)   In any such case the court must appoint the Director as the enforcement authority for the order.

Enforcement as fines etc

185   Enforcement as fines etc

(1)   This section applies if a court makes a confiscation order.

(2)   Section 35(1)(c), (2), (4) and (5) of the Criminal Justice Act (Northern Ireland) 1945 (c. 15) (functions of court as to fines) apply as if the amount ordered to be paid were a fine imposed on the defendant by the Crown Court.

(3)   An amount payable under a confiscation order is not a fine, costs, damages or compensation for the purposes of Article 35 of the Criminal Justice (Northern Ireland) Order 1998 (S.I. 1998/1504 (N.I. 9)) (parent or guardian to pay fine etc. instead of child).

186   Director's application for enforcement

(1)   If the Director believes that the conditions set out in subsection (2) are satisfied he may make an ex parte application to the Crown Court for the issue of a summons against the defendant.

(2)   The conditions are that−
    (a)   a confiscation order has been made;
    (b)   the Director has been appointed as the enforcement authority for the order;
    (c)   the order is not satisfied;
    (d)   the order is not subject to appeal;
    (e)   the Director has done all that is practicable (apart from this section) to enforce the order.

(3)   If it appears to the Crown Court that the conditions are satisfied it may issue a summons ordering the defendant to appear before the court at the time and place specified in the summons.

(4)   If the defendant fails to appear before the Crown Court in pursuance of the summons the court may issue a warrant for his arrest.

(5)   If−
    (a)   the defendant appears before the Crown Court in pursuance of the summons or of a warrant issued under subsection (4), and
    (b)   the court is satisfied that the conditions set out in subsection (2) are satisfied,
    it may issue a warrant committing the defendant to prison or to detention under section 5 of the Treatment of Offenders Act (Northern Ireland) 1968 (c. 29 (N.I.)) for default in payment of the amount ordered to be paid by the confiscation order.

(6)   Subsection (7) applies if the amount remaining to be paid under the confiscation order when the warrant under subsection (5) is issued is less than the amount ordered to be paid.

(7)   In such a case the court must substitute for the term of imprisonment or detention fixed in respect of the order under section 35(1) of the Criminal

Justice Act (Northern Ireland) 1945 (c. 15 (N.I.)) such term as bears to the original term the same proportion as the amount remaining to be paid bears to the amount ordered to be paid.

187 Provisions about imprisonment or detention

(1) Subsection (2) applies if—

    (a) a warrant committing the defendant to prison or detention is issued for a default in payment of an amount ordered to be paid under a confiscation order in respect of an offence or offences, and

    (b) at the time the warrant is issued the defendant is liable to serve a term of custody in respect of the offence (or any of the offences).

(2) In such a case the term of imprisonment or of detention to be served in default of payment of the amount does not begin to run until after the term mentioned in subsection (1)(b) above.

(3) The reference in subsection (1)(b) to the term of custody the defendant is liable to serve in respect of the offence (or any of the offences) is a reference to the term of imprisonment, or detention under section 5 of the Treatment of Offenders Act (Northern Ireland) 1968 (c. 29 (N.I.)), which he is liable to serve in respect of the offence (or any of the offences).

(4) For the purposes of subsection (3) consecutive terms and terms which are wholly or partly concurrent must be treated as a single term and the following must be ignored—

    (a) any sentence of imprisonment or order for detention suspended under section 18 of the Treatment of Offenders Act (Northern Ireland) 1968 which has not taken effect at the time the warrant is issued;

    (b) any term of imprisonment or detention fixed under section 35(1)(c) of the Criminal Justice Act (Northern Ireland) 1945 (c. 15 (N.I.)) (term to be served in default of payment of fine etc) for which a warrant committing the defendant to prison or detention has not been issued at that time.

(5) If the defendant serves a term of imprisonment or detention in default of paying any amount due under a confiscation order, his serving that term does not prevent the confiscation order from continuing to have effect so far as any other method of enforcement is concerned.

188 Reconsideration etc: variation of prison term

(1) Subsection (2) applies if—

    (a) a court varies a confiscation order under section 171, 172, 173, 179, 182 or 183,

    (b) the effect of the variation is to vary the maximum period applicable in relation to the order under section 35(2) of the Criminal Justice Act (Northern Ireland) 1945 (c. 15 (N.I.)), and

    (c) the result is that that maximum period is less than the term of imprisonment or detention fixed in respect of the order under section 35(1)(c) of that Act.

(2) In such a case the court must fix a reduced term of imprisonment or detention in respect of the confiscation order under section 35(1)(c) of that Act in place of the term previously fixed.

(3)   Subsection (4) applies if paragraphs (a) and (b) of subsection (1) apply but paragraph (c) does not.

(4)   In such a case the court may amend the term of imprisonment or detention fixed in respect of the confiscation order under section 35(1)(c) of that Act.

(5)   If the effect of section 162 is to increase the maximum period applicable in relation to a confiscation order under section 35(2) of that Act, on the application of the appropriate person the Crown Court may amend the term of imprisonment or detention fixed in respect of the order under section 35(1)(c) of that Act.

(6)   The appropriate person is –
  (a)   the Director, if he was appointed as the enforcement authority for the order under section 184;
  (b)   the prosecutor, in any other case.

Restraint orders

189   Conditions for exercise of powers

(1)   The High Court may exercise the powers conferred by section 190 if any of the following conditions is satisfied.

(2)   The first condition is that –
  (a)   a criminal investigation has been started in Northern Ireland with regard to an offence, and
  (b)   there is reasonable cause to believe that the alleged offender has benefited from his criminal conduct.

(3)   The second condition is that –
  (a)   proceedings for an offence have been started in Northern Ireland and not concluded,
  (b)   there is reasonable cause to believe that the defendant has benefited from his criminal conduct.

(4)   The third condition is that –
  (a)   an application by the prosecutor or the Director has been made under section 169, 170, 177 or 178 and not concluded, or the court believes that such an application is to be made, and
  (b)   there is reasonable cause to believe that the defendant has benefited from his criminal conduct.

(5)   The fourth condition is that –
  (a)   an application by the prosecutor or the Director has been made under section 171 and not concluded, or the court believes that such an application is to be made, and
  (b)   there is reasonable cause to believe that the court will decide under that section that the amount found under the new calculation of the defendant's benefit exceeds the relevant amount (as defined in that section).

(6)   The fifth condition is that –

(a) an application by the prosecutor or the Director has been made under section 172 and not concluded, or the court believes that such an application is to be made, and

(b) there is reasonable cause to believe that the court will decide under that section that the amount found under the new calculation of the available amount exceeds the relevant amount (as defined in that section).

(7) The second condition is not satisfied if the court believes that —

(a) there has been undue delay in continuing the proceedings, or

(b) the prosecutor does not intend to proceed.

(8) If an application mentioned in the third, fourth or fifth condition has been made the condition is not satisfied if the court believes that —

(a) there has been undue delay in continuing the application, or

(b) the prosecutor or the Director (as the case may be) does not intend to proceed.

(9) If the first condition is satisfied —

(a) references in this Part to the defendant are to the alleged offender;

(b) references in this Part to the prosecutor are to the person the court believes is to have conduct of any proceedings for the offence;

(c) section 225(9) has effect as if proceedings for the offence had been started against the defendant when the investigation was started.

190 Restraint orders

(1) If any condition set out in section 189 is satisfied the High Court may make an order (a restraint order) prohibiting any specified person from dealing with any realisable property held by him.

(2) A restraint order may provide that it applies —

(a) to all realisable property held by the specified person whether or not the property is described in the order;

(b) to realisable property transferred to the specified person after the order is made.

(3) A restraint order may be made subject to exceptions, and an exception may in particular —

(a) make provision for reasonable living expenses and reasonable legal expenses;

(b) make provision for the purpose of enabling any person to carry on any trade, business, profession or occupation;

(c) be made subject to conditions.

(4) But an exception to a restraint order may not make provision for any legal expenses which —

(a) relate to an offence which falls within subsection (5), and

(b) are incurred by the defendant or by a recipient of a tainted gift.

(5) These offences fall within this subsection —

(a) the offence mentioned in section 189(2) or (3), if the first or second condition (as the case may be) is satisfied;

    (b)   the offence (or any of the offences) concerned, if the third, fourth or fifth condition is satisfied.

(6)   Subsection (7) applies if —

    (a)   the court makes a restraint order, and

    (b)   the applicant for the order applies to the court to proceed under subsection (7) (whether as part of the application for the restraint order or at any time afterwards).

(7)   The court may make such order as it believes is appropriate for the purpose of ensuring that the restraint order is effective.

(8)   A restraint order does not affect property for the time being subject to a charge under any of these provisions —

    (a)   section 9 of the Drug Trafficking Offences Act 1986 (c. 32);

    (b)   section 78 of the Criminal Justice Act 1988 (c. 33);

    (c)   Article 14 of the Criminal Justice (Confiscation) (Northern Ireland) Order 1990 (S.I. 1990/2588 (N.I. 17));

    (d)   section 27 of the Drug Trafficking Act 1994 (c. 37);

    (e)   Article 32 of the Proceeds of Crime (Northern Ireland) Order 1996 (S.I. 1996/1299 (N.I. 9)).

(9)   Dealing with property includes removing it from Northern Ireland.

191   Application, discharge and variation

(1)   A restraint order —

    (a)   may be made only on an application by an applicant falling within subsection (2);

    (b)   may be made on an ex parte application to a judge in chambers.

(2)   These applicants fall within this subsection —

    (a)   the prosecutor;

    (b)   the Director;

    (c)   an accredited financial investigator.

(3)   An application to discharge or vary a restraint order or an order under section 190(7) may be made to the High Court by —

    (a)   the person who applied for the order;

    (b)   any person affected by the order.

(4)   Subsections (5) to (7) apply to an application under subsection (3).

(5)   The court —

    (a)   may discharge the order;

    (b)   may vary the order.

(6)   If the condition in section 189 which was satisfied was that proceedings were started or an application was made, the court must discharge the order on the conclusion of the proceedings or of the application (as the case may be).

(7)   If the condition in section 189 which was satisfied was that an investigation was started or an application was to be made, the court must discharge the order if within a reasonable time proceedings for the offence are not started or the application is not made (as the case may be).

192 Appeal to Court of Appeal

(1) If on an application for a restraint order the court decides not to make one, the person who applied for the order may appeal to the Court of Appeal against the decision.

(2) If an application is made under section 191(3) in relation to a restraint order or an order under section 190(7) the following persons may appeal to the Court of Appeal in respect of the High Court's decision on the application —
    (a) the person who applied for the order;
    (b) any person affected by the order.

(3) On an appeal under subsection (1) or (2) the Court of Appeal may —
    (a) confirm the decision, or
    (b) make such order as it believes is appropriate.

193 Appeal to House of Lords

(1) An appeal lies to the House of Lords from a decision of the Court of Appeal on an appeal under section 192.

(2) An appeal under this section lies at the instance of any person who was a party to the proceedings before the Court of Appeal.

(3) On an appeal under this section the House of Lords may —
    (a) confirm the decision of the Court of Appeal, or
    (b) make such order as it believes is appropriate.

194 Seizure

(1) If a restraint order is in force a constable or a customs officer may seize any realisable property to which it applies to prevent its removal from Northern Ireland.

(2) Property seized under subsection (1) must be dealt with in accordance with the directions of the court which made the order.

195 Supplementary

(1) The person applying for a restraint order must be treated for the purposes of section 66 of the Land Registration Act (Northern Ireland) 1970 (c. 18 (N.I.)) (cautions) as a person interested in relation to any registered land to which —
    (a) the application relates, or
    (b) a restraint order made in pursuance of the application relates.

(2) Upon being served with a copy of a restraint order, the Registrar shall, in respect of any registered land to which a restraint order or an application for a restraint order relates, make an entry inhibiting any dealing with the land without the consent of the High Court.

(3) Subsections (2) and (4) of section 67 of the Land Registration Act (Northern Ireland) 1970 (inhibitions) shall apply to an entry made under subsection (2) as they apply to an entry made on the application of any person interested in the registered land under subsection (1) of that section.

(4) Where a restraint order has been protected by an entry registered under the Land Registration Act (Northern Ireland) 1970 or the Registration of Deeds Acts, an order discharging the restraint order may require that the entry be vacated.

(5) In this section —

"Registrar" and "entry" have the same meanings as in the Land Registration Act (Northern Ireland) 1970; and

"Registration of Deeds Acts" has the meaning given by section 46(2) of the Interpretation Act (Northern Ireland) 1954 (c. 33 (N.I.)).

Management receivers

196 Appointment

(1) Subsection (2) applies if —

    (a) the High Court makes a restraint order, and

    (b) the applicant for the restraint order applies to the court to proceed under subsection (2) (whether as part of the application for the restraint order or at any time afterwards).

(2) The High Court may by order appoint a receiver in respect of any realisable property to which the restraint order applies.

197 Powers

(1) If the court appoints a receiver under section 196 it may act under this section on the application of the person who applied for the restraint order.

(2) The court may by order confer on the receiver the following powers in relation to any realisable property to which the restraint order applies —

    (a) power to take possession of the property;

    (b) power to manage or otherwise deal with the property;

    (c) power to start, carry on or defend any legal proceedings in respect of the property;

    (d) power to realise so much of the property as is necessary to meet the receiver's remuneration and expenses.

(3) The court may by order confer on the receiver power to enter any premises in Northern Ireland and to do any of the following —

    (a) search for or inspect anything authorised by the court;

    (b) make or obtain a copy, photograph or other record of anything so authorised;

    (c) remove anything which the receiver is required or authorised to take possession of in pursuance of an order of the court.

(4) The court may by order authorise the receiver to do any of the following for the purpose of the exercise of his functions —

    (a) hold property;

    (b) enter into contracts;

    (c) sue and be sued;

    (d) employ agents;

    (e) execute powers of attorney, deeds or other instruments;

     (f)   take any other steps the court thinks appropriate.

(5)   The court may order any person who has possession of realisable property to which the restraint order applies to give possession of it to the receiver.

(6)   The court —
    (a)   may order a person holding an interest in realisable property to which the restraint order applies to make to the receiver such payment as the court specifies in respect of a beneficial interest held by the defendant or the recipient of a tainted gift;
    (b)   may (on the payment being made) by order transfer, grant or extinguish any interest in the property.

(7)   Subsections (2), (5) and (6) do not apply to property for the time being subject to a charge under any of these provisions —
    (a)   section 9 of the Drug Trafficking Offences Act 1986 (c. 32);
    (b)   section 78 of the Criminal Justice Act 1988 (c. 33);
    (c)   Article 14 of the Criminal Justice (Confiscation) (Northern Ireland) Order 1990 (S.I. 1990/2588 (N.I. 17));
    (d)   section 27 of the Drug Trafficking Act 1994 (c. 37);
    (e)   Article 32 of the Proceeds of Crime (Northern Ireland) Order 1996 (S.I. 1996/1299 (N.I. 9)).

(8)   The court must not —
    (a)   confer the power mentioned in subsection (2)(b) or (d) in respect of property, or
    (b)   exercise the power conferred on it by subsection (6) in respect of property,
unless it gives persons holding interests in the property a reasonable opportunity to make representations to it.

(9)   The court may order that a power conferred by an order under this section is subject to such conditions and exceptions as it specifies.

(10)   Managing or otherwise dealing with property includes —
    (a)   selling the property or any part of it or interest in it;
    (b)   carrying on or arranging for another person to carry on any trade or business the assets of which are or are part of the property;
    (c)   incurring capital expenditure in respect of the property.

Enforcement receivers

198 Appointment

(1)   This section applies if —
    (a)   a confiscation order is made,
    (b)   it is not satisfied, and
    (c)   it is not subject to appeal.

(2)   On the application of the prosecutor the Crown Court may by order appoint a receiver in respect of realisable property.

199 Powers

(1) If the court appoints a receiver under section 198 it may act under this section on the application of the prosecutor.

(2) The court may by order confer on the receiver the following powers in relation to the realisable property –
   (a) power to take possession of the property;
   (b) power to manage or otherwise deal with the property;
   (c) power to realise the property, in such manner as the court may specify;
   (d) power to start, carry on or defend any legal proceedings in respect of the property.

(3) The court may by order confer on the receiver power to enter any premises in Northern Ireland and to do any of the following –
   (a) search for or inspect anything authorised by the court;
   (b) make or obtain a copy, photograph or other record of anything so authorised;
   (c) remove anything which the receiver is required or authorised to take possession of in pursuance of an order of the court.

(4) The court may by order authorise the receiver to do any of the following for the purpose of the exercise of his functions –
   (a) hold property;
   (b) enter into contracts;
   (c) sue and be sued;
   (d) employ agents;
   (e) execute powers of attorney, deeds or other instruments;
   (f) take any other steps the court thinks appropriate.

(5) The court may order any person who has possession of realisable property to give possession of it to the receiver.

(6) The court –
   (a) may order a person holding an interest in realisable property to make to the receiver such payment as the court specifies in respect of a beneficial interest held by the defendant or the recipient of a tainted gift;
   (b) may (on the payment being made) by order transfer, grant or extinguish any interest in the property.

(7) Subsections (2), (5) and (6) do not apply to property for the time being subject to a charge under any of these provisions –
   (a) section 9 of the Drug Trafficking Offences Act 1986 (c. 32);
   (b) section 78 of the Criminal Justice Act 1988 (c. 33);
   (c) Article 14 of the Criminal Justice (Confiscation) (Northern Ireland) Order 1990 (S.I. 1990/2588 (N.I. 17));
   (d) section 27 of the Drug Trafficking Act 1994 (c. 37);
   (e) Article 32 of the Proceeds of Crime (Northern Ireland) Order 1996 (S.I. 1996/1299 (N.I. 9)).

(8) The court must not –
   (a) confer the power mentioned in subsection (2)(b) or (c) in respect of property, or

      (b)   exercise the power conferred on it by subsection (6) in respect of property,

unless it gives persons holding interests in the property a reasonable opportunity to make representations to it.

(9)   The court may order that a power conferred by an order under this section is subject to such conditions and exceptions as it specifies.

(10)   Managing or otherwise dealing with property includes —

    (a)   selling the property or any part of it or interest in it;

    (b)   carrying on or arranging for another person to carry on any trade or business the assets of which are or are part of the property;

    (c)   incurring capital expenditure in respect of the property.

Director's receivers

200   Appointment

(1)   This section applies if —

    (a)   a confiscation order is made, and

    (b)   the Director is appointed as the enforcement authority for the order under section 184.

(2)   But this section does not apply if —

    (a)   the confiscation order was made by the Court of Appeal, and

    (b)   when the Crown Court comes to proceed under this section the confiscation order has been satisfied.

(3)   If this section applies the Crown Court must make an order for the appointment of a receiver in respect of realisable property.

(4)   An order under subsection (3) —

    (a)   must confer power on the Director to nominate the person who is to be the receiver, and

    (b)   takes effect when the Director nominates that person.

(5)   The Director must not nominate a person under subsection (4) unless at the time he does so the confiscation order —

    (a)   is not satisfied, and

    (b)   is not subject to appeal.

(6)   A person nominated to be the receiver under subsection (4) may be —

    (a)   a member of the staff of the Agency;

    (b)   a person providing services under arrangements made by the Director.

(7)   If this section applies section 198 does not apply.

201   Powers

(1)   If the court makes an order for the appointment of a receiver under section 200 it may act under this section on the application of the Director.

(2)   The court may by order confer on the receiver the following powers in relation to the realisable property —

    (a)   power to take possession of the property;

     (b)   power to manage or otherwise deal with the property;

     (c)   power to realise the property, in such manner as the court may specify;

     (d)   power to start, carry on or defend any legal proceedings in respect of the property.

(3)   The court may by order confer on the receiver power to enter any premises in Northern Ireland and to do any of the following –

     (a)   search for or inspect anything authorised by the court;

     (b)   make or obtain a copy, photograph or other record of anything so authorised;

     (c)   remove anything which the receiver is required or authorised to take possession of in pursuance of an order of the court.

(4)   The court may by order authorise the receiver to do any of the following for the purpose of the exercise of his functions –

     (a)   hold property;

     (b)   enter into contracts;

     (c)   sue and be sued;

     (d)   employ agents;

     (e)   execute powers of attorney, deeds or other instruments;

     (f)   take any other steps the court thinks appropriate.

(5)   The court may order any person who has possession of realisable property to give possession of it to the receiver.

(6)   The court –

     (a)   may order a person holding an interest in realisable property to make to the receiver such payment as the court specifies in respect of a beneficial interest held by the defendant or the recipient of a tainted gift;

     (b)   may (on the payment being made) by order transfer, grant or extinguish any interest in the property.

(7)   Subsections (2), (5) and (6) do not apply to property for the time being subject to a charge under any of these provisions –

     (a)   section 9 of the Drug Trafficking Offences Act 1986 (c. 32);

     (b)   section 78 of the Criminal Justice Act 1988 (c. 33);

     (c)   Article 14 of the Criminal Justice (Confiscation) (Northern Ireland) Order 1990 (S.I. 1990/2588 (N.I. 17));

     (d)   section 27 of the Drug Trafficking Act 1994 (c. 37);

     (e)   Article 32 of the Proceeds of Crime (Northern Ireland) Order 1996 (S.I. 1996/1299 (N.I. 9)).

(8)   The court must not –

     (a)   confer the power mentioned in subsection (2)(b) or (c) in respect of property, or

     (b)   exercise the power conferred on it by subsection (6) in respect of property,

unless it gives persons holding interests in the property a reasonable opportunity to make representations to it.

(9)   The court may order that a power conferred by an order under this section is subject to such conditions and exceptions as it specifies.

(10) Managing or otherwise dealing with property includes —
    (a) selling the property or any part of it or interest in it;
    (b) carrying on or arranging for another person to carry on any trade or business the assets of which are or are part of the property;
    (c) incurring capital expenditure in respect of the property.

Application of sums

202 Enforcement receivers

(1) This section applies to sums which are in the hands of a receiver appointed under section 198 if they are —
    (a) the proceeds of the realisation of property under section 199;
    (b) sums (other than those mentioned in paragraph (a)) in which the defendant holds an interest.

(2) The sums must be applied as follows —
    (a) first, they must be applied in payment of such expenses incurred by a person acting as an insolvency practitioner as are payable under this subsection by virtue of section 432;
    (b) second, they must be applied in making any payments directed by the Crown Court;
    (c) third, they must be applied on the defendant's behalf towards satisfaction of the confiscation order.

(3) If the amount payable under the confiscation order has been fully paid and any sums remain in the receiver's hands he must distribute them —
    (a) among such persons who held (or hold) interests in the property concerned as the Crown Court directs, and
    (b) in such proportions as it directs.

(4) Before making a direction under subsection (3) the court must give persons who held (or hold) interests in the property concerned a reasonable opportunity to make representations to it.

(5) For the purposes of subsections (3) and (4) the property concerned is —
    (a) the property represented by the proceeds mentioned in subsection (1)(a);
    (b) the sums mentioned in subsection (1)(b).

(6) The receiver applies sums as mentioned in subsection (2)(c) by paying them to the appropriate chief clerk on account of the amount payable under the order.

(7) The appropriate chief clerk is the chief clerk of the court at the place where the confiscation order was made.

203 Sums received by chief clerk

(1) This section applies if a chief clerk receives sums on account of the amount payable under a confiscation order (whether the sums are received under section 202 or otherwise).

(2) The chief clerk's receipt of the sums reduces the amount payable under the order, but he must apply the sums received as follows.

(3) First he must apply them in payment of such expenses incurred by a person acting as an insolvency practitioner as —

    (a) are payable under this subsection by virtue of section 432, but

    (b) are not already paid under section 202(2)(a).

(4) If the chief clerk received the sums under section 202 he must next apply them —

    (a) first, in payment of the remuneration and expenses of a receiver appointed under section 196, to the extent that they have not been met by virtue of the exercise by that receiver of a power conferred under section 197(2)(d);

    (b) second, in payment of the remuneration and expenses of the receiver appointed under section 198.

(5) If a direction was made under section 163(6) for an amount of compensation to be paid out of sums recovered under the confiscation order, the chief clerk must next apply the sums in payment of that amount.

(6) If any amount remains after the chief clerk makes any payments required by the preceding provisions of this section, the amount must be treated for the purposes of section 20 of the Administration of Justice Act (Northern Ireland) 1954 (c. 9 (N.I.)) (application of fines) as if it were a fine.

(7) Subsection (4) does not apply if the receiver is a member of the staff of the Director of Public Prosecutions for Northern Ireland or of the Commissioners of Customs and Excise; and it is immaterial whether he is a permanent or temporary member or he is on secondment from elsewhere.

204 Director's receivers

(1) This section applies to sums which are in the hands of a receiver appointed under section 200 if they are —

    (a) the proceeds of the realisation of property under section 201;

    (b) sums (other than those mentioned in paragraph (a)) in which the defendant holds an interest.

(2) The sums must be applied as follows —

    (a) first, they must be applied in payment of such expenses incurred by a person acting as an insolvency practitioner as are payable under this subsection by virtue of section 432;

    (b) second, they must be applied in making any payments directed by the Crown Court;

    (c) third, they must be applied on the defendant's behalf towards satisfaction of the confiscation order by being paid to the Director on account of the amount payable under it.

(3) If the amount payable under the confiscation order has been fully paid and any sums remain in the receiver's hands he must distribute them —

    (a) among such persons who held (or hold) interests in the property concerned as the Crown Court directs, and

    (b) in such proportions as it directs.

(4) Before making a direction under subsection (3) the court must give persons who held (or hold) interests in the property concerned a reasonable opportunity to make representations to it.

(5) For the purposes of subsections (3) and (4) the property concerned is—

    (a) the property represented by the proceeds mentioned in subsection (1)(a);

    (b) the sums mentioned in subsection (1)(b).

205 Sums received by Director

(1) This section applies if the Director receives sums on account of the amount payable under a confiscation order (whether the sums are received under section 204 or otherwise).

(2) The Director's receipt of the sums reduces the amount payable under the order, but he must apply the sums received as follows.

(3) First he must apply them in payment of such expenses incurred by a person acting as an insolvency practitioner as—

    (a) are payable under this subsection by virtue of section 432, but

    (b) are not already paid under section 204(2)(a).

(4) If the Director received the sums under section 204 he must next apply them—

    (a) first, in payment of the remuneration and expenses of a receiver appointed under section 196, to the extent that they have not been met by virtue of the exercise by that receiver of a power conferred under section 197(2)(d);

    (b) second, in payment of the remuneration and expenses of the receiver appointed under section 200.

(5) If a direction was made under section 163(6) for an amount of compensation to be paid out of sums recovered under the confiscation order, the Director must next apply the sums in payment of that amount.

(6) Subsection (4) does not apply if the receiver is a member of the staff of the Agency or a person providing services under arrangements made by the Director.

Restrictions

206 Restraint orders

(1) Subsections (2) and (3) apply if a court makes a restraint order.

(2) If the order applies to a tenancy of any premises, no landlord or other person to whom rent is payable may exercise a right within subsection (3) except with the leave of the High Court and subject to any terms the High Court may impose.

(3) A right is within this subsection if it is a right of forfeiture by peaceable re-entry in relation to the premises in respect of any failure by the tenant to comply with any term or condition of the tenancy.

(4) If a court in which proceedings are pending in respect of any property is satisfied that a restraint order has been applied for or made in respect of the property, the court may either stay the proceedings or allow them to continue on any terms it thinks fit.

(5)   Before exercising any power conferred by subsection (4), the court must give an opportunity to be heard to —

    (a)   the applicant for the restraint order, and

    (b)   any receiver appointed in respect of the property under section 196, 198 or 200.

207   Enforcement receivers

(1)   Subsections (2) and (3) apply if a court makes an order under section 198 appointing a receiver in respect of any realisable property.

(2)   If the receiver is appointed in respect of a tenancy of any premises, no landlord or other person to whom rent is payable may exercise a right within subsection (3) except with the leave of the Crown Court and subject to any terms the Crown Court may impose.

(3)   A right is within this subsection if it is a right of forfeiture by peaceable re-entry in relation to the premises in respect of any failure by the tenant to comply with any term or condition of the tenancy.

(4)   If a court in which proceedings are pending in respect of any property is satisfied that an order under section 198 appointing a receiver in respect of the property has been applied for or made, the court may either stay the proceedings or allow them to continue on any terms it thinks fit.

(5)   Before exercising any power conferred by subsection (4), the court must give an opportunity to be heard to —

    (a)   the prosecutor, and

    (b)   the receiver (if the order under section 198 has been made).

208   Director's receivers

(1)   Subsections (2) and (3) apply if —

    (a)   the Crown Court has made an order under section 200 for the appointment of a receiver in respect of any realisable property, and

    (b)   the order has taken effect.

(2)   If the order is for the appointment of a receiver in respect of a tenancy of any premises, no landlord or other person to whom rent is payable may exercise a right within subsection (3) except with the leave of the Crown Court and subject to any terms the Crown Court may impose.

(3)   A right is within this subsection if it is a right of forfeiture by peaceable re-entry in relation to the premises in respect of any failure by the tenant to comply with any term or condition of the tenancy.

(4)   If a court (whether the Crown Court or any other court) in which proceedings are pending in respect of any property is satisfied that an order under section 200 for the appointment of a receiver in respect of the property has taken effect, the court may either stay the proceedings or allow them to continue on any terms it thinks fit.

(5)   Before exercising any power conferred by subsection (4), the court must give an opportunity to be heard to —

    (a)   the Director, and

    (b)   the receiver.

Receivers: further provisions

209 Protection

If a receiver appointed under section 196, 198 or 200 –

(a) takes action in relation to property which is not realisable property,

(b) would be entitled to take the action if it were realisable property, and

(c) believes on reasonable grounds that he is entitled to take the action,

he is not liable to any person in respect of any loss or damage resulting from the action, except so far as the loss or damage is caused by his negligence.

210 Further applications

(1) This section applies to a receiver appointed under section 196, 198 or 200.

(2) The receiver may apply –

(a) to the High Court if he is appointed under section 196;

(b) to the Crown Court if he is appointed under section 198 or 200,

for an order giving directions as to the exercise of his powers.

(3) The following persons may apply to the High Court if the receiver is appointed under section 196 or to the Crown Court if the receiver is appointed under section 198 or 200 –

(a) any person affected by action taken by the receiver;

(b) any person who may be affected by action the receiver proposes to take.

(4) On an application under this section the court may make such order as it believes is appropriate.

211 Discharge and variation

(1) The following persons may apply to the High Court to vary or discharge an order made under section 196 or 197 or to the Crown Court to vary or discharge an order made under any of sections 198 to 201 –

(a) the receiver;

(b) the person who applied for the order or (if the order was made under section 200 or 201) the Director;

(c) any person affected by the order.

(2) On an application under this section the court –

(a) may discharge the order;

(b) may vary the order.

(3) But in the case of an order under section 196 or 197 –

(a) if the condition in section 189 which was satisfied was that proceedings were started or an application was made, the court must discharge the order on the conclusion of the proceedings or of the application (as the case may be);

(b) if the condition which was satisfied was that an investigation was started or an application was to be made, the court must discharge the order if within a reasonable time proceedings for the offence are not started or the application is not made (as the case may be).

212 Management receivers: discharge

(1) This section applies if —

    (a) a receiver stands appointed under section 196 in respect of realisable property (the management receiver), and

    (b) the court appoints a receiver under section 198 or makes an order for the appointment of a receiver under section 200.

(2) The court must order the management receiver to transfer to the other receiver all property held by the management receiver by virtue of the powers conferred on him by section 197.

(3) But in a case where the court makes an order under section 200 its order under subsection (2) above does not take effect until the order under section 200 takes effect.

(4) Subsection (2) does not apply to property which the management receiver holds by virtue of the exercise by him of his power under section 197(2)(d).

(5) If the management receiver complies with an order under subsection (2) he is discharged —

    (a) from his appointment under section 196;

    (b) from any obligation under this Act arising from his appointment.

(6) If this section applies the court may make such a consequential or incidental order as it believes is appropriate.

213 Appeal to Court of Appeal

(1) If on an application for an order under any of sections 196 to 199 or section 201 the court decides not to make one, the person who applied for the order may appeal to the Court of Appeal against the decision.

(2) If the court makes an order under any of sections 196 to 199 or section 201, the following persons may appeal to the Court of Appeal in respect of the court's decision —

    (a) the person who applied for the order;

    (b) any person affected by the order.

(3) If on an application for an order under section 210 the court decides not to make one, the person who applied for the order may appeal to the Court of Appeal against the decision.

(4) If the court makes an order under section 210, the following persons may appeal to the Court of Appeal in respect of the court's decision —

    (a) the person who applied for the order;

    (b) any person affected by the order;

    (c) the receiver.

(5) The following persons may appeal to the Court of Appeal against a decision of the court on an application under section 211 —

    (a) the person who applied for the order in respect of which the application was made or (if the order was made under section 200 or 201) the Director;

    (b) any person affected by the court's decision;

    (c) the receiver.

(6) On an appeal under this section the Court of Appeal may –
   (a) confirm the decision, or
   (b) make such order as it believes if appropriate.

214 Appeal to House of Lords

(1) An appeal lies to the House of Lords from a decision of the Court of Appeal on an appeal under section 213.

(2) An appeal under this section lies at the instance of any person who was a party to the proceedings before the Court of Appeal.

(3) On an appeal under this section the House of Lords may –
   (a) confirm the decision of the Court of Appeal, or
   (b) make such order as it believes is appropriate.

Seized money

215 Seized money

(1) This section applies to money which –
   (a) is held by a person, and
   (b) is held in an account maintained by him with a bank or a building society.

(2) This section also applies to money which is held by a person and which –
   (a) has been seized by a constable under Article 21 of the Police and Criminal Evidence (Northern Ireland) Order 1989 (S.I. 1989/1341 (N.I. 12)) (general power of seizure etc), and
   (b) is held in an account maintained by a police force with a bank or a building society.

(3) This section also applies to money which is held by a person and which –
   (a) has been seized by a customs officer under Article 21 of the 1989 Order as applied by order made under Article 85(1) of that Order, and
   (b) is held in an account maintained by the Commissioners of Customs and Excise with a bank or a building society.

(4) This section applies if the following conditions are satisfied –
   (a) a restraint order has effect in relation to money to which this section applies;
   (b) a receiver has not been appointed under section 198 in relation to the money;
   (c) a confiscation order is made against the person by whom the money is held;
   (d) the Director has not been appointed as the enforcement authority for the confiscation order;
   (e) any period allowed under section 161 for payment of the amount ordered to be paid under the confiscation order has ended.

(5) In such a case on the application of the prosecutor a magistrates' court may order the bank or building society to pay the money to the appropriate chief clerk on account of the amount payable under the confiscation order.

(6)   If a bank or building society fails to comply with an order under subsection (5) –

       (a)   the magistrates' court may order it to pay an amount not exceeding £5,000, and

       (b)   for the purposes of the Magistrates' Courts (Northern Ireland) Order 1981 (S.I. 1981/1675 (N.I. 26)) the sum is to be treated as adjudged to be paid by a conviction of the magistrates' court.

(7)   In order to take account of changes in the value of money the Secretary of State may by order substitute another sum for the sum for the time being specified in subsection (6)(a).

(8)   For the purposes of this section –

       (a)   a bank is a deposit-taking business within the meaning of the Banking Act 1987 (c. 22);

       (b)   "building society" has the same meaning as in the Building Societies Act 1986 (c. 53);

       (c)   "appropriate chief clerk" has the same meaning as in section 202(7).

Financial investigators

216   Applications and appeals

(1)   This section applies to –

       (a)   an application under section 190, 191, 196, 197 or 211;

       (b)   an appeal under section 192, 193, 213 or 214.

(2)   An accredited financial investigator must not make such an application or bring such an appeal unless he falls within subsection (3).

(3)   An accredited financial investigator falls within this subsection if he is one of the following or is authorised for the purposes of this section by one of the following –

       (a)   a police officer who is not below the rank of superintendent,

       (b)   a customs officer who is not below such grade as is designated by the Commissioners of Customs and Excise as equivalent to that rank,

       (c)   an accredited financial investigator who falls within a description specified in an order made for the purposes of this paragraph by the Secretary of State under section 453.

(4)   If such an application is made or appeal brought by an accredited financial investigator any subsequent step in the application or appeal or any further application or appeal relating to the same matter may be taken, made or brought by a different accredited financial investigator who falls within subsection (3).

(5)   If –

       (a)   an application for a restraint order is made by an accredited financial investigator, and

       (b)   a court is required under section 206(5) to give the applicant for the order an opportunity to be heard,

the court may give the opportunity to a different accredited financial investigator who falls within subsection (3).

Exercise of powers

217 Powers of court and receiver

(1) This section applies to—
    (a) the powers conferred on a court by sections 189 to 208 and sections 210 to 215;
    (b) the powers of a receiver appointed under section 196, 198 or 200.

(2) The powers—
    (a) must be exercised with a view to the value for the time being of realisable property being made available (by the property's realisation) for satisfying any confiscation order that has been or may be made against the defendant;
    (b) must be exercised, in a case where a confiscation order has not been made, with a view to securing that there is no diminution in the value of realisable property;
    (c) must be exercised without taking account of any obligation of the defendant or a recipient of a tainted gift if the obligation conflicts with the object of satisfying any confiscation order that has been or may be made against the defendant;
    (d) may be exercised in respect of a debt owed by the Crown.

(3) Subsection (2) has effect subject to the following rules—
    (a) the powers must be exercised with a view to allowing a person other than the defendant or a recipient of a tainted gift to retain or recover the value of any interest held by him;
    (b) in the case of realisable property held by a recipient of a tainted gift, the powers must be exercised with a view to realising no more than the value for the time being of the gift;
    (c) in a case where a confiscation order has not been made against the defendant, property must not be realised if the court so orders under subsection (4).

(4) If on an application by the defendant, or by the recipient of a tainted gift, the court decides that property cannot be replaced it may order that it must not be sold.

(5) An order under subsection (4) may be revoked or varied.

Committal

218 Committal by magistrates' court

(1) This section applies if—
    (a) a defendant is convicted of an offence by a magistrates' court, and
    (b) the prosecutor asks the court to commit the defendant to the Crown Court with a view to a confiscation order being considered under section 156.

(2) In such a case the magistrates' court—
    (a) must commit the defendant to the Crown Court in respect of the offence, and

    (b)   may commit him to the Crown Court in respect of any other offence falling within subsection (3).

(3)   An offence falls within this subsection if—

    (a)   the defendant has been convicted of it by the magistrates' court or any other court, and

    (b)   the magistrates' court has power to deal with him in respect of it.

(4)   If a committal is made under this section in respect of an offence or offences—

    (a)   section 156 applies accordingly, and

    (b)   the committal operates as a committal of the defendant to be dealt with by the Crown Court in accordance with section 219.

(5)   A committal under this section may be in custody or on bail.

219 Sentencing by Crown Court

(1)   If a defendant is committed to the Crown Court under section 218 in respect of an offence or offences, this section applies (whether or not the court proceeds under section 156).

(2)   The Crown Court—

    (a)   must inquire into the circumstances of the case, and

    (b)   may deal with the defendant in any way in which the magistrates' court could deal with him if it had just convicted him of the offence.

Compensation

220 Serious default

(1)   If the following three conditions are satisfied the Crown Court may order the payment of such compensation as it believes is just.

(2)   The first condition is satisfied if a criminal investigation has been started with regard to an offence and proceedings are not started for the offence.

(3)   The first condition is also satisfied if proceedings for an offence are started against a person and—

    (a)   they do not result in his conviction for the offence, or

    (b)   he is convicted of the offence but the conviction is quashed or he is pardoned in respect of it.

(4)   If subsection (2) applies the second condition is that—

    (a)   in the criminal investigation there has been a serious default by a person mentioned in subsection (9), and

    (b)   the investigation would not have continued if the default had not occurred.

(5)   If subsection (3) applies the second condition is that—

    (a)   in any criminal investigation with regard to the offence or in its prosecution there has been a serious default by a person who is mentioned in subsection (9), and

    (b)   the proceedings would not have been started or continued if the default had not occurred.

(6) The third condition is that an application is made under this section by a person who held realisable property and has suffered loss in consequence of anything done in relation to it by or in pursuance of an order under this Part.

(7) The offence referred to in subsection (2) may be one of a number of offences with regard to which the investigation is started.

(8) The offence referred to in subsection (3) may be one of a number of offences for which the proceedings are started.

(9) Compensation under this section is payable to the applicant and –

    (a) if the person in default was or was acting as a police officer within the meaning of the Police (Northern Ireland) Act 2000 (c. 32), the compensation is payable by the Chief Constable;

    (b) if the person in default was a member of the Director of Public Prosecutions for Northern Ireland or was acting on his behalf, the compensation is payable by the Director of Public Prosecutions for Northern Ireland;

    (c) if the person in default was a member of the Serious Fraud Office, the compensation is payable by the Director of that Office;

    (d) if the person in default was a customs officer, the compensation is payable by the Commissioners of Customs and Excise;

    (e) if the person in default was an officer of the Commissioners of Inland Revenue, the compensation is payable by those Commissioners.

221 Order varied or discharged

(1) This section applies if –

    (a) the court varies a confiscation order under section 179 or discharges one under section 180, and

    (b) an application is made to the Crown Court by a person who held realisable property and has suffered loss as a result of the making of the order.

(2) The court may order the payment of such compensation as it believes is just.

(3) Compensation under this section is payable –

    (a) to the applicant;

    (b) by the Lord Chancellor.

Enforcement abroad

222 Enforcement abroad

(1) This section applies if –

    (a) any of the conditions in section 189 is satisfied,

    (b) the prosecutor or the Director believes that realisable property is situated in a country or territory outside the United Kingdom (the receiving country), and

    (c) the prosecutor or the Director (as the case may be) sends a request for assistance to the Secretary of State with a view to it being forwarded under this section.

(2) In a case where no confiscation order has been made, a request for assistance is a request to the government of the receiving country to secure that any person is prohibited from dealing with realisable property.

(3) In a case where a confiscation order has been made and has not been satisfied, discharged or quashed, a request for assistance is a request to the government of the receiving country to secure that —

    (a) any person is prohibited from dealing with realisable property;

    (b) realisable property is realised and the proceeds are applied in accordance with the law of the receiving country.

(4) No request for assistance may be made for the purposes of this section in a case where a confiscation order has been made and has been satisfied, discharged or quashed.

(5) If the Secretary of State believes it is appropriate to do so he may forward the request for assistance to the government of the receiving country.

(6) If property is realised in pursuance of a request under subsection (3) the amount ordered to be paid under the confiscation order must be taken to be reduced by an amount equal to the proceeds of realisation.

(7) A certificate purporting to be issued by or on behalf of the requested government is admissible as evidence of the facts it states if it states —

    (a) that property has been realised in pursuance of a request under subsection (3),

    (b) the date of realisation, and

    (c) the proceeds of realisation.

(8) If the proceeds of realisation made in pursuance of a request under subsection (3) are expressed in a currency other than sterling, they must be taken to be the sterling equivalent calculated in accordance with the rate of exchange prevailing at the end of the day of realisation.

Interpretation

223   Criminal lifestyle

(1) A defendant has a criminal lifestyle if (and only if) the following condition is satisfied.

(2) The condition is that the offence (or any of the offences) concerned satisfies any of these tests —

    (a) it is specified in Schedule 5;

    (b) it constitutes conduct forming part of a course of criminal activity;

    (c) it is an offence committed over a period of at least six months and the defendant has benefited from the conduct which constitutes the offence.

(3) Conduct forms part of a course of criminal activity if the defendant has benefited from the conduct and —

    (a) in the proceedings in which he was convicted he was convicted of three or more other offences, each of three or more of them constituting conduct from which he has benefited, or

(b) in the period of six years ending with the day when those proceedings were started (or, if there is more than one such day, the earliest day) he was convicted on at least two separate occasions of an offence constituting conduct from which he has benefited.

(4) But an offence does not satisfy the test in subsection (2)(b) or (c) unless the defendant obtains relevant benefit of not less than £5000.

(5) Relevant benefit for the purposes of subsection (2)(b) is—
   (a) benefit from conduct which constitutes the offence;
   (b) benefit from any other conduct which forms part of the course of criminal activity and which constitutes an offence of which the defendant has been convicted;
   (c) benefit from conduct which constitutes an offence which has been or will be taken into consideration by the court in sentencing the defendant for an offence mentioned in paragraph (a) or (b).

(6) Relevant benefit for the purposes of subsection (2)(c) is—
   (a) benefit from conduct which constitutes the offence;
   (b) benefit from conduct which constitutes an offence which has been or will be taken into consideration by the court in sentencing the defendant for the offence mentioned in paragraph (a).

(7) The Secretary of State may by order amend Schedule 5.

(8) The Secretary of State may by order vary the amount for the time being specified in subsection (4).

224 Conduct and benefit

(1) Criminal conduct is conduct which—
   (a) constitutes an offence in Northern Ireland, or
   (b) would constitute such an offence if it occurred in Northern Ireland.

(2) General criminal conduct of the defendant is all his criminal conduct, and it is immaterial—
   (a) whether conduct occurred before or after the passing of this Act;
   (b) whether property constituting a benefit from conduct was obtained before or after the passing of this Act.

(3) Particular criminal conduct of the defendant is all his criminal conduct which falls within the following paragraphs—
   (a) conduct which constitutes the offence or offences concerned;
   (b) conduct which constitutes offences of which he was convicted in the same proceedings as those in which he was convicted of the offence or offences concerned;
   (c) conduct which constitutes offences which the court will be taking into consideration in deciding his sentence for the offence or offences concerned.

(4) A person benefits from conduct if he obtains property as a result of or in connection with the conduct.

(5) If a person obtains a pecuniary advantage as a result of or in connection with conduct, he is to be taken to obtain as a result of or in connection with the conduct a sum of money equal to the value of the pecuniary advantage.

(6)   References to property or a pecuniary advantage obtained in connection with conduct include references to property or a pecuniary advantage obtained both in that connection and some other.

(7)   If a person benefits from conduct his benefit is the value of the property obtained.

225   Tainted gifts

(1)   Subsections (2) and (3) apply if –
    (a)   no court has made a decision as to whether the defendant has a criminal lifestyle, or
    (b)   a court has decided that the defendant has a criminal lifestyle.

(2)   A gift is tainted if it was made by the defendant at any time after the relevant day.

(3)   A gift is also tainted if it was made by the defendant at any time and was of property –
    (a)   which was obtained by the defendant as a result of or in connection with his general criminal conduct, or
    (b)   which (in whole or part and whether directly or indirectly) represented in the defendant's hands property obtained by him as a result of or in connection with his general criminal conduct.

(4)   Subsection (5) applies if a court has decided that the defendant does not have a criminal lifestyle.

(5)   A gift is tainted if it was made by the defendant at any time after –
    (a)   the date on which the offence concerned was committed, or
    (b)   if his particular criminal conduct consists of two or more offences and they were committed on different dates, the date of the earliest.

(6)   For the purposes of subsection (5) an offence which is a continuing offence is committed on the first occasion when it is committed.

(7)   For the purposes of subsection (5) the defendant's particular criminal conduct includes any conduct which constitutes offences which the court has taken into consideration in deciding his sentence for the offence or offences concerned.

(8)   A gift may be a tainted gift whether it was made before or after the passing of this Act.

(9)   The relevant day is the first day of the period of six years ending with –
    (a)   the day when proceedings for the offence concerned were started against the defendant, or
    (b)   if there are two or more offences and proceedings for them were started on different days, the earliest of those days.

226   Gifts and their recipients

(1)   If the defendant transfers property to another person for a consideration whose value is significantly less than the value of the property at the time of the transfer, he is to be treated as making a gift.

(2)   If subsection (1) applies the property given is to be treated as such share in the property transferred as is represented by the fraction –

> (a) whose numerator is the difference between the two values mentioned in subsection (1), and
>
> (b) whose denominator is the value of the property at the time of the transfer.

(3) References to a recipient of a tainted gift are to a person to whom the defendant has made the gift.

227 Value: the basic rule

(1) This section applies for the purpose of deciding the value at any time of property then held by a person.

(2) Its value is the market value of the property at that time.

(3) But if at that time another person holds an interest in the property its value, in relation to the person mentioned in subsection (1), is the market value of his interest at that time, ignoring any charging order under a provision listed in subsection (4).

(4) The provisions are—
   (a) section 9 of the Drug Trafficking Offences Act 1986 (c. 32);
   (b) section 78 of the Criminal Justice Act 1988 (c. 33);
   (c) Article 14 of the Criminal Justice (Confiscation) (Northern Ireland) Order 1990 (S.I. 1990/2588 (N.I. 17));
   (d) section 27 of the Drug Trafficking Act 1994 (c. 37);
   (e) Article 32 of the Proceeds of Crime (Northern Ireland) Order 1996 (S.I. 1996/1299 (N.I. 9)).

(5) This section has effect subject to sections 228 and 229.

228 Value of property obtained from conduct

(1) This section applies for the purpose of deciding the value of property obtained by a person as a result of or in connection with his criminal conduct; and the material time is the time the court makes its decision.

(2) The value of the property at the material time is the greater of the following—
   (a) the value of the property (at the time the person obtained it) adjusted to take account of later changes in the value of money;
   (b) the value (at the material time) of the property found under subsection (3).

(3) The property found under this subsection is as follows—
   (a) if the person holds the property obtained, the property found under this subsection is that property;
   (b) if he holds no part of the property obtained, the property found under this subsection is any property which directly or indirectly represents it in his hands;
   (c) if he holds part of the property obtained, the property found under this subsection is that part and any property which directly or indirectly represents the other part in his hands.

(4) The references in subsection (2)(a) and (b) to the value are to the value found in accordance with section 227.

229   Value of tainted gifts

(1)   The value at any time (the material time) of a tainted gift is the greater of the following —

   (a)   the value (at the time of the gift) of the property given, adjusted to take account of later changes in the value of money;

   (b)   the value (at the material time) of the property found under subsection (2).

(2)   The property found under this subsection is as follows —

   (a)   if the recipient holds the property given, the property found under this subsection is that property;

   (b)   if the recipient holds no part of the property given, the property found under this subsection is any property which directly or indirectly represents it in his hands;

   (c)   if the recipient holds part of the property given, the property found under this subsection is that part and any property which directly or indirectly represents the other part in his hands.

(3)   The references in subsection (1)(a) and (b) to the value are to the value found in accordance with section 227.

230   Free property

Property is free unless an order is in force in respect of it under any of these provisions —

   (a)   section 27 of the Misuse of Drugs Act 1971 (c. 38) (forfeiture orders);

   (b)   Article 11 of the Criminal Justice (Northern Ireland) Order 1994 (S.I. 1994/2795 (N.I. 15)) (deprivation orders);

   (c)   Part 2 of the Proceeds of Crime (Scotland) Act 1995 (c. 43) (forfeiture of property used in crime);

   (d)   section 143 of the Powers of Criminal Courts (Sentencing) Act 2000 (c. 6) (deprivation orders);

   (e)   section 23 or 111 of the Terrorism Act 2000 (c. 11) (forfeiture orders);

   (f)   section 246, 266, 295(2) or 298(2) of this Act.

231   Realisable property

Realisable property is —

   (a)   any free property held by the defendant;

   (b)   any free property held by the recipient of a tainted gift.

232   Property: general provisions

(1)   Property is all property wherever situated and includes —

   (a)   money;

   (b)   all forms of real or personal property;

   (c)   things in action and other intangible or incorporeal property.

(2)   The following rules apply in relation to property —

   (a)   property is held by a person if he holds an interest in it;

   (b)   property is obtained by a person if he obtains an interest in it;

(c) property is transferred by one person to another if the first one transfers or grants an interest in it to the second;

(d) references to property held by a person include references to property vested in his trustee in bankruptcy, permanent or interim trustee (within the meaning of the Bankruptcy (Scotland) Act 1985 (c. 66)) or liquidator;

(e) references to an interest held by a person beneficially in property include references to an interest which would be held by him beneficially if the property were not so vested;

(f) references to an interest, in relation to land in Northern Ireland or England and Wales, are to any legal estate or equitable interest or power;

(g) references to an interest, in relation to land in Scotland, are to any estate, interest, servitude or other heritable right in or over land, including a heritable security;

(h) references to an interest, in relation to property other than land, include references to a right (including a right to possession).

233 Proceedings

(1) Proceedings for an offence are started –

    (a) when a justice of the peace issues a summons or warrant under Article 20 of the Magistrates' Courts (Northern Ireland) Order 1981 (S.I. 1981/1675 (N.I. 26)) in respect of the offence;

    (b) when a person is charged with the offence after being taken into custody without a warrant;

    (c) when an indictment is preferred under section 2(2)(c), (e) or (f) of the Grand Jury (Abolition) Act (Northern Ireland) 1969 (c. 15 (N.I.)).

(2) If more than one time is found under subsection (1) in relation to proceedings they are started at the earliest of them.

(3) If the defendant is acquitted on all counts in proceedings for an offence, the proceedings are concluded when he is acquitted.

(4) If the defendant is convicted in proceedings for an offence and the conviction is quashed or the defendant is pardoned before a confiscation order is made, the proceedings are concluded when the conviction is quashed or the defendant is pardoned.

(5) If a confiscation order is made against the defendant in proceedings for an offence (whether the order is made by the Crown Court or the Court of Appeal) the proceedings are concluded –

    (a) when the order is satisfied or discharged, or

    (b) when the order is quashed and there is no further possibility of an appeal against the decision to quash the order.

(6) If the defendant is convicted in proceedings for an offence but the Crown Court decides not to make a confiscation order against him, the following rules apply –

    (a) if an application for leave to appeal under section 181(2) is refused, the proceedings are concluded when the decision to refuse is made;

    (b) if the time for applying for leave to appeal under section 181(2) expires without an application being made, the proceedings are concluded when the time expires;

(c) if on an appeal under section 181(2) the Court of Appeal confirms the Crown Court's decision and an application for leave to appeal under section 183 is refused, the proceedings are concluded when the decision to refuse is made;

(d) if on appeal under section 181(2) the Court of Appeal confirms the Crown Court's decision, and the time for applying for leave to appeal under section 183 expires without an application being made, the proceedings are concluded when the time expires;

(e) if on appeal under section 181(2) the Court of Appeal confirms the Crown Court's decision, and on appeal under section 183 the House of Lords confirms the Court of Appeal's decision, the proceedings are concluded when the House of Lords confirms the decision;

(f) if on appeal under section 181(2) the Court of Appeal directs the Crown Court to reconsider the case, and on reconsideration the Crown Court decides not to make a confiscation order against the defendant, the proceedings are concluded when the Crown Court makes that decision;

(g) if on appeal under section 183 the House of Lords directs the Crown Court to reconsider the case, and on reconsideration the Crown Court decides not to make a confiscation order against the defendant, the proceedings are concluded when the Crown Court makes that decision.

(7) In applying subsection (6) any power to extend the time for making an application for leave to appeal must be ignored.

(8) In applying subsection (6) the fact that a court may decide on a later occasion to make a confiscation order against the defendant must be ignored.

234   Applications

(1) An application under section 169, 170, 177 or 178 is concluded —

(a) in a case where the court decides not to make a confiscation order against the defendant, when it makes the decision;

(b) in a case where a confiscation order is made against him as a result of the application, when the order is satisfied or discharged, or when the order is quashed and there is no further possibility of an appeal against the decision to quash the order;

(c) in a case where the application is withdrawn, when the person who made the application notifies the withdrawal to the court to which the application was made.

(2) An application under section 171 or 172 is concluded —

(a) in a case where the court decides not to vary the confiscation order concerned, when it makes the decision;

(b) in a case where the court varies the confiscation order as a result of the application, when the order is satisfied or discharged, or when the order is quashed and there is no further possibility of an appeal against the decision to quash the order;

(c) in a case where the application is withdrawn, when the person who made the application notifies the withdrawal to the court to which the application was made.

235   Confiscation orders

(1) A confiscation order is satisfied when no amount is due under it.

(2) A confiscation order is subject to appeal until there is no further possibility of an appeal on which the order could be varied or quashed; and for this purpose any power to grant leave to appeal out of time must be ignored.

236 Other interpretative provisions

(1) A reference to the offence (or offences) concerned must be construed in accordance with section 156(9).

(2) A criminal investigation is an investigation which police officers or other persons have a duty to conduct with a view to it being ascertained whether a person should be charged with an offence.

(3) A defendant is a person against whom proceedings for an offence have been started (whether or not he has been convicted).

(4) A reference to sentencing the defendant for an offence includes a reference to dealing with him otherwise in respect of the offence.

(5) The following paragraphs apply to references to orders —
    (a) a confiscation order is an order under section 156;
    (b) a restraint order is an order under section 190.

(6) Sections 223 to 235 and this section apply for the purposes of this Part.

General

237 Procedure on appeal to the Court of Appeal

(1) An appeal to the Court of Appeal under this Part lies only with the leave of that Court.

(2) In relation to appeals to the Court of Appeal under this Part, the Secretary of State may make an order containing provision corresponding to any provision in the Criminal Appeal (Northern Ireland) Act 1980 (c. 47) (subject to any specified modifications).

238 Procedure on appeal to the House of Lords

In relation to appeals to the House of Lords under this Part, the Secretary of State may make an order containing provision corresponding to any provision in the Criminal Appeal (Northern Ireland) Act 1980 (subject to any specified modifications).

239 Crown Court Rules

In relation to —
    (a) proceedings under this Part, or
    (b) receivers appointed under this Part,
Crown Court Rules may make provision corresponding to provision in rules of court (within the meaning of section 120(1) of the Judicature (Northern Ireland) Act 1978 (c. 23)).

150

Proceeds of Crime Act 2002 (c. 29)
Part 5 – Civil recovery of the proceeds etc. of unlawful conduct
Chapter 1 – Introductory

PART 5

CIVIL RECOVERY OF THE PROCEEDS ETC. OF UNLAWFUL CONDUCT

CHAPTER 1

INTRODUCTORY

240   General purpose of this Part

(1)   This Part has effect for the purposes of –

(a)   enabling the enforcement authority to recover, in civil proceedings before the High Court or Court of Session, property which is, or represents, property obtained through unlawful conduct,

(b)   enabling cash which is, or represents, property obtained through unlawful conduct, or which is intended to be used in unlawful conduct, to be forfeited in civil proceedings before a magistrates' court or (in Scotland) the sheriff.

(2)   The powers conferred by this Part are exercisable in relation to any property (including cash) whether or not any proceedings have been brought for an offence in connection with the property.

241   "Unlawful conduct"

(1)   Conduct occurring in any part of the United Kingdom is unlawful conduct if it is unlawful under the criminal law of that part.

(2)   Conduct which –

(a)   occurs in a country outside the United Kingdom and is unlawful under the criminal law of that country, and

(b)   if it occurred in a part of the United Kingdom, would be unlawful under the criminal law of that part,

is also unlawful conduct.

(3)   The court or sheriff must decide on a balance of probabilities whether it is proved –

(a)   that any matters alleged to constitute unlawful conduct have occurred, or

(b)   that any person intended to use any cash in unlawful conduct.

242   "Property obtained through unlawful conduct"

(1)   A person obtains property through unlawful conduct (whether his own conduct or another's) if he obtains property by or in return for the conduct.

(2)   In deciding whether any property was obtained through unlawful conduct –

(a)   it is immaterial whether or not any money, goods or services were provided in order to put the person in question in a position to carry out the conduct,

(b)   it is not necessary to show that the conduct was of a particular kind if it is shown that the property was obtained through conduct of one of a number of kinds, each of which would have been unlawful conduct.

Proceeds of Crime Act 2002 (c. 29)
Part 5 — Civil recovery of the proceeds etc. of unlawful conduct
Chapter 2 — Civil recovery in the High Court or Court of Session

151

CHAPTER 2

CIVIL RECOVERY IN THE HIGH COURT OR COURT OF SESSION

Proceedings for recovery orders

243   Proceedings for recovery orders in England and Wales or Northern Ireland

(1)   Proceedings for a recovery order may be taken by the enforcement authority in the High Court against any person who the authority thinks holds recoverable property.

(2)   The enforcement authority must serve the claim form —
    (a)   on the respondent, and
    (b)   unless the court dispenses with service, on any other person who the authority thinks holds any associated property which the authority wishes to be subject to a recovery order,
    wherever domiciled, resident or present.

(3)   If any property which the enforcement authority wishes to be subject to a recovery order is not specified in the claim form it must be described in the form in general terms; and the form must state whether it is alleged to be recoverable property or associated property.

(4)   The references above to the claim form include the particulars of claim, where they are served subsequently.

244   Proceedings for recovery orders in Scotland

(1)   Proceedings for a recovery order may be taken by the enforcement authority in the Court of Session against any person who the authority thinks holds recoverable property.

(2)   The enforcement authority must serve the application —
    (a)   on the respondent, and
    (b)   unless the court dispenses with service, on any other person who the authority thinks holds any associated property which the authority wishes to be subject to a recovery order,
    wherever domiciled, resident or present.

(3)   If any property which the enforcement authority wishes to be subject to a recovery order is not specified in the application it must be described in the application in general terms; and the application must state whether it is alleged to be recoverable property or associated property.

245   "Associated property"

(1)   "Associated property" means property of any of the following descriptions (including property held by the respondent) which is not itself the recoverable property —
    (a)   any interest in the recoverable property,
    (b)   any other interest in the property in which the recoverable property subsists,

152   *Proceeds of Crime Act 2002 (c. 29)*
                          Part 5 – Civil recovery of the proceeds etc. of unlawful conduct
                          Chapter 2 – Civil recovery in the High Court or Court of Session

    (c)   if the recoverable property is a tenancy in common, the tenancy of the other tenant,

    (d)   if (in Scotland) the recoverable property is owned in common, the interest of the other owner,

    (e)   if the recoverable property is part of a larger property, but not a separate part, the remainder of that property.

(2)   References to property being associated with recoverable property are to be read accordingly.

(3)   No property is to be treated as associated with recoverable property consisting of rights under a pension scheme (within the meaning of sections 273 to 275).

Interim receiving orders (England and Wales and Northern Ireland)

246   Application for interim receiving order

(1)   Where the enforcement authority may take proceedings for a recovery order in the High Court, the authority may apply to the court for an interim receiving order (whether before or after starting the proceedings).

(2)   An interim receiving order is an order for –

    (a)   the detention, custody or preservation of property, and

    (b)   the appointment of an interim receiver.

(3)   An application for an interim receiving order may be made without notice if the circumstances are such that notice of the application would prejudice any right of the enforcement authority to obtain a recovery order in respect of any property.

(4)   The court may make an interim receiving order on the application if it is satisfied that the conditions in subsections (5) and, where applicable, (6) are met.

(5)   The first condition is that there is a good arguable case –

    (a)   that the property to which the application for the order relates is or includes recoverable property, and

    (b)   that, if any of it is not recoverable property, it is associated property.

(6)   The second condition is that, if –

    (a)   the property to which the application for the order relates includes property alleged to be associated property, and

    (b)   the enforcement authority has not established the identity of the person who holds it,

the authority has taken all reasonable steps to do so.

(7)   In its application for an interim receiving order, the enforcement authority must nominate a suitably qualified person for appointment as interim receiver, but the nominee may not be a member of the staff of the Agency.

(8)   The extent of the power to make an interim receiving order is not limited by sections 247 to 255.

247   Functions of interim receiver

(1)   An interim receiving order may authorise or require the interim receiver –

Proceeds of Crime Act 2002 (c. 29) 153
Part 5 – Civil recovery of the proceeds etc. of unlawful conduct
Chapter 2 – Civil recovery in the High Court or Court of Session

    (a)   to exercise any of the powers mentioned in Schedule 6,

    (b)   to take any other steps the court thinks appropriate,

for the purpose of securing the detention, custody or preservation of the property to which the order applies or of taking any steps under subsection (2).

(2)   An interim receiving order must require the interim receiver to take any steps which the court thinks necessary to establish—

    (a)   whether or not the property to which the order applies is recoverable property or associated property,

    (b)   whether or not any other property is recoverable property (in relation to the same unlawful conduct) and, if it is, who holds it.

(3)   If—

    (a)   the interim receiver deals with any property which is not property to which the order applies, and

    (b)   at the time he deals with the property he believes on reasonable grounds that he is entitled to do so in pursuance of the order,

the interim receiver is not liable to any person in respect of any loss or damage resulting from his dealing with the property except so far as the loss or damage is caused by his negligence.

248   Registration

(1)   The registration Acts—

    (a)   apply in relation to interim receiving orders as they apply in relation to orders which affect land and are made by the court for the purpose of enforcing judgements or recognisances,

    (b)   apply in relation to applications for interim receiving orders as they apply in relation to other pending land actions.

(2)   The registration Acts are—

    (a)   the Land Registration Act 1925 (c. 21),

    (b)   the Land Charges Act 1972 (c. 61), and

    (c)   the Land Registration Act 2002 (c. 9).

(3)   But no notice may be entered in the register of title under the Land Registration Act 2002 in respect of an interim receiving order.

(4)   A person applying for an interim receiving order must be treated for the purposes of section 57 of the Land Registration Act 1925 (inhibitions) as a person interested in relation to any registered land to which—

    (a)   the application relates, or

    (b)   an interim receiving order made in pursuance of the application relates.

249   Registration (Northern Ireland)

(1)   A person applying for an interim receiving order must be treated for the purposes of section 66 of the Land Registration Act (Northern Ireland) 1970 (c. 18 (N.I.)) (cautions) as a person interested in relation to any registered land to which—

    (a)   the application relates, or

    (b)   an interim receiving order made in pursuance of the application relates.

154

Proceeds of Crime Act 2002 (c. 29)
Part 5 — Civil recovery of the proceeds etc. of unlawful conduct
Chapter 2 — Civil recovery in the High Court or Court of Session

(2)   Upon being served with a copy of an interim receiving order, the Registrar must, in respect of any registered land to which an interim receiving order or an application for an interim receiving order relates, make an entry inhibiting any dealing with the land without the consent of the High Court.

(3)   Subsections (2) and (4) of section 67 of the Land Registration Act (Northern Ireland) 1970 (inhibitions) apply to an entry made under subsection (2) as they apply to an entry made on the application of any person interested in the registered land under subsection (1) of that section.

(4)   Where an interim receiving order has been protected by an entry registered under the Land Registration Act (Northern Ireland) 1970 or the Registration of Deeds Acts, an order setting aside the interim receiving order may require that entry to be vacated.

(5)   In this section —

"Registrar" and "entry" have the same meanings as in the Land Registration Act (Northern Ireland) 1970, and

"Registration of Deeds Acts" has the meaning given by section 46(2) of the Interpretation Act (Northern Ireland) 1954 (c. 33 (N.I.)).

250   Duties of respondent etc.

(1)   An interim receiving order may require any person to whose property the order applies —

(a)   to bring the property to a place (in England and Wales or, as the case may be, Northern Ireland) specified by the interim receiver or place it in the custody of the interim receiver (if, in either case, he is able to do so),

(b)   to do anything he is reasonably required to do by the interim receiver for the preservation of the property.

(2)   An interim receiving order may require any person to whose property the order applies to bring any documents relating to the property which are in his possession or control to a place (in England and Wales or, as the case may be, Northern Ireland) specified by the interim receiver or to place them in the custody of the interim receiver.

"Document" means anything in which information of any description is recorded.

251   Supervision of interim receiver and variation of order

(1)   The interim receiver, any party to the proceedings and any person affected by any action taken by the interim receiver, or who may be affected by any action proposed to be taken by him, may at any time apply to the court for directions as to the exercise of the interim receiver's functions.

(2)   Before giving any directions under subsection (1), the court must (as well as giving the parties to the proceedings an opportunity to be heard) give such an opportunity to the interim receiver and to any person who may be interested in the application.

(3)   The court may at any time vary or set aside an interim receiving order.

(4)   Before exercising any power under this Chapter to vary or set aside an interim receiving order, the court must (as well as giving the parties to the proceedings

Proceeds of Crime Act 2002 (c. 29)
Part 5 — Civil recovery of the proceeds etc. of unlawful conduct
Chapter 2 — Civil recovery in the High Court or Court of Session

155

an opportunity to be heard) give such an opportunity to the interim receiver and to any person who may be affected by the court's decision.

252 Restrictions on dealing etc. with property

(1) An interim receiving order must, subject to any exclusions made in accordance with this section, prohibit any person to whose property the order applies from dealing with the property.

(2) Exclusions may be made when the interim receiving order is made or on an application to vary the order.

(3) An exclusion may, in particular, make provision for the purpose of enabling any person —
    (a)   to meet his reasonable living expenses, or
    (b)   to carry on any trade, business, profession or occupation,
and may be made subject to conditions.

(4) But an exclusion may not be made for the purpose of enabling any person to meet any legal expenses in respect of proceedings under this Part.

(5) If the excluded property is not specified in the order it must be described in the order in general terms.

(6) The power to make exclusions must be exercised with a view to ensuring, so far as practicable, that the satisfaction of any right of the enforcement authority to recover the property obtained through unlawful conduct is not unduly prejudiced.

253 Restriction on proceedings and remedies

(1) While an interim receiving order has effect —
    (a)   the court may stay any action, execution or other legal process in respect of the property to which the order applies,
    (b)   no distress may be levied against the property to which the order applies except with the leave of the court and subject to any terms the court may impose.

(2) If a court (whether the High Court or any other court) in which proceedings are pending in respect of any property is satisfied that an interim receiving order has been applied for or made in respect of the property, the court may either stay the proceedings or allow them to continue on any terms it thinks fit.

(3) If the interim receiving order applies to a tenancy of any premises, no landlord or other person to whom rent is payable may exercise any right of forfeiture by peaceable re-entry in relation to the premises in respect of any failure by the tenant to comply with any term or condition of the tenancy, except with the leave of the court and subject to any terms the court may impose.

(4) Before exercising any power conferred by this section, the court must (as well as giving the parties to any of the proceedings in question an opportunity to be heard) give such an opportunity to the interim receiver (if appointed) and any person who may be affected by the court's decision.

156

Proceeds of Crime Act 2002 (c. 29)
Part 5 — Civil recovery of the proceeds etc. of unlawful conduct
Chapter 2 — Civil recovery in the High Court or Court of Session

254   Exclusion of property which is not recoverable etc.

(1)   If the court decides that any property to which an interim receiving order applies is neither recoverable property nor associated property, it must vary the order so as to exclude it.

(2)   The court may vary an interim receiving order so as to exclude from the property to which the order applies any property which is alleged to be associated property if the court thinks that the satisfaction of any right of the enforcement authority to recover the property obtained through unlawful conduct will not be prejudiced.

(3)   The court may exclude any property within subsection (2) on any terms or conditions, applying while the interim receiving order has effect, which the court thinks necessary or expedient.

255   Reporting

(1)   An interim receiving order must require the interim receiver to inform the enforcement authority and the court as soon as reasonably practicable if he thinks that—

    (a)   any property to which the order applies by virtue of a claim that it is recoverable property is not recoverable property,

    (b)   any property to which the order applies by virtue of a claim that it is associated property is not associated property,

    (c)   any property to which the order does not apply is recoverable property (in relation to the same unlawful conduct) or associated property, or

    (d)   any property to which the order applies is held by a person who is different from the person it is claimed holds it,

or if he thinks that there has been any other material change of circumstances.

(2)   An interim receiving order must require the interim receiver—

    (a)   to report his findings to the court,

    (b)   to serve copies of his report on the enforcement authority and on any person who holds any property to which the order applies or who may otherwise be affected by the report.

Interim administration orders (Scotland)

256   Application for interim administration order

(1)   Where the enforcement authority may take proceedings for a recovery order in the Court of Session, the authority may apply to the court for an interim administration order (whether before or after starting the proceedings).

(2)   An interim administration order is an order for—

    (a)   the detention, custody or preservation of property, and

    (b)   the appointment of an interim administrator.

(3)   An application for an interim administration order may be made without notice if the circumstances are such that notice of the application would prejudice any right of the enforcement authority to obtain a recovery order in respect of any property.

Proceeds of Crime Act 2002 (c. 29) 157
Part 5 – Civil recovery of the proceeds etc. of unlawful conduct
Chapter 2 – Civil recovery in the High Court or Court of Session

(4) The court may make an interim administration order on the application if it is satisfied that the conditions in subsections (5) and, where applicable, (6) are met.

(5) The first condition is that there is a probabilis causa litigandi—
    (a) that the property to which the application for the order relates is or includes recoverable property, and
    (b) that, if any of it is not recoverable property, it is associated property.

(6) The second condition is that, if—
    (a) the property to which the application for the order relates includes property alleged to be associated property, and
    (b) the enforcement authority has not established the identity of the person who holds it,
the authority has taken all reasonable steps to do so.

(7) In its application for an interim administration order, the enforcement authority must nominate a suitably qualified person for appointment as interim administrator, but the nominee may not be a member of the staff of the Scottish Administration.

(8) The extent of the power to make an interim administration order is not limited by sections 257 to 264.

257 Functions of interim administrator

(1) An interim administration order may authorise or require the interim administrator—
    (a) to exercise any of the powers mentioned in Schedule 6,
    (b) to take any other steps the court thinks appropriate,
for the purpose of securing the detention, custody or preservation of the property to which the order applies or of taking any steps under subsection (2).

(2) An interim administration order must require the interim administrator to take any steps which the court thinks necessary to establish—
    (a) whether or not the property to which the order applies is recoverable property or associated property,
    (b) whether or not any other property is recoverable property (in relation to the same unlawful conduct) and, if it is, who holds it.

(3) If—
    (a) the interim administrator deals with any property which is not property to which the order applies, and
    (b) at the time he deals with the property he believes on reasonable grounds that he is entitled to do so in pursuance of the order,
the interim administrator is not liable to any person in respect of any loss or damage resulting from his dealing with the property except so far as the loss or damage is caused by his negligence.

258 Inhibition of property affected by order

(1) On the application of the enforcement authority, the Court of Session may, in relation to the property mentioned in subsection (2), grant warrant for inhibition against any person specified in an interim administration order.

158

Proceeds of Crime Act 2002 (c. 29)
Part 5 — Civil recovery of the proceeds etc. of unlawful conduct
Chapter 2 — Civil recovery in the High Court or Court of Session

(2)   That property is heritable property situated in Scotland to which the interim administration order applies (whether generally or such of it as is specified in the application).

(3)   The warrant for inhibition—
  (a)   has effect as if granted on the dependence of an action for debt by the enforcement authority against the person and may be executed, recalled, loosed or restricted accordingly, and
  (b)   has the effect of letters of inhibition and must forthwith be registered by the enforcement authority in the register of inhibitions and adjudications.

(4)   Section 155 of the Titles to Land Consolidation (Scotland) Act 1868 (c. 101) (effective date of inhibition) applies in relation to an inhibition for which warrant is granted under subsection (1) as it applies to an inhibition by separate letters or contained in a summons.

(5)   The execution of an inhibition under this section in respect of property does not prejudice the exercise of an interim administrator's powers under or for the purposes of this Part in respect of that property.

(6)   An inhibition executed under this section ceases to have effect when, or in so far as, the interim administration order ceases to apply in respect of the property in relation to which the warrant for inhibition was granted.

(7)   If an inhibition ceases to have effect to any extent by virtue of subsection (6) the enforcement authority must—
  (a)   apply for the recall or, as the case may be, the restriction of the inhibition, and
  (b)   ensure that the recall or restriction is reflected in the register of inhibitions and adjudications.

259   Duties of respondent etc.

(1)   An interim administration order may require any person to whose property the order applies—
  (a)   to bring the property to a place (in Scotland) specified by the interim administrator or place it in the custody of the interim administrator (if, in either case, he is able to do so),
  (b)   to do anything he is reasonably required to do by the interim administrator for the preservation of the property.

(2)   An interim administration order may require any person to whose property the order applies to bring any documents relating to the property which are in his possession or control to a place (in Scotland) specified by the interim administrator or to place them in the custody of the interim administrator.

  "Document" means anything in which information of any description is recorded.

260   Supervision of interim administrator and variation of order

(1)   The interim administrator, any party to the proceedings and any person affected by any action taken by the interim administrator, or who may be affected by any action proposed to be taken by him, may at any time apply to the court for directions as to the exercise of the interim administrator's functions.

Proceeds of Crime Act 2002 (c. 29)
Part 5 — Civil recovery of the proceeds etc. of unlawful conduct
Chapter 2 — Civil recovery in the High Court or Court of Session

159

(2) Before giving any directions under subsection (1), the court must (as well as giving the parties to the proceedings an opportunity to be heard) give such an opportunity to the interim administrator and to any person who may be interested in the application.

(3) The court may at any time vary or recall an interim administration order.

(4) Before exercising any power under this Chapter to vary or set aside an interim administration order, the court must (as well as giving the parties to the proceedings an opportunity to be heard) give such an opportunity to the interim administrator and to any person who may be affected by the court's decision.

261 Restrictions on dealing etc. with property

(1) An interim administration order must, subject to any exclusions made in accordance with this section, prohibit any person to whose property the order applies from dealing with the property.

(2) Exclusions may be made when the interim administration order is made or on an application to vary the order.

(3) An exclusion may, in particular, make provision for the purpose of enabling any person —
    (a)   to meet his reasonable living expenses, or
    (b)   to carry on any trade, business, profession or occupation,
and may be made subject to conditions.

(4) But an exclusion may not be made for the purpose of enabling any person to meet any legal expenses in respect of proceedings under this Part.

(5) If the excluded property is not specified in the order it must be described in the order in general terms.

(6) The power to make exclusions must be exercised with a view to ensuring, so far as practicable, that the satisfaction of any right of the enforcement authority to recover the property obtained through unlawful conduct is not unduly prejudiced.

262 Restriction on proceedings and remedies

(1) While an interim administration order has effect, the court may sist any action, execution or other legal process in respect of the property to which the order applies.

(2) If a court (whether the Court of Session or any other court) in which proceedings are pending in respect of any property is satisfied that an interim administration order has been applied for or made in respect of the property, the court may either sist the proceedings or allow them to continue on any terms it thinks fit.

(3) Before exercising any power conferred by this section, the court must (as well as giving the parties to any of the proceedings in question an opportunity to be heard) give such an opportunity to the interim administrator (if appointed) and any person who may be affected by the court's decision.

160

Proceeds of Crime Act 2002 (c. 29)
Part 5 — Civil recovery of the proceeds etc. of unlawful conduct
Chapter 2 — Civil recovery in the High Court or Court of Session

263   Exclusion of property which is not recoverable etc.

(1)   If the court decides that any property to which an interim administration order applies is neither recoverable property nor associated property, it must vary the order so as to exclude it.

(2)   The court may vary an interim administration order so as to exclude from the property to which the order applies any property which is alleged to be associated property if the court thinks that the satisfaction of any right of the enforcement authority to recover the property obtained through unlawful conduct will not be prejudiced.

(3)   The court may exclude any property within subsection (2) on any terms or conditions, applying while the interim administration order has effect, which the court thinks necessary or expedient.

264   Reporting

(1)   An interim administration order must require the interim administrator to inform the enforcement authority and the court as soon as reasonably practicable if he thinks that—

(a)   any property to which the order applies by virtue of a claim that it is recoverable property is not recoverable property,

(b)   any property to which the order applies by virtue of a claim that it is associated property is not associated property,

(c)   any property to which the order does not apply is recoverable property (in relation to the same unlawful conduct) or associated property, or

(d)   any property to which the order applies is held by a person who is different from the person it is claimed holds it,

or if he thinks that there has been any other material change of circumstances.

(2)   An interim administration order must require the interim administrator—

(a)   to report his findings to the court,

(b)   to serve copies of his report on the enforcement authority and on any person who holds any property to which the order applies or who may otherwise be affected by the report.

265   Arrestment of property affected by interim administration order

(1)   On the application of the enforcement authority or the interim administrator the Court of Session may, in relation to moveable recoverable property to which an interim administration order applies (whether generally or such of it as is specified in the application), grant warrant for arrestment.

(2)   An application by the enforcement authority under subsection (1) may be made at the same time as the application for the interim administration order or at any time thereafter.

(3)   Such a warrant for arrestment may be granted only if the property would be arrestable if the person entitled to it were a debtor.

(4)   A warrant under subsection (1) has effect as if granted on the dependence of an action for debt at the instance of the enforcement authority or, as the case may be, the interim administrator against the person and may be executed, recalled, loosed or restricted accordingly.

Proceeds of Crime Act 2002 (c. 29)
Part 5 – Civil recovery of the proceeds etc. of unlawful conduct
Chapter 2 – Civil recovery in the High Court or Court of Session

161

(5) The execution of an arrestment under this section in respect of property does not prejudice the exercise of an interim administrator's powers under or for the purposes of this Part in respect of that property.

(6) An arrestment executed under this section ceases to have effect when, or in so far as, the interim administration order ceases to apply in respect of the property in relation to which the warrant for arrestment was granted.

(7) If an arrestment ceases to have effect to any extent by virtue of subsection (6) the enforcement authority or, as the case may be, the interim administrator must apply to the Court of Session for an order recalling or, as the case may be, restricting the arrestment.

Vesting and realisation of recoverable property

266 Recovery orders

(1) If in proceedings under this Chapter the court is satisfied that any property is recoverable, the court must make a recovery order.

(2) The recovery order must vest the recoverable property in the trustee for civil recovery.

(3) But the court may not make in a recovery order –
   (a) any provision in respect of any recoverable property if each of the conditions in subsection (4) or (as the case may be) (5) is met and it would not be just and equitable to do so, or
   (b) any provision which is incompatible with any of the Convention rights (within the meaning of the Human Rights Act 1998 (c. 42)).

(4) In relation to a court in England and Wales or Northern Ireland, the conditions referred to in subsection (3)(a) are that –
   (a) the respondent obtained the recoverable property in good faith,
   (b) he took steps after obtaining the property which he would not have taken if he had not obtained it or he took steps before obtaining the property which he would not have taken if he had not believed he was going to obtain it,
   (c) when he took the steps, he had no notice that the property was recoverable,
   (d) if a recovery order were made in respect of the property, it would, by reason of the steps, be detrimental to him.

(5) In relation to a court in Scotland, the conditions referred to in subsection (3)(a) are that –
   (a) the respondent obtained the recoverable property in good faith,
   (b) he took steps after obtaining the property which he would not have taken if he had not obtained it or he took steps before obtaining the property which he would not have taken if he had not believed he was going to obtain it,
   (c) when he took the steps, he had no reasonable grounds for believing that the property was recoverable,
   (d) if a recovery order were made in respect of the property, it would, by reason of the steps, be detrimental to him.

162   *Proceeds of Crime Act 2002 (c. 29)*
Part 5 – Civil recovery of the proceeds etc. of unlawful conduct
Chapter 2 – Civil recovery in the High Court or Court of Session

(6)   In deciding whether it would be just and equitable to make the provision in the recovery order where the conditions in subsection (4) or (as the case may be) (5) are met, the court must have regard to—

    (a)   the degree of detriment that would be suffered by the respondent if the provision were made,

    (b)   the enforcement authority's interest in receiving the realised proceeds of the recoverable property.

(7)   A recovery order may sever any property.

(8)   A recovery order may impose conditions as to the manner in which the trustee for civil recovery may deal with any property vested by the order for the purpose of realising it.

(9)   This section is subject to sections 270 to 278.

267   Functions of the trustee for civil recovery

(1)   The trustee for civil recovery is a person appointed by the court to give effect to a recovery order.

(2)   The enforcement authority must nominate a suitably qualified person for appointment as the trustee.

(3)   The functions of the trustee are—

    (a)   to secure the detention, custody or preservation of any property vested in him by the recovery order,

    (b)   in the case of property other than money, to realise the value of the property for the benefit of the enforcement authority, and

    (c)   to perform any other functions conferred on him by virtue of this Chapter.

(4)   In performing his functions, the trustee acts on behalf of the enforcement authority and must comply with any directions given by the authority.

(5)   The trustee is to realise the value of property vested in him by the recovery order, so far as practicable, in the manner best calculated to maximise the amount payable to the enforcement authority.

(6)   The trustee has the powers mentioned in Schedule 7.

(7)   References in this section to a recovery order include an order under section 276 and references to property vested in the trustee by a recovery order include property vested in him in pursuance of an order under section 276.

268   Recording of recovery order (Scotland)

(1)   The clerk of the court must immediately after the making of a recovery order which relates to heritable property situated in Scotland send a certified copy of it to the keeper of the register of inhibitions and adjudications for recording in that register.

(2)   Recording under subsection (1) is to have the effect, as from the date of the recovery order, of an inhibition at the instance of the trustee for civil recovery against the person in whom the heritable property was vest prior to that date.

269   Rights of pre-emption, etc.

(1)   A recovery order is to have effect in relation to any property despite any provision (of whatever nature) which would otherwise prevent, penalise or restrict the vesting of the property.

(2)   A right of pre-emption, right of irritancy, right of return or other similar right does not operate or become exercisable as a result of the vesting of any property under a recovery order.

A right of return means any right under a provision for the return or reversion of property in specified circumstances.

(3)   Where property is vested under a recovery order, any such right is to have effect as if the person in whom the property is vested were the same person in law as the person who held the property and as if no transfer of the property had taken place.

(4)   References to rights in subsections (2) and (3) do not include any rights in respect of which the recovery order was made.

(5)   This section applies in relation to the creation of interests, or the doing of anything else, by a recovery order as it applies in relation to the vesting of property.

270   Associated and joint property

(1)   Sections 271 and 272 apply if the court makes a recovery order in respect of any recoverable property in a case within subsection (2) or (3).

(2)   A case is within this subsection if —

(a)   the property to which the proceedings relate includes property which is associated with the recoverable property and is specified or described in the claim form or (in Scotland) application, and

(b)   if the associated property is not the respondent's property, the claim form or application has been served on the person whose property it is or the court has dispensed with service.

(3)   A case is within this subsection if —

(a)   the recoverable property belongs to joint tenants, and

(b)   one of the tenants is an excepted joint owner.

(4)   An excepted joint owner is a person who obtained the property in circumstances in which it would not be recoverable as against him; and references to the excepted joint owner's share of the recoverable property are to so much of the recoverable property as would have been his if the joint tenancy had been severed.

(5)   Subsections (3) and (4) do not extend to Scotland.

271   Agreements about associated and joint property

(1)   Where —

(a)   this section applies, and

(b)   the enforcement authority (on the one hand) and the person who holds the associated property or who is the excepted joint owner (on the other) agree,

164

Proceeds of Crime Act 2002 (c. 29)
Part 5 – Civil recovery of the proceeds etc. of unlawful conduct
Chapter 2 – Civil recovery in the High Court or Court of Session

the recovery order may, instead of vesting the recoverable property in the trustee for civil recovery, require the person who holds the associated property or who is the excepted joint owner to make a payment to the trustee.

(2) A recovery order which makes any requirement under subsection (1) may, so far as required for giving effect to the agreement, include provision for vesting, creating or extinguishing any interest in property.

(3) The amount of the payment is to be the amount which the enforcement authority and that person agree represents—

    (a) in a case within section 270(2), the value of the recoverable property,

    (b) in a case within section 270(3), the value of the recoverable property less the value of the excepted joint owner's share.

(4) But if—

    (a) an interim receiving order or interim administration order applied at any time to the associated property or joint tenancy, and

    (b) the enforcement authority agrees that the person has suffered loss as a result of the interim receiving order or interim administration order,

the amount of the payment may be reduced by any amount the enforcement authority and that person agree is reasonable, having regard to that loss and to any other relevant circumstances.

(5) If there is more than one such item of associated property or excepted joint owner, the total amount to be paid to the trustee, and the part of that amount which is to be provided by each person who holds any such associated property or who is an excepted joint owner, is to be agreed between both (or all) of them and the enforcement authority.

(6) A recovery order which makes any requirement under subsection (1) must make provision for any recoverable property to cease to be recoverable.

272 Associated and joint property: default of agreement

(1) Where this section applies, the court may make the following provision if—

    (a) there is no agreement under section 271, and

    (b) the court thinks it just and equitable to do so.

(2) The recovery order may provide—

    (a) for the associated property to vest in the trustee for civil recovery or (as the case may be) for the excepted joint owner's interest to be extinguished, or

    (b) in the case of an excepted joint owner, for the severance of his interest.

(3) A recovery order making any provision by virtue of subsection (2)(a) may provide—

    (a) for the trustee to pay an amount to the person who holds the associated property or who is an excepted joint owner, or

    (b) for the creation of interests in favour of that person, or the imposition of liabilities or conditions, in relation to the property vested in the trustee,

or for both.

(4) In making any provision in a recovery order by virtue of subsection (2) or (3), the court must have regard to—

Proceeds of Crime Act 2002 (c. 29)
Part 5 — Civil recovery of the proceeds etc. of unlawful conduct
Chapter 2 — Civil recovery in the High Court or Court of Session

165

(a) the rights of any person who holds the associated property or who is an excepted joint owner and the value to him of that property or, as the case may be, of his share (including any value which cannot be assessed in terms of money),

(b) the enforcement authority's interest in receiving the realised proceeds of the recoverable property.

(5) If—

(a) an interim receiving order or interim administration order applied at any time to the associated property or joint tenancy, and

(b) the court is satisfied that the person who holds the associated property or who is an excepted joint owner has suffered loss as a result of the interim receiving order or interim administration order,

a recovery order making any provision by virtue of subsection (2) or (3) may require the enforcement authority to pay compensation to that person.

(6) The amount of compensation to be paid under subsection (5) is the amount the court thinks reasonable, having regard to the person's loss and to any other relevant circumstances.

273 Payments in respect of rights under pension schemes

(1) This section applies to recoverable property consisting of rights under a pension scheme.

(2) A recovery order in respect of the property must, instead of vesting the property in the trustee for civil recovery, require the trustees or managers of the pension scheme—

(a) to pay to the trustee for civil recovery within a prescribed period the amount determined by the trustees or managers to be equal to the value of the rights, and

(b) to give effect to any other provision made by virtue of this section and the two following sections in respect of the scheme.

This subsection is subject to sections 276 to 278.

(3) A recovery order made by virtue of subsection (2) overrides the provisions of the pension scheme to the extent that they conflict with the provisions of the order.

(4) A recovery order made by virtue of subsection (2) may provide for the recovery by the trustees or managers of the scheme (whether by deduction from any amount which they are required to pay to the trustee for civil recovery or otherwise) of costs incurred by them in—

(a) complying with the recovery order, or

(b) providing information, before the order was made, to the enforcement authority, interim receiver or interim administrator.

(5) None of the following provisions applies to a court making a recovery order by virtue of subsection (2)—

(a) any provision of section 159 of the Pension Schemes Act 1993 (c. 48), section 155 of the Pension Schemes (Northern Ireland) Act 1993 (c. 49), section 91 of the Pensions Act 1995 (c. 26) or Article 89 of the Pensions (Northern Ireland) Order 1995 (S.I. 1995/3213 (N.I. 22)) (which prevent assignment and the making of orders that restrain a person from receiving anything which he is prevented from assigning),

166   *Proceeds of Crime Act 2002 (c. 29)*
Part 5 — Civil recovery of the proceeds etc. of unlawful conduct
Chapter 2 — Civil recovery in the High Court or Court of Session

(b) any provision of any enactment (whenever passed or made) corresponding to any of the provisions mentioned in paragraph (a),

(c) any provision of the pension scheme in question corresponding to any of those provisions.

274 Consequential adjustment of liabilities under pension schemes

(1) A recovery order made by virtue of section 273(2) must require the trustees or managers of the pension scheme to make such reduction in the liabilities of the scheme as they think necessary in consequence of the payment made in pursuance of that subsection.

(2) Accordingly, the order must require the trustees or managers to provide for the liabilities of the pension scheme in respect of the respondent's recoverable property to which section 273 applies to cease.

(3) So far as the trustees or managers are required by the recovery order to provide for the liabilities of the pension scheme in respect of the respondent's recoverable property to which section 273 applies to cease, their powers include (in particular) power to reduce the amount of —

(a) any benefit or future benefit to which the respondent is or may be entitled under the scheme,

(b) any future benefit to which any other person may be entitled under the scheme in respect of that property.

275 Pension schemes: supplementary

(1) Regulations may make provision as to the exercise by trustees or managers of their powers under sections 273 and 274, including provision about the calculation and verification of the value at any time of rights or liabilities.

(2) The power conferred by subsection (1) includes power to provide for any values to be calculated or verified —

(a) in a manner which, in the particular case, is approved by a prescribed person, or

(b) in accordance with guidance from time to time prepared by a prescribed person.

(3) Regulations means regulations made by the Secretary of State after consultation with the Scottish Ministers; and prescribed means prescribed by regulations.

(4) A pension scheme means an occupational pension scheme or a personal pension scheme; and those expressions have the same meaning as in the Pension Schemes Act 1993 (c. 48) or, in relation to Northern Ireland, the Pension Schemes (Northern Ireland) Act 1993 (c. 49).

(5) In relation to an occupational pension scheme or a personal pension scheme, the trustees or managers means —

(a) in the case of a scheme established under a trust, the trustees,

(b) in any other case, the managers.

(6) References to a pension scheme include —

(a) a retirement annuity contract (within the meaning of Part 3 of the Welfare Reform and Pensions Act 1999 (c. 30) or, in relation to Northern

Proceeds of Crime Act 2002 (c. 29)
Part 5 — Civil recovery of the proceeds etc. of unlawful conduct
Chapter 2 — Civil recovery in the High Court or Court of Session

167

Ireland, Part 4 of the Welfare Reform and Pensions (Northern Ireland) Order 1999),

    (b)   an annuity or insurance policy purchased, or transferred, for the purpose of giving effect to rights under an occupational pension scheme or a personal pension scheme,

    (c)   an annuity purchased, or entered into, for the purpose of discharging any liability in respect of a pension credit under section 29(1)(b) of the Welfare Reform and Pensions Act 1999 (c. 30) or, in relation to Northern Ireland, Article 26(1)(b) of the Welfare Reform and Pensions (Northern Ireland) Order 1999.

(7)   References to the trustees or managers—

    (a)   in relation to a retirement annuity contract or other annuity, are to the provider of the annuity,

    (b)   in relation to an insurance policy, are to the insurer.

(8)   Subsections (3) to (7) have effect for the purposes of this group of sections (that is, sections 273 and 274 and this section).

276   Consent orders

(1)   The court may make an order staying (in Scotland, sisting) any proceedings for a recovery order on terms agreed by the parties for the disposal of the proceedings if each person to whose property the proceedings, or the agreement, relates is a party both to the proceedings and the agreement.

(2)   An order under subsection (1) may, as well as staying (or sisting) the proceedings on terms—

    (a)   make provision for any property which may be recoverable property to cease to be recoverable,

    (b)   make any further provision which the court thinks appropriate.

(3)   Section 280 applies to property vested in the trustee for civil recovery, or money paid to him, in pursuance of the agreement as it applies to property vested in him by a recovery order or money paid under section 271.

277   Consent orders: pensions

(1)   This section applies where recoverable property to which proceedings under this Chapter relate includes rights under a pension scheme.

(2)   An order made under section 276—

    (a)   may not stay (in Scotland, sist) the proceedings on terms that the rights are vested in any other person, but

    (b)   may include provision imposing the following requirement, if the trustees or managers of the scheme are parties to the agreement by virtue of which the order is made.

(3)   The requirement is that the trustees or managers of the pension scheme—

    (a)   make a payment in accordance with the agreement, and

    (b)   give effect to any other provision made by virtue of this section in respect of the scheme.

168

Proceeds of Crime Act 2002 (c. 29)
Part 5 – Civil recovery of the proceeds etc. of unlawful conduct
Chapter 2 – Civil recovery in the High Court or Court of Session

(4) The trustees or managers of the pension scheme have power to enter into an agreement in respect of the proceedings on any terms on which an order made under section 276 may stay (in Scotland, sist) the proceedings.

(5) The following provisions apply in respect of an order under section 276, so far as it includes the requirement mentioned in subsection (3).

(6) The order overrides the provisions of the pension scheme to the extent that they conflict with the requirement.

(7) The order may provide for the recovery by the trustees or managers of the scheme (whether by deduction from any amount which they are required to pay in pursuance of the agreement or otherwise) of costs incurred by them in –

   (a) complying with the order, or

   (b) providing information, before the order was made, to the enforcement authority, interim receiver or interim administrator.

(8) Sections 273(5) and 274 (read with section 275) apply as if the requirement were included in an order made by virtue of section 273(2).

(9) Section 275(4) to (7) has effect for the purposes of this section.

278 Limit on recovery

(1) This section applies if the enforcement authority seeks a recovery order –

   (a) in respect of both property which is or represents property obtained through unlawful conduct and related property, or

   (b) in respect of property which is or represents property obtained through unlawful conduct where such an order, or an order under section 276, has previously been made in respect of related property.

(2) For the purposes of this section –

   (a) the original property means the property obtained through unlawful conduct,

   (b) the original property, and any items of property which represent the original property, are to be treated as related to each other.

(3) The court is not to make a recovery order if it thinks that the enforcement authority's right to recover the original property has been satisfied by a previous recovery order or order under section 276.

(4) Subject to subsection (3), the court may act under subsection (5) if it thinks that –

   (a) a recovery order may be made in respect of two or more related items of recoverable property, but

   (b) the making of a recovery order in respect of both or all of them is not required in order to satisfy the enforcement authority's right to recover the original property.

(5) The court may in order to satisfy that right to the extent required make a recovery order in respect of –

   (a) only some of the related items of property, or

   (b) only a part of any of the related items of property,

   or both.

Proceeds of Crime Act 2002 (c. 29)
Part 5 – Civil recovery of the proceeds etc. of unlawful conduct
Chapter 2 – Civil recovery in the High Court or Court of Session

169

(6) Where the court may make a recovery order in respect of any property, this section does not prevent the recovery of any profits which have accrued in respect of the property.

(7) If—

    (a) an order is made under section 298 for the forfeiture of recoverable property, and

    (b) the enforcement authority subsequently seeks a recovery order in respect of related property,

the order under section 298 is to be treated for the purposes of this section as if it were a recovery order obtained by the enforcement authority in respect of the forfeited property.

(8) If—

    (a) in pursuance of a judgment in civil proceedings (whether in the United Kingdom or elsewhere), the claimant has obtained property from the defendant ("the judgment property"),

    (b) the claim was based on the defendant's having obtained the judgment property or related property through unlawful conduct, and

    (c) the enforcement authority subsequently seeks a recovery order in respect of property which is related to the judgment property,

the judgment is to be treated for the purposes of this section as if it were a recovery order obtained by the enforcement authority in respect of the judgment property.

In relation to Scotland, "claimant" and "defendant" are to be read as "pursuer" and "defender".

(9) If—

    (a) property has been taken into account in deciding the amount of a person's benefit from criminal conduct for the purpose of making a confiscation order, and

    (b) the enforcement authority subsequently seeks a recovery order in respect of related property,

the confiscation order is to be treated for the purposes of this section as if it were a recovery order obtained by the enforcement authority in respect of the property referred to in paragraph (a).

(10) In subsection (9), a confiscation order means—

    (a) an order under section 6, 92 or 156, or

    (b) an order under a corresponding provision of an enactment mentioned in section 8(7)(a) to (g),

and, in relation to an order mentioned in paragraph (b), the reference to the amount of a person's benefit from criminal conduct is to be read as a reference to the corresponding amount under the enactment in question.

279 Section 278: supplementary

(1) Subsections (2) and (3) give examples of the satisfaction of the enforcement authority's right to recover the original property.

(2) If—

    (a) there is a disposal, other than a part disposal, of the original property, and

    (b) other property (the representative property) is obtained in its place,

170

Proceeds of Crime Act 2002 (c. 29)
Part 5 – Civil recovery of the proceeds etc. of unlawful conduct
Chapter 2 – Civil recovery in the High Court or Court of Session

the enforcement authority's right to recover the original property is satisfied by the making of a recovery order in respect of either the original property or the representative property.

(3) If—

    (a) there is a part disposal of the original property, and

    (b) other property (the representative property) is obtained in place of the property disposed of,

the enforcement authority's right to recover the original property is satisfied by the making of a recovery order in respect of the remainder of the original property together with either the representative property or the property disposed of.

(4) In this section—

    (a) a part disposal means a disposal to which section 314(1) applies,

    (b) the original property has the same meaning as in section 278.

280 Applying realised proceeds

(1) This section applies to—

    (a) sums which represent the realised proceeds of property which was vested in the trustee for civil recovery by a recovery order or which he obtained in pursuance of a recovery order,

    (b) sums vested in the trustee by a recovery order or obtained by him in pursuance of a recovery order.

(2) The trustee is to make out of the sums—

    (a) first, any payment required to be made by him by virtue of section 272,

    (b) second, any payment of expenses incurred by a person acting as an insolvency practitioner which are payable under this subsection by virtue of section 432(10),

and any sum which remains is to be paid to the enforcement authority.

Exemptions etc.

281 Victims of theft, etc.

(1) In proceedings for a recovery order, a person who claims that any property alleged to be recoverable property, or any part of the property, belongs to him may apply for a declaration under this section.

(2) If the applicant appears to the court to meet the following condition, the court may make a declaration to that effect.

(3) The condition is that—

    (a) the person was deprived of the property he claims, or of property which it represents, by unlawful conduct,

    (b) the property he was deprived of was not recoverable property immediately before he was deprived of it, and

    (c) the property he claims belongs to him.

(4) Property to which a declaration under this section applies is not recoverable property.

Proceeds of Crime Act 2002 (c. 29)
Part 5 — Civil recovery of the proceeds etc. of unlawful conduct
Chapter 2 — Civil recovery in the High Court or Court of Session

171

282 Other exemptions

(1) Proceedings for a recovery order may not be taken against any person in circumstances of a prescribed description; and the circumstances may relate to the person himself or to the property or to any other matter.

In this subsection, prescribed means prescribed by an order made by the Secretary of State after consultation with the Scottish Ministers.

(2) Proceedings for a recovery order may not be taken in respect of cash found at any place in the United Kingdom unless the proceedings are also taken in respect of property other than cash which is property of the same person.

(3) Proceedings for a recovery order may not be taken against the Financial Services Authority in respect of any recoverable property held by the authority.

(4) Proceedings for a recovery order may not be taken in respect of any property which is subject to any of the following charges—

    (a) a collateral security charge, within the meaning of the Financial Markets and Insolvency (Settlement Finality) Regulations 1999 (S.I. 1999/2979),

    (b) a market charge, within the meaning of Part 7 of the Companies Act 1989 (c. 40),

    (c) a money market charge, within the meaning of the Financial Markets and Insolvency (Money Market) Regulations 1995 (S.I. 1995/2049),

    (d) a system charge, within the meaning of the Financial Markets and Insolvency Regulations 1996 (S.I. 1996/1469) or the Financial Markets and Insolvency Regulations (Northern Ireland) 1996 (S.R. 1996/252).

(5) Proceedings for a recovery order may not be taken against any person in respect of any recoverable property which he holds by reason of his acting, or having acted, as an insolvency practitioner.

Acting as an insolvency practitioner has the same meaning as in section 433.

Miscellaneous

283 Compensation

(1) If, in the case of any property to which an interim receiving order or interim administration order has at any time applied, the court does not in the course of the proceedings decide that the property is recoverable property or associated property, the person whose property it is may make an application to the court for compensation.

(2) Subsection (1) does not apply if the court—

    (a) has made a declaration in respect of the property by virtue of section 281, or

    (b) makes an order under section 276.

(3) If the court has made a decision by reason of which no recovery order could be made in respect of the property, the application for compensation must be made within the period of three months beginning—

    (a) in relation to a decision of the High Court in England and Wales, with the date of the decision or, if any application is made for leave to appeal, with the date on which the application is withdrawn or refused

172   *Proceeds of Crime Act 2002 (c. 29)*
Part 5 — Civil recovery of the proceeds etc. of unlawful conduct
Chapter 2 — Civil recovery in the High Court or Court of Session

or (if the application is granted) on which any proceedings on appeal
are finally concluded,

(b)   in relation to a decision of the Court of Session or of the High Court in
Northern Ireland, with the date of the decision or, if there is an appeal
against the decision, with the date on which any proceedings on appeal
are finally concluded.

(4)   If, in England and Wales or Northern Ireland, the proceedings in respect of the
property have been discontinued, the application for compensation must be
made within the period of three months beginning with the discontinuance.

(5)   If the court is satisfied that the applicant has suffered loss as a result of the
interim receiving order or interim administration order, it may require the
enforcement authority to pay compensation to him.

(6)   If, but for section 269(2), any right mentioned there would have operated in
favour of, or become exercisable by, any person, he may make an application
to the court for compensation.

(7)   The application for compensation under subsection (6) must be made within
the period of three months beginning with the vesting referred to in section
269(2).

(8)   If the court is satisfied that, in consequence of the operation of section 269, the
right in question cannot subsequently operate in favour of the applicant or (as
the case may be) become exercisable by him, it may require the enforcement
authority to pay compensation to him.

(9)   The amount of compensation to be paid under this section is the amount the
court thinks reasonable, having regard to the loss suffered and any other
relevant circumstances.

284   Payment of interim administrator or trustee (Scotland)

Any fees or expenses incurred by an interim administrator, or a trustee for civil
recovery appointed by the Court of Session, in the exercise of his functions are
to be reimbursed by the Scottish Ministers as soon as is practicable after they
have been incurred.

285   Effect on diligence of recovery order (Scotland)

(1)   An arrestment or poinding of any recoverable property executed on or after the
appointment of the trustee for civil recovery is ineffectual in a question with
the trustee.

(2)   Any recoverable property so arrested or poinded, or (if the property has been
sold) the proceeds of sale, must be handed over to the trustee for civil recovery.

(3)   A poinding of the ground in respect of recoverable property on or after such an
appointment is ineffectual in a question with the trustee for civil recovery
except for the interest mentioned in subsection (4).

(4)   That interest is —
(a)   interest on the debt of a secured creditor for the current half yearly
term, and
(b)   arrears of interest on that debt for one year immediately before the
commencement of that term.

Proceeds of Crime Act 2002 (c. 29)
Part 5 — Civil recovery of the proceeds etc. of unlawful conduct
Chapter 2 — Civil recovery in the High Court or Court of Session

173

(5)   On and after such appointment no other person may raise or insist in an adjudication against recoverable property or be confirmed as an executor-creditor on that property.

(6)   An inhibition on recoverable property shall cease to have effect in relation to any heritable property comprised in the recoverable property on such appointment.

(7)   The provisions of this section apply in relation to —
    (a)   an action of maills and duties, and
    (b)   an action for sequestration of rent,
as they apply in relation to an arrestment or poinding.

286   Scope of powers (Scotland)

(1)   Orders under this Chapter may be made by the Court of Session in respect of a person wherever domiciled, resident or present.

(2)   Such an order may be made by the Court of Session in respect of moveable property wherever situated.

(3)   But such an order in respect of a person's moveable property may not be made by the Court of Session where —
    (a)   the person is not domiciled, resident or present in Scotland, and
    (b)   the property is not situated in Scotland,
unless the unlawful conduct took place in Scotland.

287   Financial threshold

(1)   At any time when an order specifying an amount for the purposes of this section has effect, the enforcement authority may not start proceedings for a recovery order unless the authority reasonably believes that the aggregate value of the recoverable property which the authority wishes to be subject to a recovery order is not less than the specified amount.

(2)   The power to make an order under subsection (1) is exercisable by the Secretary of State after consultation with the Scottish Ministers.

(3)   If the authority applies for an interim receiving order or interim administration order before starting the proceedings, subsection (1) applies to the application instead of to the start of the proceedings.

(4)   This section does not affect the continuation of proceedings for a recovery order which have been properly started or the making or continuing effect of an interim receiving order or interim administration order which has been properly applied for.

288   Limitation

(1)   After section 27 of the Limitation Act 1980 (c. 58) there is inserted —

174 *Proceeds of Crime Act 2002 (c. 29)*
Part 5 — Civil recovery of the proceeds etc. of unlawful conduct
Chapter 2 — Civil recovery in the High Court or Court of Session

"27A Actions for recovery of property obtained through unlawful conduct etc.

(1) None of the time limits given in the preceding provisions of this Act applies to any proceedings under Chapter 2 of Part 5 of the Proceeds of Crime Act 2002 (civil recovery of proceeds of unlawful conduct).

(2) Proceedings under that Chapter for a recovery order in respect of any recoverable property shall not be brought after the expiration of the period of twelve years from the date on which the Director's cause of action accrued.

(3) Proceedings under that Chapter are brought when—
    (a) a claim form is issued, or
    (b) an application is made for an interim receiving order,
    whichever is the earlier.

(4) The Director's cause of action accrues in respect of any recoverable property—
    (a) in the case of proceedings for a recovery order in respect of property obtained through unlawful conduct, when the property is so obtained,
    (b) in the case of proceedings for a recovery order in respect of any other recoverable property, when the property obtained through unlawful conduct which it represents is so obtained.

(5) If—
    (a) a person would (but for the preceding provisions of this Act) have a cause of action in respect of the conversion of a chattel, and
    (b) proceedings are started under that Chapter for a recovery order in respect of the chattel,
    section 3(2) of this Act does not prevent his asserting on an application under section 281 of that Act that the property belongs to him, or the court making a declaration in his favour under that section.

(6) If the court makes such a declaration, his title to the chattel is to be treated as not having been extinguished by section 3(2) of this Act.

(7) Expressions used in this section and Part 5 of that Act have the same meaning in this section as in that Part."

(2) After section 19A of the Prescription and Limitation (Scotland) Act 1973 (c. 52) there is inserted—

"19B Actions for recovery of property obtained through unlawful conduct etc.

(1) None of the time limits given in the preceding provisions of this Act applies to any proceedings under Chapter 2 of Part 5 of the Proceeds of Crime Act 2002 (civil recovery of proceeds of unlawful conduct).

(2) Proceedings under that Chapter for a recovery order in respect of any recoverable property shall not be commenced after the expiration of the period of twelve years from the date on which the Scottish Ministers' right of action accrued.

Proceeds of Crime Act 2002 (c. 29)
Part 5 – Civil recovery of the proceeds etc. of unlawful conduct
Chapter 2 – Civil recovery in the High Court or Court of Session

175

(3) Proceedings under that Chapter are commenced when—

(a) the proceedings are served, or

(b) an application is made for an interim administration order,

whichever is the earlier.

(4) The Scottish Ministers' right of action accrues in respect of any recoverable property—

(a) in the case of proceedings for a recovery order in respect of property obtained through unlawful conduct, when the property is so obtained,

(b) in the case of proceedings for a recovery order in respect of any other recoverable property, when the property obtained through unlawful conduct which it represents is so obtained.

(5) Expressions used in this section and Part 5 of that Act have the same meaning in this section as in that Part."

(3) After Article 72 of the Limitation (Northern Ireland) Order 1989 (SI 1989/1339 (N.I. 11)) there is inserted—

"72A Actions for recovery of property obtained through unlawful conduct etc.

(1) None of the time limits fixed by Parts II and III applies to any proceedings under Chapter 2 of Part 5 of the Proceeds of Crime Act 2002 (civil recovery of proceeds of unlawful conduct).

(2) Proceedings under that Chapter for a recovery order in respect of any recoverable property shall not be brought after the expiration of the period of twelve years from the date on which the Director's cause of action accrued.

(3) Proceedings under that Chapter are brought when—

(a) a claim form is issued, or

(b) an application is made for an interim receiving order,

whichever is the earlier.

(4) The Director's cause of action accrues in respect of any recoverable property—

(a) in the case of proceedings for a recovery order in respect of property obtained through unlawful conduct, when the property is so obtained,

(b) in the case of proceedings for a recovery order in respect of any other recoverable property, when the property obtained through unlawful conduct which it represents is so obtained.

(5) If—

(a) a person would (but for a time limit fixed by this Order) have a cause of action in respect of the conversion of a chattel, and

(b) proceedings are started under that Chapter for a recovery order in respect of the chattel,

Article 17(2) does not prevent his asserting on an application under section 281 of that Act that the property belongs to him, or the court making a declaration in his favour under that section.

176

Proceeds of Crime Act 2002 (c. 29)
Part 5 — Civil recovery of the proceeds etc. of unlawful conduct
Chapter 2 — Civil recovery in the High Court or Court of Session

(6) If the court makes such a declaration, his title to the chattel is to be treated as not having been extinguished by Article 17(2).

(7) Expressions used in this Article and Part 5 of that Act have the same meaning in this Article as in that Part."

CHAPTER 3

RECOVERY OF CASH IN SUMMARY PROCEEDINGS

Searches

289   Searches

(1) If a customs officer or constable who is lawfully on any premises has reasonable grounds for suspecting that there is on the premises cash —

    (a) which is recoverable property or is intended by any person for use in unlawful conduct, and

    (b) the amount of which is not less than the minimum amount,

he may search for the cash there.

(2) If a customs officer or constable has reasonable grounds for suspecting that a person (the suspect) is carrying cash —

    (a) which is recoverable property or is intended by any person for use in unlawful conduct, and

    (b) the amount of which is not less than the minimum amount,

he may exercise the following powers.

(3) The officer or constable may, so far as he thinks it necessary or expedient, require the suspect —

    (a) to permit a search of any article he has with him,

    (b) to permit a search of his person.

(4) An officer or constable exercising powers by virtue of subsection (3)(b) may detain the suspect for so long as is necessary for their exercise.

(5) The powers conferred by this section —

    (a) are exercisable only so far as reasonably required for the purpose of finding cash,

    (b) are exercisable by a customs officer only if he has reasonable grounds for suspecting that the unlawful conduct in question relates to an assigned matter (within the meaning of the Customs and Excise Management Act 1979 (c. 2)).

(6) Cash means —

    (a) notes and coins in any currency,

    (b) postal orders,

    (c) cheques of any kind, including travellers' cheques,

    (d) bankers' drafts,

    (e) bearer bonds and bearer shares,

found at any place in the United Kingdom.

Proceeds of Crime Act 2002 (c. 29)
Part 5 – Civil recovery of the proceeds etc. of unlawful conduct
Chapter 3 – Recovery of cash in summary proceedings

177

(7) Cash also includes any kind of monetary instrument which is found at any place in the United Kingdom, if the instrument is specified by the Secretary of State by an order made after consultation with the Scottish Ministers.

(8) This section does not require a person to submit to an intimate search or strip search (within the meaning of section 164 of the Customs and Excise Management Act 1979 (c. 2)).

290 Prior approval

(1) The powers conferred by section 289 may be exercised only with the appropriate approval unless, in the circumstances, it is not practicable to obtain that approval before exercising the power.

(2) The appropriate approval means the approval of a judicial officer or (if that is not practicable in any case) the approval of a senior officer.

(3) A judicial officer means –
   (a) in relation to England and Wales and Northern Ireland, a justice of the peace,
   (b) in relation to Scotland, the sheriff.

(4) A senior officer means –
   (a) in relation to the exercise of the power by a customs officer, a customs officer of a rank designated by the Commissioners of Customs and Excise as equivalent to that of a senior police officer,
   (b) in relation to the exercise of the power by a constable, a senior police officer.

(5) A senior police officer means a police officer of at least the rank of inspector.

(6) If the powers are exercised without the approval of a judicial officer in a case where –
   (a) no cash is seized by virtue of section 294, or
   (b) any cash so seized is not detained for more than 48 hours,
   the customs officer or constable who exercised the powers must give a written report to the appointed person.

(7) The report must give particulars of the circumstances which led him to believe that –
   (a) the powers were exercisable, and
   (b) it was not practicable to obtain the approval of a judicial officer.

(8) In this section and section 291, the appointed person means –
   (a) in relation to England and Wales and Northern Ireland, a person appointed by the Secretary of State,
   (b) in relation to Scotland, a person appointed by the Scottish Ministers.

(9) The appointed person must not be a person employed under or for the purposes of a government department or of the Scottish Administration; and the terms and conditions of his appointment, including any remuneration or expenses to be paid to him, are to be determined by the person appointing him.

178

Proceeds of Crime Act 2002 (c. 29)
Part 5 – Civil recovery of the proceeds etc. of unlawful conduct
Chapter 3 – Recovery of cash in summary proceedings

291   Report on exercise of powers

(1)   As soon as possible after the end of each financial year, the appointed person must prepare a report for that year.

"Financial year" means—

    (a)   the period beginning with the day on which this section comes into force and ending with the next 31 March (which is the first financial year), and

    (b)   each subsequent period of twelve months beginning with 1 April.

(2)   The report must give his opinion as to the circumstances and manner in which the powers conferred by section 289 are being exercised in cases where the customs officer or constable who exercised them is required to give a report under section 290(6).

(3)   In the report, he may make any recommendations he considers appropriate.

(4)   He must send a copy of his report to the Secretary of State or, as the case may be, the Scottish Ministers, who must arrange for it to be published.

(5)   The Secretary of State must lay a copy of any report he receives under this section before Parliament; and the Scottish Ministers must lay a copy of any report they receive under this section before the Scottish Parliament.

292   Code of practice

(1)   The Secretary of State must make a code of practice in connection with the exercise by customs officers and (in relation to England and Wales and Northern Ireland) constables of the powers conferred by virtue of section 289.

(2)   Where he proposes to issue a code of practice he must—

    (a)   publish a draft,

    (b)   consider any representations made to him about the draft by the Scottish Ministers or any other person,

    (c)   if he thinks it appropriate, modify the draft in the light of any such representations.

(3)   He must lay a draft of the code before Parliament.

(4)   When he has laid a draft of the code before Parliament he may bring it into operation by order.

(5)   He may revise the whole or any part of the code issued by him and issue the code as revised; and subsections (2) to (4) apply to such a revised code as they apply to the original code.

(6)   A failure by a customs officer or constable to comply with a provision of the code does not of itself make him liable to criminal or civil proceedings.

(7)   The code is admissible in evidence in criminal or civil proceedings and is to be taken into account by a court or tribunal in any case in which it appears to the court or tribunal to be relevant.

Proceeds of Crime Act 2002 (c. 29)
Part 5 – Civil recovery of the proceeds etc. of unlawful conduct
Chapter 3 – Recovery of cash in summary proceedings

179

293 Code of practice (Scotland)

(1) The Scottish Ministers must make a code of practice in connection with the exercise by constables in relation to Scotland of the powers conferred by virtue of section 289.

(2) Where they propose to issue a code of practice they must –
    (a) publish a draft,
    (b) consider any representations made to them about the draft,
    (c) if they think it appropriate, modify the draft in the light of any such representations.

(3) They must lay a draft of the code before the Scottish Parliament.

(4) When they have laid a draft of the code before the Scottish Parliament they may bring it into operation by order.

(5) They may revise the whole or any part of the code issued by them and issue the code as revised; and subsections (2) to (4) apply to such a revised code as they apply to the original code.

(6) A failure by a constable to comply with a provision of the code does not of itself make him liable to criminal or civil proceedings.

(7) The code is admissible in evidence in criminal or civil proceedings and is to be taken into account by a court or tribunal in any case in which it appears to the court or tribunal to be relevant.

Seizure and detention

294 Seizure of cash

(1) A customs officer or constable may seize any cash if he has reasonable grounds for suspecting that it is –
    (a) recoverable property, or
    (b) intended by any person for use in unlawful conduct.

(2) A customs officer or constable may also seize cash part of which he has reasonable grounds for suspecting to be –
    (a) recoverable property, or
    (b) intended by any person for use in unlawful conduct,
if it is not reasonably practicable to seize only that part.

(3) This section does not authorise the seizure of an amount of cash if it or, as the case may be, the part to which his suspicion relates, is less than the minimum amount.

295 Detention of seized cash

(1) While the customs officer or constable continues to have reasonable grounds for his suspicion, cash seized under section 294 may be detained initially for a period of 48 hours.

(2) The period for which the cash or any part of it may be detained may be extended by an order made by a magistrates' court or (in Scotland) the sheriff; but the order may not authorise the detention of any of the cash –

180

Proceeds of Crime Act 2002 (c. 29)
Part 5 — Civil recovery of the proceeds etc. of unlawful conduct
Chapter 3 — Recovery of cash in summary proceedings

    (a)   beyond the end of the period of three months beginning with the date of the order,

    (b)   in the case of any further order under this section, beyond the end of the period of two years beginning with the date of the first order.

(3)   A justice of the peace may also exercise the power of a magistrates' court to make the first order under subsection (2) extending the period.

(4)   An application for an order under subsection (2) —

    (a)   in relation to England and Wales and Northern Ireland, may be made by the Commissioners of Customs and Excise or a constable,

    (b)   in relation to Scotland, may be made by the Scottish Ministers in connection with their functions under section 298 or by a procurator fiscal,

and the court, sheriff or justice may make the order if satisfied, in relation to any cash to be further detained, that either of the following conditions is met.

(5)   The first condition is that there are reasonable grounds for suspecting that the cash is recoverable property and that either —

    (a)   its continued detention is justified while its derivation is further investigated or consideration is given to bringing (in the United Kingdom or elsewhere) proceedings against any person for an offence with which the cash is connected, or

    (b)   proceedings against any person for an offence with which the cash is connected have been started and have not been concluded.

(6)   The second condition is that there are reasonable grounds for suspecting that the cash is intended to be used in unlawful conduct and that either —

    (a)   its continued detention is justified while its intended use is further investigated or consideration is given to bringing (in the United Kingdom or elsewhere) proceedings against any person for an offence with which the cash is connected, or

    (b)   proceedings against any person for an offence with which the cash is connected have been started and have not been concluded.

(7)   An application for an order under subsection (2) may also be made in respect of any cash seized under section 294(2), and the court, sheriff or justice may make the order if satisfied that —

    (a)   the condition in subsection (5) or (6) is met in respect of part of the cash, and

    (b)   it is not reasonably practicable to detain only that part.

(8)   An order under subsection (2) must provide for notice to be given to persons affected by it.

296   Interest

(1)   If cash is detained under section 295 for more than 48 hours, it is at the first opportunity to be paid into an interest-bearing account and held there; and the interest accruing on it is to be added to it on its forfeiture or release.

(2)   In the case of cash detained under section 295 which was seized under section 294(2), the customs officer or constable must, on paying it into the account, release the part of the cash to which the suspicion does not relate.

Proceeds of Crime Act 2002 (c. 29)
Part 5 – Civil recovery of the proceeds etc. of unlawful conduct
Chapter 3 – Recovery of cash in summary proceedings

181

(3) Subsection (1) does not apply if the cash or, as the case may be, the part to which the suspicion relates is required as evidence of an offence or evidence in proceedings under this Chapter.

297 Release of detained cash

(1) This section applies while any cash is detained under section 295.

(2) A magistrates' court or (in Scotland) the sheriff may direct the release of the whole or any part of the cash if the following condition is met.

(3) The condition is that the court or sheriff is satisfied, on an application by the person from whom the cash was seized, that the conditions in section 295 for the detention of the cash are no longer met in relation to the cash to be released.

(4) A customs officer, constable or (in Scotland) procurator fiscal may, after notifying the magistrates' court, sheriff or justice under whose order cash is being detained, release the whole or any part of it if satisfied that the detention of the cash to be released is no longer justified.

Forfeiture

298 Forfeiture

(1) While cash is detained under section 295, an application for the forfeiture of the whole or any part of it may be made –
   (a) to a magistrates' court by the Commissioners of Customs and Excise or a constable,
   (b) (in Scotland) to the sheriff by the Scottish Ministers.

(2) The court or sheriff may order the forfeiture of the cash or any part of it if satisfied that the cash or part –
   (a) is recoverable property, or
   (b) is intended by any person for use in unlawful conduct.

(3) But in the case of recoverable property which belongs to joint tenants, one of whom is an excepted joint owner, the order may not apply to so much of it as the court thinks is attributable to the excepted joint owner's share.

(4) Where an application for the forfeiture of any cash is made under this section, the cash is to be detained (and may not be released under any power conferred by this Chapter) until any proceedings in pursuance of the application (including any proceedings on appeal) are concluded.

299 Appeal against forfeiture

(1) Any party to proceedings in which an order is made under section 298 for the forfeiture of cash who is aggrieved by the order may appeal –
   (a) in relation to England and Wales, to the Crown Court,
   (b) in relation to Scotland, to the Court of Session,
   (c) in relation to Northern Ireland, to a county court.

(2) An appeal under subsection (1) must be made within the period of 30 days beginning with the date on which the order is made.

(3) The appeal is to be by way of a rehearing.

182   *Proceeds of Crime Act 2002 (c. 29)*
Part 5 — Civil recovery of the proceeds etc. of unlawful conduct
Chapter 3 — Recovery of cash in summary proceedings

(4)   The court hearing the appeal may make any order it thinks appropriate.

(5)   If the court upholds the appeal, it may order the release of the cash.

300   Application of forfeited cash

(1)   Cash forfeited under this Chapter, and any accrued interest on it —
   (a)   if forfeited by a magistrates' court in England and Wales or Northern
           Ireland, is to be paid into the Consolidated Fund,
   (b)   if forfeited by the sheriff, is to be paid into the Scottish Consolidated
           Fund.

(2)   But it is not to be paid in —
   (a)   before the end of the period within which an appeal under section 299
           may be made, or
   (b)   if a person appeals under that section, before the appeal is determined
           or otherwise disposed of.

Supplementary

301   Victims and other owners

(1)   A person who claims that any cash detained under this Chapter, or any part of
        it, belongs to him may apply to a magistrates' court or (in Scotland) the sheriff
        for the cash or part to be released to him.

(2)   The application may be made in the course of proceedings under section 295 or
        298 or at any other time.

(3)   If it appears to the court or sheriff concerned that —
   (a)   the applicant was deprived of the cash to which the application relates,
           or of property which it represents, by unlawful conduct,
   (b)   the property he was deprived of was not, immediately before he was
           deprived of it, recoverable property, and
   (c)   that cash belongs to him,
        the court or sheriff may order the cash to which the application relates to be
        released to the applicant.

(4)   If —
   (a)   the applicant is not the person from whom the cash to which the
           application relates was seized,
   (b)   it appears to the court or sheriff that that cash belongs to the applicant,
   (c)   the court or sheriff is satisfied that the conditions in section 295 for the
           detention of that cash are no longer met or, if an application has been
           made under section 298, the court or sheriff decides not to make an
           order under that section in relation to that cash, and
   (d)   no objection to the making of an order under this subsection has been
           made by the person from whom that cash was seized,
        the court or sheriff may order the cash to which the application relates to be
        released to the applicant or to the person from whom it was seized.

Proceeds of Crime Act 2002 (c. 29) 183
Part 5 — Civil recovery of the proceeds etc. of unlawful conduct
Chapter 3 — Recovery of cash in summary proceedings

302 Compensation

(1) If no forfeiture order is made in respect of any cash detained under this Chapter, the person to whom the cash belongs or from whom it was seized may make an application to the magistrates' court or (in Scotland) the sheriff for compensation.

(2) If, for any period beginning with the first opportunity to place the cash in an interest-bearing account after the initial detention of the cash for 48 hours, the cash was not held in an interest-bearing account while detained, the court or sheriff may order an amount of compensation to be paid to the applicant.

(3) The amount of compensation to be paid under subsection (2) is the amount the court or sheriff thinks would have been earned in interest in the period in question if the cash had been held in an interest-bearing account.

(4) If the court or sheriff is satisfied that, taking account of any interest to be paid under section 296 or any amount to be paid under subsection (2), the applicant has suffered loss as a result of the detention of the cash and that the circumstances are exceptional, the court or sheriff may order compensation (or additional compensation) to be paid to him.

(5) The amount of compensation to be paid under subsection (4) is the amount the court or sheriff thinks reasonable, having regard to the loss suffered and any other relevant circumstances.

(6) If the cash was seized by a customs officer, the compensation is to be paid by the Commissioners of Customs and Excise.

(7) If the cash was seized by a constable, the compensation is to be paid as follows—

    (a) in the case of a constable of a police force in England and Wales, it is to be paid out of the police fund from which the expenses of the police force are met,

    (b) in the case of a constable of a police force in Scotland, it is to be paid by the police authority or joint police board for the police area for which that force is maintained,

    (c) in the case of a police officer within the meaning of the Police (Northern Ireland) Act 2000 (c. 32), it is to be paid out of money provided by the Chief Constable.

(8) If a forfeiture order is made in respect only of a part of any cash detained under this Chapter, this section has effect in relation to the other part.

303 "The minimum amount"

(1) In this Chapter, the minimum amount is the amount in sterling specified in an order made by the Secretary of State after consultation with the Scottish Ministers.

(2) For that purpose the amount of any cash held in a currency other than sterling must be taken to be its sterling equivalent, calculated in accordance with the prevailing rate of exchange.

184

Proceeds of Crime Act 2002 (c. 29)
Part 5 – Civil recovery of the proceeds etc. of unlawful conduct
Chapter 4 – General

CHAPTER 4

GENERAL

Recoverable property

304 Property obtained through unlawful conduct

(1) Property obtained through unlawful conduct is recoverable property.

(2) But if property obtained through unlawful conduct has been disposed of (since it was so obtained), it is recoverable property only if it is held by a person into whose hands it may be followed.

(3) Recoverable property obtained through unlawful conduct may be followed into the hands of a person obtaining it on a disposal by –
  (a) the person who through the conduct obtained the property, or
  (b) a person into whose hands it may (by virtue of this subsection) be followed.

305 Tracing property, etc.

(1) Where property obtained through unlawful conduct ("the original property") is or has been recoverable, property which represents the original property is also recoverable property.

(2) If a person enters into a transaction by which –
  (a) he disposes of recoverable property, whether the original property or property which (by virtue of this Chapter) represents the original property, and
  (b) he obtains other property in place of it,
  the other property represents the original property.

(3) If a person disposes of recoverable property which represents the original property, the property may be followed into the hands of the person who obtains it (and it continues to represent the original property).

306 Mixing property

(1) Subsection (2) applies if a person's recoverable property is mixed with other property (whether his property or another's).

(2) The portion of the mixed property which is attributable to the recoverable property represents the property obtained through unlawful conduct.

(3) Recoverable property is mixed with other property if (for example) it is used –
  (a) to increase funds held in a bank account,
  (b) in part payment for the acquisition of an asset,
  (c) for the restoration or improvement of land,
  (d) by a person holding a leasehold interest in the property to acquire the freehold.

Proceeds of Crime Act 2002 (c. 29)
Part 5 – Civil recovery of the proceeds etc. of unlawful conduct
Chapter 4 – General

185

307 Recoverable property: accruing profits

(1) This section applies where a person who has recoverable property obtains further property consisting of profits accruing in respect of the recoverable property.

(2) The further property is to be treated as representing the property obtained through unlawful conduct.

308 General exceptions

(1) If—
   (a) a person disposes of recoverable property, and
   (b) the person who obtains it on the disposal does so in good faith, for value and without notice that it was recoverable property,

   the property may not be followed into that person's hands and, accordingly, it ceases to be recoverable.

(2) If recoverable property is vested, forfeited or otherwise disposed of in pursuance of powers conferred by virtue of this Part, it ceases to be recoverable.

(3) If—
   (a) in pursuance of a judgment in civil proceedings (whether in the United Kingdom or elsewhere), the defendant makes a payment to the claimant or the claimant otherwise obtains property from the defendant,
   (b) the claimant's claim is based on the defendant's unlawful conduct, and
   (c) apart from this subsection, the sum received, or the property obtained, by the claimant would be recoverable property,

   the property ceases to be recoverable.
   In relation to Scotland, "claimant" and "defendant" are to be read as "pursuer" and "defender".

(4) If—
   (a) a payment is made to a person in pursuance of a compensation order under Article 14 of the Criminal Justice (Northern Ireland) Order 1994 (S.I. 1994/2795 (N.I. 15)), section 249 of the Criminal Procedure (Scotland) Act 1995 (c. 46) or section 130 of the Powers of Criminal Courts (Sentencing) Act 2000 (c. 6), and
   (b) apart from this subsection, the sum received would be recoverable property,

   the property ceases to be recoverable.

(5) If—
   (a) a payment is made to a person in pursuance of a restitution order under section 27 of the Theft Act (Northern Ireland) 1969 (c. 16 (N.I.)) or section 148(2) of the Powers of Criminal Courts (Sentencing) Act 2000 or a person otherwise obtains any property in pursuance of such an order, and
   (b) apart from this subsection, the sum received, or the property obtained, would be recoverable property,

   the property ceases to be recoverable.

(6) If—

186

Proceeds of Crime Act 2002 (c. 29)
Part 5 – Civil recovery of the proceeds etc. of unlawful conduct
Chapter 4 – General

(a) in pursuance of an order made by the court under section 382(3) or 383(5) of the Financial Services and Markets Act 2000 (c. 8) (restitution orders), an amount is paid to or distributed among any persons in accordance with the court's directions, and

(b) apart from this subsection, the sum received by them would be recoverable property,

the property ceases to be recoverable.

(7) If —

(a) in pursuance of a requirement of the Financial Services Authority under section 384(5) of the Financial Services and Markets Act 2000 (power of authority to require restitution), an amount is paid to or distributed among any persons, and

(b) apart from this subsection, the sum received by them would be recoverable property,

the property ceases to be recoverable.

(8) Property is not recoverable while a restraint order applies to it, that is —

(a) an order under section 41, 120 or 190, or

(b) an order under any corresponding provision of an enactment mentioned in section 8(7)(a) to (g).

(9) Property is not recoverable if it has been taken into account in deciding the amount of a person's benefit from criminal conduct for the purpose of making a confiscation order, that is —

(a) an order under section 6, 92 or 156, or

(b) an order under a corresponding provision of an enactment mentioned in section 8(7)(a) to (g),

and, in relation to an order mentioned in paragraph (b), the reference to the amount of a person's benefit from criminal conduct is to be read as a reference to the corresponding amount under the enactment in question.

(10) Where —

(a) a person enters into a transaction to which section 305(2) applies, and

(b) the disposal is one to which subsection (1) or (2) applies,

this section does not affect the recoverability (by virtue of section 305(2)) of any property obtained on the transaction in place of the property disposed of.

309 Other exemptions

(1) An order may provide that property is not recoverable or (as the case may be) associated property if —

(a) it is prescribed property, or

(b) it is disposed of in pursuance of a prescribed enactment or an enactment of a prescribed description.

(2) An order may provide that if property is disposed of in pursuance of a prescribed enactment or an enactment of a prescribed description, it is to be treated for the purposes of section 278 as if it had been disposed of in pursuance of a recovery order.

(3) An order under this section may be made so as to apply to property, or a disposal of property, only in prescribed circumstances; and the circumstances

Proceeds of Crime Act 2002 (c. 29)
Part 5 — Civil recovery of the proceeds etc. of unlawful conduct
Chapter 4 — General

187

may relate to the property or disposal itself or to a person who holds or has held the property or to any other matter.

(4) In this section, an order means an order made by the Secretary of State after consultation with the Scottish Ministers, and prescribed means prescribed by the order.

310 Granting interests

(1) If a person grants an interest in his recoverable property, the question whether the interest is also recoverable is to be determined in the same manner as it is on any other disposal of recoverable property.

(2) Accordingly, on his granting an interest in the property ("the property in question") —

    (a) where the property in question is property obtained through unlawful conduct, the interest is also to be treated as obtained through that conduct,

    (b) where the property in question represents in his hands property obtained through unlawful conduct, the interest is also to be treated as representing in his hands the property so obtained.

Insolvency

311 Insolvency

(1) Proceedings for a recovery order may not be taken or continued in respect of property to which subsection (3) applies unless the appropriate court gives leave and the proceedings are taken or (as the case may be) continued in accordance with any terms imposed by that court.

(2) An application for an order for the further detention of any cash to which subsection (3) applies may not be made under section 295 unless the appropriate court gives leave.

(3) This subsection applies to recoverable property, or property associated with it, if —

    (a) it is an asset of a company being wound up in pursuance of a resolution for voluntary winding up,

    (b) it is an asset of a company and a voluntary arrangement under Part 1 of the 1986 Act, or Part 2 of the 1989 Order, has effect in relation to the company,

    (c) an order under section 2 of the 1985 Act, section 286 of the 1986 Act or Article 259 of the 1989 Order (appointment of interim trustee or interim receiver) has effect in relation to the property,

    (d) it is an asset comprised in the estate of an individual who has been adjudged bankrupt or, in relation to Scotland, of a person whose estate has been sequestrated,

    (e) it is an asset of an individual and a voluntary arrangement under Part 8 of the 1986 Act, or Part 8 of the 1989 Order, has effect in relation to him, or

    (f) in relation to Scotland, it is property comprised in the estate of a person who has granted a trust deed within the meaning of the 1985 Act.

188   *Proceeds of Crime Act 2002 (c. 29)*
Part 5 − Civil recovery of the proceeds etc. of unlawful conduct
Chapter 4 − General

(4)   An application under this section, or under any provision of the 1986 Act or the 1989 Order, for leave to take proceedings for a recovery order may be made without notice to any person.

(5)   Subsection (4) does not affect any requirement for notice of an application to be given to any person acting as an insolvency practitioner or to the official receiver (whether or not acting as an insolvency practitioner).

(6)   References to the provisions of the 1986 Act in sections 420 and 421 of that Act, or to the provisions of the 1989 Order in Articles 364 or 365 of that Order, (insolvent partnerships and estates of deceased persons) include subsections (1) to (3) above.

(7)   In this section −

     (a)   the 1985 Act means the Bankruptcy (Scotland) Act 1985 (c. 66),

     (b)   the 1986 Act means the Insolvency Act 1986 (c. 45),

     (c)   the 1989 Order means the Insolvency (Northern Ireland) Order 1989 (S.I. 1989/2405 (N.I. 19)),

and in subsection (8) "the applicable enactment" means whichever enactment mentioned in paragraphs (a) to (c) is relevant to the resolution, arrangement, order or trust deed mentioned in subsection (3).

(8)   In this section −

     (a)   an asset means any property within the meaning of the applicable enactment or, where the 1985 Act is the applicable enactment, any property comprised in an estate to which the 1985 Act applies,

     (b)   the appropriate court means the court which, in relation to the resolution, arrangement, order or trust deed mentioned in subsection (3), is the court for the purposes of the applicable enactment or, in relation to Northern Ireland, the High Court,

     (c)   acting as an insolvency practitioner has the same meaning as in section 433,

     (d)   other expressions used in this section and in the applicable enactment have the same meaning as in that enactment.

Delegation of enforcement functions

312   Performance of functions of Scottish Ministers by constables in Scotland

(1)   In Scotland, a constable engaged in temporary service with the Scottish Ministers in connection with their functions under this Part may perform functions, other than those specified in subsection (2), on behalf of the Scottish Ministers.

(2)   The specified functions are the functions conferred on the Scottish Ministers by −

     (a)   sections 244(1) and (2) and 256(1) and (7) (proceedings in the Court of Session),

     (b)   section 267(2) (trustee for civil recovery),

     (c)   sections 271(3) and (4) and 272(5) (agreements about associated and joint property),

     (d)   section 275(3) (pension schemes),

     (e)   section 282(1) (exemptions),

     (f)   section 283(5) and (8) (compensation),

Proceeds of Crime Act 2002 (c. 29)
Part 5 – Civil recovery of the proceeds etc. of unlawful conduct
Chapter 4 – General

189

(g)   section 287(2) (financial threshold),

(h)   section 293(1) (code of practice),

(i)   section 298(1) (forfeiture),

(j)   section 303(1) (minimum amount).

313   Restriction on performance of Director's functions by police

(1)   In spite of section 1(6), nothing which the Director is authorised or required to do for the purposes of this Part may be done by –

(a)   a member of a police force,

(b)   a member of the Police Service of Northern Ireland,

(c)   a person appointed as a police member of the National Criminal Intelligence Service under section 9(1)(b) of the Police Act 1997 (c. 50),

(d)   a person appointed as a police member of the National Crime Squad under section 55(1)(b) of that Act.

(2)   In this section –

(a)   "member of a police force" has the same meaning as in the Police Act 1996 (c. 16) and includes a person who would be a member of a police force but for section 97(3) of that Act (police officers engaged on service outside their force),

(b)   "member of the Police Service of Northern Ireland" includes a person who would be a member of the Police Service of Northern Ireland but for section 27(3) of the Police (Northern Ireland) Act 1998 (c. 32) (members of that service engaged on other police service).

Interpretation

314   Obtaining and disposing of property

(1)   References to a person disposing of his property include a reference –

(a)   to his disposing of a part of it, or

(b)   to his granting an interest in it,

(or to both); and references to the property disposed of are to any property obtained on the disposal.

(2)   A person who makes a payment to another is to be treated as making a disposal of his property to the other, whatever form the payment takes.

(3)   Where a person's property passes to another under a will or intestacy or by operation of law, it is to be treated as disposed of by him to the other.

(4)   A person is only to be treated as having obtained his property for value in a case where he gave unexecuted consideration if the consideration has become executed consideration.

315   Northern Ireland courts

In relation to the practice and procedure of courts in Northern Ireland, expressions used in this Part are to be read in accordance with rules of court.

190

Proceeds of Crime Act 2002 (c. 29)
Part 5 — Civil recovery of the proceeds etc. of unlawful conduct
Chapter 4 — General

316   General interpretation

(1)   In this Part—

"associated property" has the meaning given by section 245,

"cash" has the meaning given by section 289(6) or (7),

"constable", in relation to Northern Ireland, means a police officer within the meaning of the Police (Northern Ireland) Act 2000 (c. 32),

"country" includes territory,

"the court" (except in sections 253(2) and (3) and 262(2) and (3) and Chapter 3) means the High Court or (in relation to proceedings in Scotland) the Court of Session,

"dealing" with property includes disposing of it, taking possession of it or removing it from the United Kingdom,

"enforcement authority"—

(a)   in relation to England and Wales and Northern Ireland, means the Director,

(b)   in relation to Scotland, means the Scottish Ministers,

"excepted joint owner" has the meaning given by section 270(4),

"interest", in relation to land—

(a)   in the case of land in England and Wales or Northern Ireland, means any legal estate and any equitable interest or power,

(b)   in the case of land in Scotland, means any estate, interest, servitude or other heritable right in or over land, including a heritable security,

"interest", in relation to property other than land, includes any right (including a right to possession of the property),

"interim administration order" has the meaning given by section 256(2),

"interim receiving order" has the meaning given by section 246(2),

"the minimum amount" (in Chapter 3) has the meaning given by section 303,

"part", in relation to property, includes a portion,

"premises" has the same meaning as in the Police and Criminal Evidence Act 1984 (c. 60),

"property obtained through unlawful conduct" has the meaning given by section 242,

"recoverable property" is to be read in accordance with sections 304 to 310,

"recovery order" means an order made under section 266,

"respondent" means—

(a)   where proceedings are brought by the enforcement authority by virtue of Chapter 2, the person against whom the proceedings are brought,

(b)   where no such proceedings have been brought but the enforcement authority has applied for an interim receiving order or interim administration order, the person against whom he intends to bring such proceedings,

"share", in relation to an excepted joint owner, has the meaning given by section 270(4),

"unlawful conduct" has the meaning given by section 241,

"value" means market value.

Proceeds of Crime Act 2002 (c. 29)
Part 5 – Civil recovery of the proceeds etc. of unlawful conduct
Chapter 4 – General

191

(2) The following provisions apply for the purposes of this Part.

(3) For the purpose of deciding whether or not property was recoverable at any time (including times before commencement), it is to be assumed that this Part was in force at that and any other relevant time.

(4) Property is all property wherever situated and includes –
    (a) money,
    (b) all forms of property, real or personal, heritable or moveable,
    (c) things in action and other intangible or incorporeal property.

(5) Any reference to a person's property (whether expressed as a reference to the property he holds or otherwise) is to be read as follows.

(6) In relation to land, it is a reference to any interest which he holds in the land.

(7) In relation to property other than land, it is a reference –
    (a) to the property (if it belongs to him), or
    (b) to any other interest which he holds in the property.

(8) References to the satisfaction of the enforcement authority's right to recover property obtained through unlawful conduct are to be read in accordance with section 279.

(9) Proceedings against any person for an offence are concluded when –
    (a) the person is convicted or acquitted,
    (b) the prosecution is discontinued or, in Scotland, the trial diet is deserted simpliciter, or
    (c) the jury is discharged without a finding.

PART 6

REVENUE FUNCTIONS

General functions

317 Director's general Revenue functions

(1) For the purposes of this section the qualifying condition is that the Director has reasonable grounds to suspect that –
    (a) income arising or a gain accruing to a person in respect of a chargeable period is chargeable to income tax or is a chargeable gain (as the case may be) and arises or accrues as a result of the person's or another's criminal conduct (whether wholly or partly and whether directly or indirectly), or
    (b) a company is chargeable to corporation tax on its profits arising in respect of a chargeable period and the profits arise as a result of the company's or another person's criminal conduct (whether wholly or partly and whether directly or indirectly).

(2) If the qualifying condition is satisfied the Director may serve on the Commissioners of Inland Revenue (the Board) a notice which –
    (a) specifies the person or the company (as the case may be) and the period, and

(b)   states that the Director intends to carry out, in relation to the person or the company (as the case may be) and in respect of the period, such of the general Revenue functions as are specified in the notice.

(3)   Service of a notice under subsection (2) vests in the Director, in relation to the person or the company (as the case may be) and in respect of the period, such of the general Revenue functions as are specified in the notice; but this is subject to section 318.

(4)   The Director—

    (a)   may at any time serve on the Board a notice of withdrawal of the notice under subsection (2);

    (b)   must serve such a notice of withdrawal on the Board if the qualifying condition ceases to be satisfied.

(5)   A notice under subsection (2) and a notice of withdrawal under subsection (4) may be in respect of one or more periods.

(6)   Service of a notice under subsection (4) divests the Director of the functions concerned in relation to the person or the company (as the case may be) and in respect of the period or periods specified in the notice.

(7)   The vesting of a function in the Director under this section does not divest the Board or an officer of the Board of the function.

(8)   If—

    (a)   apart from this section the Board's authorisation would be required for the exercise of a function, and

    (b)   the function is vested in the Director under this section,

the authorisation is not required in relation to the function as so vested.

(9)   It is immaterial whether a chargeable period or any part of it falls before or after the passing of this Act.

318   Revenue functions regarding employment

(1)   Subsection (2) applies if—

    (a)   the Director serves a notice or notices under section 317(2) in relation to a company and in respect of a period or periods, and

    (b)   the company is an employer.

(2)   The general Revenue functions vested in the Director do not include functions relating to any requirement which—

    (a)   is imposed on the company in its capacity as employer, and

    (b)   relates to a year of assessment which does not fall wholly within the period or periods.

(3)   Subsection (4) applies if—

    (a)   the Director serves a notice or notices under section 317(2) in relation to an individual and in respect of a year or years of assessment, and

    (b)   the individual is a self-employed earner.

(4)   The general Revenue functions vested in the Director do not include functions relating to any liability to pay Class 2 contributions in respect of a period which does not fall wholly within the year or years of assessment.

(5)   In this section in its application to Great Britain—

    (a)   "self-employed earner" has the meaning given by section 2(1)(b) of the Social Security Contributions and Benefits Act 1992 (c. 4);

    (b)   "Class 2 contributions" must be construed in accordance with section 1(2)(c) of that Act.

(6)   In this section in its application to Northern Ireland —

    (a)   "self-employed earner" has the meaning given by section 2(1)(b) of the Social Security Contributions and Benefits (Northern Ireland) Act 1992 (c. 7);

    (b)   "Class 2 contributions" must be construed in accordance with section 1(2)(c) of that Act.

319 Source of income

(1)   For the purpose of the exercise by the Director of any function vested in him by virtue of this Part it is immaterial that he cannot identify a source for any income.

(2)   An assessment made by the Director under section 29 of the Taxes Management Act 1970 (c. 9) (assessment where loss of tax discovered) in respect of income charged to tax under Case 6 of Schedule D must not be reduced or quashed only because it does not specify (to any extent) the source of the income.

(3)   If the Director serves on the Board a notice of withdrawal under section 317(4), any assessment made by him under section 29 of the Taxes Management Act 1970 is invalid to the extent that it does not specify a source for the income.

(4)   Subsections (2) and (3) apply in respect of years of assessment whenever occurring.

320 Appeals

(1)   An appeal in respect of the exercise by the Director of general Revenue functions shall be to the Special Commissioners.

(2)   The Presiding Special Commissioner may nominate one or more assessors to assist the Special Commissioners in any appeal to be heard by them in respect of the exercise by the Director of any of his Revenue functions.

(3)   An assessor nominated under subsection (2) —

    (a)   must have special knowledge and experience of the matter to which the appeal relates, and

    (b)   must be selected from a panel of persons appointed for the purposes of this section by the Lord Chancellor after consultation with the Scottish Ministers.

(4)   Regulations made under section 56B of the Taxes Management Act 1970 may include provision as to the manner in which an assessor nominated under subsection (2) is to assist the Special Commissioners.

(5)   The remuneration of an assessor nominated under subsection (2) must be paid by the Lord Chancellor and must be at such rate as he decides.

Inheritance tax functions

321   Director's functions: transfers of value

(1)   For the purposes of this section the qualifying condition is that the Director has
       reasonable grounds to suspect that—

       (a)   there has been a transfer of value within the meaning of the Inheritance
              Tax Act 1984 (c. 51), and

       (b)   the value transferred by it is attributable (in whole or part) to criminal
              property.

(2)   If the qualifying condition is satisfied the Director may serve on the Board a
       notice which—

       (a)   specifies the transfer of value, and

       (b)   states that the Director intends to carry out the Revenue inheritance tax
              functions in relation to the transfer.

(3)   Service of a notice under subsection (2) vests in the Director the Revenue
       inheritance tax functions in relation to the transfer.

(4)   The Director—

       (a)   may at any time serve on the Board a notice of withdrawal of the notice
              under subsection (2);

       (b)   must serve such a notice of withdrawal on the Board if the qualifying
              condition ceases to be satisfied.

(5)   Service of a notice under subsection (4) divests the Director of the Revenue
       inheritance tax functions in relation to the transfer.

(6)   The vesting of a function in the Director under this section does not divest the
       Board or an officer of the Board of the function.

(7)   It is immaterial whether a transfer of value is suspected to have occurred before
       or after the passing of this Act.

322   Director's functions: certain settlements

(1)   For the purposes of this section the qualifying condition is that the Director has
       reasonable grounds to suspect that—

       (a)   all or part of the property comprised in a settlement is relevant
              property for the purposes of Chapter 3 of Part 3 of the Inheritance Tax
              Act 1984 (settlements without interest in possession), and

       (b)   the relevant property is (in whole or part) criminal property.

(2)   If the qualifying condition is satisfied the Director may serve on the Board a
       notice which—

       (a)   specifies the settlement concerned,

       (b)   states that the Director intends to carry out the Revenue inheritance tax
              functions in relation to the settlement, and

       (c)   states the period for which he intends to carry them out.

(3)   Service of a notice under subsection (2) vests in the Director the Revenue
       inheritance tax functions in relation to the settlement for the period.

(4)   The Director—

>   (a)   may at any time serve on the Board a notice of withdrawal of the notice under subsection (2);
>
>   (b)   must serve such a notice of withdrawal on the Board if the qualifying condition ceases to be satisfied.

(5)   Service of a notice under subsection (4) divests the Director of the Revenue inheritance tax functions in relation to the settlement for the period.

(6)   The vesting of a function in the Director under this section does not divest the Board or an officer of the Board of the function.

(7)   It is immaterial whether the settlement is commenced or a charge to tax arises or a period or any part of it falls before or after the passing of this Act.

General

323   Functions

(1)   The general Revenue functions are such of the functions vested in the Board or in an officer of the Board as relate to any of the following matters —
>   (a)   income tax;
>   (b)   capital gains tax;
>   (c)   corporation tax;
>   (d)   national insurance contributions;
>   (e)   statutory sick pay;
>   (f)   statutory maternity pay;
>   (g)   statutory paternity pay;
>   (h)   statutory adoption pay;
>   (i)   student loans.

(2)   The Revenue inheritance tax functions are such functions vested in the Board or in an officer of the Board as relate to inheritance tax.

(3)   But the general Revenue functions and the Revenue inheritance tax functions do not include any of the following functions —
>   (a)   functions relating to the making of subordinate legislation (within the meaning given by section 21(1) of the Interpretation Act 1978 (c. 30));
>   (b)   the function of the prosecution of offences;
>   (c)   the function of authorising an officer for the purposes of section 20BA of the Taxes Management Act 1970 (c. 9) (orders for delivery of documents);
>   (d)   the function of giving information under that section;
>   (e)   the function of approving an officer's application for the purposes of section 20C of the Taxes Management Act 1970 (warrant to enter and search premises);
>   (f)   the function of applying under that section.

(4)   For the purposes of this section in its application to Great Britain —
>   (a)   national insurance contributions are contributions payable under Part 1 of the Social Security Contributions and Benefits Act 1992 (c. 4);
>   (b)   "statutory sick pay" must be construed in accordance with section 151(1) of that Act;

(c)　"statutory maternity pay" must be construed in accordance with section 164(1) of that Act;

(d)　"statutory paternity pay" must be construed in accordance with section 171ZA of that Act;

(e)　"statutory adoption pay" must be construed in accordance with section 171ZL of that Act;

(f)　"student loans" must be construed in accordance with the Education (Student Loans) (Repayment) Regulations 2000 (S.I. 2000/944).

(5)　For the purposes of this section in its application to Northern Ireland –

(a)　national insurance contributions are contributions payable under Part 1 of the Social Security Contributions and Benefits (Northern Ireland) Act 1992 (c. 7);

(b)　"statutory sick pay" must be construed in accordance with section 147(1) of that Act;

(c)　"statutory maternity pay" must be construed in accordance with section 160(1) of that Act;

(d)　"statutory paternity pay" must be construed in accordance with any Northern Ireland legislation which corresponds to Part 12ZA of the Social Security Contributions and Benefits Act 1992;

(e)　"statutory adoption pay" must be construed in accordance with any Northern Ireland legislation which corresponds to Part 12ZB of that Act;

(f)　"student loans" must be construed in accordance with the Education (Student Loans) (Repayment) Regulations (Northern Ireland) 2000 (S.R. 2000/121).

324　Exercise of Revenue functions

(1)　This section applies in relation to the exercise by the Director of –
　　(a)　general Revenue functions;
　　(b)　Revenue inheritance tax functions.

(2)　Paragraph (b) of section 1(6) does not apply.

(3)　The Director must apply –
　　(a)　any interpretation of the law which has been published by the Board;
　　(b)　any concession which has been published by the Board and which is available generally to any person falling within its terms.

(4)　The Director must also take account of any material published by the Board which does not fall within subsection (3).

(5)　The Director must provide the Board with such documents and information as they consider appropriate.

(6)　"Concession" includes any practice, interpretation or other statement in the nature of a concession.

325　Declarations

(1)　As soon as practicable after the appointment of a person as the Director he must make a declaration in the form set out in Schedule 8 before a member of the Board.

(2) Every member of the staff of the Agency who is authorised under section 1(6)(a) to carry out any of the functions of the Director under this Part must, as soon as practicable after being so authorised, make a declaration in the form set out in Schedule 8 before a person nominated by the Director for the purpose.

326 Interpretation

(1) Criminal conduct is conduct which —
    (a) constitutes an offence in any part of the United Kingdom, or
    (b) would constitute an offence in any part of the United Kingdom if it occurred there.

(2) But criminal conduct does not include conduct constituting an offence relating to a matter under the care and management of the Board.

(3) In applying subsection (1) it is immaterial whether conduct occurred before or after the passing of this Act.

(4) Property is criminal property if it constitutes a person's benefit from criminal conduct or it represents such a benefit (in whole or part and whether directly or indirectly); and it is immaterial —
    (a) who carried out the conduct;
    (b) who benefited from it.

(5) A person benefits from conduct if he obtains property as a result of or in connection with the conduct.

(6) If a person obtains a pecuniary advantage as a result of or in connection with conduct, he is to be taken to obtain as a result of or in connection with the conduct a sum of money equal to the value of the pecuniary advantage.

(7) References to property or a pecuniary advantage obtained in connection with conduct include references to property or a pecuniary advantage obtained in both that connection and some other.

(8) If a person benefits from conduct his benefit is the property obtained as a result of or in connection with the conduct.

(9) Property is all property wherever situated and includes —
    (a) money;
    (b) all forms of property, real or personal, heritable or moveable;
    (c) things in action and other intangible or incorporeal property.

(10) The following rules apply in relation to property —
    (a) property is obtained by a person if he obtains an interest in it;
    (b) references to an interest, in relation to land in England and Wales or Northern Ireland, are to any legal estate or equitable interest or power;
    (c) references to an interest, in relation to land in Scotland, are to any estate, interest, servitude or other heritable right in or over land, including a heritable security;
    (d) references to an interest, in relation to property other than land, include references to a right (including a right to possession).

(11) Any reference to an officer of the Board includes a reference to —
    (a) a collector of taxes;
    (b) an inspector of taxes.

(12)   Expressions used in this Part and in the Taxes Acts have the same meaning as
       in the Taxes Acts (within the meaning given by section 118 of the Taxes
       Management Act 1970 (c. 9)).

(13)   This section applies for the purposes of this Part.

PART 7

MONEY LAUNDERING

Offences

327   Concealing etc

(1)   A person commits an offence if he—
      (a)   conceals criminal property;
      (b)   disguises criminal property;
      (c)   converts criminal property;
      (d)   transfers criminal property;
      (e)   removes criminal property from England and Wales or from Scotland
            or from Northern Ireland.

(2)   But a person does not commit such an offence if—
      (a)   he makes an authorised disclosure under section 338 and (if the
            disclosure is made before he does the act mentioned in subsection (1))
            he has the appropriate consent;
      (b)   he intended to make such a disclosure but had a reasonable excuse for
            not doing so;
      (c)   the act he does is done in carrying out a function he has relating to the
            enforcement of any provision of this Act or of any other enactment
            relating to criminal conduct or benefit from criminal conduct.

(3)   Concealing or disguising criminal property includes concealing or disguising
      its nature, source, location, disposition, movement or ownership or any rights
      with respect to it.

328   Arrangements

(1)   A person commits an offence if he enters into or becomes concerned in an
      arrangement which he knows or suspects facilitates (by whatever means) the
      acquisition, retention, use or control of criminal property by or on behalf of
      another person.

(2)   But a person does not commit such an offence if—
      (a)   he makes an authorised disclosure under section 338 and (if the
            disclosure is made before he does the act mentioned in subsection (1))
            he has the appropriate consent;
      (b)   he intended to make such a disclosure but had a reasonable excuse for
            not doing so;
      (c)   the act he does is done in carrying out a function he has relating to the
            enforcement of any provision of this Act or of any other enactment
            relating to criminal conduct or benefit from criminal conduct.

329 Acquisition, use and possession

(1) A person commits an offence if he—
    (a) acquires criminal property;
    (b) uses criminal property;
    (c) has possession of criminal property.

(2) But a person does not commit such an offence if—
    (a) he makes an authorised disclosure under section 338 and (if the disclosure is made before he does the act mentioned in subsection (1)) he has the appropriate consent;
    (b) he intended to make such a disclosure but had a reasonable excuse for not doing so;
    (c) he acquired or used or had possession of the property for adequate consideration;
    (d) the act he does is done in carrying out a function he has relating to the enforcement of any provision of this Act or of any other enactment relating to criminal conduct or benefit from criminal conduct.

(3) For the purposes of this section—
    (a) a person acquires property for inadequate consideration if the value of the consideration is significantly less than the value of the property;
    (b) a person uses or has possession of property for inadequate consideration if the value of the consideration is significantly less than the value of the use or possession;
    (c) the provision by a person of goods or services which he knows or suspects may help another to carry out criminal conduct is not consideration.

330 Failure to disclose: regulated sector

(1) A person commits an offence if each of the following three conditions is satisfied.

(2) The first condition is that he—
    (a) knows or suspects, or
    (b) has reasonable grounds for knowing or suspecting,
that another person is engaged in money laundering.

(3) The second condition is that the information or other matter—
    (a) on which his knowledge or suspicion is based, or
    (b) which gives reasonable grounds for such knowledge or suspicion,
came to him in the course of a business in the regulated sector.

(4) The third condition is that he does not make the required disclosure as soon as is practicable after the information or other matter comes to him.

(5) The required disclosure is a disclosure of the information or other matter—
    (a) to a nominated officer or a person authorised for the purposes of this Part by the Director General of the National Criminal Intelligence Service;
    (b) in the form and manner (if any) prescribed for the purposes of this subsection by order under section 339.

(6) But a person does not commit an offence under this section if—

- (a) he has a reasonable excuse for not disclosing the information or other matter;
- (b) he is a professional legal adviser and the information or other matter came to him in privileged circumstances;
- (c) subsection (7) applies to him.

(7) This subsection applies to a person if—
- (a) he does not know or suspect that another person is engaged in money laundering, and
- (b) he has not been provided by his employer with such training as is specified by the Secretary of State by order for the purposes of this section.

(8) In deciding whether a person committed an offence under this section the court must consider whether he followed any relevant guidance which was at the time concerned—
- (a) issued by a supervisory authority or any other appropriate body,
- (b) approved by the Treasury, and
- (c) published in a manner it approved as appropriate in its opinion to bring the guidance to the attention of persons likely to be affected by it.

(9) A disclosure to a nominated officer is a disclosure which—
- (a) is made to a person nominated by the alleged offender's employer to receive disclosures under this section, and
- (b) is made in the course of the alleged offender's employment and in accordance with the procedure established by the employer for the purpose.

(10) Information or other matter comes to a professional legal adviser in privileged circumstances if it is communicated or given to him—
- (a) by (or by a representative of) a client of his in connection with the giving by the adviser of legal advice to the client,
- (b) by (or by a representative of) a person seeking legal advice from the adviser, or
- (c) by a person in connection with legal proceedings or contemplated legal proceedings.

(11) But subsection (10) does not apply to information or other matter which is communicated or given with the intention of furthering a criminal purpose.

(12) Schedule 9 has effect for the purpose of determining what is—
- (a) a business in the regulated sector;
- (b) a supervisory authority.

(13) An appropriate body is any body which regulates or is representative of any trade, profession, business or employment carried on by the alleged offender.

331 Failure to disclose: nominated officers in the regulated sector

(1) A person nominated to receive disclosures under section 330 commits an offence if the conditions in subsections (2) to (4) are satisfied.

(2) The first condition is that he—
- (a) knows or suspects, or
- (b) has reasonable grounds for knowing or suspecting,

that another person is engaged in money laundering.

(3)   The second condition is that the information or other matter —
    (a)   on which his knowledge or suspicion is based, or
    (b)   which gives reasonable grounds for such knowledge or suspicion,
came to him in consequence of a disclosure made under section 330.

(4)   The third condition is that he does not make the required disclosure as soon as is practicable after the information or other matter comes to him.

(5)   The required disclosure is a disclosure of the information or other matter —
    (a)   to a person authorised for the purposes of this Part by the Director General of the National Criminal Intelligence Service;
    (b)   in the form and manner (if any) prescribed for the purposes of this subsection by order under section 339.

(6)   But a person does not commit an offence under this section if he has a reasonable excuse for not disclosing the information or other matter.

(7)   In deciding whether a person committed an offence under this section the court must consider whether he followed any relevant guidance which was at the time concerned —
    (a)   issued by a supervisory authority or any other appropriate body,
    (b)   approved by the Treasury, and
    (c)   published in a manner it approved as appropriate in its opinion to bring the guidance to the attention of persons likely to be affected by it.

(8)   Schedule 9 has effect for the purpose of determining what is a supervisory authority.

(9)   An appropriate body is a body which regulates or is representative of a trade, profession, business or employment.

332   Failure to disclose: other nominated officers

(1)   A person nominated to receive disclosures under section 337 or 338 commits an offence if the conditions in subsections (2) to (4) are satisfied.

(2)   The first condition is that he knows or suspects that another person is engaged in money laundering.

(3)   The second condition is that the information or other matter on which his knowledge or suspicion is based came to him in consequence of a disclosure made under section 337 or 338.

(4)   The third condition is that he does not make the required disclosure as soon as is practicable after the information or other matter comes to him.

(5)   The required disclosure is a disclosure of the information or other matter —
    (a)   to a person authorised for the purposes of this Part by the Director General of the National Criminal Intelligence Service;
    (b)   in the form and manner (if any) prescribed for the purposes of this subsection by order under section 339.

(6)   But a person does not commit an offence under this section if he has a reasonable excuse for not disclosing the information or other matter.

333   Tipping off

(1)   A person commits an offence if —

    (a)   he knows or suspects that a disclosure falling within section 337 or 338 has been made, and

    (b)   he makes a disclosure which is likely to prejudice any investigation which might be conducted following the disclosure referred to in paragraph (a).

(2)   But a person does not commit an offence under subsection (1) if —

    (a)   he did not know or suspect that the disclosure was likely to be prejudicial as mentioned in subsection (1);

    (b)   the disclosure is made in carrying out a function he has relating to the enforcement of any provision of this Act or of any other enactment relating to criminal conduct or benefit from criminal conduct;

    (c)   he is a professional legal adviser and the disclosure falls within subsection (3).

(3)   A disclosure falls within this subsection if it is a disclosure —

    (a)   to (or to a representative of) a client of the professional legal adviser in connection with the giving by the adviser of legal advice to the client, or

    (b)   to any person in connection with legal proceedings or contemplated legal proceedings.

(4)   But a disclosure does not fall within subsection (3) if it is made with the intention of furthering a criminal purpose.

334   Penalties

(1)   A person guilty of an offence under section 327, 328 or 329 is liable —

    (a)   on summary conviction, to imprisonment for a term not exceeding six months or to a fine not exceeding the statutory maximum or to both, or

    (b)   on conviction on indictment, to imprisonment for a term not exceeding 14 years or to a fine or to both.

(2)   A person guilty of an offence under section 330, 331, 332 or 333 is liable —

    (a)   on summary conviction, to imprisonment for a term not exceeding six months or to a fine not exceeding the statutory maximum or to both, or

    (b)   on conviction on indictment, to imprisonment for a term not exceeding five years or to a fine or to both.

Consent

335   Appropriate consent

(1)   The apropriate consent is —

    (a)   the consent of a nominated officer to do a prohibited act if an authorised disclosure is made to the nominated officer;

    (b)   the consent of a constable to do a prohibited act if an authorised disclosure is made to a constable;

    (c)   the consent of a customs officer to do a prohibited act if an authorised disclosure is made to a customs officer.

(2)   A person must be treated as having the appropriate consent if —

      (a) he makes an authorised disclosure to a constable or a customs officer, and

      (b) the condition in subsection (3) or the condition in subsection (4) is satisfied.

(3)   The condition is that before the end of the notice period he does not receive notice from a constable or customs officer that consent to the doing of the act is refused.

(4)   The condition is that—

      (a) before the end of the notice period he receives notice from a constable or customs officer that consent to the doing of the act is refused, and

      (b) the moratorium period has expired.

(5)   The notice period is the period of seven working days starting with the first working day after the person makes the disclosure.

(6)   The moratorium period is the period of 31 days starting with the day on which the person receives notice that consent to the doing of the act is refused.

(7)   A working day is a day other than a Saturday, a Sunday, Christmas Day, Good Friday or a day which is a bank holiday under the Banking and Financial Dealings Act 1971 (c. 80) in the part of the United Kingdom in which the person is when he makes the disclosure.

(8)   References to a prohibited act are to an act mentioned in section 327(1), 328(1) or 329(1) (as the case may be).

(9)   A nominated officer is a person nominated to receive disclosures under section 338.

(10) Subsections (1) to (4) apply for the purposes of this Part.

336   Nominated officer: consent

(1)   A nominated officer must not give the appropriate consent to the doing of a prohibited act unless the condition in subsection (2), the condition in subsection (3) or the condition in subsection (4) is satisfied.

(2)   The condition is that—

      (a) he makes a disclosure that property is criminal property to a person authorised for the purposes of this Part by the Director General of the National Criminal Intelligence Service, and

      (b) such a person gives consent to the doing of the act.

(3)   The condition is that—

      (a) he makes a disclosure that property is criminal property to a person authorised for the purposes of this Part by the Director General of the National Criminal Intelligence Service, and

      (b) before the end of the notice period he does not receive notice from such a person that consent to the doing of the act is refused.

(4)   The condition is that—

      (a) he makes a disclosure that property is criminal property to a person authorised for the purposes of this Part by the Director General of the National Criminal Intelligence Service,

    (b)   before the end of the notice period he receives notice from such a person that consent to the doing of the act is refused, and

    (c)   the moratorium period has expired.

(5)   A person who is a nominated officer commits an offence if—

    (a)   he gives consent to a prohibited act in circumstances where none of the conditions in subsections (2), (3) and (4) is satisfied, and

    (b)   he knows or suspects that the act is a prohibited act.

(6)   A person guilty of such an offence is liable—

    (a)   on summary conviction, to imprisonment for a term not exceeding six months or to a fine not exceeding the statutory maximum or to both, or

    (b)   on conviction on indictment, to imprisonment for a term not exceeding five years or to a fine or to both.

(7)   The notice period is the period of seven working days starting with the first working day after the nominated officer makes the disclosure.

(8)   The moratorium period is the period of 31 days starting with the day on which the nominated officer is given notice that consent to the doing of the act is refused.

(9)   A working day is a day other than a Saturday, a Sunday, Christmas Day, Good Friday or a day which is a bank holiday under the Banking and Financial Dealings Act 1971 (c. 80) in the part of the United Kingdom in which the nominated officer is when he gives the appropriate consent.

(10)   References to a prohibited act are to an act mentioned in section 327(1), 328(1) or 329(1) (as the case may be).

(11)   A nominated officer is a person nominated to receive disclosures under section 338.

Disclosures

337   Protected disclosures

(1)   A disclosure which satisfies the following three conditions is not to be taken to breach any restriction on the disclosure of information (however imposed).

(2)   The first condition is that the information or other matter disclosed came to the person making the disclosure (the discloser) in the course of his trade, profession, business or employment.

(3)   The second condition is that the information or other matter—

    (a)   causes the discloser to know or suspect, or

    (b)   gives him reasonable grounds for knowing or suspecting,

that another person is engaged in money laundering.

(4)   The third condition is that the disclosure is made to a constable, a customs officer or a nominated officer as soon as is practicable after the information or other matter comes to the discloser.

(5)   A disclosure to a nominated officer is a disclosure which—

    (a)   is made to a person nominated by the discloser's employer to receive disclosures under this section, and

(b)   is made in the course of the discloser's employment and in accordance with the procedure established by the employer for the purpose.

338   Authorised disclosures

(1)   For the purposes of this Part a disclosure is authorised if —

  (a)   it is a disclosure to a constable, a customs officer or a nominated officer by the alleged offender that property is criminal property,

  (b)   it is made in the form and manner (if any) prescribed for the purposes of this subsection by order under section 339, and

  (c)   the first or second condition set out below is satisfied.

(2)   The first condition is that the disclosure is made before the alleged offender does the prohibited act.

(3)   The second condition is that —

  (a)   the disclosure is made after the alleged offender does the prohibited act,

  (b)   there is a good reason for his failure to make the disclosure before he did the act, and

  (c)   the disclosure is made on his own initiative and as soon as it is practicable for him to make it.

(4)   An authorised disclosure is not to be taken to breach any restriction on the disclosure of information (however imposed).

(5)   A disclosure to a nominated officer is a disclosure which —

  (a)   is made to a person nominated by the alleged offender's employer to receive authorised disclosures, and

  (b)   is made in the course of the alleged offender's employment and in accordance with the procedure established by the employer for the purpose.

(6)   References to the prohibited act are to an act mentioned in section 327(1), 328(1) or 329(1) (as the case may be).

339   Form and manner of disclosures

(1)   The Secretary of State may by order prescribe the form and manner in which a disclosure under section 330, 331, 332 or 338 must be made.

(2)   An order under this section may also provide that the form may include a request to the discloser to provide additional information specified in the form.

(3)   The additional information must be information which is necessary to enable the person to whom the disclosure is made to decide whether to start a money laundering investigation.

(4)   A disclosure made in pursuance of a request under subsection (2) is not to be taken to breach any restriction on the disclosure of information (however imposed).

(5)   The discloser is the person making a disclosure mentioned in subsection (1).

(6)   Money laundering investigation must be construed in accordance with section 341(4).

(7) Subsection (2) does not apply to a disclosure made to a nominated officer.

340 Interpretation

(1) This section applies for the purposes of this Part.

(2) Criminal conduct is conduct which—
  (a) constitutes an offence in any part of the United Kingdom, or
  (b) would constitute an offence in any part of the United Kingdom if it occurred there.

(3) Property is criminal property if—
  (a) it constitutes a person's benefit from criminal conduct or it represents such a benefit (in whole or part and whether directly or indirectly), and
  (b) the alleged offender knows or suspects that it constitutes or represents such a benefit.

(4) It is immaterial—
  (a) who carried out the conduct;
  (b) who benefited from it;
  (c) whether the conduct occurred before or after the passing of this Act.

(5) A person benefits from conduct if he obtains property as a result of or in connection with the conduct.

(6) If a person obtains a pecuniary advantage as a result of or in connection with conduct, he is to be taken to obtain as a result of or in connection with the conduct a sum of money equal to the value of the pecuniary advantage.

(7) References to property or a pecuniary advantage obtained in connection with conduct include references to property or a pecuniary advantage obtained in both that connection and some other.

(8) If a person benefits from conduct his benefit is the property obtained as a result of or in connection with the conduct.

(9) Property is all property wherever situated and includes—
  (a) money;
  (b) all forms of property, real or personal, heritable or moveable;
  (c) things in action and other intangible or incorporeal property.

(10) The following rules apply in relation to property—
  (a) property is obtained by a person if he obtains an interest in it;
  (b) references to an interest, in relation to land in England and Wales or Northern Ireland, are to any legal estate or equitable interest or power;
  (c) references to an interest, in relation to land in Scotland, are to any estate, interest, servitude or other heritable right in or over land, including a heritable security;
  (d) references to an interest, in relation to property other than land, include references to a right (including a right to possession).

(11) Money laundering is an act which—
  (a) constitutes an offence under section 327, 328 or 329,

> (b) constitutes an attempt, conspiracy or incitement to commit an offence specified in paragraph (a),
>
> (c) constitutes aiding, abetting, counselling or procuring the commission of an offence specified in paragraph (a), or
>
> (d) would constitute an offence specified in paragraph (a), (b) or (c) if done in the United Kingdom.

(12) For the purposes of a disclosure to a nominated officer—

> (a) references to a person's employer include any body, association or organisation (including a voluntary organisation) in connection with whose activities the person exercises a function (whether or not for gain or reward), and
>
> (b) references to employment must be construed accordingly.

(13) References to a constable include references to a person authorised for the purposes of this Part by the Director General of the National Criminal Intelligence Service.

PART 8

INVESTIGATIONS

CHAPTER 1

INTRODUCTION

341 Investigations

(1) For the purposes of this Part a confiscation investigation is an investigation into—

> (a) whether a person has benefited from his criminal conduct, or
>
> (b) the extent or whereabouts of his benefit from his criminal conduct.

(2) For the purposes of this Part a civil recovery investigation is an investigation into—

> (a) whether property is recoverable property or associated property,
>
> (b) who holds the property, or
>
> (c) its extent or whereabouts.

(3) But an investigation is not a civil recovery investigation if—

> (a) proceedings for a recovery order have been started in respect of the property in question,
>
> (b) an interim receiving order applies to the property in question,
>
> (c) an interim administration order applies to the property in question, or
>
> (d) the property in question is detained under section 295.

(4) For the purposes of this Part a money laundering investigation is an investigation into whether a person has committed a money laundering offence.

342 Offences of prejudicing investigation

(1) This section applies if a person knows or suspects that an appropriate officer or (in Scotland) a proper person is acting (or proposing to act) in connection

with a confiscation investigation, a civil recovery investigation or a money laundering investigation which is being or is about to be conducted.

(2) The person commits an offence if—

   (a) he makes a disclosure which is likely to prejudice the investigation, or

   (b) he falsifies, conceals, destroys or otherwise disposes of, or causes or permits the falsification, concealment, destruction or disposal of, documents which are relevant to the investigation.

(3) A person does not commit an offence under subsection (2)(a) if—

   (a) he does not know or suspect that the disclosure is likely to prejudice the investigation,

   (b) the disclosure is made in the exercise of a function under this Act or any other enactment relating to criminal conduct or benefit from criminal conduct or in compliance with a requirement imposed under or by virtue of this Act, or

   (c) he is a professional legal adviser and the disclosure falls within subsection (4).

(4) A disclosure falls within this subsection if it is a disclosure—

   (a) to (or to a representative of) a client of the professional legal adviser in connection with the giving by the adviser of legal advice to the client, or

   (b) to any person in connection with legal proceedings or contemplated legal proceedings.

(5) But a disclosure does not fall within subsection (4) if it is made with the intention of furthering a criminal purpose.

(6) A person does not commit an offence under subsection (2)(b) if—

   (a) he does not know or suspect that the documents are relevant to the investigation, or

   (b) he does not intend to conceal any facts disclosed by the documents from any appropriate officer or (in Scotland) proper person carrying out the investigation.

(7) A person guilty of an offence under subsection (2) is liable—

   (a) on summary conviction, to imprisonment for a term not exceeding six months or to a fine not exceeding the statutory maximum or to both, or

   (b) on conviction on indictment, to imprisonment for a term not exceeding five years or to a fine or to both.

(8) For the purposes of this section—

   (a) "appropriate officer" must be construed in accordance with section 378;

   (b) "proper person" must be construed in accordance with section 412.

Proceeds of Crime Act 2002 (c. 29)
Part 8 – Investigations
Chapter 2 – England and Wales and Northern Ireland

209

CHAPTER 2

ENGLAND AND WALES AND NORTHERN IRELAND

Judges and courts

343 Judges

(1) In this Chapter references to a judge in relation to an application must be construed in accordance with this section.

(2) In relation to an application for the purposes of a confiscation investigation or a money laundering investigation a judge is –
   (a) in England and Wales, a judge entitled to exercise the jurisdiction of the Crown Court;
   (b) in Northern Ireland, a Crown Court judge.

(3) In relation to an application for the purposes of a civil recovery investigation a judge is a judge of the High Court.

344 Courts

In this Chapter references to the court are to –
   (a) the Crown Court, in relation to an order for the purposes of a confiscation investigation or a money laundering investigation;
   (b) the High Court, in relation to an order for the purposes of a civil recovery investigation.

Production orders

345 Production orders

(1) A judge may, on an application made to him by an appropriate officer, make a production order if he is satisfied that each of the requirements for the making of the order is fulfilled.

(2) The application for a production order must state that –
   (a) a person specified in the application is subject to a confiscation investigation or a money laundering investigation, or
   (b) property specified in the application is subject to a civil recovery investigation.

(3) The application must also state that –
   (a) the order is sought for the purposes of the investigation;
   (b) the order is sought in relation to material, or material of a description, specified in the application;
   (c) a person specified in the application appears to be in possession or control of the material.

(4) A production order is an order either –
   (a) requiring the person the application for the order specifies as appearing to be in possession or control of material to produce it to an appropriate officer for him to take away, or

210

Proceeds of Crime Act 2002 (c. 29)
Part 8 – Investigations
Chapter 2 – England and Wales and Northern Ireland

(b)   requiring that person to give an appropriate officer access to the material,

within the period stated in the order.

(5)   The period stated in a production order must be a period of seven days beginning with the day on which the order is made, unless it appears to the judge by whom the order is made that a longer or shorter period would be appropriate in the particular circumstances.

346   Requirements for making of production order

(1)   These are the requirements for the making of a production order.

(2)   There must be reasonable grounds for suspecting that—

(a)   in the case of a confiscation investigation, the person the application for the order specifies as being subject to the investigation has benefited from his criminal conduct;

(b)   in the case of a civil recovery investigation, the property the application for the order specifies as being subject to the investigation is recoverable property or associated property;

(c)   in the case of a money laundering investigation, the person the application for the order specifies as being subject to the investigation has committed a money laundering offence.

(3)   There must be reasonable grounds for believing that the person the application specifies as appearing to be in possession or control of the material so specified is in possession or control of it.

(4)   There must be reasonable grounds for believing that the material is likely to be of substantial value (whether or not by itself) to the investigation for the purposes of which the order is sought.

(5)   There must be reasonable grounds for believing that it is in the public interest for the material to be produced or for access to it to be given, having regard to—

(a)   the benefit likely to accrue to the investigation if the material is obtained;

(b)   the circumstances under which the person the application specifies as appearing to be in possession or control of the material holds it.

347   Order to grant entry

(1)   This section applies if a judge makes a production order requiring a person to give an appropriate officer access to material on any premises.

(2)   The judge may, on an application made to him by an appropriate officer and specifying the premises, make an order to grant entry in relation to the premises.

(3)   An order to grant entry is an order requiring any person who appears to an appropriate officer to be entitled to grant entry to the premises to allow him to enter the premises to obtain access to the material.

Proceeds of Crime Act 2002 (c. 29)
Part 8 – Investigations
Chapter 2 – England and Wales and Northern Ireland

211

348 Further provisions

(1) A production order does not require a person to produce, or give access to, privileged material.

(2) Privileged material is any material which the person would be entitled to refuse to produce on grounds of legal professional privilege in proceedings in the High Court.

(3) A production order does not require a person to produce, or give access to, excluded material.

(4) A production order has effect in spite of any restriction on the disclosure of information (however imposed).

(5) An appropriate officer may take copies of any material which is produced, or to which access is given, in compliance with a production order.

(6) Material produced in compliance with a production order may be retained for so long as it is necessary to retain it (as opposed to copies of it) in connection with the investigation for the purposes of which the order was made.

(7) But if an appropriate officer has reasonable grounds for believing that—
    (a) the material may need to be produced for the purposes of any legal proceedings, and
    (b) it might otherwise be unavailable for those purposes,
    it may be retained until the proceedings are concluded.

349 Computer information

(1) This section applies if any of the material specified in an application for a production order consists of information contained in a computer.

(2) If the order is an order requiring a person to produce the material to an appropriate officer for him to take away, it has effect as an order to produce the material in a form in which it can be taken away by him and in which it is visible and legible.

(3) If the order is an order requiring a person to give an appropriate officer access to the material, it has effect as an order to give him access to the material in a form in which it is visible and legible.

350 Government departments

(1) A production order may be made in relation to material in the possession or control of an authorised government department.

(2) An order so made may require any officer of the department (whether named in the order or not) who may for the time being be in possession or control of the material to comply with it.

(3) An order containing such a requirement must be served as if the proceedings were civil proceedings against the department.

(4) If an order contains such a requirement—
    (a) the person on whom it is served must take all reasonable steps to bring it to the attention of the officer concerned;

212   *Proceeds of Crime Act 2002 (c. 29)*
Part 8 — Investigations
Chapter 2 — England and Wales and Northern Ireland

      (b)   any other officer of the department who is in receipt of the order must also take all reasonable steps to bring it to the attention of the officer concerned.

(5)   If the order is not brought to the attention of the officer concerned within the period stated in the order (in pursuance of section 345(4)) the person on whom it is served must report the reasons for the failure to —

      (a)   a judge entitled to exercise the jurisdiction of the Crown Court or (in Northern Ireland) a Crown Court judge, in the case of an order made for the purposes of a confiscation investigation or a money laundering investigation;

      (b)   a High Court judge, in the case of an order made for the purposes of a civil recovery investigation.

(6)   An authorised government department is a government department, or a Northern Ireland department, which is an authorised department for the purposes of the Crown Proceedings Act 1947 (c. 44).

351   Supplementary

(1)   An application for a production order or an order to grant entry may be made ex parte to a judge in chambers.

(2)   Rules of court may make provision as to the practice and procedure to be followed in connection with proceedings relating to production orders and orders to grant entry.

(3)   An application to discharge or vary a production order or an order to grant entry may be made to the court by —

      (a)   the person who applied for the order;

      (b)   any person affected by the order.

(4)   The court —

      (a)   may discharge the order;

      (b)   may vary the order.

(5)   If an accredited financial investigator, a constable or a customs officer applies for a production order or an order to grant entry, an application to discharge or vary the order need not be by the same accredited financial investigator, constable or customs officer.

(6)   References to a person who applied for a production order or an order to grant entry must be construed accordingly.

(7)   Production orders and orders to grant entry have effect as if they were orders of the court.

(8)   Subsections (2) to (7) do not apply to orders made in England and Wales for the purposes of a civil recovery investigation.

Proceeds of Crime Act 2002 (c. 29)
Part 8 — Investigations
Chapter 2 — England and Wales and Northern Ireland

213

Search and seizure warrants

352 Search and seizure warrants

(1) A judge may, on an application made to him by an appropriate officer, issue a search and seizure warrant if he is satisfied that either of the requirements for the issuing of the warrant is fulfilled.

(2) The application for a search and seizure warrant must state that —
    (a) a person specified in the application is subject to a confiscation investigation or a money laundering investigation, or
    (b) property specified in the application is subject to a civil recovery investigation.

(3) The application must also state —
    (a) that the warrant is sought for the purposes of the investigation;
    (b) that the warrant is sought in relation to the premises specified in the application;
    (c) that the warrant is sought in relation to material specified in the application, or that there are reasonable grounds for believing that there is material falling within section 353(6), (7) or (8) on the premises.

(4) A search and seizure warrant is a warrant authorising an appropriate person —
    (a) to enter and search the premises specified in the application for the warrant, and
    (b) to seize and retain any material found there which is likely to be of substantial value (whether or not by itself) to the investigation for the purposes of which the application is made.

(5) An appropriate person is —
    (a) a constable or a customs officer, if the warrant is sought for the purposes of a confiscation investigation or a money laundering investigation;
    (b) a named member of the staff of the Agency, if the warrant is sought for the purposes of a civil recovery investigation.

(6) The requirements for the issue of a search and seizure warrant are —
    (a) that a production order made in relation to material has not been complied with and there are reasonable grounds for believing that the material is on the premises specified in the application for the warrant, or
    (b) that section 353 is satisfied in relation to the warrant.

353 Requirements where production order not available

(1) This section is satisfied in relation to a search and seizure warrant if —
    (a) subsection (2) applies, and
    (b) either the first or the second set of conditions is complied with.

(2) This subsection applies if there are reasonable grounds for suspecting that —
    (a) in the case of a confiscation investigation, the person specified in the application for the warrant has benefited from his criminal conduct;

214

Proceeds of Crime Act 2002 (c. 29)
Part 8 – Investigations
Chapter 2 – England and Wales and Northern Ireland

(b) in the case of a civil recovery investigation, the property specified in the application for the warrant is recoverable property or associated property;

(c) in the case of a money laundering investigation, the person specified in the application for the warrant has committed a money laundering offence.

(3) The first set of conditions is that there are reasonable grounds for believing that—

(a) any material on the premises specified in the application for the warrant is likely to be of substantial value (whether or not by itself) to the investigation for the purposes of which the warrant is sought,

(b) it is in the public interest for the material to be obtained, having regard to the benefit likely to accrue to the investigation if the material is obtained, and

(c) it would not be appropriate to make a production order for any one or more of the reasons in subsection (4).

(4) The reasons are—

(a) that it is not practicable to communicate with any person against whom the production order could be made;

(b) that it is not practicable to communicate with any person who would be required to comply with an order to grant entry to the premises;

(c) that the investigation might be seriously prejudiced unless an appropriate person is able to secure immediate access to the material.

(5) The second set of conditions is that—

(a) there are reasonable grounds for believing that there is material on the premises specified in the application for the warrant and that the material falls within subsection (6), (7) or (8),

(b) there are reasonable grounds for believing that it is in the public interest for the material to be obtained, having regard to the benefit likely to accrue to the investigation if the material is obtained, and

(c) any one or more of the requirements in subsection (9) is met.

(6) In the case of a confiscation investigation, material falls within this subsection if it cannot be identified at the time of the application but it—

(a) relates to the person specified in the application, the question whether he has benefited from his criminal conduct or any question as to the extent or whereabouts of his benefit from his criminal conduct, and

(b) is likely to be of substantial value (whether or not by itself) to the investigation for the purposes of which the warrant is sought.

(7) In the case of a civil recovery investigation, material falls within this subsection if it cannot be identified at the time of the application but it—

(a) relates to the property specified in the application, the question whether it is recoverable property or associated property, the question as to who holds any such property, any question as to whether the person who appears to hold any such property holds other property which is recoverable property, or any question as to the extent or whereabouts of any property mentioned in this paragraph, and

(b) is likely to be of substantial value (whether or not by itself) to the investigation for the purposes of which the warrant is sought.

Proceeds of Crime Act 2002 (c. 29)
Part 8 – Investigations
Chapter 2 – England and Wales and Northern Ireland

215

(8) In the case of a money laundering investigation, material falls within this subsection if it cannot be identified at the time of the application but it—

    (a) relates to the person specified in the application or the question whether he has committed a money laundering offence, and

    (b) is likely to be of substantial value (whether or not by itself) to the investigation for the purposes of which the warrant is sought.

(9) The requirements are—

    (a) that it is not practicable to communicate with any person entitled to grant entry to the premises;

    (b) that entry to the premises will not be granted unless a warrant is produced;

    (c) that the investigation might be seriously prejudiced unless an appropriate person arriving at the premises is able to secure immediate entry to them.

(10) An appropriate person is—

    (a) a constable or a customs officer, if the warrant is sought for the purposes of a confiscation investigation or a money laundering investigation;

    (b) a member of the staff of the Agency, if the warrant is sought for the purposes of a civil recovery investigation.

354 Further provisions: general

(1) A search and seizure warrant does not confer the right to seize privileged material.

(2) Privileged material is any material which a person would be entitled to refuse to produce on grounds of legal professional privilege in proceedings in the High Court.

(3) A search and seizure warrant does not confer the right to seize excluded material.

355 Further provisions: confiscation and money laundering

(1) This section applies to—

    (a) search and seizure warrants sought for the purposes of a confiscation investigation or a money laundering investigation, and

    (b) powers of seizure under them.

(2) In relation to such warrants and powers, the Secretary of State may make an order which applies the provisions to which subsections (3) and (4) apply subject to any specified modifications.

(3) This subsection applies to the following provisions of the Police and Criminal Evidence Act 1984 (c. 60)—

    (a) section 15 (search warrants - safeguards);

    (b) section 16 (execution of warrants);

    (c) section 21 (access and copying);

    (d) section 22 (retention).

(4) This subsection applies to the following provisions of the Police and Criminal Evidence (Northern Ireland) Order 1989 (S.I. 1989/1341 (N.I. 12))—

216 *Proceeds of Crime Act 2002 (c. 29)*
Part 8 – Investigations
Chapter 2 – England and Wales and Northern Ireland

    (a)   Article 17 (search warrants - safeguards);

    (b)   Article 18 (execution of warrants);

    (c)   Article 23 (access and copying);

    (d)   Article 24 (retention).

356 Further provisions: civil recovery

(1) This section applies to search and seizure warrants sought for the purposes of civil recovery investigations.

(2) An application for a warrant may be made ex parte to a judge in chambers.

(3) A warrant may be issued subject to conditions.

(4) A warrant continues in force until the end of the period of one month starting with the day on which it is issued.

(5) A warrant authorises the person it names to require any information which is held in a computer and is accessible from the premises specified in the application for the warrant, and which the named person believes relates to any matter relevant to the investigation, to be produced in a form—

    (a)   in which it can be taken away, and

    (b)   in which it is visible and legible.

(6) If—

    (a)   the Director gives written authority for members of staff of the Agency to accompany the person a warrant names when executing it, and

    (b)   a warrant is issued,

the authorised members have the same powers under it as the person it names.

(7) A warrant may include provision authorising a person who is exercising powers under it to do other things which—

    (a)   are specified in the warrant, and

    (b)   need to be done in order to give effect to it.

(8) Copies may be taken of any material seized under a warrant.

(9) Material seized under a warrant may be retained for so long as it is necessary to retain it (as opposed to copies of it) in connection with the investigation for the purposes of which the warrant was issued.

(10) But if the Director has reasonable grounds for believing that—

    (a)   the material may need to be produced for the purposes of any legal proceedings, and

    (b)   it might otherwise be unavailable for those purposes,

it may be retained until the proceedings are concluded.

Disclosure orders

357 Disclosure orders

(1) A judge may, on an application made to him by the Director, make a disclosure order if he is satisfied that each of the requirements for the making of the order is fulfilled.

Proceeds of Crime Act 2002 (c. 29)
Part 8 – Investigations
Chapter 2 – England and Wales and Northern Ireland

217

(2) No application for a disclosure order may be made in relation to a money laundering investigation.

(3) The application for a disclosure order must state that—

    (a) a person specified in the application is subject to a confiscation investigation which is being carried out by the Director and the order is sought for the purposes of the investigation, or

    (b) property specified in the application is subject to a civil recovery investigation and the order is sought for the purposes of the investigation.

(4) A disclosure order is an order authorising the Director to give to any person the Director considers has relevant information notice in writing requiring him to do, with respect to any matter relevant to the investigation for the purposes of which the order is sought, any or all of the following—

    (a) answer questions, either at a time specified in the notice or at once, at a place so specified;

    (b) provide information specified in the notice, by a time and in a manner so specified;

    (c) produce documents, or documents of a description, specified in the notice, either at or by a time so specified or at once, and in a manner so specified.

(5) Relevant information is information (whether or not contained in a document) which the Director considers to be relevant to the investigation.

(6) A person is not bound to comply with a requirement imposed by a notice given under a disclosure order unless evidence of authority to give the notice is produced to him.

358 Requirements for making of disclosure order

(1) These are the requirements for the making of a disclosure order.

(2) There must be reasonable grounds for suspecting that—

    (a) in the case of a confiscation investigation, the person specified in the application for the order has benefited from his criminal conduct;

    (b) in the case of a civil recovery investigation, the property specified in the application for the order is recoverable property or associated property.

(3) There must be reasonable grounds for believing that information which may be provided in compliance with a requirement imposed under the order is likely to be of substantial value (whether or not by itself) to the investigation for the purposes of which the order is sought.

(4) There must be reasonable grounds for believing that it is in the public interest for the information to be provided, having regard to the benefit likely to accrue to the investigation if the information is obtained.

359 Offences

(1) A person commits an offence if without reasonable excuse he fails to comply with a requirement imposed on him under a disclosure order.

(2) A person guilty of an offence under subsection (1) is liable on summary conviction to—

218
Proceeds of Crime Act 2002 (c. 29)
Part 8 – Investigations
Chapter 2 – England and Wales and Northern Ireland

    (a)   imprisonment for a term not exceeding six months,

    (b)   a fine not exceeding level 5 on the standard scale, or

    (c)   both.

(3)   A person commits an offence if, in purported compliance with a requirement imposed on him under a disclosure order, he—

    (a)   makes a statement which he knows to be false or misleading in a material particular, or

    (b)   recklessly makes a statement which is false or misleading in a material particular.

(4)   A person guilty of an offence under subsection (3) is liable—

    (a)   on summary conviction, to imprisonment for a term not exceeding six months or to a fine not exceeding the statutory maximum or to both, or

    (b)   on conviction on indictment, to imprisonment for a term not exceeding two years or to a fine or to both.

360   Statements

(1)   A statement made by a person in response to a requirement imposed on him under a disclosure order may not be used in evidence against him in criminal proceedings.

(2)   But subsection (1) does not apply—

    (a)   in the case of proceedings under Part 2 or 4,

    (b)   on a prosecution for an offence under section 359(1) or (3),

    (c)   on a prosecution for an offence under section 5 of the Perjury Act 1911 (c. 6) or Article 10 of the Perjury (Northern Ireland) Order 1979 (S.I. 1979/1714 (N.I. 19)) (false statements), or

    (d)   on a prosecution for some other offence where, in giving evidence, the person makes a statement inconsistent with the statement mentioned in subsection (1).

(3)   A statement may not be used by virtue of subsection (2)(d) against a person unless—

    (a)   evidence relating to it is adduced, or

    (b)   a question relating to it is asked,

by him or on his behalf in the proceedings arising out of the prosecution.

361   Further provisions

(1)   A disclosure order does not confer the right to require a person to answer any privileged question, provide any privileged information or produce any privileged document, except that a lawyer may be required to provide the name and address of a client of his.

(2)   A privileged question is a question which the person would be entitled to refuse to answer on grounds of legal professional privilege in proceedings in the High Court.

(3)   Privileged information is any information which the person would be entitled to refuse to provide on grounds of legal professional privilege in proceedings in the High Court.

Proceeds of Crime Act 2002 (c. 29)
Part 8 – Investigations
Chapter 2 – England and Wales and Northern Ireland

219

(4) Privileged material is any material which the person would be entitled to refuse to produce on grounds of legal professional privilege in proceedings in the High Court.

(5) A disclosure order does not confer the right to require a person to produce excluded material.

(6) A disclosure order has effect in spite of any restriction on the disclosure of information (however imposed).

(7) The Director may take copies of any documents produced in compliance with a requirement to produce them which is imposed under a disclosure order.

(8) Documents so produced may be retained for so long as it is necessary to retain them (as opposed to a copy of them) in connection with the investigation for the purposes of which the order was made.

(9) But if the Director has reasonable grounds for believing that –
  (a) the documents may need to be produced for the purposes of any legal proceedings, and
  (b) they might otherwise be unavailable for those purposes,
they may be retained until the proceedings are concluded.

362 Supplementary

(1) An application for a disclosure order may be made ex parte to a judge in chambers.

(2) Rules of court may make provision as to the practice and procedure to be followed in connection with proceedings relating to disclosure orders.

(3) An application to discharge or vary a disclosure order may be made to the court by –
  (a) the Director;
  (b) any person affected by the order.

(4) The court –
  (a) may discharge the order;
  (b) may vary the order.

(5) Subsections (2) to (4) do not apply to orders made in England and Wales for the purposes of a civil recovery investigation.

Customer information orders

363 Customer information orders

(1) A judge may, on an application made to him by an appropriate officer, make a customer information order if he is satisfied that each of the requirements for the making of the order is fulfilled.

(2) The application for a customer information order must state that –
  (a) a person specified in the application is subject to a confiscation investigation or a money laundering investigation, or

220   *Proceeds of Crime Act 2002 (c. 29)*
Part 8 — Investigations
Chapter 2 — England and Wales and Northern Ireland

    (b)   property specified in the application is subject to a civil recovery investigation and a person specified in the application appears to hold the property.

(3)   The application must also state that —

    (a)   the order is sought for the purposes of the investigation;

    (b)   the order is sought against the financial institution or financial institutions specified in the application.

(4)   An application for a customer information order may specify —

    (a)   all financial institutions,

    (b)   a particular description, or particular descriptions, of financial institutions, or

    (c)   a particular financial institution or particular financial institutions.

(5)   A customer information order is an order that a financial institution covered by the application for the order must, on being required to do so by notice in writing given by an appropriate officer, provide any such customer information as it has relating to the person specified in the application.

(6)   A financial institution which is required to provide information under a customer information order must provide the information to an appropriate officer in such manner, and at or by such time, as an appropriate officer requires.

(7)   If a financial institution on which a requirement is imposed by a notice given under a customer information order requires the production of evidence of authority to give the notice, it is not bound to comply with the requirement unless evidence of the authority has been produced to it.

364   Meaning of customer information

(1)   "Customer information", in relation to a person and a financial institution, is information whether the person holds, or has held, an account or accounts at the financial institution (whether solely or jointly with another) and (if so) information as to —

    (a)   the matters specified in subsection (2) if the person is an individual;

    (b)   the matters specified in subsection (3) if the person is a company or limited liability partnership or a similar body incorporated or otherwise established outside the United Kingdom.

(2)   The matters referred to in subsection (1)(a) are —

    (a)   the account number or numbers;

    (b)   the person's full name;

    (c)   his date of birth;

    (d)   his most recent address and any previous addresses;

    (e)   the date or dates on which he began to hold the account or accounts and, if he has ceased to hold the account or any of the accounts, the date or dates on which he did so;

    (f)   such evidence of his identity as was obtained by the financial institution under or for the purposes of any legislation relating to money laundering;

    (g)   the full name, date of birth and most recent address, and any previous addresses, of any person who holds, or has held, an account at the financial institution jointly with him;

Proceeds of Crime Act 2002 (c. 29)
Part 8 – Investigations
Chapter 2 – England and Wales and Northern Ireland

221

     (h)   the account number or numbers of any other account or accounts held at the financial institution to which he is a signatory and details of the person holding the other account or accounts.

(3)   The matters referred to in subsection (1)(b) are —

     (a)   the account number or numbers;

     (b)   the person's full name;

     (c)   a description of any business which the person carries on;

     (d)   the country or territory in which it is incorporated or otherwise established and any number allocated to it under the Companies Act 1985 (c. 6) or the Companies (Northern Ireland) Order 1986 (S.I. 1986/1032 (N.I. 6)) or corresponding legislation of any country or territory outside the United Kingdom;

     (e)   any number assigned to it for the purposes of value added tax in the United Kingdom;

     (f)   its registered office, and any previous registered offices, under the Companies Act 1985 or the Companies (Northern Ireland) Order 1986 (S.I. 1986/1032 (N.I. 6)) or anything similar under corresponding legislation of any country or territory outside the United Kingdom;

     (g)   its registered office, and any previous registered offices, under the Limited Liability Partnerships Act 2000 (c. 12) or anything similar under corresponding legislation of any country or territory outside Great Britain;

     (h)   the date or dates on which it began to hold the account or accounts and, if it has ceased to hold the account or any of the accounts, the date or dates on which it did so;

     (i)   such evidence of its identity as was obtained by the financial institution under or for the purposes of any legislation relating to money laundering;

     (j)   the full name, date of birth and most recent address and any previous addresses of any person who is a signatory to the account or any of the accounts.

(4)   The Secretary of State may by order provide for information of a description specified in the order —

     (a)   to be customer information, or

     (b)   no longer to be customer information.

(5)   Money laundering is an act which —

     (a)   constitutes an offence under section 327, 328 or 329 of this Act or section 18 of the Terrorism Act 2000 (c. 11), or

     (b)   would constitute an offence specified in paragraph (a) if done in the United Kingdom.

365 Requirements for making of customer information order

(1)   These are the requirements for the making of a customer information order.

(2)   In the case of a confiscation investigation, there must be reasonable grounds for suspecting that the person specified in the application for the order has benefited from his criminal conduct.

(3)   In the case of a civil recovery investigation, there must be reasonable grounds for suspecting that —

222

Proceeds of Crime Act 2002 (c. 29)
Part 8 – Investigations
Chapter 2 – England and Wales and Northern Ireland

    (a)   the property specified in the application for the order is recoverable property or associated property;

    (b)   the person specified in the application holds all or some of the property.

(4)   In the case of a money laundering investigation, there must be reasonable grounds for suspecting that the person specified in the application for the order has committed a money laundering offence.

(5)   In the case of any investigation, there must be reasonable grounds for believing that customer information which may be provided in compliance with the order is likely to be of substantial value (whether or not by itself) to the investigation for the purposes of which the order is sought.

(6)   In the case of any investigation, there must be reasonable grounds for believing that it is in the public interest for the customer information to be provided, having regard to the benefit likely to accrue to the investigation if the information is obtained.

366 Offences

(1)   A financial institution commits an offence if without reasonable excuse it fails to comply with a requirement imposed on it under a customer information order.

(2)   A financial institution guilty of an offence under subsection (1) is liable on summary conviction to a fine not exceeding level 5 on the standard scale.

(3)   A financial institution commits an offence if, in purported compliance with a customer information order, it—

    (a)   makes a statement which it knows to be false or misleading in a material particular, or

    (b)   recklessly makes a statement which is false or misleading in a material particular.

(4)   A financial institution guilty of an offence under subsection (3) is liable—

    (a)   on summary conviction, to a fine not exceeding the statutory maximum, or

    (b)   on conviction on indictment, to a fine.

367 Statements

(1)   A statement made by a financial institution in response to a customer information order may not be used in evidence against it in criminal proceedings.

(2)   But subsection (1) does not apply—

    (a)   in the case of proceedings under Part 2 or 4,

    (b)   on a prosecution for an offence under section 366(1) or (3), or

    (c)   on a prosecution for some other offence where, in giving evidence, the financial institution makes a statement inconsistent with the statement mentioned in subsection (1).

(3)   A statement may not be used by virtue of subsection (2)(c) against a financial institution unless—

    (a)   evidence relating to it is adduced, or

    (b)   a question relating to it is asked,

Proceeds of Crime Act 2002 (c. 29)
Part 8 — Investigations
Chapter 2 — England and Wales and Northern Ireland

223

by or on behalf of the financial institution in the proceedings arising out of the prosecution.

368 Disclosure of information

A customer information order has effect in spite of any restriction on the disclosure of information (however imposed).

369 Supplementary

(1) An application for a customer information order may be made ex parte to a judge in chambers.

(2) Rules of court may make provision as to the practice and procedure to be followed in connection with proceedings relating to customer information orders.

(3) An application to discharge or vary a customer information order may be made to the court by—
    (a) the person who applied for the order;
    (b) any person affected by the order.

(4) The court—
    (a) may discharge the order;
    (b) may vary the order.

(5) If an accredited financial investigator, a constable or a customs officer applies for a customer information order, an application to discharge or vary the order need not be by the same accredited financial investigator, constable or customs officer.

(6) References to a person who applied for a customer information order must be construed accordingly.

(7) An accredited financial investigator, a constable or a customs officer may not make an application for a customer information order or an application to vary such an order unless he is a senior appropriate officer or he is authorised to do so by a senior appropriate officer.

(8) Subsections (2) to (6) do not apply to orders made in England and Wales for the purposes of a civil recovery investigation.

Account monitoring orders

370 Account monitoring orders

(1) A judge may, on an application made to him by an appropriate officer, make an account monitoring order if he is satisfied that each of the requirements for the making of the order is fulfilled.

(2) The application for an account monitoring order must state that—
    (a) a person specified in the application is subject to a confiscation investigation or a money laundering investigation, or
    (b) property specified in the application is subject to a civil recovery investigation and a person specified in the application appears to hold the property.

224

Proceeds of Crime Act 2002 (c. 29)
Part 8 — Investigations
Chapter 2 — England and Wales and Northern Ireland

(3)   The application must also state that—

    (a)   the order is sought for the purposes of the investigation;

    (b)   the order is sought against the financial institution specified in the application in relation to account information of the description so specified.

(4)   Account information is information relating to an account or accounts held at the financial institution specified in the application by the person so specified (whether solely or jointly with another).

(5)   The application for an account monitoring order may specify information relating to—

    (a)   all accounts held by the person specified in the application for the order at the financial institution so specified,

    (b)   a particular description, or particular descriptions, of accounts so held, or

    (c)   a particular account, or particular accounts, so held.

(6)   An account monitoring order is an order that the financial institution specified in the application for the order must, for the period stated in the order, provide account information of the description specified in the order to an appropriate officer in the manner, and at or by the time or times, stated in the order.

(7)   The period stated in an account monitoring order must not exceed the period of 90 days beginning with the day on which the order is made.

371   Requirements for making of account monitoring order

(1)   These are the requirements for the making of an account monitoring order.

(2)   In the case of a confiscation investigation, there must be reasonable grounds for suspecting that the person specified in the application for the order has benefited from his criminal conduct.

(3)   In the case of a civil recovery investigation, there must be reasonable grounds for suspecting that—

    (a)   the property specified in the application for the order is recoverable property or associated property;

    (b)   the person specified in the application holds all or some of the property.

(4)   In the case of a money laundering investigation, there must be reasonable grounds for suspecting that the person specified in the application for the order has committed a money laundering offence.

(5)   In the case of any investigation, there must be reasonable grounds for believing that account information which may be provided in compliance with the order is likely to be of substantial value (whether or not by itself) to the investigation for the purposes of which the order is sought.

(6)   In the case of any investigation, there must be reasonable grounds for believing that it is in the public interest for the account information to be provided, having regard to the benefit likely to accrue to the investigation if the information is obtained.

Proceeds of Crime Act 2002 (c. 29)
Part 8 – Investigations
Chapter 2 – England and Wales and Northern Ireland

225

372 Statements

(1) A statement made by a financial institution in response to an account monitoring order may not be used in evidence against it in criminal proceedings.

(2) But subsection (1) does not apply —
  (a) in the case of proceedings under Part 2 or 4,
  (b) in the case of proceedings for contempt of court, or
  (c) on a prosecution for an offence where, in giving evidence, the financial institution makes a statement inconsistent with the statement mentioned in subsection (1).

(3) A statement may not be used by virtue of subsection (2)(c) against a financial institution unless —
  (a) evidence relating to it is adduced, or
  (b) a question relating to it is asked,
by or on behalf of the financial institution in the proceedings arising out of the prosecution.

373 Applications

An application for an account monitoring order may be made ex parte to a judge in chambers.

374 Disclosure of information

An account monitoring order has effect in spite of any restriction on the disclosure of information (however imposed).

375 Supplementary

(1) Rules of court may make provision as to the practice and procedure to be followed in connection with proceedings relating to account monitoring orders.

(2) An application to discharge or vary an account monitoring order may be made to the court by —
  (a) the person who applied for the order;
  (b) any person affected by the order.

(3) The court —
  (a) may discharge the order;
  (b) may vary the order.

(4) If an accredited financial investigator, a constable or a customs officer applies for an account monitoring order, an application to discharge or vary the order need not be by the same accredited financial investigator, constable or customs officer.

(5) References to a person who applied for an account monitoring order must be construed accordingly.

(6) Account monitoring orders have effect as if they were orders of the court.

226

Proceeds of Crime Act 2002 (c. 29)
Part 8 – Investigations
Chapter 2 – England and Wales and Northern Ireland

(7)   This section does not apply to orders made in England and Wales for the purposes of a civil recovery investigation.

Evidence overseas

376   Evidence overseas

(1)   This section applies if the Director is carrying out a confiscation investigation.

(2)   A judge on the application of the Director or a person subject to the investigation may issue a letter of request if he thinks that there is evidence in a country or territory outside the United Kingdom—

   (a)   that such a person has benefited from his criminal conduct, or

   (b)   of the extent or whereabouts of that person's benefit from his criminal conduct.

(3)   The Director may issue a letter of request if he thinks that there is evidence in a country or territory outside the United Kingdom—

   (a)   that a person subject to the investigation has benefited from his criminal conduct, or

   (b)   of the extent or whereabouts of that person's benefit from his criminal conduct.

(4)   A letter of request is a letter requesting assistance in obtaining outside the United Kingdom such evidence as is specified in the letter for use in the investigation.

(5)   The person issuing a letter of request must send it to the Secretary of State.

(6)   If the Secretary of State believes it is appropriate to do so he may forward a letter received under subsection (5)—

   (a)   to a court or tribunal which is specified in the letter and which exercises jurisdiction in the place where the evidence is to be obtained, or

   (b)   to an authority recognised by the government of the country or territory concerned as the appropriate authority for receiving letters of request.

(7)   But in a case of urgency the person issuing the letter of request may send it directly to the court or tribunal mentioned in subsection (6)(a).

(8)   Evidence obtained in pursuance of a letter of request must not be used—

   (a)   by any person other than the Director or a person subject to the investigation;

   (b)   for any purpose other than that for which it is obtained.

(9)   Subsection (8) does not apply if the authority mentioned in subsection (6)(b) consents to the use.

(10) Evidence includes documents and other articles.

(11) Rules of court may make provision as to the practice and procedure to be followed in connection with proceedings relating to the issue of letters of request by a judge under this section.

Proceeds of Crime Act 2002 (c. 29)
Part 8 — Investigations
Chapter 2 — England and Wales and Northern Ireland

227

Code of practice

377 Code of practice

(1)   The Secretary of State must prepare a code of practice as to the exercise by all of the following of functions they have under this Chapter —
    (a)   the Director;
    (b)   members of the staff of the Agency;
    (c)   accredited financial investigators;
    (d)   constables;
    (e)   customs officers.

(2)   After preparing a draft of the code the Secretary of State—
    (a)   must publish the draft;
    (b)   must consider any representations made to him about the draft;
    (c)   may amend the draft accordingly.

(3)   After the Secretary of State has proceeded under subsection (2) he must lay the code before Parliament.

(4)   When he has done so the Secretary of State may bring the code into operation on such day as he may appoint by order.

(5)   A person specified in subsection (1)(a) to (e) must comply with a code of practice which is in operation under this section in the exercise of any function he has under this Chapter.

(6)   If such a person fails to comply with any provision of such a code of practice he is not by reason only of that failure liable in any criminal or civil proceedings.

(7)   But the code of practice is admissible in evidence in such proceedings and a court may take account of any failure to comply with its provisions in determining any question in the proceedings.

(8)   The Secretary of State may from time to time revise a code previously brought into operation under this section; and the preceding provisions of this section apply to a revised code as they apply to the code as first prepared.

(9)   The following provisions do not apply to an appropriate officer in the exercise of any function he has under this Chapter —
    (a)   section 67(9) of the Police and Criminal Evidence Act 1984 (c. 60) (application of codes of practice under that Act to persons other than police officers);
    (b)   Article 66(8) of the Police and Criminal Evidence (Northern Ireland) Order 1989 (S.I. 1989/1341 (N.I. 12)) (which makes similar provision for Northern Ireland).

Interpretation

378 Officers

(1)   In relation to a confiscation investigation these are appropriate officers —
    (a)   the Director;
    (b)   an accredited financial investigator;

228

Proceeds of Crime Act 2002 (c. 29)
Part 8 – Investigations
Chapter 2 – England and Wales and Northern Ireland

      (c)   a constable;

      (d)   a customs officer.

(2)   In relation to a confiscation investigation these are senior appropriate officers –

      (a)   the Director;

      (b)   a police officer who is not below the rank of superintendent;

      (c)   a customs officer who is not below such grade as is designated by the Commissioners of Customs and Excise as equivalent to that rank;

      (d)   an accredited financial investigator who falls within a description specified in an order made for the purposes of this paragraph by the Secretary of State under section 453.

(3)   In relation to a civil recovery investigation the Director (and only the Director) is –

      (a)   an appropriate officer;

      (b)   a senior appropriate officer.

(4)   In relation to a money laundering investigation these are appropriate officers –

      (a)   an accredited financial investigator;

      (b)   a constable;

      (c)   a customs officer.

(5)   For the purposes of section 342, in relation to a money laundering investigation a person authorised for the purposes of money laundering investigations by the Director General of the National Criminal Intelligence Service is also an appropriate officer.

(6)   In relation to a money laundering investigation these are senior appropriate officers –

      (a)   a police officer who is not below the rank of superintendent;

      (b)   a customs officer who is not below such grade as is designated by the Commissioners of Customs and Excise as equivalent to that rank;

      (c)   an accredited financial investigator who falls within a description specified in an order made for the purposes of this paragraph by the Secretary of State under section 453.

(7)   But a person is not an appropriate officer or a senior appropriate officer in relation to a money laundering investigation if he is –

      (a)   a member of the staff of the Agency, or

      (b)   a person providing services under arrangements made by the Director.

379   Miscellaneous

"Document", "excluded material" and "premises" have the same meanings as in the Police and Criminal Evidence Act 1984 (c. 60) or (in relation to Northern Ireland) the Police and Criminal Evidence (Northern Ireland) Order 1989 (S.I. 1989/1341 (N.I. 12)).

CHAPTER 3

SCOTLAND

Production orders

380 Production orders

(1) The sheriff may, on an application made to him by the appropriate person, make a production order if he is satisfied that each of the requirements for the making of the order is fulfilled.

(2) In making a production order in relation to property subject to a civil recovery investigation, the sheriff shall act in the exercise of his civil jurisdiction.

(3) The application for a production order must state that—
   (a) a person specified in the application is subject to a confiscation investigation or a money laundering investigation, or
   (b) property specified in the application is subject to a civil recovery investigation.

(4) The application must also state that—
   (a) the order is sought for the purposes of the investigation;
   (b) the order is sought in relation to material, or material of a description, specified in the application;
   (c) a person specified in the application appears to be in possession or control of the material.

(5) A production order is an order either—
   (a) requiring the person the application for the order specifies as appearing to be in possession or control of material to produce it to a proper person for him to take away, or
   (b) requiring that person to give a proper person access to the material,
   within the period stated in the order.

(6) The period stated in a production order must be a period of seven days beginning with the day on which the order is made, unless it appears to the sheriff that a longer or shorter period would be appropriate in the particular circumstances.

381 Requirements for making of production order

(1) These are the requirements for the making of a production order.

(2) There must be reasonable grounds for suspecting that—
   (a) in the case of a confiscation investigation, the person the application for the order specifies as being subject to the investigation has benefited from his criminal conduct;
   (b) in the case of a civil recovery investigation, the property the application for the order specifies as being subject to the investigation is recoverable property or associated property;
   (c) in the case of a money laundering investigation, the person the application for the order specifies as being subject to the investigation has committed a money laundering offence.

(3)   There must be reasonable grounds for believing that the person the application specifies as appearing to be in possession or control of the material so specified is in possession or control of it.

(4)   There must be reasonable grounds for believing that the material is likely to be of substantial value (whether or not by itself) to the investigation for the purposes of which the order is sought.

(5)   There must be reasonable grounds for believing that it is in the public interest for the material to be produced or for access to it to be given, having regard to —
      (a)   the benefit likely to accrue to the investigation if the material is obtained,
      (b)   the circumstances under which the person the application specifies as appearing to be in possession or control of the material holds it.

382   Order to grant entry

(1)   This section applies if a sheriff makes a production order requiring a person to give a proper person access to material on any premises.

(2)   The sheriff may, on an application made to him by the appropriate person and specifying the premises, make an order to grant entry in relation to the premises.

(3)   An order to grant entry is an order requiring any person who appears to the appropriate person to be entitled to grant entry to the premises to allow a proper person to enter the premises to obtain access to the material.

383   Further provisions

(1)   A production order does not require a person to produce, or give access to, any items subject to legal privilege.

(2)   A production order has effect in spite of any restriction on the disclosure of information (however imposed).

(3)   A proper person may take copies of any material which is produced, or to which access is given, in compliance with a production order.

(4)   Material produced in compliance with a production order may be retained for so long as it is necessary to retain it (as opposed to copies of it) in connection with the investigation for the purposes of which the order was made.

(5)   But if a proper person has reasonable grounds for believing that —
      (a)   the material may need to be produced for the purposes of any legal proceedings, and
      (b)   it might otherwise be unavailable for those purposes,
      it may be retained until the proceedings are concluded.

384   Computer information

(1)   This section applies if any of the material specified in an application for a production order consists of information contained in a computer.

(2)   If the order is an order requiring a person to produce the material to a proper person for him to take away, it has effect as an order to produce the material in

a form in which it can be taken away by him and in which it is visible and legible.

(3) If the order is an order requiring a person to give a proper person access to the material, it has effect as an order to give him access to the material in a form in which it is visible and legible.

385 Government departments

(1) A production order may be made in relation to material in the possession or control of an authorised government department.

(2) An order so made may require any officer of the department (whether named in the order or not) who may for the time being be in possession or control of the material to comply with it.

(3) If an order contains such a requirement –
   (a) the person on whom it is served must take all reasonable steps to bring it to the attention of the officer concerned;
   (b) any other officer of the department who is in receipt of the order must also take all reasonable steps to bring it to the attention of the officer concerned.

(4) If the order is not brought to the attention of the officer concerned within the period stated in the order (in pursuance of section 380(5)) the person on whom it is served must report the reasons for the failure to –
   (a) the sheriff in the case of an order made for the purposes of a confiscation investigation or a money laundering investigation;
   (b) the sheriff exercising a civil jurisdiction in the case of an order made for the purposes of a civil recovery investigation.

(5) In this section, "authorised government department" includes a government department which is an authorised department for the purposes of the Crown Proceedings Act 1947 (c. 44) and the Scottish Administration.

386 Supplementary

(1) An application for a production order or an order to grant entry may be made ex parte to a sheriff in chambers.

(2) Provision may be made by rules of court as to the discharge and variation of production orders and orders to grant entry.

(3) Rules of court under subsection (2) relating to production orders and orders to grant entry –
   (a) made in a confiscation investigation or a money laundering investigation shall, without prejudice to section 305 of the Criminal Procedure (Scotland) Act 1995 (c. 46) be made by act of adjournal;
   (b) made in a civil recovery investigation shall, without prejudice to section 32 of the Sheriff Courts (Scotland) Act 1971 (c. 58) be made by act of sederunt.

(4) An application to discharge or vary a production order or an order to grant entry may be made to the sheriff by –
   (a) the person who applied for the order;
   (b) any person affected by the order.

(5) The sheriff may –
    (a) discharge the order;
    (b) vary the order.

Search warrants

387 Search warrants

(1) The sheriff may, on an application made to him by the appropriate person, issue a search warrant if he is satisfied that either of the requirements for the issuing of the warrant is fulfilled.

(2) In issuing a search warrant in relation to property subject to a civil recovery investigation, the sheriff shall act in the exercise of his civil jurisdiction.

(3) The application for a search warrant must state that –
    (a) a person specified in the application is subject to a confiscation investigation or a money laundering investigation, or
    (b) property specified in the application is subject to a civil recovery investigation.

(4) A search warrant is a warrant authorising a proper person –
    (a) to enter and search the premises specified in the application for the warrant, and
    (b) to seize and retain any material specified in the warrant which is found there and which is likely to be of substantial value (whether or not by itself) to the investigation for the purposes of which the application is made.

(5) The requirements for the issue of a search warrant are –
    (a) that a production order made in relation to material has not been complied with and there are reasonable grounds for believing that the material is on the premises specified in the application for the warrant, or
    (b) that section 388 is satisfied in relation to the warrant.

(6) An application for a search warrant may be made ex parte to a sheriff in chambers.

388 Requirements where production order not available

(1) This section is satisfied in relation to a search warrant if –
    (a) subsection (2) applies, and
    (b) either the first or the second set of conditions is complied with.

(2) This subsection applies if there are reasonable grounds for suspecting that –
    (a) in the case of a confiscation investigation, the person specified in the application for the warrant has benefited from his criminal conduct;
    (b) in the case of a civil recovery investigation, the property specified in the application for the warrant is recoverable property or associated property;
    (c) in the case of a money laundering investigation, the person specified in the application for the warrant has committed a money laundering offence.

(3)   The first set of conditions is that there are reasonable grounds for believing that —

(a)   any material on the premises specified in the application for the warrant is likely to be of substantial value (whether or not by itself) to the investigation for the purposes of which the warrant is sought,

(b)   it is in the public interest for the material to be obtained, having regard to the benefit likely to accrue to the investigation if the material is obtained, and

(c)   it would not be appropriate to make a production order for any one or more of the reasons in subsection (4).

(4)   The reasons are —

(a)   that it is not practicable to communicate with any person against whom the production order could be made;

(b)   that it is not practicable to communicate with any person who would be required to comply with an order to grant access to the material or to grant entry to the premises on which the material is situated;

(c)   that the investigation might be seriously prejudiced unless a proper person is able to secure immediate access to the material.

(5)   The second set of conditions is that —

(a)   there are reasonable grounds for believing that there is material on the premises specified in the application for the warrant and that the material falls within subsection (6), (7) or (8),

(b)   there are reasonable grounds for believing that it is in the public interest for the material to be obtained, having regard to the benefit likely to accrue to the investigation if the material is obtained, and

(c)   any one or more of the requirements in subsection (9) is met.

(6)   In the case of a confiscation investigation, material falls within this subsection if it cannot be identified at the time of the application but it —

(a)   relates to the person specified in the application, the question whether he has benefited from his criminal conduct or any question as to the extent or whereabouts of his benefit from his criminal conduct, and

(b)   is likely to be of substantial value (whether or not by itself) to the investigation for the purposes of which the warrant is sought.

(7)   In the case of a civil recovery investigation, material falls within this subsection if it cannot be identified at the time of the application but it —

(a)   relates to the property specified in the application, the question whether it is recoverable property or associated property, the question as to who holds any such property, any question as to whether the person who appears to hold any such property holds other property which is recoverable property, or any question as to the extent or whereabouts of any property mentioned in this paragraph, and

(b)   is likely to be of substantial value (whether or not by itself) to the investigation for the purposes of which the warrant is sought.

(8)   In the case of a money laundering investigation, material falls within this subsection if it cannot be identified at the time of the application but it —

(a)   relates to the person specified in the application or the question whether he has committed a money laundering offence, and

(b)   is likely to be of substantial value (whether or not by itself) to the investigation for the purposes of which the warrant is sought.

(9) The requirements are—

    (a) that it is not practicable to communicate with any person entitled to grant entry to the premises;

    (b) that entry to the premises will not be granted unless a warrant is produced;

    (c) that the investigation might be seriously prejudiced unless a proper person arriving at the premises is able to secure immediate entry to them.

389 Further provisions: general

A search warrant does not confer the right to seize any items subject to legal privilege.

390 Further provisions: confiscation, civil recovery and money laundering

(1) This section applies to search warrants sought for the purposes of confiscation investigations, civil recovery investigations or money laundering investigations.

(2) A warrant continues in force until the end of the period of one month starting with the day on which it is issued.

(3) A warrant authorises the person executing it to require any information which is held in a computer and is accessible from the premises specified in the application for the warrant, and which the proper person believes relates to any matter relevant to the investigation, to be produced in a form—

    (a) in which it can be taken away, and

    (b) in which it is visible and legible.

(4) Copies may be taken of any material seized under a warrant.

(5) A warrant issued in relation to a civil recovery investigation may be issued subject to conditions.

(6) A warrant issued in relation to a civil recovery investigation may include provision authorising the person executing it to do other things which—

    (a) are specified in the warrant, and

    (b) need to be done in order to give effect to it.

(7) Material seized under a warrant issued in relation to a civil recovery investigation may be retained for so long as it is necessary to retain it (as opposed to copies of it) in connection with the investigation for the purposes of which the warrant was issued.

(8) But if the Scottish Ministers have reasonable grounds for believing that—

    (a) the material may need to be produced for the purposes of any legal proceedings, and

    (b) it might otherwise be unavailable for those purposes,

it may be retained until the proceedings are concluded.

Disclosure orders

391 Disclosure orders

(1) The High Court of Justiciary, on an application made to it by the Lord Advocate in relation to confiscation investigations, or the Court of Session, on an application made to it by the Scottish Ministers in relation to civil recovery investigations, may make a disclosure order if it is satisfied that each of the requirements for the making of the order is fulfilled.

(2) No application for a disclosure order may be made in relation to a money laundering investigation.

(3) The application for a disclosure order must state that —
   (a) a person specified in the application is subject to a confiscation investigation and the order is sought for the purposes of the investigation, or
   (b) property specified in the application is subject to a civil recovery investigation and the order is sought for the purposes of the investigation.

(4) A disclosure order is an order authorising the Lord Advocate or the Scottish Ministers to give to any person the Lord Advocate considers or the Scottish Ministers consider has relevant information, notice in writing requiring him to do, with respect to any matter relevant to the investigation for the purposes of which the order is sought, any or all of the following —
   (a) answer questions, either at a time specified in the notice or at once, at a place so specified;
   (b) provide information specified in the notice, by a time and in a manner so specified;
   (c) produce documents, or documents of a description, specified in the notice, either at or by a time so specified or at once, and in a manner so specified.

(5) Relevant information is information (whether or not contained in a document) which the Lord Advocate considers or the Scottish Ministers consider to be relevant to the investigation.

(6) A person is not bound to comply with a requirement imposed by a notice given under a disclosure order unless evidence of authority to give the notice is produced to him.

392 Requirements for making of disclosure order

(1) These are the requirements for the making of a disclosure order.

(2) There must be reasonable grounds for suspecting that —
   (a) in the case of a confiscation investigation, the person specified in the application for the order has benefited from his criminal conduct;
   (b) in the case of a civil recovery investigation, the property specified in the application for the order is recoverable property or associated property.

(3) There must be reasonable grounds for believing that information which may be provided in compliance with a requirement imposed under the order is likely to be of substantial value (whether or not by itself) to the investigation for the purposes of which the order is sought.

(4)   There must be reasonable grounds for believing that it is in the public interest for the information to be provided, having regard to the benefit likely to accrue to the investigation if the information is obtained.

393   Offences

(1)   A person commits an offence if without reasonable excuse he fails to comply with a requirement imposed on him under a disclosure order.

(2)   A person guilty of an offence under subsection (1) is liable on summary conviction to —

    (a)   imprisonment for a term not exceeding six months,

    (b)   a fine not exceeding level 5 on the standard scale, or

    (c)   both.

(3)   A person commits an offence if, in purported compliance with a requirement imposed on him under a disclosure order, he —

    (a)   makes a statement which he knows to be false or misleading in a material particular, or

    (b)   recklessly makes a statement which is false or misleading in a material particular.

(4)   A person guilty of an offence under subsection (3) is liable —

    (a)   on summary conviction, to imprisonment for a term not exceeding six months or to a fine not exceeding the statutory maximum or to both, or

    (b)   on conviction on indictment, to imprisonment for a term not exceeding two years or to a fine or to both.

394   Statements

(1)   A statement made by a person in response to a requirement imposed on him under a disclosure order may not be used in evidence against him in criminal proceedings.

(2)   But subsection (1) does not apply —

    (a)   in the case of proceedings under Part 3,

    (b)   on a prosecution for an offence under section 393(1) or (3),

    (c)   on a prosecution for perjury, or

    (d)   on a prosecution for some other offence where, in giving evidence, the person makes a statement inconsistent with the statement mentioned in subsection (1).

(3)   A statement may not be used by virtue of subsection (2)(d) against a person unless —

    (a)   evidence relating to it is adduced, or

    (b)   a question relating to it is asked,

by him or on his behalf in the proceedings arising out of the prosecution.

395   Further provisions

(1)   A disclosure order does not confer the right to require a person to answer any question, provide any information or produce any document which he would be entitled to refuse to answer, provide or produce on grounds of legal privilege.

(2) A disclosure order has effect in spite of any restriction on the disclosure of information (however imposed).

(3) The Lord Advocate and the Scottish Ministers may take copies of any documents produced in compliance with a requirement to produce them which is imposed under a disclosure order.

(4) Documents so produced may be retained for so long as it is necessary to retain them (as opposed to a copy of them) in connection with the investigation for the purposes of which the order was made.

(5) But if the Lord Advocate has, or the Scottish Ministers have, reasonable grounds for believing that—
    (a) the documents may need to be produced for the purposes of any legal proceedings, and
    (b) they might otherwise be unavailable for those purposes,
they may be retained until the proceedings are concluded.

396 Supplementary

(1) An application for a disclosure order may be made ex parte to—
    (a) in the case of an order made in a confiscation investigation, a judge of the High Court of Justiciary;
    (b) in the case of an order made in a civil recovery investigation, a judge of the Court of Session,
in chambers.

(2) Provision may be made by rules of court as to the discharge and variation of disclosure orders.

(3) Rules of court under subsection (2) relating to disclosure orders—
    (a) made in a confiscation investigation shall, without prejudice to section 305 of the Criminal Procedure (Scotland) Act 1995 (c. 46) be made by act of adjournal;
    (b) made in a civil recovery investigation shall, without prejudice to section 5 of the Court of Session Act 1988 (c. 36), be made by act of sederunt.

(4) An application to discharge or vary a disclosure order may be made to a judge of the court which made the order by—
    (a) the Lord Advocate or the Scottish Ministers;
    (b) any person affected by the order.

(5) The court may—
    (a) discharge the order;
    (b) vary the order.

Customer information orders

397 Customer information orders

(1) The sheriff may, on an application made to him by the appropriate person, make a customer information order if he is satisfied that each of the requirements for the making of the order is fulfilled.

(2) In making a customer information order in relation to property subject to a civil recovery investigation the sheriff shall act in the exercise of his civil jurisdiction.

(3) The application for a customer information order must state that—

    (a) a person specified in the application is subject to a confiscation investigation or a money laundering investigation, or

    (b) property specified in the application is subject to a civil recovery investigation and a person specified in the application appears to hold the property.

(4) The application must also state that—

    (a) the order is sought for the purposes of the investigation;

    (b) the order is sought against the financial institution or financial institutions specified in the application.

(5) An application for a customer information order may specify—

    (a) all financial institutions,

    (b) a particular description, or particular descriptions, of financial institutions, or

    (c) a particular financial institution or particular financial institutions.

(6) A customer information order is an order that a financial institution covered by the application for the order must, on being required to do so by notice in writing given by the appropriate person, provide any such customer information as it has relating to the person specified in the application.

(7) A financial institution which is required to provide information under a customer information order must provide the information to a proper person in such manner, and at or by such time, as that person requires.

(8) If a financial institution on which a requirement is imposed by a notice given under a customer information order requires the production of evidence of authority to give the notice, it is not bound to comply with the requirement unless evidence of the authority has been produced to it.

398 Meaning of customer information

(1) "Customer information", in relation to a person and a financial institution, is information whether the person holds, or has held, an account or accounts at the financial institution (whether solely or jointly with another) and (if so) information as to—

    (a) the matters specified in subsection (2) if the person is an individual;

    (b) the matters specified in subsection (3) if the person is a company or limited liability partnership or a similar body incorporated or otherwise established outside the United Kingdom.

(2) The matters referred to in subsection (1)(a) are—

    (a) the account number or numbers;

    (b) the person's full name;

    (c) his date of birth;

    (d) his most recent address and any previous addresses;

    (e) the date or dates on which he began to hold the account or accounts and, if he has ceased to hold the account or any of the accounts, the date or dates on which he did so;

(f) such evidence of his identity as was obtained by the financial institution under or for the purposes of any legislation relating to money laundering;

(g) the full name, date of birth and most recent address, and any previous addresses, of any person who holds, or has held, an account at the financial institution jointly with him;

(h) the account number or numbers of any other account or accounts held at the financial institution to which he is a signatory and details of the person holding the other account or accounts.

(3) The matters referred to in subsection (1)(b) are—

(a) the account number or numbers;

(b) the person's full name;

(c) a description of any business which the person carries on;

(d) the country or territory in which it is incorporated or otherwise established and any number allocated to it under the Companies Act 1985 (c. 6) or the Companies (Northern Ireland) Order 1986 (S.I. 1986/ 1032 (N.I. 6)) or corresponding legislation of any country or territory outside the United Kingdom;

(e) any number assigned to it for the purposes of value added tax in the United Kingdom;

(f) its registered office, and any previous registered offices, under the Companies Act 1985 or the Companies (Northern Ireland) Order 1986 (S.I. 1986/1032 (N.I. 6)) or anything similar under corresponding legislation of any country or territory outside the United Kingdom;

(g) its registered office, and any previous registered offices, under the Limited Liability Partnerships Act 2000 (c. 12) or anything similar under corresponding legislation of any country or territory outside Great Britain;

(h) the date or dates on which it began to hold the account or accounts and, if it has ceased to hold the account or any of the accounts, the date or dates on which it did so;

(i) such evidence of its identity as was obtained by the financial institution under or for the purposes of any legislation relating to money laundering;

(j) the full name, date of birth and most recent address and any previous addresses of any person who is a signatory to the account or any of the accounts.

(4) The Scottish Ministers may by order provide for information of a description specified in the order—

(a) to be customer information, or

(b) no longer to be customer information.

(5) Money laundering is an act which—

(a) constitutes an offence under section 327, 328 or 329 of this Act or section 18 of the Terrorism Act 2000 (c. 11), or

(b) would constitute an offence specified in paragraph (a) if done in the United Kingdom.

399 Requirements for making of customer information order

(1) These are the requirements for the making of a customer information order.

(2) In the case of a confiscation investigation, there must be reasonable grounds for suspecting that the person specified in the application for the order has benefited from his criminal conduct.

(3) In the case of a civil recovery investigation, there must be reasonable grounds for suspecting that—

  (a) the property specified in the application for the order is recoverable property or associated property;

  (b) the person specified in the application holds all or some of the property.

(4) In the case of a money laundering investigation, there must be reasonable grounds for suspecting that the person specified in the application for the order has committed a money laundering offence.

(5) In the case of any investigation, there must be reasonable grounds for believing that customer information which may be provided in compliance with the order is likely to be of substantial value (whether or not by itself) to the investigation for the purposes of which the order is sought.

(6) In the case of any investigation there must be reasonable grounds for believing that it is in the public interest for the customer information to be provided, having regard to the benefit likely to accrue to the investigation if the information is obtained.

400 Offences

(1) A financial institution commits an offence if without reasonable excuse it fails to comply with a requirement imposed on it under a customer information order.

(2) A financial institution guilty of an offence under subsection (1) is liable on summary conviction to a fine not exceeding level 5 on the standard scale.

(3) A financial institution commits an offence if, in purported compliance with a customer information order, it—

  (a) makes a statement which it knows to be false or misleading in a material particular, or

  (b) recklessly makes a statement which is false or misleading in a material particular.

(4) A financial institution guilty of an offence under subsection (3) is liable—

  (a) on summary conviction, to a fine not exceeding the statutory maximum, or

  (b) on conviction on indictment, to a fine.

401 Statements

(1) A statement made by a financial institution in response to a customer information order may not be used in evidence against it in criminal proceedings.

(2) But subsection (1) does not apply—

  (a) in the case of proceedings under Part 3,

  (b) on a prosecution for an offence under section 400(1) or (3), or

(c)   on a prosecution for some other offence where, in giving evidence, the financial institution makes a statement inconsistent with the statement mentioned in subsection (1).

(3)   A statement may not be used by virtue of subsection (2)(c) against a financial institution unless –

(a)   evidence relating to it is adduced, or

(b)   a question relating to it is asked,

by or on behalf of the financial institution in the proceedings arising out of the prosecution.

402   Further provisions

A customer information order has effect in spite of any restriction on the disclosure of information (however imposed).

403   Supplementary

(1)   An application for a customer information order may be made ex parte to a sheriff in chambers.

(2)   Provision may be made by rules of court as to the discharge and variation of customer information orders.

(3)   Rules of court under subsection (2) relating to customer information orders –

(a)   made in a confiscation investigation or a money laundering investigation shall, without prejudice to section 305 of the Criminal Procedure (Scotland) Act 1995 (c. 46), be made by act of adjournal;

(b)   made in a civil recovery investigation shall, without prejudice to section 32 of the Sheriff Courts (Scotland) Act 1971 (c. 58), be made by act of sederunt.

(4)   An application to discharge or vary a customer information order may be made to the sheriff by –

(a)   the person who applied for the order;

(b)   any person affected by the order.

(5)   The sheriff may –

(a)   discharge the order;

(b)   vary the order.

Account monitoring orders

404   Account monitoring orders

(1)   The sheriff may, on an application made to him by the appropriate person, make an account monitoring order if he is satisfied that each of the requirements for the making of the order is fulfilled.

(2)   In making an account monitoring order in relation to property subject to a civil recovery investigation, the sheriff shall act in the exercise of his civil jurisdiction.

(3)   The application for an account monitoring order must state that –

> > (a) a person specified in the application is subject to a confiscation investigation or a money laundering investigation, or
> >
> > (b) property specified in the application is subject to a civil recovery investigation and a person specified in the application appears to hold the property.

> (4) The application must also state that—
> > (a) the order is sought for the purposes of the investigation;
> > (b) the order is sought against the financial institution specified in the application in relation to account information of the description so specified.

> (5) Account information is information relating to an account or accounts held at the financial institution specified in the application by the person so specified (whether solely or jointly with another).

> (6) The application for an account monitoring order may specify information relating to—
> > (a) all accounts held by the person specified in the application for the order at the financial institution so specified,
> > (b) a particular description, or particular descriptions, of accounts so held, or
> > (c) a particular account, or particular accounts, so held.

> (7) An account monitoring order is an order that the financial institution specified in the application for the order must, for the period stated in the order, provide account information of the description specified in the order to the proper person in the manner, and at or by the time or times, stated in the order.

> (8) The period stated in an account monitoring order must not exceed the period of 90 days beginning with the day on which the order is made.

405 Requirements for making of account monitoring order

> (1) These are the requirements for the making of an account monitoring order.

> (2) In the case of a confiscation investigation, there must be reasonable grounds for suspecting that the person specified in the application for the order has benefited from his criminal conduct.

> (3) In the case of a civil recovery investigation, there must be reasonable grounds for suspecting that—
> > (a) the property specified in the application for the order is recoverable property or associated property;
> > (b) the person specified in the application holds all or some of the property.

> (4) In the case of a money laundering investigation, there must be reasonable grounds for suspecting that the person specified in the application for the order has committed a money laundering offence.

> (5) In the case of any investigation, there must be reasonable grounds for believing that account information which may be provided in compliance with the order is likely to be of substantial value (whether or not by itself) to the investigation for the purposes of which the order is sought.

> (6) In the case of any investigation, there must be reasonable grounds for believing that it is in the public interest for the account information to be provided,

having regard to the benefit likely to accrue to the investigation if the information is obtained.

406 Statements

(1) A statement made by a financial institution in response to an account monitoring order may not be used in evidence against it in criminal proceedings.

(2) But subsection (1) does not apply –
    (a) in the case of proceedings under Part 3;
    (b) in the case of proceedings for contempt of court, or
    (c) on a prosecution for an offence where, in giving evidence, the financial institution makes a statement inconsistent with the statement mentioned in subsection (1).

(3) A statement may not be used by virtue of subsection (2)(c) against a financial institution unless –
    (a) evidence relating to it is adduced, or
    (b) a question relating to it is asked,
by or on behalf of the financial institution in the proceedings arising out of the prosecution.

407 Further provisions

An account monitoring order has effect in spite of any restriction on the disclosure of information (however imposed).

408 Supplementary

(1) An application for an account monitoring order may be made ex parte to a sheriff in chambers.

(2) Provision may be made by rules of court as to the discharge and variation of account monitoring orders.

(3) Rules of court under subsection (2) relating to account monitoring orders –
    (a) made in a confiscation investigation or a money laundering investigation shall, without prejudice to section 305 of the Criminal Procedure (Scotland) Act 1995 (c. 46), be made by act of adjournal;
    (b) made in a civil recovery investigation shall, without prejudice to section 32 of the Sheriff Courts (Scotland) Act 1971 (c. 58), be made by act of sederunt.

(4) An application to discharge or vary an account monitoring order may be made to the sheriff by –
    (a) the person who applied for the order;
    (b) any person affected by the order.

(5) The sheriff may –
    (a) discharge the order;
    (b) vary the order.

General

409 Jurisdiction of sheriff

(1) A sheriff may grant a production order, search warrant, customer information order or account monitoring order under this Act in relation to property situated in any area of Scotland notwithstanding that it is outside the area of that sheriff.

(2) Any such order or warrant may, without being backed or endorsed by another sheriff, be executed throughout Scotland in the same way as it may be executed within the sheriffdom of the sheriff who granted it.

(3) This section is without prejudice to any existing rule of law or to any other provision of this Act.

410 Code of practice

(1) The Scottish Ministers must prepare a code of practice as to the exercise by proper persons of functions they have under this Chapter.

(2) After preparing a draft of the code the Scottish Ministers—
    (a) must publish the draft;
    (b) must consider any representations made to them about the draft;
    (c) may amend the draft accordingly.

(3) After the Scottish Ministers have proceeded under subsection (2) they must lay the code before the Scottish Parliament.

(4) When they have done so, the Scottish Ministers may bring the code into operation on such day as they may appoint by order.

(5) A proper person must compy with a code of practice which is in operation under this section in the exercise of any function he has under this Chapter.

(6) If a proper person fails to comply with any provision of a code of practice issued under this section he is not by reason only of that failure liable in any criminal or civil proceedings.

(7) But the code of practice is admissible in evidence in such proceedings and a court may take account of any failure to comply with its provisions in determining any questions in the proceedings.

(8) The Scottish Ministers may from time to time revise a code previously brought into operation under this section; and the preceding provisions of this section apply to a revised code as they apply to the code as first prepared.

411 Performance of functions of Scottish Ministers by constables in Scotland

(1) In Scotland, a constable engaged in temporary service with the Scottish Ministers in connection with their functions under this Part may perform functions, other than those specified in subsection (2), on behalf of the Scottish Ministers.

(2) The specified functions are the functions conferred on the Scottish Ministers by—
    (a) section 380(1) (production orders),

    (b)   section 382(2) (entry orders),

    (c)   section 386(4) (supplementary to production and entry orders),

    (d)   section 387(1) (search warrants),

    (e)   section 391(1) (disclosure orders),

    (f)   section 396(4) (supplementary to disclosure orders),

    (g)   section 397(1) (customer information orders),

    (h)   section 403(4) (supplementary to customer information orders),

    (i)   section 404(1) (account monitoring orders),

    (j)   section 408(4) (supplementary to account monitoring orders).

412 Interpretation

In this Chapter, unless the context otherwise requires —

    "appropriate person" means —

        (a)   the procurator fiscal, in relation to a confiscation investigation or a money laundering investigation,

        (b)   the Scottish Ministers, in relation to a civil recovery investigation;

    references to a "constable" include references to a customs and excise officer;

    "legal privilege" means protection in legal proceedings from disclosure, by virtue of any rule of law relating to the confidentiality of communications; and "items subject to legal privilege" are —

        (a)   communications between a professional legal adviser and his client, or

        (b)   communications made in connection with or in contemplation of legal proceedings and for the purposes of those proceedings,

    which would be so protected.

    "premises" include any place and, in particular, include —

        (a)   any vehicle, vessel, aircraft or hovercraft;

        (b)   any offshore installation within the meaning of section 1 of the Mineral Workings (Offshore Installations) Act 1971 (c. 61) and any tent or movable structure;

    "proper person" means —

        (a)   a constable, in relation to a confiscation investigation or a money laundering investigation;

        (b)   the Scottish Ministers or a person named by them, in relation to a civil recovery investigation.

CHAPTER 4

INTERPRETATION

413 Criminal conduct

(1)   Criminal conduct is conduct which —

    (a)   constitutes an offence in any part of the United Kingdom, or

    (b)   would constitute an offence in any part of the United Kingdom if it occurred there.

(2)   A person benefits from conduct if he obtains property or a pecuniary advantage as a result of or in connection with the conduct.

(3)   References to property or a pecuniary advantage obtained in connection with conduct include references to property or a pecuniary advantage obtained in both that connection and some other.

(4)   If a person benefits from conduct his benefit is the property or pecuniary advantage obtained as a result of or in connection with the conduct.

(5)   It is immaterial—
     (a)   whether conduct occurred before or after the passing of this Act, and
     (b)   whether property or a pecuniary advantage constituting a benefit from conduct was obtained before or after the passing of this Act.

414   Property

(1)   Property is all property wherever situated and includes—
     (a)   money;
     (b)   all forms of property, real or personal, heritable or moveable;
     (c)   things in action and other intangible or incorporeal property.

(2)   "Recoverable property" and "associated property" have the same meanings as in Part 5.

(3)   The following rules apply in relation to property—
     (a)   property is obtained by a person if he obtains an interest in it;
     (b)   references to an interest, in relation to land in England and Wales or Northern Ireland, are to any legal estate or equitable interest or power;
     (c)   references to an interest, in relation to land in Scotland, are to any estate, interest, servitude or other heritable right in or over land, including a heritable security;
     (d)   references to an interest, in relation to property other than land, include references to a right (including a right to possession).

415   Money laundering offences

(1)   An offence under section 327, 328 or 329 is a money laundering offence.

(2)   Each of the following is a money laundering offence—
     (a)   an attempt, conspiracy or incitement to commit an offence specified in subsection (1);
     (b)   aiding, abetting, counselling or procuring the commission of an offence specified in subsection (1).

416   Other interpretative provisions

(1)   These expressions are to be construed in accordance with these provisions of this Part—
       civil recovery investigation: section 341(2) and (3)
       confiscation investigation: section 341(1)
       money laundering investigation: section 341(4)

(2)   In the application of this Part to England and Wales and Northern Ireland, these expressions are to be construed in accordance with these provisions of this Part—

account information: section 370(4)
account monitoring order: section 370(6)
appropriate officer: section 378
customer information: section 364
customer information order: section 363(5)
disclosure order: section 357(4)
document: section 379
order to grant entry: section 347(3)
production order: section 345(4)
search and seizure warrant: section 352(4)
senior appropriate officer: section 378.

(3)   In the application of this Part to Scotland, these expressions are to be construed in accordance with these provisions of this Part—

account information: section 404(5)
account monitoring order: section 404(7)
customer information: section 398
customer information order: section 397(6)
disclosure order: section 391(4)
production order: section 380(5)
proper person: section 412
search warrant: section 387(4).

(4)   "Financial institution" means a person carrying on a business in the regulated sector.

(5)   But a person who ceases to carry on a business in the regulated sector (whether by virtue of paragraph 5 of Schedule 9 or otherwise) is to continue to be treated as a financial institution for the purposes of any requirement under—

(a)   a customer information order, or

(b)   an account monitoring order,

to provide information which relates to a time when the person was a financial institution.

(6)   References to a business in the regulated sector must be construed in accordance with Schedule 9.

(7)   "Recovery order", "interim receiving order" and "interim administration order" have the same meanings as in Part 5.

(8)   References to notice in writing include references to notice given by electronic means.

(9)   This section and sections 413 to 415 apply for the purposes of this Part.

PART 9

INSOLVENCY ETC.

Bankruptcy in England and Wales

417 Modifications of the 1986 Act

(1) This section applies if a person is adjudged bankrupt in England and Wales.

(2) The following property is excluded from his estate for the purposes of Part 9 of the 1986 Act—

   (a) property for the time being subject to a restraint order which was made under section 41, 120 or 190 before the order adjudging him bankrupt;

   (b) any property in respect of which an order under section 50 or 52 is in force;

   (c) any property in respect of which an order under section 128(3) is in force;

   (d) any property in respect of which an order under section 198 or 200 is in force.

(3) Subsection (2)(a) applies to heritable property in Scotland only if the restraint order is recorded in the General Register of Sasines or registered in the Land Register of Scotland before the order adjudging the person bankrupt.

(4) If in the case of a debtor an interim receiver stands at any time appointed under section 286 of the 1986 Act and any property of the debtor is then subject to a restraint order made under section 41, 120 or 190 the powers conferred on the receiver by virtue of that Act do not apply to property then subject to the restraint order.

418 Restriction of powers

(1) If a person is adjudged bankrupt in England and Wales the powers referred to in subsection (2) must not be exercised in relation to the property referred to in subsection (3).

(2) These are the powers—

   (a) the powers conferred on a court by sections 41 to 67 and the powers of a receiver appointed under section 48, 50 or 52;

   (b) the powers conferred on a court by sections 120 to 136 and Schedule 3 and the powers of an administrator appointed under section 125 or 128(3);

   (c) the powers conferred on a court by sections 190 to 215 and the powers of a receiver appointed under section 196, 198 or 200.

(3) This is the property—

   (a) property which is for the time being comprised in the bankrupt's estate for the purposes of Part 9 of the 1986 Act;

   (b) property in respect of which his trustee in bankruptcy may (without leave of the court) serve a notice under section 307, 308 or 308A of the 1986 Act (after-acquired property, tools, tenancies etc);

    (c)   property which is to be applied for the benefit of creditors of the bankrupt by virtue of a condition imposed under section 280(2)(c) of the 1986 Act;

    (d)   in a case where a confiscation order has been made under section 6 or 156 of this Act, any sums remaining in the hands of a receiver appointed under section 50, 52, 198 or 200 of this Act after the amount required to be paid under the confiscation order has been fully paid;

    (e)   in a case where a confiscation order has been made under section 92 of this Act, any sums remaining in the hands of an administrator appointed under section 128 of this Act after the amount required to be paid under the confiscation order has been fully paid.

(4)   But nothing in the 1986 Act must be taken to restrict (or enable the restriction of) the powers referred to in subsection (2).

(5)   In a case where a petition in bankruptcy was presented or a receiving order or adjudication in bankruptcy was made before 29 December 1986 (when the 1986 Act came into force) this section has effect with these modifications –

    (a)   for the reference in subsection (3)(a) to the bankrupt's estate for the purposes of Part 9 of that Act substitute a reference to the property of the bankrupt for the purposes of the 1914 Act;

    (b)   omit subsection (3)(b);

    (c)   for the reference in subsection (3)(c) to section 280(2)(c) of the 1986 Act substitute a reference to section 26(2) of the 1914 Act;

    (d)   for the reference in subsection (4) to the 1986 Act substitute a reference to the 1914 Act.

419   Tainted gifts

(1)   This section applies if a person who is adjudged bankrupt in England and Wales has made a tainted gift (whether directly or indirectly).

(2)   No order may be made under section 339, 340 or 423 of the 1986 Act (avoidance of certain transactions) in respect of the making of the gift at any time when –

    (a)   any property of the recipient of the tainted gift is subject to a restraint order under section 41, 120 or 190, or

    (b)   there is in force in respect of such property an order under section 50, 52, 128(3), 198 or 200.

(3)   Any order made under section 339, 340 or 423 of the 1986 Act after an order mentioned in subsection (2)(a) or (b) is discharged must take into account any realisation under Part 2, 3 or 4 of this Act of property held by the recipient of the tainted gift.

(4)   A person makes a tainted gift for the purposes of this section if he makes a tainted gift within the meaning of Part 2, 3 or 4.

(5)   In a case where a petition in bankruptcy was presented or a receiving order or adjudication in bankruptcy was made before 29 December 1986 (when the 1986 Act came into force) this section has effect with the substitution for a reference to section 339, 340 or 423 of the 1986 Act of a reference to section 27, 42 or 44 of the 1914 Act.

Sequestration in Scotland

420   Modifications of the 1985 Act

(1)   This section applies if an award of sequestration is made in Scotland.

(2)   The following property is excluded from the debtor's estate for the purposes of
the 1985 Act—

  (a)   property for the time being subject to a restraint order which was made
under section 41, 120 or 190 before the award of sequestration;

  (b)   any property in respect of which an order under section 50 or 52 is in
force;

  (c)   any property in respect of which an order under section 128(3) is in
force;

  (d)   any property in respect of which an order under section 198 or 200 is in
force.

(3)   Subsection (2)(a) applies to heritable property in Scotland only if the restraint
order is recorded in the General Register of Sasines or registered in the Land
Register of Scotland before the award of sequestration.

(4)   It shall not be competent to submit a claim in relation to a confiscation order to
the permanent trustee in accordance with section 48 of the 1985 Act; and the
reference here to a confiscation order is to any confiscation order that has been
or may be made against the debtor under Part 2, 3 or 4 of this Act.

(5)   If at any time in the period before the award of sequestration is made an
interim trustee stands appointed under section 2(5) of the 1985 Act and any
property in the debtor's estate is at that time subject to a restraint order made
under section 41, 120 or 190, the powers conferred on the trustee by virtue of
that Act do not apply to property then subject to the restraint order.

421   Restriction of powers

(1)   If an award of sequestration is made in Scotland the powers referred to in
subsection (2) must not be exercised in relation to the property referred to in
subsection (3).

(2)   These are the powers—

  (a)   the powers conferred on a court by sections 41 to 67 and the powers of
a receiver appointed under section 48, 50 or 52;

  (b)   the powers conferred on a court by sections 120 to 136 and Schedule 3
and the powers of an administrator appointed under section 125 or
128(3);

  (c)   the powers conferred on a court by sections 190 to 215 and the powers
of a receiver appointed under section 196, 198 or 200.

(3)   This is the property—

  (a)   property which is for the time being comprised in the whole estate of
the debtor within the meaning of section 31(8) of the 1985 Act;

  (b)   any income of the debtor which has been ordered under section 32(2) of
that Act to be paid to the permanent trustee;

  (c)   any estate which under section 31(10) or 32(6) of that Act vests in the
permanent trustee;

(d) in a case where a confiscation order has been made under section 6 or 156 of this Act, any sums remaining in the hands of a receiver appointed under section 50, 52, 198 or 200 of this Act after the amount required to be paid under the confiscation order has been fully paid;

(e) in a case where a confiscation order has been made under section 92 of this Act, any sums remaining in the hands of an administrator appointed under section 128 of this Act after the amount required to be paid under the confiscation order has been fully paid.

(4) But nothing in the 1985 Act must be taken to restrict (or enable the restriction of) the powers referred to in subsection (2).

(5) In a case where (despite the coming into force of the 1985 Act) the 1913 Act applies to a sequestration, subsection (3) above has effect as if for paragraphs (a) to (c) there were substituted –

"(a) property which is for the time being comprised in the whole property of the debtor which vests in the trustee under section 97 of the 1913 Act;

(b) any income of the bankrupt which has been ordered under section 98(2) of that Act to be paid to the trustee;

(c) any estate which under section 98(1) of that Act vests in the trustee."

(6) In a case where subsection (5) applies, subsection (4) has effect as if for the reference to the 1985 Act there were substituted a reference to the 1913 Act.

422   Tainted gifts

(1) This section applies if a person whose estate is sequestrated in Scotland has made a tainted gift (whether directly or indirectly).

(2) No decree may be granted under the Bankruptcy Act 1621 (c. 18) or section 34 or 36 of the 1985 Act (gratuitous alienations and unfair preferences), or otherwise, in respect of the making of the gift at any time when –

(a) any property of the recipient of the tainted gift is subject to a restraint order under section 41, 120 or 190, or

(b) there is in force in respect of such property an order under section 50, 52, 128(3), 198 or 200.

(3) Any decree made under the Bankruptcy Act 1621 (c. 18) or section 34 or 36 of the 1985 Act, or otherwise, after an order mentioned in subsection (2)(a) or (b) is discharged must take into account any realisation under Part 2, 3 or 4 of this Act of property held by the recipient of the tainted gift.

(4) A person makes a tainted gift for the purposes of this section if he makes a tainted gift within the meaning of Part 2, 3 or 4.

Bankruptcy in Northern Ireland

423   Modifications of the 1989 Order

(1) This section applies if a person is adjudged bankrupt in Northern Ireland.

(2) The following property is excluded from his estate for the purposes of Part 9 of the 1989 Order –

    (a)   property for the time being subject to a restraint order which was made under section 41, 120 or 190 before the order adjudging him bankrupt;

    (b)   any property in respect of which an order under section 50 or 52 is in force;

    (c)   any property in respect of which an order under section 128(3) is in force;

    (d)   any property in respect of which an order under section 198 or 200 is in force.

(3)   Subsection (2)(a) applies to heritable property in Scotland only if the restraint order is recorded in the General Register of Sasines or registered in the Land Register of Scotland before the order adjudging the person bankrupt.

(4)   If in the case of a debtor an interim receiver stands at any time appointed under Article 259 of the 1989 Order and any property of the debtor is then subject to a restraint order made under section 41, 120 or 190, the powers conferred on the receiver by virtue of that Order do not apply to property then subject to the restraint order.

424   Restriction of powers

(1)   If a person is adjudged bankrupt in Northern Ireland the powers referred to in subsection (2) must not be exercised in relation to the property referred to in subsection (3).

(2)   These are the powers —

    (a)   the powers conferred on a court by sections 41 to 67 and the powers of a receiver appointed under section 48, 50 or 52;

    (b)   the powers conferred on a court by sections 120 to 136 and Schedule 3 and the powers of an administrator appointed under section 125 or 128(3);

    (c)   the powers conferred on a court by sections 190 to 215 and the powers of a receiver appointed under section 196, 198 or 200.

(3)   This is the property —

    (a)   property which is for the time being comprised in the bankrupt's estate for the purposes of Part 9 of the 1989 Order;

    (b)   property in respect of which his trustee in bankruptcy may (without leave of the court) serve a notice under Article 280 or 281 of the 1989 Order (after-acquired property etc);

    (c)   property which is to be applied for the benefit of creditors of the bankrupt by virtue of a condition imposed under Article 254(2)(c) of the 1989 Order;

    (d)   in a case where a confiscation order has been made under section 6 or 156 of this Act, any sums remaining in the hands of a receiver appointed under section 50, 52, 198 or 200 of this Act after the amount required to be paid under the confiscation order has been fully paid;

    (e)   in a case where a confiscation order has been made under section 92 of this Act, any sums remaining in the hands of an administrator appointed under section 128 of this Act after the amount required to be paid under the confiscation order has been fully paid.

(4)   But nothing in the 1989 Order must be taken to restrict (or enable the restriction of) the powers mentioned in subsection (2).

(5) In a case where a petition in bankruptcy was presented or an adjudication in bankruptcy was made before 1 October 1991 (when the 1989 Order came into force) this section has effect with these modifications—

  (a) for the reference in subsection (3)(a) to the bankrupt's estate for the purposes of Part 9 of that Order substitute a reference to the property of the bankrupt for the purposes of the Bankruptcy Acts (Northern Ireland) 1857 to 1980;

  (b) omit subsection (3)(b);

  (c) for the reference in subsection (3)(c) to Article 254(2)(c) of the 1989 Order substitute a reference to Articles 28(4), (5)(c) and (11) and 30(6)(c) of the Bankruptcy Amendment (Northern Ireland) Order 1980 (S.I. 1980/561 (N.I. 4));

  (d) for the reference in subsection (4) to the 1989 Order substitute a reference to the Bankruptcy Acts (Northern Ireland) 1857 to 1980.

425 Tainted gifts

(1) This section applies if a person who is adjudged bankrupt in Northern Ireland has made a tainted gift (whether directly or indirectly).

(2) No order may be made under Article 312, 313 or 367 of the 1989 Order (avoidance of certain transactions) in respect of the making of the gift at any time when—

  (a) any property of the recipient of the tainted gift is subject to a restraint order under section 41, 120 or 190, or

  (b) there is in force in respect of such property an order under section 50, 52, 128(3), 198 or 200.

(3) Any order made under Article 312, 313 or 367 of the 1989 Order after an order mentioned in subsection (2)(a) or (b) is discharged must take into account any realisation under Part 2, 3 or 4 of this Act of property held by the recipient of the tainted gift.

(4) A person makes a tainted gift for the purposes of this section if he makes a tainted gift within the meaning of Part 2, 3 or 4.

(5) In a case where a petition in bankruptcy was presented or an adjudication in bankruptcy was made before 1 October 1991 (when the 1989 Order came into force) this section has effect with these modifications—

  (a) for a reference to Article 312 of the 1989 Order substitute a reference to section 12 of the Bankruptcy Amendment Act (Northern Ireland) 1929 (c. 1 (N.I.));

  (b) for a reference to Article 367 of the 1989 Order substitute a reference to section 10 of the Conveyancing Act (Ireland) 1634 (c. 3).

Winding up in England and Wales and Scotland

426 Winding up under the 1986 Act

(1) In this section "company" means any company which may be wound up under the 1986 Act.

(2) If an order for the winding up of a company is made or it passes a resolution for its voluntary winding up, the functions of the liquidator (or any provisional liquidator) are not exercisable in relation to the following property—

(a) property for the time being subject to a restraint order which was made under section 41, 120 or 190 before the relevant time;

(b) any property in respect of which an order under section 50 or 52 is in force;

(c) any property in respect of which an order under section 128(3) is in force;

(d) any property in respect of which an order under section 198 or 200 is in force.

(3) Subsection (2)(a) applies to heritable property in Scotland only if the restraint order is recorded in the General Register of Sasines or registered in the Land Register of Scotland before the relevant time.

(4) If an order for the winding up of a company is made or it passes a resolution for its voluntary winding up the powers referred to in subsection (5) must not be exercised in the way mentioned in subsection (6) in relation to any property –

(a) which is held by the company, and

(b) in relation to which the functions of the liquidator are exercisable.

(5) These are the powers –

(a) the powers conferred on a court by sections 41 to 67 and the powers of a receiver appointed under section 48, 50 or 52;

(b) the powers conferred on a court by sections 120 to 136 and Schedule 3 and the powers of an administrator appointed under section 125 or 128(3);

(c) the powers conferred on a court by sections 190 to 215 and the powers of a receiver appointed under section 196, 198 or 200.

(6) The powers must not be exercised –

(a) so as to inhibit the liquidator from exercising his functions for the purpose of distributing property to the company's creditors;

(b) so as to prevent the payment out of any property of expenses (including the remuneration of the liquidator or any provisional liquidator) properly incurred in the winding up in respect of the property.

(7) But nothing in the 1986 Act must be taken to restrict (or enable the restriction of) the exercise of the powers referred to in subsection (5).

(8) For the purposes of the application of Parts 4 and 5 of the 1986 Act (winding up) to a company which the Court of Session has jurisdiction to wind up, a person is not a creditor in so far as any sum due to him by the company is due in respect of a confiscation order made under section 6, 92 or 156.

(9) The relevant time is –

(a) if no order for the winding up of the company has been made, the time of the passing of the resolution for voluntary winding up;

(b) if such an order has been made, but before the presentation of the petition for the winding up of the company by the court such a resolution has been passed by the company, the time of the passing of the resolution;

(c) if such an order has been made, but paragraph (b) does not apply, the time of the making of the order.

(10) In a case where a winding up of a company commenced or is treated as having commenced before 29 December 1986, this section has effect with the following modifications—

    (a) in subsections (1) and (7) for "the 1986 Act" substitute "the Companies Act 1985";

    (b) in subsection (8) for "Parts 4 and 5 of the 1986 Act" substitute "Parts 20 and 21 of the Companies Act 1985".

427 Tainted gifts

(1) In this section "company" means any company which may be wound up under the 1986 Act.

(2) This section applies if—

    (a) an order for the winding up of a company is made or it passes a resolution for its voluntary winding up, and

    (b) it has made a tainted gift (whether directly or indirectly).

(3) No order may be made under section 238, 239 or 423 of the 1986 Act (avoidance of certain transactions) and no decree may be granted under section 242 or 243 of that Act (gratuitous alienations and unfair preferences), or otherwise, in respect of the making of the gift at any time when—

    (a) any property of the recipient of the tainted gift is subject to a restraint order under section 41, 120 or 190, or

    (b) there is in force in respect of such property an order under section 50, 52, 128(3), 198 or 200.

(4) Any order made under section 238, 239 or 423 of the 1986 Act or decree granted under section 242 or 243 of that Act, or otherwise, after an order mentioned in subsection (3)(a) or (b) is discharged must take into account any realisation under Part 2, 3 or 4 of this Act of property held by the recipient of the tainted gift.

(5) A person makes a tainted gift for the purposes of this section if he makes a tainted gift within the meaning of Part 2, 3 or 4.

(6) In a case where the winding up of a company commenced or is treated as having commenced before 29 December 1986 this section has effect with the substitution—

    (a) for references to section 239 of the 1986 Act of references to section 615 of the Companies Act 1985 (c. 6);

    (b) for references to section 242 of the 1986 Act of references to section 615A of the Companies Act 1985;

    (c) for references to section 243 of the 1986 Act of references to section 615B of the Companies Act 1985.

Winding up in Northern Ireland

428 Winding up under the 1989 Order

(1) In this section "company" means any company which may be wound up under the 1989 Order.

(2)   If an order for the winding up of a company is made or it passes a resolution
for its voluntary winding up, the functions of the liquidator (or any provisional
liquidator) are not exercisable in relation to the following property—

   (a)   property for the time being subject to a restraint order which was made
under section 41, 120 or 190 before the relevant time;

   (b)   any property in respect of which an order under section 50 or 52 is in
force;

   (c)   any property in respect of which an order under section 128(3) is in
force;

   (d)   any property in respect of which an order under section 198 or 200 is in
force.

(3)   Subsection (2)(a) applies to heritable property in Scotland only if the restraint
order is recorded in the General Register of Sasines or registered in the Land
Register of Scotland before the relevant time.

(4)   If an order for the winding up of a company is made or it passes a resolution
for its voluntary winding up the powers referred to in subsection (5) must not
be exercised in the way mentioned in subsection (6) in relation to any
property—

   (a)   which is held by the company, and

   (b)   in relation to which the functions of the liquidator are exercisable.

(5)   These are the powers—

   (a)   the powers conferred on a court by sections 41 to 67 and the powers of
a receiver appointed under section 48, 50 or 52;

   (b)   the powers conferred on a court by sections 120 to 136 and Schedule 3
and the powers of an administrator appointed under section 125 or
128(3);

   (c)   the powers conferred on a court by sections 190 to 215 and the powers
of a receiver appointed under section 196, 198 or 200.

(6)   The powers must not be exercised—

   (a)   so as to inhibit the liquidator from exercising his functions for the
purpose of distributing property to the company's creditors;

   (b)   so as to prevent the payment out of any property of expenses (including
the remuneration of the liquidator or any provisional liquidator)
properly incurred in the winding up in respect of the property.

(7)   But nothing in the 1989 Order must be taken to restrict (or enable the restriction
of) the exercise of the powers referred to in subsection (5).

(8)   The relevant time is—

   (a)   if no order for the winding up of the company has been made, the time
of the passing of the resolution for voluntary winding up;

   (b)   if such an order has been made, but before the presentation of the
petition for the winding up of the company by the court such a
resolution has been passed by the company, the time of the passing of
the resolution;

   (c)   if such an order has been made, but paragraph (b) does not apply, the
time of the making of the order.

(9)   In a case where a winding up of a company commenced or is treated as having
commenced before 1 October 1991, this section has effect with the substitution

for references to the 1989 Order of references to the Companies (Northern Ireland) Order 1986 (S.I. 1986/1032 (N.I. 6)).

429 Tainted gifts

(1) In this section "company" means any company which may be wound up under the 1989 Order.

(2) This section applies if –

    (a) an order for the winding up of a company is made or it passes a resolution for its voluntary winding up, and

    (b) it has made a tainted gift (whether directly or indirectly).

(3) No order may be made under Article 202, 203 or 367 of the 1989 Order (avoidance of certain transactions) in respect of the making of the gift at any time when –

    (a) any property of the recipient of the tainted gift is subject to a restraint order under section 41, 120 or 190, or

    (b) there is in force in respect of such property an order under section 50, 52, 128(3), 198 or 200.

(4) Any order made under Article 202, 203 or 367 of the 1989 Order after an order mentioned in subsection (3)(a) or (b) is discharged must take into account any realisation under Part 2, 3 or 4 of this Act of property held by the recipient of the tainted gift.

(5) A person makes a tainted gift for the purposes of this section if he makes a tainted gift within the meaning of Part 2, 3 or 4.

Floating charges

430 Floating charges

(1) In this section "company" means a company which may be wound up under

    (a) the 1986 Act, or

    (b) the 1989 Order.

(2) If a company holds property which is subject to a floating charge, and a receiver has been appointed by or on the application of the holder of the charge, the functions of the receiver are not exercisable in relation to the following property –

    (a) property for the time being subject to a restraint order which was made under section 41, 120 or 190 before the appointment of the receiver;

    (b) any property in respect of which an order under section 50 or 52 is in force;

    (c) any property in respect of which an order under section 128(3) is in force;

    (d) any property in respect of which an order under section 198 or 200 is in force.

(3) Subsection (2)(a) applies to heritable property in Scotland only if the restraint order is recorded in the General Register of Sasines or registered in the Land Register of Scotland before the appointment of the receiver.

(4)   If a company holds property which is subject to a floating charge, and a receiver has been appointed by or on the application of the holder of the charge, the powers referred to in subsection (5) must not be exercised in the way mentioned in subsection (6) in relation to any property –

   (a)   which is held by the company, and

   (b)   in relation to which the functions of the receiver are exercisable.

(5)   These are the powers –

   (a)   the powers conferred on a court by sections 41 to 67 and the powers of a receiver appointed under section 48, 50 or 52;

   (b)   the powers conferred on a court by sections 120 to 136 and Schedule 3 and the powers of an administrator appointed under section 125 or 128(3);

   (c)   the powers conferred on a court by sections 190 to 215 and the powers of a receiver appointed under section 196, 198 or 200.

(6)   The powers must not be exercised –

   (a)   so as to inhibit the receiver from exercising his functions for the purpose of distributing property to the company's creditors;

   (b)   so as to prevent the payment out of any property of expenses (including the remuneration of the receiver) properly incurred in the exercise of his functions in respect of the property.

(7)   But nothing in the 1986 Act or the 1989 Order must be taken to restrict (or enable the restriction of) the exercise of the powers referred to in subsection (5).

(8)   In this section "floating charge" includes a floating charge within the meaning of section 462 of the Companies Act 1985 (c. 6).

Limited liability partnerships

431   Limited liability partnerships

(1)   In sections 426, 427 and 430 "company" includes a limited liability partnership which may be wound up under the 1986 Act.

(2)   A reference in those sections to a company passing a resolution for its voluntary winding up is to be construed in relation to a limited liability partnership as a reference to the partnership making a determination for its voluntary winding up.

Insolvency practitioners

432   Insolvency practitioners

(1)   Subsections (2) and (3) apply if a person acting as an insolvency practitioner seizes or disposes of any property in relation to which his functions are not exercisable because –

   (a)   it is for the time being subject to a restraint order made under section 41, 120 or 190, or

   (b)   it is for the time being subject to an interim receiving order made under section 246 or an interim administration order made under section 256, and at the time of the seizure or disposal he believes on reasonable grounds that he is entitled (whether in pursuance of an order of a court or otherwise) to seize or dispose of the property.

(2) He is not liable to any person in respect of any loss or damage resulting from the seizure or disposal, except so far as the loss or damage is caused by his negligence.

(3) He has a lien on the property or the proceeds of its sale —
   (a) for such of his expenses as were incurred in connection with the liquidation, bankruptcy, sequestration or other proceedings in relation to which he purported to make the seizure or disposal, and
   (b) for so much of his remuneration as may reasonably be assigned to his acting in connection with those proceedings.

(4) Subsection (2) does not prejudice the generality of any provision of the 1985 Act, the 1986 Act, the 1989 Order or any other Act or Order which confers protection from liability on him.

(5) Subsection (7) applies if —
   (a) property is subject to a restraint order made under section 41, 120 or 190,
   (b) a person acting as an insolvency practitioner incurs expenses in respect of property subject to the restraint order, and
   (c) he does not know (and has no reasonable grounds to believe) that the property is subject to the restraint order.

(6) Subsection (7) also applies if —
   (a) property is subject to a restraint order made under section 41, 120 or 190,
   (b) a person acting as an insolvency practitioner incurs expenses which are not ones in respect of property subject to the restraint order, and
   (c) the expenses are ones which (but for the effect of the restraint order) might have been met by taking possession of and realising property subject to it.

(7) Whether or not he has seized or disposed of any property, he is entitled to payment of the expenses under —
   (a) section 54(2), 55(3), 56(2) or 57(3) if the restraint order was made under section 41;
   (b) section 130(3) or 131(3) if the restraint order was made under section 120;
   (c) section 202(2), 203(3), 204(2) or 205(3) if the restraint order was made under section 190.

(8) Subsection (10) applies if —
   (a) property is subject to an interim receiving order made under section 246 or an interim administration order made under section 256,
   (b) a person acting as an insolvency practitioner incurs expenses in respect of property subject to the order, and
   (c) he does not know (and has no reasonable grounds to believe) that the property is subject to the order.

(9) Subsection (10) also applies if —

(a)   property is subject to an interim receiving order made under section 246 or an interim administration order made under section 256,

(b)   a person acting as an insolvency practitioner incurs expenses which are not ones in respect of property subject to the order, and

(c)   the expenses are ones which (but for the effect of the order) might have been met by taking possession of and realising property subject to it.

(10)   Whether or not he has seized or disposed of any property, he is entitled to payment of the expenses under section 280.

433   Meaning of insolvency practitioner

(1)   This section applies for the purposes of section 432.

(2)   A person acts as an insolvency practitioner if he so acts within the meaning given by section 388 of the 1986 Act or Article 3 of the 1989 Order; but this is subject to subsections (3) to (5).

(3)   The expression "person acting as an insolvency practitioner" includes the official receiver acting as receiver or manager of the property concerned.

(4)   In applying section 388 of the 1986 Act under subsection (2) above —

(a)   the reference in section 388(2)(a) to a permanent or interim trustee in sequestration must be taken to include a reference to a trustee in sequestration;

(b)   section 388(5) (which includes provision that nothing in the section applies to anything done by the official receiver or the Accountant in Bankruptcy) must be ignored.

(5)   In applying Article 3 of the 1989 Order under subsection (2) above, paragraph (5) (which includes provision that nothing in the Article applies to anything done by the official receiver) must be ignored.

Interpretation

434   Interpretation

(1)   The following paragraphs apply to references to Acts or Orders —

(a)   the 1913 Act is the Bankruptcy (Scotland) Act 1913 (c. 20);

(b)   the 1914 Act is the Bankruptcy Act 1914 (c. 59);

(c)   the 1985 Act is the Bankruptcy (Scotland) Act 1985 (c. 66);

(d)   the 1986 Act is the Insolvency Act 1986 (c. 45);

(e)   the 1989 Order is the Insolvency (Northern Ireland) Order 1989 (S.I. 1989/2405 (N.I. 19)).

(2)   An award of sequestration is made on the date of sequestration within the meaning of section 12(4) of the 1985 Act.

(3)   This section applies for the purposes of this Part.

PART 10

INFORMATION

England and Wales and Northern Ireland

435 Use of information by Director

Information obtained by or on behalf of the Director in connection with the exercise of any of his functions may be used by him in connection with his exercise of any of his other functions.

436 Disclosure of information to Director

(1) Information which is held by or on behalf of a permitted person (whether it was obtained before or after the coming into force of this section) may be disclosed to the Director for the purpose of the exercise by the Director of his functions.

(2) A disclosure under this section is not to be taken to breach any restriction on the disclosure of information (however imposed).

(3) But nothing in this section authorises the making of a disclosure −
    (a) which contravenes the Data Protection Act 1998 (c. 29);
    (b) which is prohibited by Part 1 of the Regulation of Investigatory Powers Act 2000 (c. 23).

(4) This section does not affect a power to disclose which exists apart from this section.

(5) These are permitted persons −
    (a) a constable;
    (b) the Director General of the National Criminal Intelligence Service;
    (c) the Director General of the National Crime Squad;
    (d) the Director of the Serious Fraud Office;
    (e) the Commissioners of Inland Revenue;
    (f) the Commissioners of Customs and Excise;
    (g) the Director of Public Prosecutions;
    (h) the Director of Public Prosecutions for Northern Ireland.

(6) The Secretary of State may by order designate as permitted persons other persons who exercise functions which he believes are of a public nature.

(7) But an order under subsection (6) must specify the functions in respect of which the designation is made.

(8) Information must not be disclosed under this section on behalf of the Commissioners of Inland Revenue or on behalf of the Commissioners of Customs and Excise unless the Commissioners concerned authorise the disclosure.

(9) The power to authorise a disclosure under subsection (8) may be delegated (either generally or for a specified purpose) −
    (a) in the case of the Commissioners of Inland Revenue, to an officer of the Board of Inland Revenue;

(b)   in the case of the Commissioners of Customs and Excise, to a customs officer.

437   Further disclosure

(1)   Subsection (2) applies to information obtained under section 436 from the Commissioners of Inland Revenue or from the Commissioners of Customs and Excise or from a person acting on behalf of either of them.

(2)   Such information must not be further disclosed except—
(a)   for a purpose connected with the exercise of the Director's functions, and
(b)   with the consent of the Commissioners concerned.

(3)   Consent under subsection (2) may be given—
(a)   in relation to a particular disclosure;
(b)   in relation to disclosures made in circumstances specified or described in the consent.

(4)   The power to consent to further disclosure under subsection (2)(b) may be delegated (either generally or for a specified purpose)—
(a)   in the case of the Commissioners of Inland Revenue, to an officer of the Board of Inland Revenue;
(b)   in the case of the Commissioners of Customs and Excise, to a customs officer.

(5)   Subsection (6) applies to information obtained under section 436 from a permitted person other than the Commissioners of Inland Revenue or the Commissioners of Customs and Excise or a person acting on behalf of either of them.

(6)   A permitted person who discloses such information to the Director may make the disclosure subject to such conditions as to further disclosure by the Director as the permitted person thinks appropriate; and the information must not be further disclosed in contravention of the conditions.

438   Disclosure of information by Director

(1)   Information obtained by or on behalf of the Director in connection with the exercise of any of his functions may be disclosed by him if the disclosure is for the purposes of any of the following—
(a)   any criminal investigation which is being or may be carried out, whether in the United Kingdom or elsewhere;
(b)   any criminal proceedings which have been or may be started, whether in the United Kingdom or elsewhere;
(c)   the exercise of the Director's functions;
(d)   the exercise by the prosecutor of functions under Parts 2, 3 and 4;
(e)   the exercise by the Scottish Ministers of their functions under Part 5;
(f)   the exercise by a customs officer or a constable of his functions under Chapter 3 of Part 5;
(g)   safeguarding national security;
(h)   investigations or proceedings outside the United Kingdom which have led or may lead to the making of an external order within the meaning of section 447;

      (i)   the exercise of a designated function.

(2) Subsection (1) does not apply to information obtained by the Director or on his behalf in connection with the exercise of his functions under Part 6.

(3) But such information may be disclosed by the Director –
    (a)   to the Commissioners of Inland Revenue;
    (b)   to the Lord Advocate for the purpose of the exercise by the Lord Advocate of his functions under Part 3.

(4) Information disclosed to the Lord Advocate under subsection (3)(b) may be further disclosed by him only to the Scottish Ministers for the purpose of the exercise by them of their functions under Part 5.

(5) If the Director makes a disclosure of information for a purpose specified in subsection (1) he may make any further disclosure of the information by the person to whom he discloses it subject to such conditions as he thinks fit.

(6) Such a person must not further disclose the information in contravention of the conditions.

(7) A disclosure under this section is not to be taken to breach any restriction on the disclosure of information (however imposed).

(8) But nothing in this section authorises the making of a disclosure –
    (a)   which contravenes the Data Protection Act 1998 (c. 29);
    (b)   which is prohibited by Part 1 of the Regulation of Investigatory Powers Act 2000 (c. 23).

(9) A designated function is a function which the Secretary of State thinks is a function of a public nature and which he designates by order.

Scotland

439   Disclosure of information to Lord Advocate and to Scottish Ministers

(1) Information which is held by or on behalf of a permitted person (whether it was obtained before or after the coming into force of this section) may be disclosed to the Lord Advocate in connection with the exercise of any of his functions under Part 3 or to the Scottish Ministers in connection with the exercise of any of their functions under Part 5.

(2) A disclosure under this section is not to be taken to breach any restriction on the disclosure of information (however imposed).

(3) But nothing in this section authorises the making of a disclosure –
    (a)   which contravenes the Data Protection Act 1998;
    (b)   which is prohibited by Part 1 of the Regulation of Investigatory Powers Act 2000.

(4) This section does not affect a power to disclose which exists apart from this section.

(5) These are permitted persons –
    (a)   a constable;
    (b)   the Director General of the National Criminal Intelligence Service;
    (c)   the Director General of the National Crime Squad;

      (d)   the Director of the Serious Fraud Office;

      (e)   the Commissioners of Inland Revenue;

      (f)   the Commissioners of Customs and Excise;

      (g)   the Director of Public Prosecutions;

      (h)   the Director of Public Prosecutions for Northern Ireland.

(6)   The Scottish Ministers may by order designate as permitted persons other persons who exercise functions which they believe are of a public nature.

(7)   But an order under subsection (6) must specify the functions in respect of which the designation is made.

(8)   Information must not be disclosed under this section on behalf of the Commissioners of Inland Revenue or on behalf of the Commissioners of Customs and Excise unless the Commissioners concerned authorise the disclosure.

(9)   The power to authorise a disclosure under subsection (8) may be delegated (either generally or for a specified purpose) –

      (a)   in the case of the Commissioners of Inland Revenue, to an officer of the Board of Inland Revenue;

      (b)   in the case of the Commissioners of Customs and Excise, to a customs officer.

440   Further disclosure

(1)   Subsection (2) applies to information obtained under section 439 from the Commissioners of Inland Revenue or from the Commissioners of Customs and Excise or from a person acting on behalf of either of them.

(2)   Such information must not be further disclosed except –

      (a)   for a purpose connected with the exercise of the functions of the Lord Advocate under Part 3 and of the Scottish Ministers under Part 5, and

      (b)   with the consent of the Commissioners concerned.

(3)   Consent under subsection (2) may be given –

      (a)   in relation to a particular disclosure;

      (b)   in relation to disclosures made in circumstances specified or described in the consent.

(4)   The power to consent to further disclosure under subsection (2)(b) may be delegated (either generally or for a specified purpose) –

      (a)   in the case of the Commissioners of Inland Revenue, to an officer of the Board of Inland Revenue;

      (b)   in the case of the Commissioners of Customs and Excise, to a customs officer.

(5)   Subsection (6) applies to information obtained under section 439 from a permitted person other than the Commissioners of Inland Revenue or the Commissioners of Customs and Excise or a person acting on behalf of either of them.

(6)   A permitted person who discloses such information to the Lord Advocate or to the Scottish Ministers may make the disclosure subject to such conditions as to further disclosure by the Lord Advocate or by the Scottish Ministers as the

permitted person thinks appropriate; and the information must not be further disclosed in contravention of the conditions.

441   Disclosure of information by Lord Advocate and by Scottish Ministers

(1) Information obtained by or on behalf of the Lord Advocate in connection with the exercise of any of his functions under Chapter 3 of Part 5 may be disclosed to the Scottish Ministers in connection with the exercise of any of their functions under that Part.

(2) Information obtained by or on behalf of the Lord Advocate in connection with the exercise of any of his functions under Part 3 or by or on behalf of the Scottish Ministers in connection with the exercise of any of their functions under Part 5 may be disclosed by him or by them if the disclosure is for the purposes of any of the following –

   (a) any criminal investigation which is being or may be carried out whether in the United Kingdom or elsewhere;

   (b) any criminal proceedings which have been or may be started, whether in the United Kingdom or elsewhere;

   (c) the exercise of the functions of the Lord Advocate under Part 3;

   (d) the exercise of the functions of the Scottish Ministers under Part 5;

   (e) the exercise by the prosecutor of functions under Parts 2, 3 and 4;

   (f) the exercise of the Director's functions;

   (g) the exercise by a customs officer or a constable of his functions under Chapter 3 of Part 5;

   (h) safeguarding national security;

   (i) investigations or proceedings outside the United Kingdom which have led or may lead to the making of an external order within the meaning of section 447;

   (j) the exercise of a designated function.

(3) If the Lord Advocate makes a disclosure of information for a purpose specified in subsection (2) he may make any further disclosure of the information by the person to whom he discloses it subject to such conditions as he thinks fit.

(4) If the Scottish Ministers make a disclosure of information for a purpose specified in subsection (2) they may make any further disclosure of the information by the person to whom they disclose it subject to such conditions as they think fit.

(5) A person mentioned in subsection (3) or (4) must not further disclose the information in contravention of the conditions.

(6) A disclosure under this section is not to be taken to breach any restriction on the disclosure of information (however imposed).

(7) But nothing in this section authorises the making of a disclosure –

   (a) which contravenes the Data Protection Act 1998 (c. 29);

   (b) which is prohibited by Part 1 of the Regulation of Investigatory Powers Act 2000 (c. 23).

(8) This section does not affect a power to disclose which exists apart from this section.

(9) A designated function is a function which the Scottish Ministers think is a function of a public nature and which they designate by order.

Overseas purposes

442   Restriction on disclosure for overseas purposes

(1)   Section 18 of the Anti-terrorism, Crime and Security Act 2001 (c. 24)
(restrictions on disclosure of information for overseas purposes) applies to a
disclosure of information authorised by section 438(1)(a) or (b) or 441(2)(a) or
(b).

(2)   In the application of section 18 of the Anti-terrorism, Crime and Security Act
2001 by virtue of subsection (1) section 20 of that Act must be ignored and the
following subsection is substituted for subsection (2) of section 18 of that Act—

"(2)   In subsection (1) the reference, in relation to a direction, to a relevant
disclosure is a reference to a disclosure which—

(a)   is made for a purpose authorised by section 438(1)(a) or (b) or
441(2)(a) or (b) of the Proceeds of Crime Act 2002, and

(b)   is of any such information as is described in the direction.".

PART 11

CO-OPERATION

443   Enforcement in different parts of the United Kingdom

(1)   Her Majesty may by Order in Council make provision—

(a)   for an order made by a court under Part 2 to be enforced in Scotland or
Northern Ireland;

(b)   for an order made by a court under Part 3 to be enforced in England and
Wales or Northern Ireland;

(c)   for an order made by a court under Part 4 to be enforced in England and
Wales or Scotland;

(d)   for an order made under Part 8 in one part of the United Kingdom to be
enforced in another part;

(e)   for a warrant issued under Part 8 in one part of the United Kingdom to
be executed in another part.

(2)   Her Majesty may by Order in Council make provision—

(a)   for a function of a receiver appointed in pursuance of Part 2 to be
exercisable in Scotland or Northern Ireland;

(b)   for a function of an administrator appointed in pursuance of Part 3 to
be exercisable in England and Wales or Northern Ireland;

(c)   for a function of a receiver appointed in pursuance of Part 4 to be
exercisable in England and Wales or Scotland.

(3)   An Order under this section may include—

(a)   provision conferring and imposing functions on the prosecutor and the
Director;

(b)   provision about the registration of orders and warrants;

(c)   provision allowing directions to be given in one part of the United
Kingdom about the enforcement there of an order made or warrant
issued in another part;

(d)   provision about the authentication in one part of the United Kingdom
of an order made or warrant issued in another part.

    (4)   An Order under this section may –

        (a)   amend an enactment;

        (b)   apply an enactment (with or without modifications).

444   External requests and orders

    (1)   Her Majesty may by Order in Council –

        (a)   make provision for a prohibition on dealing with property which is the subject of an external request;

        (b)   make provision for the realisation of property for the purpose of giving effect to an external order.

    (2)   An Order under this section may include provision which (subject to any specified modifications) corresponds to any provision of Part 2, 3 or 4 or Part 5 except Chapter 3.

    (3)   An Order under this section may include –

        (a)   provision about the functions of the Secretary of State, the Lord Advocate, the Scottish Ministers and the Director in relation to external requests and orders;

        (b)   provision about the registration of external orders;

        (c)   provision about the authentication of any judgment or order of an overseas court, and of any other document connected with such a judgment or order or any proceedings relating to it;

        (d)   provision about evidence (including evidence required to establish whether proceedings have been started or are likely to be started in an overseas court);

        (e)   provision to secure that any person affected by the implementation of an external request or the enforcement of an external order has an opportunity to make representations to a court in the part of the United Kingdom where the request is being implemented or the order is being enforced.

445   External investigations

    (1)   Her Majesty may by Order in Council make –

        (a)   provision to enable orders equivalent to those under Part 8 to be made, and warrants equivalent to those under Part 8 to be issued, for the purposes of an external investigation;

        (b)   provision creating offences in relation to external investigations which are equivalent to offences created by Part 8.

    (2)   An Order under this section may include –

        (a)   provision corresponding to any provision of Part 8 (subject to any specified modifications);

        (b)   provision about the functions of the Secretary of State, the Lord Advocate, the Scottish Ministers, the Director, the Director General of the National Criminal Intelligence Service, the Director of the Serious Fraud Office, constables and customs officers;

        (c)   provision about evidence (including evidence required to establish whether an investigation is being carried out in a country or territory outside the United Kingdom).

(3) But an Order under this section must not provide for a disclosure order to be made for the purposes of an external investigation into whether a money laundering offence has been committed.

446 Rules of court

Rules of court may make such provision as is necessary or expedient to give effect to an Order in Council made under this Part (including provision about the exercise of functions of a judge conferred or imposed by the Order).

447 Interpretation

(1) An external request is a request by an overseas authority to prohibit dealing with relevant property which is identified in the request.

(2) An external order is an order which –

    (a) is made by an overseas court where property is found or believed to have been obtained as a result of or in connection with criminal conduct, and

    (b) is for the recovery of specified property or a specified sum of money.

(3) An external investigation is an investigation by an overseas authority into –

    (a) whether property has been obtained as a result of or in connection with criminal conduct, or

    (b) whether a money laundering offence has been committed.

(4) Property is all property wherever situated and includes –

    (a) money;

    (b) all forms of property, real or personal, heritable or moveable;

    (c) things in action and other intangible or incorporeal property.

(5) Property is obtained by a person if he obtains an interest in it.

(6) References to an interest, in relation to property other than land, include references to a right (including a right to possession).

(7) Property is relevant property if there are reasonable grounds to believe that it may be needed to satisfy an external order which has been or which may be made.

(8) Criminal conduct is conduct which –

    (a) constitutes an offence in any part of the United Kingdom, or

    (b) would constitute an offence in any part of the United Kingdom if it occurred there.

(9) A money laundering offence is conduct carried out in a country or territory outside the United Kingdom and which if carried out in the United Kingdom would constitute any of the following offences –

    (a) an offence under section 327, 328 or 329;

    (b) an attempt, conspiracy or incitement to commit an offence specified in paragraph (a);

    (c) aiding, abetting, counselling or procuring the commission of an offence specified in paragraph (a).

(10) An overseas court is a court of a country or territory outside the United Kingdom.

(11) An overseas authority is an authority which has responsibility in a country or territory outside the United Kingdom—

    (a) for making a request to an authority in another country or territory (including the United Kingdom) to prohibit dealing with relevant property,

    (b) for carrying out an investigation into whether property has been obtained as a result of or in connection with criminal conduct, or

    (c) for carrying out an investigation into whether a money laundering offence has been committed.

(12) This section applies for the purposes of this Part.

PART 12

MISCELLANEOUS AND GENERAL

Miscellaneous

448 Tax

Schedule 10 contains provisions about tax.

449 Agency staff: pseudonyms

(1) This section applies to a member of the staff of the Agency if—

    (a) he is authorised (generally or specifically) by the Director to do anything for the purposes of this Act, and

    (b) it is necessary or expedient for the purpose of doing the thing for the member of the staff of the Agency to identify himself by name.

(2) The Director may direct that such a member of the staff of the Agency may for that purpose identify himself by means of a pseudonym.

(3) For the purposes of any proceedings or application under this Act a certificate signed by the Director which sufficiently identifies the member of the staff of the Agency by reference to the pseudonym is conclusive evidence that that member of the staff of the Agency is authorised to use the pseudonym.

(4) In any proceedings or application under this Act a member of the staff of the Agency in respect of whom a direction under this section is in force must not be asked (and if asked is not required to answer) any question which is likely to reveal his true identity.

(5) Section 1(6) does not apply to anything done by the Director under this section.

450 Pseudonyms: Scotland

(1) This section applies to—

    (a) any person named by the Scottish Ministers for the purpose of a civil recovery investigation under Part 8, or

    (b) any person authorised by the Scottish Ministers for the purpose of such a civil recovery investigation to receive relevant information under section 391, if it is necessary or expedient for the person to identify himself by name for that purpose.

(2)   The Scottish Ministers may direct that such a person may for that purpose identify himself by means of a pseudonym.

(3)   For the purposes of any proceedings or application under this Act, a certificate signed by the Scottish Ministers which sufficiently identifies the person by reference to the pseudonym is conclusive evidence that the person is authorised to use the pseudonym.

(4)   In any proceedings or application under this Act a person in respect of whom a direction under this section is in force must not be asked (and if asked is not required to answer) any question which is likely to reveal his true identity.

451   Customs and Excise prosecutions

(1)   Proceedings for a specified offence may be started by order of the Commissioners of Customs and Excise (the Commissioners).

(2)   Such proceedings must be brought in the name of a customs officer.

(3)   If the customs officer in whose name the proceedings are brought —
   (a)   dies,
   (b)   is removed or discharged, or
   (c)   is absent,
the proceedings may be continued by a different customs officer.

(4)   If the Commissioners investigate, or propose to investigate, any matter to help them to decide —
   (a)   whether there are grounds for believing that a specified offence has been committed, or
   (b)   whether a person is to be prosecuted for such an offence,
the matter must be treated as an assigned matter within the meaning of the Customs and Excise Management Act 1979 (c. 2).

(5)   This section —
   (a)   does not prevent any person (including a customs officer) who has power to arrest, detain or prosecute a person for a specified offence from doing so;
   (b)   does not prevent a court from dealing with a person brought before it following his arrest by a customs officer for a specified offence, even if the proceedings were not started by an order under subsection (1).

(6)   The following are specified offences —
   (a)   an offence under Part 7;
   (b)   an offence under section 342;
   (c)   an attempt, conspiracy or incitement to commit an offence specified in paragraph (a) or (b);
   (d)   aiding, abetting, counselling or procuring the commission of an offence specified in paragraph (a) or (b).

(7)   This section does not apply to proceedings on indictment in Scotland.

452   Crown servants

(1)   The Secretary of State may by regulations provide that any of the following provisions apply to persons in the public service of the Crown.

(2)   The provisions are—
    (a)   the provisions of Part 7;
    (b)   section 342.

453   References to financial investigators

(1)   The Secretary of State may by order provide that a specified reference in this Act to an accredited financial investigator is a reference to such an investigator who falls within a specified description.

(2)   A description may be framed by reference to a grade designated by a specified person.

454   Customs officers

For the purposes of this Act a customs officer is a person commissioned by the Commissioners of Customs and Excise under section 6(3) of the Customs and Excise Management Act 1979 (c. 2).

455   Enactment

In this Act (except in section 460(1)) a reference to an enactment includes a reference to—
    (a)   an Act of the Scottish Parliament;
    (b)   Northern Ireland legislation.

General

456   Amendments

Schedule 11 contains miscellaneous and consequential amendments.

457   Repeals and revocations

Schedule 12 contains repeals and revocations.

458   Commencement

(1)   The preceding provisions of this Act (except the provisions specified in subsection (3)) come into force in accordance with provision made by the Secretary of State by order.

(2)   But no order may be made which includes provision for the commencement of Part 5, 8 or 10 unless the Secretary of State has consulted the Scottish Ministers.

(3)   The following provisions come into force in accordance with provision made by the Scottish Ministers by order after consultation with the Secretary of State—
    (a)   Part 3;

(b)   this Part, to the extent that it relates to Part 3.

459   Orders and regulations

(1)   References in this section to subordinate legislation are to—
  (a)   any Order in Council under this Act;
  (b)   any order under this Act (other than one falling to be made by a court);
  (c)   any regulations under this Act.

(2)   Subordinate legislation—
  (a)   may make different provision for different purposes;
  (b)   may include supplementary, incidental, saving or transitional provisions.

(3)   Any power to make subordinate legislation is exercisable by statutory instrument.

(4)   A statutory instrument is subject to annulment in pursuance of a resolution of either House of Parliament if it contains subordinate legislation other than—
  (a)   an order under section 75(7) or (8), 223(7) or (8), 282, 292(4), 309, 364(4), 377(4), 436(6), 438(9) or 458;
  (b)   subordinate legislation made by the Scottish Ministers;
  (c)   an Order in Council made under section 443 which makes provision only in relation to Scotland.

(5)   A statutory instrument is subject to annulment in pursuance of a resolution of the Scottish Parliament if it contains—
  (a)   subordinate legislation made by the Scottish Ministers other than an order under section 142(6) or (7), 293(4), 398(4), 410(4), 439(6), 441(9) or 458;
  (b)   an Order in Council made under section 443 which makes provision only in relation to Scotland.

(6)   No order may be made—
  (a)   by the Secretary of State under section 75(7) or (8), 223(7) or (8), 282, 292(4), 309, 364(4), 377(4), 436(6) or 438(9) unless a draft of the order has been laid before Parliament and approved by a resolution of each House;
  (b)   by the Scottish Ministers under section 142(6) or (7), 293(4), 398(4), 410(4), 439(6) or 441(9) unless a draft of the order has been laid before and approved by a resolution of the Scottish Parliament.

(7)   The Scottish Ministers must lay before the Scottish Parliament a copy of every statutory instrument containing an Order in Council made under section 444 or 445.

460   Finance

(1)   The following are to be paid out of money provided by Parliament—
  (a)   any expenditure incurred by any Minister of the Crown under this Act;
  (b)   any increase attributable to this Act in the sums payable out of money so provided under any other enactment.

(2)   Any sums received by the Secretary of State in consequence of this Act are to be paid into the Consolidated Fund.

461 Extent

(1) Part 2 extends to England and Wales only.

(2) In Part 8, Chapter 2 extends to England and Wales and Northern Ireland only.

(3) These provisions extend to Scotland only —
    (a) Part 3;
    (b) in Part 8, Chapter 3.

(4) Part 4 extends to Northern Ireland only.

(5) The amendments in Schedule 11 have the same extent as the provisions amended.

(6) The repeals and revocations in Schedule 12 have the same extent as the provisions repealed or revoked.

462 Short title

This Act may be cited as the Proceeds of Crime Act 2002.

SCHEDULES

SCHEDULE 1   Section 1

ASSETS RECOVERY AGENCY

Director's terms of appointment

1   (1) The Director holds office for the period determined by the Secretary of State on his appointment (or re-appointment) to the office.

    (2) But—

        (a) the Director may at any time resign by giving notice to the Secretary of State;

        (b) the Secretary of State may at any time remove the Director from office if satisfied that he is unable or unfit to exercise his functions.

2   Subject to that, the Director holds office on the terms determined by the Secretary of State with the approval of the Minister for the Civil Service.

Staff

3   (1) The members of staff of the Agency must include—

        (a) a deputy to the Director who is to act as Director during any vacancy in that office or if the Director is absent, subject to suspension or unable to act, and

        (b) an assistant to the Director with responsibilities in relation to the exercise of the Director's functions in Northern Ireland.

    (2) But the Director must not appoint a person under sub-paragraph (1)(b) unless he first consults the Secretary of State.

4   The members of staff of the Agency hold office on the terms determined by the Director with the approval of the Minister for the Civil Service.

Finances

5   (1) These amounts are to be paid out of money provided by Parliament—

        (a) the remuneration of the Director and the staff of the Agency;

        (b) any expenses incurred by the Director or any of the staff in the exercise of his or their functions.

    (2) Subject to anything in this Act any sums received by the Director are to be paid into the Consolidated Fund.

Annual plan

6 (1) The Director must, before the beginning of each financial year apart from the first, prepare a plan setting out how he intends to exercise his functions during the financial year (an annual plan).

   (2) The annual plan must, in particular, set out how the Director intends to exercise his functions in Northern Ireland.

   (3) The annual plan must also include a statement of —
       (a) the Director's objectives for the financial year;
       (b) any performance targets which he has for the financial year (whether or not relating to his objectives);
       (c) his priorities for the financial year;
       (d) the financial resources expected to be available to him for the financial year;
       (e) his proposed allocation of those resources.

   (4) Once the annual plan has been prepared the Director must send a copy to the Secretary of State for his approval.

   (5) If the Secretary of State does not approve the annual plan —
       (a) he must give the Director his reasons for not approving it, and
       (b) he may require the Director to revise it in the manner specified by the Secretary of State.

   (6) The Director must revise the annual plan, but if sub-paragraph (5)(b) applies he must do so in the manner specified by the Secretary of State.

   (7) The Director must send a copy of the revised annual plan to the Secretary of State for his approval.

Annual report

7 (1) The Director must, as soon as possible after the end of each financial year, prepare a report on how he has exercised his functions during the financial year.

   (2) The report for any financial year apart from the first must include —
       (a) the Director's annual plan for the financial year, and
       (b) an assessment of the extent to which it has been carried out.

   (3) The Director must send a copy of each report to the Secretary of State who must —
       (a) lay a copy of it before each House of Parliament, and
       (b) arrange for it to be published.

Meaning of "financial year"

8   In this Schedule "financial year" means —
       (a) the period beginning with the day on which section 1 comes into force and ending with the next 31 March (which is the first financial year), and
       (b) each subsequent period of twelve months beginning with 1 April.

SCHEDULE 2   Section 75

LIFESTYLE OFFENCES: ENGLAND AND WALES

Drug trafficking

1   (1) An offence under any of the following provisions of the Misuse of Drugs Act
         1971 (c. 38) —
         (a)   section 4(2) or (3) (unlawful production or supply of controlled
               drugs);
         (b)   section 5(3) (possession of controlled drug with intent to supply);
         (c)   section 8 (permitting certain activities relating to controlled drugs);
         (d)   section 20 (assisting in or inducing the commission outside the UK of
               an offence punishable under a corresponding law).

     (2) An offence under any of the following provisions of the Customs and Excise
         Management Act 1979 (c. 2) if it is committed in connection with a
         prohibition or restriction on importation or exportation which has effect by
         virtue of section 3 of the Misuse of Drugs Act 1971 —
         (a)   section 50(2) or (3) (improper importation of goods);
         (b)   section 68(2) (exploration of prohibited or restricted goods);
         (c)   section 170 (fraudulent evasion).

     (3) An offence under either of the following provisions of the Criminal Justice
         (International Co-operation) Act 1990 (c. 5) —
         (a)   section 12 (manufacture or supply of a substance for the time being
               specified in Schedule 2 to that Act);
         (b)   section 19 (using a ship for illicit traffic in controlled drugs).

Money laundering

2   An offence under either of the following provisions of this Act —
         (a)   section 327 (concealing etc criminal property);
         (b)   section 328 (assisting another to retain criminal property).

Directing terrorism

3   An offence under section 56 of the Terrorism Act 2000 (c. 11) (directing the
         activities of a terrorist organisation).

People trafficking

4   An offence under section 25(1) of the Immigration Act 1971 (c. 77) (assisting
         illegal entry etc).

Arms trafficking

5   (1) An offence under either of the following provisions of the Customs and
         Excise Management Act 1979 if it is committed in connection with a firearm
         or ammunition —
         (a)   section 68(2) (exportation of prohibited goods);
         (b)   section 170 (fraudulent evasion).

     (2) An offence under section 3(1) of the Firearms Act 1968 (c. 27) (dealing in
         firearms or ammunition by way of trade or business).

(3) In this paragraph "firearm" and "ammunition" have the same meanings as in section 57 of the Firearms Act 1968 (c. 27).

Counterfeiting

6   An offence under any of the following provisions of the Forgery and Counterfeiting Act 1981 (c. 45)—

    (a)   section 14 (making counterfeit notes or coins);
    (b)   section 15 (passing etc counterfeit notes or coins);
    (c)   section 16 (having counterfeit notes or coins);
    (d)   section 17 (making or possessing materials or equipment for counterfeiting).

Intellectual property

7   (1) An offence under any of the following provisions of the Copyright, Designs and Patents Act 1988 (c. 48)—

    (a)   section 107(1) (making or dealing in an article which infringes copyright);
    (b)   section 107(2) (making or possessing an article designed or adapted for making a copy of a copyright work);
    (c)   section 198(1) (making or dealing in an illicit recording);
    (d)   section 297A (making or dealing in unauthorised decoders).

    (2) An offence under section 92(1), (2) or (3) of the Trade Marks Act 1994 (c. 26) (unauthorised use etc of trade mark).

Pimps and brothels

8   (1) An offence under any of the following provisions of the Sexual Offences Act 1956 (c. 69)—

    (a)   section 2 (procuring a woman by threats);
    (b)   section 3 (procuring a woman by false pretences);
    (c)   section 9 (procuring a defective woman to have sexual intercourse);
    (d)   section 22 (procuring a woman for prostitution);
    (e)   section 24 (detaining a woman in a brothel);
    (f)   section 28 (causing or encouraging prostitution etc of girl under 16);
    (g)   section 29 (causing or encouraging prostitution of defective woman);
    (h)   section 30 (man living on earnings of prostitution);
    (i)   section 31 (woman exercising control over prostitute);
    (j)   section 33 (keeping a brothel);
    (k)   section 34 (letting premises for use as brothel).

    (2) An offence under section 5 of the Sexual Offences Act 1967 (c. 60) (living on the earnings of male prostitute).

Blackmail

9   An offence under section 21 of the Theft Act 1968 (c. 60) (blackmail).

Inchoate offences

10 (1) An offence of attempting, conspiring or inciting the commission of an offence specified in this Schedule.

    (2) An offence of aiding, abetting, counselling or procuring the commission of such an offence.

SCHEDULE 3

ADMINISTRATORS: FURTHER PROVISION

General

1   In this Schedule, unless otherwise expressly provided –

        (a) references to an administrator are to an administrator appointed under section 125 or 128(3);

        (b) references to realisable property are to the realisable property in respect of which the administrator is appointed.

Appointment etc

2 (1) If the office of administrator is vacant, for whatever reason, the court must appoint a new administrator.

   (2) Any property vested in the previous administrator by virtue of paragraph 5(4) vests in the new administrator.

   (3) Any order under section 125 or 128(7) in relation to the previous administrator applies in relation to the new administrator when he gives written notice of his appointment to the person subject to the order.

   (4) The administration of property by an administrator must be treated as continuous despite any temporary vacancy in that office.

   (5) The appointment of an administrator is subject to such conditions as to caution as the accountant of court may impose.

   (6) The premium of any bond of caution or other security required by such conditions must be treated as part of the administrator's expenses in the exercise of his functions.

Functions

3 (1) An administrator –

        (a) may, if appointed under section 125, and

        (b) must, if appointed under section 128(3),

        as soon as practicable take possession of the realisable property and of the documents mentioned in sub-paragraph (2).

   (2) Those documents are any document which –

        (a) is in the possession or control of the person ("A") in whom the property is vested (or would be vested but for an order made under paragraph 5(4)), and

        (b) relates to the property or to A's assets, business or financial affairs.

(3) An administrator is entitled to have access to, and to copy, any document relating to the property or to A's assets, business or financial affairs and not falling within sub-paragraph (2)(a).

(4) An administrator may bring, defend or continue any legal proceedings relating to the property.

(5) An administrator may borrow money so far as it is necessary to do so to safeguard the property and may for the purposes of such borrowing create a security over any part of the property.

(6) An administrator may, if he considers that it would be beneficial for the management or realisation of the property—
    (a) carry on any business of A;
    (b) exercise any right of A as holder of securities in a company;
    (c) grant a lease of the property or take on lease any other property;
    (d) enter into any contract, or execute any deed, as regards the property or as regards A's business.

(7) An administrator may, where any right, option or other power forms part of A's estate, make payments or incur liabilities with a view to—
    (a) obtaining property which is the subject of, or
    (b) maintaining,
the right, option or power.

(8) An administrator may effect or maintain insurance policies as regards the property on A's business.

(9) An administrator may, if appointed under section 128(3), complete any uncompleted title which A has to any heritable estate; but completion of title in A's name does not validate by accretion any unperfected right in favour of any person other than the administrator.

(10) An administrator may sell, purchase or exchange property or discharge any security for an obligation due to A; but it is incompetent for the administrator or an associate of his (within the meaning of section 74 of the Bankruptcy (Scotland) Act 1985 (c. 66)) to purchase any of A's property in pursuance of this sub-paragraph.

(11) An administrator may claim, vote and draw dividends in the sequestration of the estate (or bankruptcy or liquidation) of a debtor of A and may accede to a voluntary trust deed for creditors of such a debtor.

(12) An administrator may discharge any of his functions through agents or employees, but is personally liable to meet the fees and expenses of any such agent or employee out of such remuneration as is payable to the administrator on a determination by the accountant of court.

(13) An administrator may take such professional advice as he considers necessary in connection with the exercise of his functions.

(14) An administrator may at any time apply to the court for directions as regards the exercise of his functions.

(15) An administrator may exercise any power specifically conferred on him by the court, whether conferred on his appointment or subsequently.

(16) An administrator may—
    (a) enter any premises;
    (b) search for or inspect anything authorised by the court;

> (c) make or obtain a copy, photograph or other record of anything so authorised;
>
> (d) remove anything which the administrator is required or authorised to take possession of in pursuance of an order of the court.

(17) An administrator may do anything incidental to the powers and duties listed in the previous provisions of this paragraph.

Consent of accountant of court

4   An administrator proposing to exercise any power conferred by paragraph 3(4) to (17) must first obtain the consent of the accountant of court.

Dealings in good faith with administrator

5   (1) A person dealing with an administrator in good faith and for value is not concerned to enquire whether the administrator is acting within the powers mentioned in paragraph 3.

(2) Sub-paragraph (1) does not apply where the administrator or an associate purchases property in contravention of paragraph 3(10).

(3) The validity of any title is not challengeable by reason only of the administrator having acted outwith the powers mentioned in paragraph 3.

(4) The exercise of a power mentioned in paragraph 3(4) to (11) must be in A's name except where and in so far as an order made by the court under this sub-paragraph vests the property in the administrator (or in a previous administrator).

(5) The court may make an order under sub-paragraph (4) on the application of the administrator or on its own motion.

Money received by administrator

6   (1) All money received by an administrator in the exercise of his functions must be deposited by him, in the name (unless vested in the administrator by virtue of paragraph 5(4)) of the holder of the property realised, in an appropriate bank or institution.

(2) But the administrator may at any time retain in his hands a sum not exceeding £200 or such other sum as may be prescribed by the Scottish Ministers by regulations.

(3) In sub-paragraph (1), "appropriate bank or institution" means a bank or institution mentioned in section 3(1) of the Banking Act 1987 (c. 22) or for the time being specified in Schedule 2 to that Act.

Effect of appointment of administrator on diligence

7   (1) An arrestment or poinding of realisable property executed on or after the appointment of an administrator does not create a preference for the arrester or poinder.

(2) Any realisable property so arrested or poinded, or (if the property has been sold) the proceeds of sale, must be handed over to the administrator.

(3) A poinding of the ground in respect of realisable property on or after such appointment is ineffectual in a question with the administrator except for the interest mentioned in sub-paragraph (4).

(4) That interest is—

    (a) interest on the debt of a secured creditor for the current half-yearly term, and

    (b) arrears of interest on that debt for one year immediately before the commencement of that term.

(5) On and after such appointment no other person may raise or insist in an adjudication against realisable property or be confirmed as executor-creditor on that property.

(6) An inhibition on realisable property which takes effect on or after such appointment does not create a preference for the inhibitor in a question with the administrator.

(7) This paragraph is without prejudice to sections 123 and 124.

(8) In this paragraph, the reference to an administrator is to an administrator appointed under section 128(3).

Supervision

8   (1) If the accountant of court reports to the court that an administrator has failed to perform any duty imposed on him, the court may, after giving the administrator an opportunity to be heard as regards the matter—

    (a) remove him from office,

    (b) censure him, or

    (c) make such other order as it thinks fit.

(2) Section 6 of the Judicial Factors (Scotland) Act 1889 (c. 39) (supervision of judicial factors) does not apply in relation to an administrator.

Accounts and remuneration

9   (1) Not later than two weeks after the issuing of any determination by the accountant of court as to the remuneration and expenses payable to the administrator, the administrator or the Lord Advocate may appeal against it to the court.

(2) The amount of remuneration payable to the administrator must be determined on the basis of the value of the work reasonably undertaken by him, regard being had to the extent of the responsibilities involved.

(3) The accountant of court may authorise the administrator to pay without taxation an account in respect of legal services incurred by the administrator.

Discharge of administrator

10   (1) After an administrator has lodged his final accounts under paragraph 9(1), he may apply to the accountant of court to be discharged from office.

(2) A discharge, if granted, frees the administrator from all liability (other than liability arising from fraud) in respect of any act or omission of his in exercising his functions as administrator.

SCHEDULE 4

Section 142

LIFESTYLE OFFENCES: SCOTLAND

Money laundering

1   An offence under either of the following provisions of this Act—

      (a)   section 327 (concealing etc. criminal property);

      (b)   section 328 (assisting another person to retain criminal property).

Drug trafficking

2   (1)   An offence under any of the following provisions of the Misuse of Drugs Act 1971 (c. 38)—

      (a)   section 4(2) or (3) (unlawful production or supply of controlled drugs);

      (b)   section 5(3) (possession of controlled drug with intent to supply);

      (c)   section 8 (permitting certain activities relating to controlled drugs);

      (d)   section 20 (assisting in or inducing the commission outside the UK of an offence punishable under a corresponding law).

    (2)   An offence under any of the following provisions of the Customs and Excise Management Act 1979 (c. 2) if it is committed in connection with a prohibition or restriction on importation or exportation which has effect by virtue of section 3 of the Misuse of Drugs Act 1971—

      (a)   section 50(2) or (3) (improper importation of goods);

      (b)   section 68(2) (exploration of prohibited or restricted goods);

      (c)   section 170 (fraudulent evasion).

    (3)   An offence under either of the following provisions of the Criminal Justice (International Co-operation) Act 1990 (c. 5)—

      (a)   section 12 (manufacture or supply of a substance for the time being specified in Schedule 2 to that Act);

      (b)   section 19 (using a ship for illicit traffic in controlled drugs).

Directing terrorism

3   An offence under section 56 of the Terrorism Act 2000 (c. 11) (directing the activities of a terrorist organisation).

People trafficking

4   An offence under section 25(1) of the Immigration Act 1971 (c. 77) (assisting illegal entry etc).

Arms trafficking

5   (1)   An offence under either of the following provisions of the Customs and Excise Management Act 1979 if it is committed in connection with a firearm or ammunition—

      (a)   section 68(2) (exportation of prohibited goods);

      (b)   section 170 (fraudulent evasion).

    (2)   An offence under section 3(1) of the Firearms Act 1968 (c. 27)(dealing in firearms or ammunition by way of trade or business).

(3) In this paragraph "firearm" and "ammunition" have the same meanings as in section 57 of the Firearms Act 1968 (c. 27).

Counterfeiting

6   An offence under any of the following provisions of the Forgery and Counterfeiting Act 1981 (c. 45) –
     (a)   section 14 (making counterfeit notes or coins);
     (b)   section 15 (passing etc counterfeit notes or coins);
     (c)   section 16 (having counterfeit notes or coins);
     (d)   section 17 (making or possessing materials or equipment for counterfeiting).

Intellectual property

7   (1) An offence under any of the following provisions of the Copyright, Designs and Patents Act 1988 (c. 48) –
     (a)   section 107(1) (making or dealing in an article which infringes copyright);
     (b)   section 107(2) (making or possessing an article designed or adapted for making a copy of a copyright work);
     (c)   section 198(1) (making or dealing in an illicit recording);
     (d)   section 297A (making or dealing in unauthorised decoders).
     (2) An offence under section 92(1), (2), or (3) of the Trade Marks Act 1994 (c. 26)(unauthorised use etc of trade mark).

Pimps and brothels

8   An offence under either of the following provisions of the Criminal Law (Consolidation) (Scotland) Act 1995 (c. 39) –
     (a)   section 11(1) (living on earnings of prostitution or soliciting for immoral purposes);
     (b)   section 11(5) (running of brothels).

Blackmail

9   An offence of blackmail or extortion.

Inchoate offences

10   (1) An offence of conspiring or inciting the commission of an offence specified in this Schedule.
     (2) An offence of aiding, abetting, counselling or procuring the commission of such an offence.

SCHEDULE 5 Section 223

LIFESTYLE OFFENCES: NORTHERN IRELAND

Drug trafficking

1   (1) An offence under any of the following provisions of the Misuse of Drugs Act 1971 (c. 38) –

    (a) section 4(2) or (3) (unlawful production or supply of controlled drugs);

    (b) section 5(3) (possession of controlled drug with intent to supply);

    (c) section 8 (permitting certain activities relating to controlled drugs);

    (d) section 20 (assisting in or inducing the commission outside the UK of an offence punishable under a corresponding law).

  (2) An offence under any of the following provisions of the Customs and Excise Management Act 1979 (c. 2) if it is committed in connection with a prohibition or restriction on importation or exportation which has effect by virtue of section 3 of the Misuse of Drugs Act 1971 –

    (a) section 50(2) or (3) (improper importation of goods);

    (b) section 68(2) (exportation of prohibited or restricted goods);

    (c) section 170 (fraudulent evasion).

  (3) An offence under either of the following provisions of the Criminal Justice (International Co-operation) Act 1990 (c. 5) –

    (a) section 12 (manufacture or supply of a substance for the time being specified in Schedule 2 to that Act);

    (b) section 19 (using a ship for illicit traffic in controlled drugs).

Money laundering

2   An offence under either of the following provisions of this Act –

    (a) section 327 (concealing etc. criminal property);

    (b) section 328 (assisting another to retain criminal property).

Directing terrorism

3   An offence under section 56 of the Terrorism Act 2000 (c. 11) (directing the activities of a terrorist organisation).

People trafficking

4   An offence under section 25(1) of the Immigration Act 1971 (c. 77) (assisting illegal entry etc.).

Arms trafficking

5   (1) An offence under either of the following provisions of the Customs and Excise Management Act 1979 if it is committed in connection with a firearm or ammunition –

    (a) section 68(2) (exportation of prohibited goods);

    (b) section 170 (fraudulent evasion).

(2) An offence under Article 4(1) of the Firearms (Northern Ireland) Order 1981 (S.I. 1981/155 (N.I. 2) (dealing in firearms or ammunition by way of trade or business).

(3) In this paragraph "firearm" and "ammunition" have the same meanings as in Article 2(2) of that Order.

Counterfeiting

6   An offence under any of the following provisions of the Forgery and Counterfeiting Act 1981 (c. 45) —
- (a) section 14 (making counterfeit notes or coins);
- (b) section 15 (passing etc counterfeit notes or coins);
- (c) section 16 (having counterfeit notes or coins);
- (d) section 17 (making or possessing materials or equipment for counterfeiting).

Intellectual property

7   (1) An offence under any of the following provisions of the Copyright, Designs and Patents Act 1988 (c. 48) —
- (a) section 107(1) (making or dealing in an article which infringes copyright);
- (b) section 107(2) (making or possessing an article designed or adapted for making a copy of a copyright work);
- (c) section 198(1) (making or dealing in an illicit recording);
- (d) section 297A (making or dealing in unauthorised decoders).

(2) An offence under section 92(1), (2) or (3) of the Trade Marks Act 1994 (c. 26) (unauthorised use etc of trade mark).

Pimps and brothels

8   (1) An offence under any of the following provisions of the Criminal Law Amendment Act 1885 (c. 69) —
- (a) section 2 (procuring a woman or girl);
- (b) section 3 (procuring a woman or girl by threats or false pretences);
- (c) section 8 (detaining a woman in a brothel);
- (d) section 13(3) (letting premises for use as a brothel).

(2) An offence under section 1(1) of the Vagrancy Act 1898 (c. 39) (man living on the earnings of prostitution).

(3) An offence under that Act as extended by section 7(4) of the Criminal Law Amendment Act 1912 (c. 20) (woman exercising control over prostitute)).

(4) An offence under section 21 of the Children and Young Persons Act (Northern Ireland) 1968 (c. 34) (causing or encouraging prostitution etc of girl under 17).

(5) An offence under Article 8 of the Homosexual Offences (Northern Ireland) Order 1982 (S.I. 1982/1536 (N.I. 19)) (living on the earnings of male prostitute).

(6) An offence under Article 122(1)(b) or (c) of the Mental Health (Northern Ireland) Order 1986 (S.I. 1986/595 (N.I. 4)) (procuring or causing prostitution by woman suffering from severe mental handicap).

(7) An offence of keeping a bawdy house.

Blackmail

9   An offence under section 20 of the Theft Act (Northern Ireland) 1969 (c. 16)
          (blackmail).

Inchoate offences

10   (1) An offence of attempting, conspiring or inciting the commission of an
          offence specified in this Schedule.

     (2) An offence of aiding, abetting, counselling or procuring the commission of
          such an offence.

                              SCHEDULE 6   Sections 247 and 257

                    POWERS OF INTERIM RECEIVER OR ADMINISTRATOR

Seizure

1   Power to seize property to which the order applies.

Information

2   (1) Power to obtain information or to require a person to answer any question.

     (2) A requirement imposed in the exercise of the power has effect in spite of any
          restriction on the disclosure of information (however imposed).

     (3) An answer given by a person in pursuance of such a requirement may not
          be used in evidence against him in criminal proceedings.

     (4) Sub-paragraph (3) does not apply —
          (a) on a prosecution for an offence under section 5 of the Perjury Act
               1911, section 44(2) of the Criminal Law (Consolidation) (Scotland)
               Act 1995 or Article 10 of the Perjury (Northern Ireland) Order 1979
               (false statements), or
          (b) on a prosecution for some other offence where, in giving evidence, he
               makes a statement inconsistent with it.

     (5) But an answer may not be used by virtue of sub-paragraph (4)(b) against a
          person unless —
          (a) evidence relating to it is adduced, or
          (b) a question relating to it is asked,
          by him or on his behalf in the proceedings arising out of the prosecution.

Entry, search, etc.

3   (1) Power to —
          (a) enter any premises in the United Kingdom to which the interim
               order applies, and
          (b) take any of the following steps.

     (2) Those steps are —

      (a)   to carry out a search for or inspection of anything described in the order,

      (b)   to make or obtain a copy, photograph or other record of anything so described,

      (c)   to remove anything which he is required to take possession of in pursuance of the order or which may be required as evidence in the proceedings under Chapter 2 of Part 5.

  (3) The order may describe anything generally, whether by reference to a class or otherwise.

Supplementary

4   (1) An order making any provision under paragraph 2 or 3 must make provision in respect of legal professional privilege (in Scotland, legal privilege within the meaning of Chapter 3 of Part 8).

    (2) An order making any provision under paragraph 3 may require any person —

      (a)   to give the interim receiver or administrator access to any premises which he may enter in pursuance of paragraph 3,

      (b)   to give the interim receiver or administrator any assistance he may require for taking the steps mentioned in that paragraph.

Management

5   (1) Power to manage any property to which the order applies.

    (2) Managing property includes —

      (a)   selling or otherwise disposing of assets comprised in the property which are perishable or which ought to be disposed of before their value diminishes,

      (b)   where the property comprises assets of a trade or business, carrying on, or arranging for another to carry on, the trade or business,

      (c)   incurring capital expenditure in respect of the property.

SCHEDULE 7

Section 267

POWERS OF TRUSTEE FOR CIVIL RECOVERY

Sale

1   Power to sell the property or any part of it or interest in it.

Expenditure

2   Power to incur expenditure for the purpose of —

      (a)   acquiring any part of the property, or any interest in it, which is not vested in him,

      (b)   discharging any liabilities, or extinguishing any rights, to which the property is subject.

Management

3   (1) Power to manage property.

       (2) Managing property includes doing anything mentioned in paragraph 5(2) of
            Schedule 6.

Legal proceedings

4   Power to start, carry on or defend any legal proceedings in respect of the
            property.

Compromise

5   Power to make any compromise or other arrangement in connection with
            any claim relating to the property.

Supplementary

6   (1) For the purposes of, or in connection with, the exercise of any of his
            powers –
            (a) power by his official name to do any of the things mentioned in sub-
                 paragraph (2),
            (b)   power to do any other act which is necessary or expedient.

       (2) Those things are –
            (a)   holding property,
            (b)   entering into contracts,
            (c)   suing and being sued,
            (d)   employing agents,
            (e)   executing a power of attorney, deed or other instrument.

SCHEDULE 8   Section 325

FORMS OF DECLARATIONS

The Director

"I, A.B., do solemnly declare that I will not disclose any information received
by me in carrying out my functions under Part 6 of the Proceeds of Crime
Act 2002 except for the purposes of those functions or for the purposes of any
prosecution for an offence relating to inland revenue, or in such other cases
as may be required or permitted by law."

Members of the staff of the Agency

"I, A.B., do solemnly declare that I will not disclose any information received
by me in carrying out the functions under Part 6 of the Proceeds of Crime Act
2002 which I may from time to time be authorised by the Director of the
Assets Recovery Agency to carry out except for the purposes of those
functions, or to the Director or in accordance with his instructions, or for the
purposes of any prosecution for an offence relating to inland revenue, or in
such other cases as may be required or permitted by law."

Proceeds of Crime Act 2002 (c. 29)
Schedule 9 – Regulated sector and supervisory authorities
Part 1 – Regulated sector

289

SCHEDULE 9 Section 330

REGULATED SECTOR AND SUPERVISORY AUTHORITIES

PART 1

REGULATED SECTOR

Business in the regulated sector

1 (1) A business is in the regulated sector to the extent that it engages in any of the following activities –

   (a) accepting deposits by a person with permission under Part 4 of the Financial Services and Markets Act 2000 (c. 8) to accept deposits (including, in the case of a building society, the raising of money from members of the society by the issue of shares);

   (b) the business of the National Savings Bank;

   (c) business carried on by a credit union;

   (d) any home-regulated activity carried on by a European institution in respect of which the establishment conditions in paragraph 13 of Schedule 3 to the Financial Services and Markets Act 2000, or the service conditions in paragraph 14 of that Schedule, are satisfied;

   (e) any activity carried on for the purpose of raising money authorised to be raised under the National Loans Act 1968 (c. 13) under the auspices of the Director of Savings;

   (f) the activity of operating a bureau de change, transmitting money (or any representation of monetary value) by any means or cashing cheques which are made payable to customers;

   (g) any activity falling within sub-paragraph (2);

   (h) any of the activities in points 1 to 12 or 14 of Annex 1 to the Banking Consolidation Directive, ignoring an activity described in any of sub-paragraphs (a) to (g) above;

   (i) business which consists of effecting or carrying out contracts of long term insurance by a person who has received official authorisation pursuant to Article 6 or 27 of the First Life Directive.

(2) An activity falls within this sub-paragraph if it constitutes any of the following kinds of regulated activity in the United Kingdom –

   (a) dealing in investments as principal or as agent;

   (b) arranging deals in investments;

   (c) managing investments;

   (d) safeguarding and administering investments;

   (e) sending dematerialised instructions;

   (f) establishing (and taking other steps in relation to) collective investment schemes;

   (g) advising on investments.

(3) Paragraphs (a) and (i) of sub-paragraph (1) and sub-paragraph (2) must be read with section 22 of the Financial Services and Markets Act 2000, any relevant order under that section and Schedule 2 to that Act.

2 (1) This paragraph has effect for the purposes of paragraph 1.

(2) "Building society" has the meaning given by the Building Societies Act 1986 (c. 53).

290

Proceeds of Crime Act 2002 (c. 29)
Schedule 9 — Regulated sector and supervisory authorities
Part 1 — Regulated sector

(3) "Credit union" has the meaning given by the Credit Unions Act 1979 (c. 34) or the Credit Unions (Northern Ireland) Order 1985 (S.I. 1985/1205 (N.I. 12)).

(4) "European institution" means an EEA firm of the kind mentioned in paragraph 5(b) or (c) of Schedule 3 to the Financial Services and Markets Act 2000 (c. 8) which qualifies for authorisation for the purposes of that Act under paragraph 12 of that Schedule.

(5) "Home-regulated activity" in relation to a European institution, means an activity —

   (a) which is specified in Annex 1 to the Banking Consolidation Directive and in respect of which a supervisory authority in the home State of the institution has regulatory functions, and

   (b) if the institution is an EEA firm of the kind mentioned in paragraph 5(c) of Schedule 3 to the Financial Services and Markets Act 2000, which the institution carries on in its home State.

(6) "Home State", in relation to a person incorporated in or formed under the law of another member State, means that State.

(7) The Banking Consolidation Directive is the Directive of the European Parliament and Council relating to the taking up and pursuit of the business of credit institutions (No. 2000/12 EC).

(8) The First Life Directive is the First Council Directive on the co-ordination of laws, regulations and administrative provisions relating to the taking up and pursuit of the business of direct life assurance (No. 79/267/EEC).

Excluded activities

3   A business is not in the regulated sector to the extent that it engages in any of the following activities —

   (a) the issue of withdrawable share capital within the limit set by section 6 of the Industrial and Provident Societies Act 1965 (c. 12) by a society registered under that Act;

   (b) the acceptance of deposits from the public within the limit set by section 7(3) of that Act by such a society;

   (c) the issue of withdrawable share capital within the limit set by section 6 of the Industrial and Provident Societies Act (Northern Ireland) 1969 by a society registered under that Act;

   (d) the acceptance of deposits from the public within the limit set by section 7(3) of that Act by such a society;

   (e) activities carried on by the Bank of England;

   (f) any activity in respect of which an exemption order under section 38 of the Financial Services and Markets Act 2000 has effect if it is carried on by a person who is for the time being specified in the order or falls within a class of persons so specified.

PART 2

SUPERVISORY AUTHORITIES

4   (1) Each of the following is a supervisory authority —

   (a) the Bank of England;

   (b) the Financial Services Authority;

   (c) the Council of Lloyd's;

Proceeds of Crime Act 2002 (c. 29)
Schedule 9 — Regulated sector and supervisory authorities
Part 2 — Supervisory authorities

291

> (d)   the Director General of Fair Trading;
>
> (e)   a body which is a designated professional body for the purposes of Part 20 of the Financial Services and Markets Act 2000 (c. 8).

(2)   The Secretary of State is also a supervisory authority in the exercise, in relation to a person carrying on a business in the regulated sector, of his functions under the enactments relating to companies or insolvency or under the Financial Services and Markets Act 2000.

(3)   The Treasury are also a supervisory authority in the exercise, in relation to a person carrying on a business in the regulated sector, of their functions under the enactments relating to companies or insolvency or under the Financial Services and Markets Act 2000.

PART 3

POWER TO AMEND

5   The Treasury may by order amend Part 1 or 2 of this Schedule.

SCHEDULE 10   Section 448

TAX

PART 1

GENERAL

1   Sections 75 and 77 of the Taxes Management Act 1970 (c. 9) (receivers: income tax and capital gains tax) shall not apply in relation to—

> (a)   a receiver appointed under section 48, 50 or 52;
>
> (b)   an administrator appointed under section 125 or 128;
>
> (c)   a receiver appointed under section 196, 198 or 200;
>
> (d)   an interim receiver appointed under section 246;
>
> (e)   an interim administrator appointed under section 256.

PART 2

PROVISIONS RELATING TO PART 5

INTRODUCTORY

2   (1)   The vesting of property in the trustee for civil recovery or any other person by a recovery order or in pursuance of an order under section 276 is referred to as a Part 5 transfer.

(2)   The person who holds the property immediately before the vesting is referred to as the transferor; and the person in whom the property is vested is referred to as the transferee.

(3)   Any amount paid in respect of the transfer by the trustee for civil recovery, or another, to a person who holds the property immediately before the vesting is referred to (in relation to that person) as a compensating payment.

292

Proceeds of Crime Act 2002 (c. 29)
Schedule 10 – Tax
Part 2 – Provisions relating to Part 5

(4) If the recovery order provides or (as the case may be) the terms on which the order under section 276 is made provide for the creation of any interest in favour of a person who holds the property immediately before the vesting, he is to be treated instead as receiving (in addition to any payment referred to in sub-paragraph (3)) a compensating payment of an amount equal to the value of the interest.

(5) Where the property belongs to joint tenants immediately before the vesting and a compensating payment is made to one or more (but not both or all) of the joint tenants, this Part has effect separately in relation to each joint tenant.

(6) Expressions used in this paragraph have the same meaning as in Part 5 of this Act.

(7) "The Taxes Act 1988" means the Income and Corporation Taxes Act 1988 (c. 1), and "the Allowances Act 2001" means the Capital Allowances Act 2001 (c. 2).

(8) This paragraph applies for the purposes of this Part.

CAPITAL GAINS TAX

3   (1) If a gain attributable to a Part 5 transfer accrues to the transferor, it is not a chargeable gain.

(2) But if a compensating payment is made to the transferor –
   (a) sub-paragraph (1) does not apply, and
   (b) the consideration for the transfer is the amount of the compensating payment.

(3) If a gain attributable to the forfeiture under section 298 of property consisting of –
   (a) notes or coins in any currency other than sterling,
   (b) anything mentioned in section 289(6)(b) to (d), if expressed in any currency other than sterling, or
   (c) bearer bonds or bearer shares,
   accrues to the person who holds the property immediately before the forfeiture, it is not a chargeable gain.

(4) This paragraph has effect as if it were included in Chapter 1 of Part 2 of the Taxation of Chargeable Gains Act 1992 (c. 12).

INCOME TAX AND CORPORATION TAX

Accrued income scheme

4   If a Part 5 transfer is a transfer of securities within the meaning of sections 711 to 728 of the Taxes Act 1988 (transfers with or without accrued interest), sections 713(2) and (3) and 716 of that Act do not apply to the transfer.

Discounted securities

5   In the case of a Part 5 transfer of property consisting of a relevant discounted security (within the meaning of Schedule 13 to the Finance Act 1996 (c. 8)), it is not to be treated as a transfer for the purposes of that Schedule.

Proceeds of Crime Act 2002 (c. 29)
Schedule 10 — Tax
Part 2 — Provisions relating to Part 5

293

Rights to receive amounts stated in certificates of deposit etc.

6   In the case of a Part 5 transfer of property consisting of a right to which
         section 56(2) of the Taxes Act 1988 applies, or a right mentioned in section
         56A(1) of that Act, (rights stated in certificates of deposit etc.) it is not to be
         treated as a disposal of the right for the purposes of section 56(2) of that Act.

Non-qualifying offshore funds

7   In the case of a Part 5 transfer of property consisting of an asset mentioned
         in section 757(1)(a) or (b) of the Taxes Act 1988 (interests in non-qualifying
         offshore funds etc.), it is not to be treated as a disposal for the purposes of
         that section.

Futures and options

8   In the case of a Part 5 transfer of property consisting of futures or options
         (within the meaning of paragraph 4 of Schedule 5AA to the Taxes Act 1988),
         it is not to be treated as a disposal of the futures or options for the purposes
         of that Schedule.

Loan relationships

9   (1) Sub-paragraph (2) applies if, apart from this paragraph, a Part 5 transfer
         would be a related transaction for the purposes of section 84 of the Finance
         Act 1996 (c. 8) (debits and credits brought into account for the purpose of
         taxing loan relationships under Chapter 2 of Part 4 of that Act).

     (2) The Part 5 transfer is to be disregarded for the purposes of that Chapter,
         except for the purpose of identifying any person in whose case any debit or
         credit not relating to the transaction is to be brought into account.

Exception from paragraphs 4 to 9

10   Paragraphs 4 to 9 do not apply if a compensating payment is made to the
         transferor.

Trading stock

11   (1) Sub-paragraph (2) applies, in the case of a Part 5 transfer of property
         consisting of the trading stock of a trade, for the purpose of computing any
         profits of the trade for tax purposes.

     (2) If, because of the transfer, the trading stock is to be treated for that purpose
         as if it had been sold in the course of the trade, the amount realised on the
         sale is to be treated for that purpose as equal to its acquisition cost.

     (3) Sub-paragraph (2) has effect in spite of anything in section 100 of the Taxes
         Act 1988 (valuation of trading stock at discontinuance).

     (4) In this paragraph, trading stock and trade have the same meaning as in that
         section.

CAPITAL ALLOWANCES

294

Proceeds of Crime Act 2002 (c. 29)
Schedule 10 – Tax
Part 2 – Provisions relating to Part 5

Plant and machinery

12 (1) If there is a Part 5 transfer of plant or machinery, Part 2 of the Allowances Act 2001 is to have effect as if a transferor who has incurred qualifying expenditure were required to bring the disposal value of the plant or machinery into account in accordance with section 61 of that Act for the chargeable period in which the transfer occurs.

   (2) But the Part 5 transfer is not to be treated as a disposal event for the purposes of Part 2 of that Act other than by virtue of sub-paragraph (1).

13 (1) If a compensating payment is made to the transferor, the disposal value to be brought into account is the amount of the payment.

   (2) Otherwise, the disposal value to be brought into account is the amount which would give rise neither to a balancing allowance nor to a balancing charge.

14 (1) Paragraph 13(2) does not apply if the qualifying expenditure has been allocated to the main pool or a class pool.

   (2) Instead, the disposal value to be brought into account is the notional written-down value of the qualifying expenditure incurred by the transferor on the provision of the plant or machinery.

   (3) The notional written-down value is –

$$QE - A$$

where –

QE is the qualifying expenditure incurred by the transferor on the provision of the plant or machinery,

A is the total of all allowances which could have been made to the transferor in respect of the expenditure if –

   (a) that expenditure had been the only expenditure that had ever been taken into account in determining his available qualifying expenditure, and

   (b) all allowances had been made in full.

   (4) But if –

   (a) the Part 5 transfer of the plant or machinery occurs in the same chargeable period as that in which the qualifying expenditure is incurred, and

   (b) a first-year allowance is made in respect of an amount of the expenditure,

the disposal value to be brought into account is that which is equal to the balance left after deducting the first year allowance.

15 (1) Paragraph 13 does not apply if –

   (a) a qualifying activity is carried on in partnership,

   (b) the Part 5 transfer is a transfer of plant or machinery which is partnership property, and

   (c) compensating payments are made to one or more, but not both or all, of the partners.

Proceeds of Crime Act 2002 (c. 29)
Schedule 10 – Tax
Part 2 – Provisions relating to Part 5

295

    (2) Instead, the disposal value to be brought into account is the sum of –

        (a) any compensating payments made to any of the partners, and

        (b) in the case of each partner to whom a compensating payment has not been made, his share of the tax-neutral amount.

    (3) A partner's share of the tax-neutral amount is to be determined according to the profit-sharing arrangements for the twelve months ending immediately before the date of the Part 5 transfer.

16   (1) Paragraph 13 does not apply if –

        (a) a qualifying activity is carried on in partnership,

        (b) the Part 5 transfer is a transfer of plant or machinery which is not partnership property but is owned by two or more of the partners ("the owners"),

        (c) the plant or machinery is used for the purposes of the qualifying activity, and

        (d) compensating payments are made to one or more, but not both or all, of the owners.

    (2) Instead, the disposal value to be brought into account is the sum of –

        (a) any compensating payments made to any of the owners, and

        (b) in the case of each owner to whom a compensating payment has not been made, his share of the tax-neutral amount.

    (3) An owner's share of the tax-neutral amount is to be determined in proportion to the value of his interest in the plant or machinery.

17   (1) Paragraphs 12 to 16 have effect as if they were included in section 61 of the Allowances Act 2001.

    (2) In paragraphs 15 and 16, the tax-neutral amount is the amount that would be brought into account as the disposal value under paragraph 13(2) or (as the case may be) 14 if the provision in question were not disapplied.

Industrial buildings

18   (1) If there is a Part 5 transfer of a relevant interest in an industrial building, Part 3 of the Allowances Act 2001 is to have effect as if the transfer were a balancing event within section 315(1) of that Act.

    (2) But the Part 5 transfer is not to be treated as a balancing event for the purposes of Part 3 of that Act other than by virtue of sub-paragraph (1).

19   (1) If a compensating payment is made to the transferor, the proceeds from the balancing event are the amount of the payment.

    (2) Otherwise –

        (a) the proceeds from the balancing event are the amount which is equal to the residue of qualifying expenditure immediately before the transfer, and

        (b) no balancing adjustment is to be made as a result of the event under section 319 of the Allowances Act 2001.

20   (1) Paragraph 19 does not apply to determine the proceeds from the balancing event if –

        (a) the relevant interest in the industrial building is partnership property, and

        (b) compensating payments are made to one or more, but not both or all, of the partners.

296 *Proceeds of Crime Act 2002 (c. 29)*
Schedule 10 – Tax
Part 2 – Provisions relating to Part 5

    (2) Instead, the proceeds from the balancing event are the sum of —

      (a)   any compensating payments made to any of the partners, and

      (b)   in the case of each partner to whom a compensating payment has not been made, his share of the amount which is equal to the residue of qualifying expenditure immediately before the Part 5 transfer.

    (3) A partner's share of that amount is to be determined according to the profit-sharing arrangements for the twelve months ending immediately before the date of the Part 5 transfer.

21   Paragraphs 18 to 20 have effect as if they were included in Part 3 of the Allowances Act 2001.

Flat conversion

22   (1) If there is a Part 5 transfer of a relevant interest in a flat, Part 4A of the Allowances Act 2001 is to have effect as if the transfer were a balancing event within section 393N of that Act.

    (2) But the Part 5 transfer is not to be treated as a balancing event for the purposes of Part 4A of that Act other than by virtue of sub-paragraph (1).

23   (1) If a compensating payment is made to the transferor, the proceeds from the balancing event are the amount of the payment.

    (2) Otherwise, the proceeds from the balancing event are the amount which is equal to the residue of qualifying expenditure immediately before the transfer.

24   (1) Paragraph 23 does not apply to determine the proceeds from the balancing event if —

      (a)   the relevant interest in the flat is partnership property, and

      (b)   compensating payments are made to one or more, but not both or all, of the partners.

    (2) Instead, the proceeds from the balancing event are the sum of —

      (a)   any compensating payments made to any of the partners, and

      (b)   in the case of each partner to whom a compensating payment has not been made, his share of the amount which is equal to the residue of qualifying expenditure immediately before the transfer.

    (3) A partner's share of that amount is to be determined according to the profit-sharing arrangements for the twelve months ending immediately before the date of the transfer.

25   Paragraphs 22 to 24 have effect as if they were included in Part 4A of the Allowances Act 2001.

Research and development

26   If there is a Part 5 transfer of an asset representing qualifying expenditure incurred by a person, the disposal value he is required to bring into account under section 443(1) of the Allowances Act 2001 for any chargeable period is to be determined as follows (and not in accordance with subsection (4) of that section).

27   (1) If a compensating payment is made to the transferor, the disposal value he is required to bring into account is the amount of the payment.

    (2) Otherwise, the disposal value he is required to bring into account is nil.

Proceeds of Crime Act 2002 (c. 29)
Schedule 10 — Tax
Part 2 — Provisions relating to Part 5

297

28   (1) Paragraph 27 does not apply to determine the disposal value to be brought into account if—

    (a)   the asset is partnership property, and

    (b)   compensating payments are made to one or more, but not both or all, of the partners.

    (2) Instead, the disposal value to be brought into account is equal to the sum of any compensating payments.

29   Paragraphs 26 to 28 have effect as if they were included in Part 6 of the Allowances Act 2001.

EMPLOYEE ETC. SHARE SCHEMES

Share options

30   Section 135(6) of the Taxes Act 1988 (gains by directors and employees) does not make any person chargeable to tax in respect of any gain realised by the trustee for civil recovery.

Conditional acquisition of shares

31   Section 140A(4) of the Taxes Act 1988 (disposal etc. of shares) does not make the transferor chargeable to income tax in respect of a Part 5 transfer of shares or an interest in shares.

Shares acquired at an undervalue

32   Section 162(5) of the Taxes Act 1988 (employee shareholdings) does not make the transferor chargeable to income tax in respect of a Part 5 transfer of shares.

Shares in dependent subsidiaries

33   Section 79 of the Finance Act 1988 (c. 39) (charge on increase in value of shares) does not make the transferor chargeable to income tax in respect of a Part 5 transfer of shares or an interest in shares.

SCHEDULE 11

Section 456

AMENDMENTS

Introduction

1   The amendments specified in this Schedule shall have effect.

Parliamentary Commissioner Act 1967 (c. 13)

2   (1) The Parliamentary Commissioner Act 1967 is amended as follows.

    (2) In Schedule 2 (Departments etc. subject to investigation) at the appropriate place insert—

        "Director of the Assets Recovery Agency."

    (3) In the Notes to that Schedule before paragraph 1 insert—

"A1   In the case of the Director of the Assets Recovery Agency an investigation under this Act may be conducted only in respect of the exercise of functions vested in him by virtue of a notice served on the Commissioners of Inland Revenue under section 317(2), 321(2) or 322(2) of the Proceeds of Crime Act 2002 (Inland Revenue functions)."

Police (Scotland) Act 1967 (c. 77)

3   (1)   The Police (Scotland) Act 1967 is amended as follows.

(2)   In section 38(3B)(liability of Scottish Ministers for constables on central service) after "central service" insert "or on temporary service as mentioned in section 38A(1)(aa) of this Act".

(3)   In section 38A(1) (meaning of "relevant service") after paragraph (a) insert –

"(aa)   temporary service with the Scottish Ministers in connection with their functions under Part 5 or 8 of the Proceeds of Crime Act 2002, on which a person is engaged with the consent of the appropriate authority;".

Criminal Appeal Act 1968 (c. 19)

4   (1)   The Criminal Appeal Act 1968 is amended as follows.

(2)   In section 33 (appeal to House of Lords) after subsection (1) insert –

"(1A)   In subsection (1) above the reference to the prosecutor includes a reference to the Director of the Assets Recovery Agency in a case where (and to the extent that) he is a party to the appeal to the Court of Appeal."

(3)   In section 50(1) (meaning of sentence) after paragraph (c) insert –

"(ca)   a confiscation order under Part 2 of the Proceeds of Crime Act 2002;

(cb)   an order which varies a confiscation order made under Part 2 of the Proceeds of Crime Act 2002 if the varying order is made under section 21, 22 or 29 of that Act (but not otherwise);".

Misuse of Drugs Act 1971 (c. 38)

5   (1)   Section 27 of the Misuse of Drugs Act 1971 (forfeiture) is amended as follows.

(2)   In subsection (1) for "a drug trafficking offence, as defined in section 1(3) of the Drug Trafficking Act 1994" substitute "an offence falling within subsection (3) below".

(3)   After subsection (2) insert –

"(3)   An offence falls within this subsection if it is an offence which is specified in –

(a)   paragraph 1 of Schedule 2 to the Proceeds of Crime Act 2002 (drug trafficking offences), or

(b)   so far as it relates to that paragraph, paragraph 10 of that Schedule."

Immigration Act 1971 (c. 77)

6   In section 28L of the Immigration Act 1971, in paragraph (c) for the words "33 of the Criminal Law (Consolidation) (Scotland) Act 1995" substitute "412 of the Proceeds of Crime Act 2002".

Rehabilitation of Offenders Act 1974 (c. 53)

7   In section 1 of the Rehabilitation of Offenders Act 1974 (rehabilitated persons and spent convictions) after subsection (2A) insert—

        "(2B) In subsection (2)(a) above the reference to a fine or other sum adjudged to be paid by or imposed on a conviction does not include a reference to an amount payable under a confiscation order made under Part 2 or 3 of the Proceeds of Crime Act 2002."

Rehabilitation of Offenders (Northern Ireland) Order 1978 (S.I. 1978/1908 (N.I. 27))

8   In Article 3 of the Rehabilitation of Offenders (Northern Ireland) Order 1978 (rehabilitated persons and spent convictions) after paragraph (2) insert—

        "(2A) In paragraph (2)(a) the reference to a fine or other sum adjudged to be paid by or imposed on a conviction does not include a reference to an amount payable under a confiscation order made under Part 4 of the Proceeds of Crime Act 2002."

Criminal Appeal (Northern Ireland) Act 1980 (c. 47)

9   (1) The Criminal Appeal (Northern Ireland) Act 1980 is amended as follows.

     (2) In section 30(3) (meaning of sentence) omit "and" after paragraph (b) and after paragraph (c) insert—
              "(d)   a confiscation order under Part 4 of the Proceeds of Crime Act 2002;
               (e)   an order which varies a confiscation order made under Part 4 of the Proceeds of Crime Act 2002 if the varying order is made under section 171, 172 or 179 of that Act (but not otherwise)."

     (3) In section 31 (appeal to House of Lords) after subsection (1) insert—

          "(1A) In subsection (1) above the reference to the prosecutor includes a reference to the Director of the Assets Recovery Agency in a case where (and to the extent that) he is a party to the appeal to the Court of Appeal."

Legal Aid, Advice and Assistance (Northern Ireland) Order 1981 (S.I. 1981/228 (N.I. 8))

10   (1) Part I of Schedule 1 to the Legal Aid, Advice and Assistance (Northern Ireland) Order 1981 (proceedings for which legal aid may be given under Part II of the Order) is amended as follows.

     (2) After paragraph 2 insert—
          "2A.(1) The following proceedings in the Crown Court under the Proceeds of Crime Act 2002—
              (a)   proceedings which relate to a direction under section 202(3) or 204(3) as to the distribution of funds in the hands of a receiver;

> > (b) applications under section 210 relating to action taken or proposed to be taken by a receiver;
> >
> > (c) applications under section 211 to vary or discharge an order under any of sections 196 to 201 for the appointment of or conferring powers on a receiver;
> >
> > (d) applications under section 220 or 221 for the payment of compensation;
> >
> > (e) applications under sections 351(3), 362(3), 369(3) or 375(2) to vary or discharge certain orders made under Part 8.
>
> (2) But sub-paragraph (1) does not apply in relation to a defendant (within the meaning of Part 4 of that Act) in the following proceedings —
>
> > (a) proceedings mentioned in head (b) of that sub-paragraph;
> >
> > (b) an application under section 221 for the payment of compensation if the confiscation order was varied under section 179."

(3) In paragraph 3 (courts of summary jurisdiction), after sub-paragraph (i) insert —

> > "(j) proceedings under sections 295, 297, 298, 301 and 302 of the Proceeds of Crime Act 2002".

(4) The amendments made by this paragraph are without prejudice to the power to make regulations under Article 10(2) of the Legal Aid, Advice and Assistance (Northern Ireland) Order 1981 amending or revoking the provisions inserted by this paragraph.

Civil Jurisdiction and Judgments Act 1982 (c. 27)

11   In section 18 of the Civil Jurisdiction and Judgments Act 1982 (enforcement of United Kingdom judgments in other parts of the United Kingdom) in subsection (3) (exceptions) insert after paragraph (c) —

> > "(d) an order made under Part 2, 3 or 4 of the Proceeds of Crime Act 2002 (confiscation)."

Civic Government (Scotland) Act 1982 (c. 45)

12 (1) The Civic Government (Scotland) Act 1982 is amended as follows.

    (2) In section 86A(3) (application of Part VIIA) for "sections 21(2) and 28(1) of the Proceeds of Crime (Scotland) Act 1995" substitute "section 21(2) of the Proceeds of Crime (Scotland) Act 1995 and Part 3 of the Proceeds of Crime Act 2002".

    (3) In paragraph 8 of Schedule 2A (interpretation) for the definition of "restraint order" substitute —

> > ""restraint order" means a restraint order made under Part 3 of the Proceeds of Crime Act 2002".

Criminal Justice Act 1982 (c. 48)

13   In Part 2 of Schedule 1 to the Criminal Justice Act 1982 (offences excluded from early release provisions) after the entry relating to the Drug Trafficking Act 1994 insert —

"PROCEEDS OF CRIME ACT 2002

Section 327 (concealing criminal property etc).

Section 328 (arrangements relating to criminal property).

Section 329 (acquisition, use and possession of criminal property)."

Police and Criminal Evidence Act 1984 (c. 60)

14   (1) The Police and Criminal Evidence Act 1984 is amended as follows.

(2) In section 56 (right to have someone informed when arrested) for subsection (5A) substitute—

"(5A) An officer may also authorise delay where he has reasonable grounds for believing that—

(a) the person detained for the serious arrestable offence has benefited from his criminal conduct, and

(b) the recovery of the value of the property constituting the benefit will be hindered by telling the named person of the arrest.

(5B) For the purposes of subsection (5A) above the question whether a person has benefited from his criminal conduct is to be decided in accordance with Part 2 of the Proceeds of Crime Act 2002."

(3) In section 58 (access to legal advice) for subsection (8A) substitute—

"(8A) An officer may also authorise delay where he has reasonable grounds for believing that—

(a) the person detained for the serious arrestable offence has benefited from his criminal conduct, and

(b) the recovery of the value of the property constituting the benefit will be hindered by the exercise of the right conferred by subsection (1) above.

(8B) For the purposes of subsection (8A) above the question whether a person has benefited from his criminal conduct is to be decided in accordance with Part 2 of the Proceeds of Crime Act 2002."

(4) In section 116 (meaning of serious arrestable offence) in subsection (2) for paragraph (c) and the word "and" immediately preceding it substitute—

"(c) any offence which is specified in paragraph 1 of Schedule 2 to the Proceeds of Crime Act 2002 (drug trafficking offences),

(d) any offence under section 327, 328 or 329 of that Act (certain money laundering offences)."

Bankruptcy (Scotland) Act 1985 (c. 66)

15   (1) The Bankruptcy (Scotland) Act 1985 is amended as follows.

(2) In section 5(4) (meaning of "qualified creditor") for the words from "has the meaning" to "1995" substitute "means a confiscation order under Part 2, 3 or 4 of the Proceeds of Crime Act 2002".

(3) In section 7(1) (meaning of "apparent insolvency") for the words from "has the meaning assigned" where second occurring to "said Act of 1994" where second occurring substitute " "confiscation order" and "restraint order"

mean a confiscation order or a restraint order made under Part 2, 3 or 4 of the Proceeds of Crime Act 2002".

(4) After section 31 (vesting of estate at date of sequestration) insert—

"31A Property subject to restraint order

(1) This section applies where—

    (a) property is excluded from the debtor's estate by virtue of section 420(2)(a) of the Proceeds of Crime Act 2002 (property subject to a restraint order),

    (b) an order under section 50, 52, 128, 198 or 200 of that Act has not been made in respect of the property, and

    (c) the restraint order is discharged.

(2) On the discharge of the restraint order the property vests in the permanent trustee as part of the debtor's estate.

(3) But subsection (2) does not apply to the proceeds of property realised by a management receiver under section 49(2)(d) or 197(2)(d) of that Act (realisation of property to meet receiver's remuneration and expenses).

31B Property in respect of which receivership or administration order is made

(1) This section applies where—

    (a) property is excluded from the debtor's estate by virtue of section 420(2)(b), (c) or (d) of the Proceeds of Crime Act 2002 (property in respect of which an order for the appointment of a receiver or administrator under certain provisions of that Act is in force), and

    (b) a confiscation order is made under section 6, 92 or 156 of that Act,

    (c) the amount payable under the confiscation order is fully paid, and

    (d) any of the property remains in the hands of the receiver or administrator (as the case may be).

(2) The property vests in the permanent trustee as part of the debtor's estate.

31C Property subject to certain orders where confiscation order discharged or quashed

(1) This section applies where—

    (a) property is excluded from the debtor's estate by virtue of section 420(2)(a), (b), (c) or (d) of the Proceeds of Crime Act 2002 (property in respect of which a restraint order or an order for the appointment of a receiver or administrator under that Act is in force),

    (b) a confiscation order is made under section 6, 92 or 156 of that Act, and

        (c)   the confiscation order is discharged under section 30, 114 or 180 of that Act (as the case may be) or quashed under that Act or in pursuance of any enactment relating to appeals against conviction or sentence.

   (2)   Any property in the hands of a receiver appointed under Part 2 or 4 of that Act or an administrator appointed under Part 3 of that Act vests in the permanent trustee as part of the debtor's estate.

   (3)   But subsection (2) does not apply to the proceeds of property realised by a management receiver under section 49(2)(d) or 197(2)(d) of that Act (realisation of property to meet receiver's remuneration and expenses)."

  (5) In section 55 (effect of discharge) after subsection (2) insert –

     "(3)   In subsection (2)(a) above the reference to a fine or other penalty due to the Crown includes a reference to a confiscation order made under Part 2, 3 or 4 of the Proceeds of Crime Act 2002.".

Insolvency Act 1986 (c. 45)

16   (1) The Insolvency Act 1986 is amended as follows.

   (2) In section 281 (effect of discharge) after subsection (4) insert –

    "(4A)   In subsection (4) the reference to a fine includes a reference to a confiscation order under Part 2, 3 or 4 of the Proceeds of Crime Act 2002."

   (3) After section 306 insert –

"306A   Property subject to restraint order

   (1)   This section applies where –
        (a)   property is excluded from the bankrupt's estate by virtue of section 417(2)(a) of the Proceeds of Crime Act 2002 (property subject to a restraint order),
        (b)   an order under section 50, 52, 128, 198 or 200 of that Act has not been made in respect of the property, and
        (c)   the restraint order is discharged.

   (2)   On the discharge of the restraint order the property vests in the trustee as part of the bankrupt's estate.

   (3)   But subsection (2) does not apply to the proceeds of property realised by a management receiver under section 49(2)(d) or 197(2)(d) of that Act (realisation of property to meet receiver's remuneration and expenses).

306B   Property in respect of which receivership or administration order made

   (1)   This section applies where –
        (a)   property is excluded from the bankrupt's estate by virtue of section 417(2)(b), (c) or (d) of the Proceeds of Crime Act 2002 (property in respect of which an order for the appointment of

a receiver or administrator under certain provisions of that Act is in force),

(b)   a confiscation order is made under section 6, 92 or 156 of that Act,

(c)   the amount payable under the confiscation order is fully paid, and

(d)   any of the property remains in the hands of the receiver or administrator (as the case may be).

(2)   The property vests in the trustee as part of the bankrupt's estate.

306C   Property subject to certain orders where confiscation order discharged or quashed

(1)   This section applies where—

(a)   property is excluded from the bankrupt's estate by virtue of section 417(2)(a), (b), (c) or (d) of the Proceeds of Crime Act 2002 (property in respect of which a restraint order or an order for the appointment of a receiver or administrator under that Act is in force),

(b)   a confiscation order is made under section 6, 92 or 156 of that Act, and

(c)   the confiscation order is discharged under section 30, 114 or 180 of that Act (as the case may be) or quashed under that Act or in pursuance of any enactment relating to appeals against conviction or sentence.

(2)   Any such property in the hands of a receiver appointed under Part 2 or 4 of that Act or an administrator appointed under Part 3 of that Act vests in the trustee as part of the bankrupt's estate.

(3)   But subsection (2) does not apply to the proceeds of property realised by a management receiver under section 49(2)(d) or 197(2)(d) of that Act (realisation of property to meet receiver's remuneration and expenses)."

Criminal Justice Act 1988 (c. 33)

17   (1)   The Criminal Justice Act 1988 is amended as follows.

(2)   The following provisions shall cease to have effect—

(a)   sections 71 to 102;

(b)   Schedule 4.

(3)   In section 151(4) (Customs and Excise power of arrest) omit "and" after paragraph (a), and after paragraph (b) insert—

"(c)   a money laundering offence;"

(4)   In section 151(5) for the words after "means" substitute "any offence which is specified in—

(a)   paragraph 1 of Schedule 2 to the Proceeds of Crime Act 2002 (drug trafficking offences), or

(b)   so far as it relates to that paragraph, paragraph 10 of that Schedule.

(5)   In section 151 after subsection (5) insert—

"(6)   In this section "money laundering offence" means any offence which by virtue of section 415 of the Proceeds of Crime Act 2002 is a money laundering offence for the purposes of Part 8 of that Act."

(6) In section 152(4) (remands of suspected drugs offenders to customs detention) for the words after "means" substitute "any offence which is specified in —

(a)   paragraph 1 of Schedule 5 to the Proceeds of Crime Act 2002 (drug trafficking offences), or

(b)   so far as it relates to that paragraph, paragraph 10 of that Schedule."

Extradition Act 1989 (c. 33)

18   (1)   The Extradition Act 1989 is amended as follows.

(2)   In section 22 (extension of purposes of extradition for offences under Acts giving effect to international conventions) in subsection (4)(h) —

(a)   for sub-paragraph (i) substitute —

"(i)   any offence which is specified in —

(a)   paragraph 1 of Schedule 2 to the Proceeds of Crime Act 2002 (drug trafficking offences), or

(b)   so far as it relates to that paragraph, paragraph 10 of that Schedule;

(ia)   any offence which by virtue of section 415 of the Proceeds of Crime Act 2002 is a money laundering offence for the purposes of Part 8 of that Act;";

(b)   for sub-paragraph (ii) substitute —

"(ii)   any offence which is specified in —

(a)   paragraph 2 of Schedule 4 to the Proceeds of Crime Act 2002, or

(b)   so far as it relates to that paragraph, paragraph 10 of that Schedule;

(iia)   any offence which by virtue of section 415 of the Proceeds of Crime Act 2002 is a money laundering offence for the purposes of Part 8 of that Act;";

(c)   omit "and" after sub-paragraph (ii) and for sub-paragraph (iii) substitute —

"(iii)   any offence which is specified in —

(a)   paragraph 1 of Schedule 5 to the Proceeds of Crime Act 2002 (drug trafficking offences), or

(b)   so far as it relates to that paragraph, paragraph 10 of that Schedule; and

(iv)   any offence which by virtue of section 415 of the Proceeds of Crime Act 2002 is a money laundering offence for the purposes of Part 8 of that Act;".

(3)   In paragraph 15 of Schedule 1 (deemed extension of jurisdiction of foreign states) —

(a)   for paragraph (j) substitute —

"(j) any offence which is specified in —

    (i) paragraph 1 of Schedule 2 to the Proceeds of Crime Act 2002 (drug trafficking offences), or

    (ii) so far as it relates to that paragraph, paragraph 10 of that Schedule;

(ja) any offence which by virtue of section 415 of the Proceeds of Crime Act 2002 is a money laundering offence for the purposes of Part 8 of that Act;";

(b) for paragraph (k) substitute —

"(k) any offence which is specified in —

    (i) paragraph 2 of Schedule 4 to the Proceeds of Crime Act 2002, or

    (ii) so far as it relates to that paragraph, paragraph 10 of that Schedule;

(ka) any offence which by virtue of section 415 of the Proceeds of Crime Act 2002 is a money laundering offence for the purposes of Part 8 of that Act;";

(c) for paragraph (m) substitute —

"(m) any offence which is specified in —

    (i) paragraph 1 of Schedule 5 to the Proceeds of Crime Act 2002 (drug trafficking offences), or

    (ii) so far as it relates to that paragraph, paragraph 10 of that Schedule;

(ma) any offence which by virtue of section 415 of the Proceeds of Crime Act 2002 is a money laundering offence for the purposes of Part 8 of that Act;".

Police and Criminal Evidence (Northern Ireland) Order 1989 (S.I. 1989/1341 (N.I. 12))

19 (1) The Police and Criminal Evidence (Northern Ireland) Order 1989 is amended as follows.

(2) In Article 57 (right to have someone informed when arrested) for paragraph (5A) substitute —

"(5A) An officer may also authorise delay where he has reasonable grounds for believing that —

    (a) the person detained for the serious arrestable offence has benefited from his criminal conduct, and

    (b) the recovery of the value of the property constituting the benefit will be hindered by telling the named person of the arrest.

(5B) For the purposes of paragraph (5A) the question whether a person has benefited from his criminal conduct is to be decided in accordance with Part 4 of the Proceeds of Crime Act 2002."

(3) In Article 59 (access to legal advice) for paragraph (8A) substitute —

"(8A) An officer may also authorise delay where he has reasonable grounds for believing that —

    (a) the person detained for the serious arrestable offence has benefited from his criminal conduct, and

(b) the recovery of the value of the property constituting the benefit will be hindered by the exercise of the right conferred by paragraph (1).

(8B) For the purposes of paragraph (8A) the question whether a person has benefited from his criminal conduct is to be decided in accordance with Part 4 of the Proceeds of Crime Act 2002."

(4) In Article 87 (meaning of serious arrestable offence) in paragraph (2) for sub-paragraph (aa) substitute—

"(aa) any offence which is specified in paragraph 1 of Schedule 5 to the Proceeds of Crime Act 2002 (drug trafficking offences);

(ab) any offence under section 327, 328 or 329 of that Act (certain money laundering offences);".

Insolvency (Northern Ireland) Order 1989 (S.I. 1989/2405 (N.I. 19))

20 (1) The Insolvency (Northern Ireland) Order 1989 is amended as follows.

(2) In Article 255 (effect of discharge) after paragraph (4) insert—

"(4A) In paragraph (4) the reference to a fine includes a reference to a confiscation order under Part 2, 3 or 4 of the Proceeds of Crime Act 2002."

(3) After Article 279 insert—

"279A Property subject to restraint order

(1) This Article applies where—

(a) property is excluded from the bankrupt's estate by virtue of section 423(2)(a) of the Proceeds of Crime Act 2002 (property subject to a restraint order),

(b) an order under section 50, 52, 128, 198 or 200 of that Act has not been made in respect of the property, and

(c) the restraint order is discharged.

(2) On the discharge of the restraint order the property vests in the trustee as part of the bankrupt's estate.

(3) But paragraph (2) does not apply to the proceeds of property realised by a management receiver under section 49(2)(d) or 197(2)(d) of that Act (realisation of property to meet receiver's remuneration and expenses).

279B Property in respect of which receivership or administration order made

(1) This Article applies where—

(a) property is excluded from the bankrupt's estate by virtue of section 423(2)(b), (c) or (d) of the Proceeds of Crime Act 2002 (property in respect of which an order for the appointment of a receiver or administrator under certain provisions of that Act is in force),

(b) a confiscation order is made under section 6, 92 or 156 of that Act,

> (c) the amount payable under the confiscation order is fully paid, and
>
> (d) any of the property remains in the hands of the receiver or administrator (as the case may be).
>
> (2) The property vests in the trustee as part of the bankrupt's estate.

279C Property subject to certain orders where confiscation order discharged or quashed

> (1) This Article applies where—
>
> (a) property is excluded from the bankrupt's estate by virtue of section 423(2)(a), (b), (c) or (d) of the Proceeds of Crime Act 2002 (property in respect of which a restraint order or an order for the appointment of a receiver or administrator under that Act is in force),
>
> (b) a confiscation order is made under section 6, 92 or 156 of that Act, and
>
> (c) the confiscation order is discharged under section 30, 114 or 180 of that Act (as the case may be) or quashed under that Act or in pursuance of any enactment relating to appeals against conviction or sentence.
>
> (2) Any such property in the hands of a receiver appointed under Part 2 or 4 of that Act or an administrator appointed under Part 3 of that Act vests in the trustee as part of the bankrupt's estate.
>
> (3) But paragraph (2) does not apply to the proceeds of property realised by a management receiver under section 49(2)(d) or 197(2)(d) of that Act (realisation of property to meet receiver's remuneration and expenses)."

Criminal Justice (International Co-operation) Act 1990 (c. 5)

21   In section 13(6) of the Criminal Justice (International Co-operation) Act 1990 (information not to be disclosed except for certain purposes) –

(a) omit "the Drug Trafficking Act 1994 or the Criminal Justice (Scotland) Act 1987";

(b) at the end insert "or of proceedings under Part 2, 3 or 4 of the Proceeds of Crime Act 2002".

Pension Schemes Act 1993 (c. 48)

22   (1) The Pension Schemes Act 1993 is amended as follows.

(2) In section 10 (protected rights and money purchase benefits), after subsection (5) insert –

"(6) Where, in the case of a scheme which makes such provision as is mentioned in subsection (2) or (3), any liability of the scheme in respect of a member's protected rights ceases by virtue of a civil recovery order, his protected rights are extinguished or reduced accordingly."

(3) In section 14 (earner's guaranteed minimum), after subsection (2) insert –

"(2A) Where any liability of a scheme in respect of an earner's guaranteed minimum pension ceases by virtue of a civil recovery order, his guaranteed minimum in relation to the scheme is extinguished or reduced accordingly."

(4) In section 47 (further provisions relating to guaranteed minimum pensions), in subsection (6), after "but for" insert "section 14(2A) and".

(5) In section 68B (safeguarded rights), at the end insert "including provision for such rights to be extinguished or reduced in consequence of a civil recovery order made in respect of such rights".

(6) In section 181(1) (general interpretation), after the definition of "Category A retirement pension" insert—

""civil recovery order" means an order under section 266 of the Proceeds of Crime Act 2002 or an order under section 276 imposing the requirement mentioned in section 277(3)."

Pension Schemes (Northern Ireland) Act 1993 (c. 49)

23   (1) The Pension Schemes (Northern Ireland) Act 1993 is amended as follows.

(2) In section 6 (protected rights and money purchase benefits), after subsection (5) insert—

"(6) Where, in the case of a scheme which makes such provision as is mentioned in subsection (2) or (3), any liability of the scheme in respect of a member's protected rights ceases by virtue of a civil recovery order, his protected rights are extinguished or reduced accordingly."

(3) In section 10 (earner's guaranteed minimum), after subsection (2) insert—

"(2A) Where any liability of a scheme in respect of an earner's guaranteed minimum pension ceases by virtue of a civil recovery order, his guaranteed minimum in relation to the scheme is extinguished or reduced accordingly."

(4) In section 43 (further provisions relating to guaranteed minimum pensions), in subsection (6), after "but for" insert "section 10(2A) and".

(5) In section 64B (safeguarded rights), at the end insert "including provision for such rights to be extinguished or reduced in consequence of a civil recovery order made in respect of such rights".

(6) In section 176(1) (general interpretation), after the definition of "Category A retirement pension" insert—

""civil recovery order" means an order under section 266 of the Proceeds of Crime Act 2002 or an order under section 276 imposing the requirement mentioned in section 277(3)."

Criminal Justice and Public Order Act 1994 (c. 31)

24   In section 139(12) of the Criminal Justice and Public Order Act 1994 (search powers) in paragraph (b) of the definition of "items subject to legal privilege" for "section 40 of the Criminal Justice (Scotland) Act 1987" substitute "section 412 of the Proceeds of Crime Act 2002".

Drug Trafficking Act 1994 (c. 37)

25   (1) The Drug Trafficking Act 1994 is amended as follows.

    (2) The following provisions shall cease to have effect—

       (a)   sections 1 to 54;

       (b)   in sections 55(4)(a) (orders to make material available) and 56(3)(a) and (4)(a) (authority for search) the words "or has benefited from";

       (c)   in section 59 (disclosure of information held by government departments), subsections (1) to (10) and in subsection (11) the words "An order under subsection (1) above, and,";

       (d)   in section 60(6) (Customs and Excise prosecution powers), in the definition of "specified offence", in paragraph (a) the words "Part III or" and paragraph (c) and the word "or" immediately preceding it;

       (e)   in section 60(6) the words from "and references to the institution of proceedings" to the end;

       (f)   in section 60, subsections (7) and (8);

       (g)   in section 61 (extension of certain offences to the Crown), subsections (2) to (4);

       (h)   sections 62, 63(1), (2) and (3)(a) and 64 (interpretation);

       (i)   in section 68(2) (extent - Scotland), paragraphs (a) to (c) and in paragraph (g) the words "1, 41, 62" and "64";

       (j)   in section 68(3) (extent - Northern Ireland), paragraph (a) and in paragraph (d) the word "64".

    (3) In section 59(12)(b) for the words "referred to in subsection (1) above" substitute "specified in an order under section 55(2)".

    (4) After section 59 insert the following section—

"59A Construction of sections 55 to 59

    (1) This section has effect for the purposes of sections 55 to 59.

    (2) A reference to a constable includes a reference to a customs officer.

    (3) A customs officer is a person commissioned by the Commissioners of Customs and Excise under section 6(3) of the Customs and Excise Management Act 1979 (c. 2).

    (4) Drug trafficking means doing or being concerned in any of the following (whether in England and Wales or elsewhere)—

       (a)   producing or supplying a controlled drug where the production or supply contravenes section 4(1) of the Misuse of Drugs Act 1971 or a corresponding law;

       (b)   transporting or storing a controlled drug where possession of the drug contravenes section 5(1) of that Act or a corresponding law;

       (c)   importing or exporting a controlled drug where the importation or exportation is prohibited by section 3(1) of that Act or a corresponding law;

       (d)   manufacturing or supplying a scheduled substance within the meaning of section 12 of the Criminal Justice (International Co-operation) Act 1990 where the manufacture or supply is an offence under that section or would be such an offence if it took place in England and Wales;

(e) using any ship for illicit traffic in controlled drugs in circumstances which amount to the commission of an offence under section 19 of that Act.

(5) In this section "corresponding law" has the same meaning as in the Misuse of Drugs Act 1971."

(5) In section 60 after subsection (6) insert—

"(6A) Proceedings for an offence are instituted —

(a) when a justice of the peace issues a summons or warrant under section 1 of the Magistrates' Courts Act 1980 (issue of summons to, or warrant for arrest of, accused) in respect of the offence;

(b) when a person is charged with the offence after being taken into custody without a warrant;

(c) when a bill of indictment is preferred under section 2 of the Administration of Justice (Miscellaneous Provisions) Act 1933 in a case falling within paragraph (b) of subsection (2) of that section (preferment by direction of the criminal division of the Court of Appeal or by direction, or with the consent, of a High Court judge).

(6B) Where the application of subsection (6A) would result in there being more than one time for the institution of proceedings they must be taken to have been instituted at the earliest of those times."

(6) In section 61(1) for "sections 49(2), 50 to 53 and 58" substitute "section 58".

(7) In section 68(2)(d), for "59(10)" substitute "59(11)".

Criminal Justice (Northern Ireland) Order 1994 (S.I. 1994/2795 (N.I. 15))

26   In Article 16 of the Criminal Justice (Northern Ireland) Order 1994 in paragraph (a) after "Proceeds of Crime (Northern Ireland) Order 1996" insert "or Part 4 of the Proceeds of Crime Act 2002".

Proceeds of Crime Act 1995 (c. 11)

27   Section 15(2) and (3) of the Proceeds of Crime Act 1995 (investigation into benefit to be treated as the investigation of an offence for the purposes of sections 21 and 22 of the Police and Criminal Evidence Act 1984) shall cease to have effect.

Proceeds of Crime (Scotland) Act 1995 (c. 43)

28   (1) The Proceeds of Crime (Scotland) Act 1995 is amended as follows.

(2) The following provisions in the Act shall cease to have effect—

(a) Part I, except section 2(7);

(b) in section 28, subsections (1)(a) and (2) and in subsection (5) the words "(including a restraint order made under and within the meaning of the 1994 Act)";

(c) section 29;

(d) in section 31, subsection (2) and in subsection (4) the words "or (2)";

(e)   sections 35 to 39;

(f)   in section 40, subsections (1)(a), (2) and (4);

(g)   in section 42, subsections (1)(a) and (b);

(h)   in section 43, in subsection (1) the words ", confiscation order" and subsection (2);

(i)   in section 45, subsection (1)(a);

(j)   section 47;

(k)   in section 49, in subsection (1) the definitions of "the 1988 Act", "the 1994 Act" and "confiscation order" and subsection (4).

(3) The following provisions in Schedule 1 to the Act shall cease to have effect —

(a)   in paragraph 1(1)(b) the words "or a confiscation order", in paragraph 1(2)(a) the words "subject to paragraph (b) below", paragraph 1(2)(b) and in paragraph 1(3)(a)(i) the words "or confiscation order";

(b)   in paragraph 2(1)(a) the words ", and if appointed (or empowered) under paragraph 1(1)(b) above where a confiscation order has been made";

(c)   paragraph 4;

(d)   in paragraph 5(1) the words "Part I of";

(e)   in paragraph 8(2) the words ", unless in a case where a confiscation order has been made there are sums available to be applied in payment of it under paragraph 4(4)(b) above,";

(f)   in paragraph 10(1) the words "or the recipient of a gift caught by Part I of this Act or an implicative gift" and paragraphs 10(2) and 10(3);

(g)   in paragraph 12(1)(a) the words "paragraph (a) or (b) of section 4(1) or".

(4) The following provisions in Schedule 2 to the Act shall cease to have effect —

(a)   in paragraph 1(2) the words "and 35 to 38";

(b)   in paragraph 2, in sub-paragraph (1) the words "realisable or", in sub-paragraph (2) the words "and 35 to 38", sub-paragraph (5).

(c)   in paragraph 3(2) the words "and 35 to 38" and paragraphs 3(4) and (5);

(d)   in paragraph 4(2) the words "and 35 to 38";

(e)   paragraph 6(2)(a).

(5) In section 28(9) (restraint orders) for "Subsections (2)(a) and" substitute "Subsection".

(6) In section 42 (enforcement) in subsections (2)(a), (c) and (d) for "Part I," substitute "Part".

Criminal Procedure (Scotland) Act 1995 (c. 46)

29 (1) The Criminal Procedure (Scotland) Act 1995 is amended as follows.

(2) In section 109(1) (intimation of appeal) for "section 10 of the Proceeds of Crime (Scotland) Act 1995 (postponed confiscation orders)" substitute "section 99 of the Proceeds of Crime Act 2002 (postponement)".

(3) In section 205B(5) (minimum sentence for third drug trafficking offence) for the definition of "drug trafficking offence" substitute —

"""drug trafficking offence" means an offence specified in paragraph 2 or (so far as it relates to that paragraph) paragraph 10 of Schedule 4 to the Proceeds of Crime Act 2002;".

(4) In section 219(8)(b) (fines: imprisonment for non-payment) for "14(2) of the Proceeds of Crime (Scotland) Act 1995" substitute "118(2) of the Proceeds of Crime Act 2002".

Police Act 1996 (c. 16)

30 (1) Section 97 of the Police Act 1996 (police officers engaged on service outside their force) is amended as follows.

(2) In subsection (1) after paragraph (cc) insert—
   "(cd)   temporary service with the Assets Recovery Agency on which a person is engaged with the consent of the appropriate authority;".

(3) In subsection (6)(a) after "(cc)" insert "(cd)".

(4) In subsection (8) after "(cc)" insert "(cd)".

Proceeds of Crime (Northern Ireland) Order 1996 (S.I. 1996/1299 (N.I. 9)

31 (1) The Proceeds of Crime (Northern Ireland) Order 1996 is amended as follows.

(2) Parts II and III shall cease to have effect.

(3) The following provisions shall also cease to have effect—
   (a)   in Article 2 (interpretation) in paragraph (2) from the definition of "charging order" to the definition of "external confiscation order" and from the definition of "modifications" to the definition of "restraint order" and paragraphs (3) to (10) and (12);
   (b)   Article 3 (definition of "property" etc.);
   (c)   in Article 49 (additional investigation powers), in paragraph (1) sub-paragraph (c) and the word "and" immediately preceding it, in paragraph (1A) sub-paragraph (c) and the word "and" immediately preceding it, paragraph (4) and in paragraph (5) the definitions of "customs officer" and "relevant property";
   (d)   in Article 52 (supplementary provisions) in paragraph (2) sub-paragraph (b) and the word "and" immediately preceding it, and paragraph (3);
   (e)   in Article 54 (disclosure of information held by government departments) paragraphs (1) to (10) and (13) and in paragraph (11) the words "An order under paragraph (1) and,";
   (f)   in Article 55 (Customs and Excise prosecution powers), in paragraph (6) in the definition of "specified offence" in paragraph (a) the words "Part III or" and paragraph (c) and the word "or" immediately preceding it, and paragraph (7);
   (g)   Article 56(2) to (4) (extension of certain offences to the Crown);
   (h)   in Schedule 2 paragraph 3.

(4) In Article 49(1) (additional investigation powers)—
   (a)   for "county court" substitute "Crown Court";
   (b)   in sub-paragraph (a) for the words from "an investigation" to the end of head (ii) substitute "a confiscation investigation";

(c) in sub-paragraph (b) after "and who is" insert "an accredited financial investigator".

(5) In Article 49(1A) —

(a) after "application made by" insert "the Director of the Assets Recovery Agency or";

(b) for "county court" substitute "Crown Court";

(c) in sub-paragraph (a) for the words from "an investigation" to the end of head (ii) substitute "a confiscation investigation";

(d) in sub-paragraph (b) after "if" insert "the Director or";

(e) after "authorise" insert "the Director or";

(f) for "paragraphs 3 and 3A" where it twice occurs substitute "paragraph 3A".

(6) In Article 49(5) insert at the appropriate place in alphabetical order —

""accredited financial investigator" has the meaning given by section 3(5) of the Proceeds of Crime Act 2002;

"confiscation investigation" has the same meaning as it has for the purposes of Part 8 of that Act by virtue of section 341(1);".

(7) In Article 50(1) (order to make material available) —

(a) for sub-paragraphs (a) and (b) substitute "drug trafficking";

(b) for "county court" substitute "Crown Court".

(8) In Article 50(4)(a), for heads (i) to (iii) substitute "has carried on drug trafficking".

(9) In Article 50(8) for "county court" substitute "Crown Court".

(10) In Article 51(1) (authority for search) —

(a) for sub-paragraphs (a) and (b) substitute "drug trafficking";

(b) for "county court" substitute "Crown Court".

(11) In Article 51(3)(a) for heads (i) to (iii) substitute "has carried on drug trafficking".

(12) In Article 51(4) —

(a) in sub-paragraph (a) for heads (i) to (iii) substitute "has carried on drug trafficking";

(b) in sub-paragraph (b)(i) for the words from "the question" to the end substitute "drug trafficking".

(13) In Article 52(1)(a) (supplementary provisions), for heads (i) to (ii) substitute "drug trafficking".

(14) In Article 54 (disclosure of information held by government departments) in paragraph (12)(b) for "referred to in paragraph (1)" substitute "specified in an order under Article 50(2)".

(15) After Article 54 insert the following Article —

"54A Construction of Articles 49 to 54

(1) This Article has effect for the purposes of Articles 49 to 54.

(2) A reference to a constable includes a reference to a customs officer.

(3) A customs officer is a person commissioned by the Commissioners of Customs and Excise under section 6(3) of the Customs and Excise Management Act 1979.

(4) Drug trafficking means doing or being concerned in any of the following (whether in Northern Ireland or elsewhere) –

    (a) producing or supplying a controlled drug where the production or supply contravenes section 4(1) of the Misuse of Drugs Act 1971 or a corresponding law;

    (b) transporting or storing a controlled drug where possession of the drug contravenes section 5(1) of that Act or a corresponding law;

    (c) importing or exporting a controlled drug where the importation or exportation is prohibited by section 3(1) of that Act or a corresponding law;

    (d) manufacturing or supplying a scheduled substance within the meaning of section 12 of the Criminal Justice (International Co-operation) Act 1990 where the manufacture or supply is an offence under that section or would be such an offence if it took place in Northern Ireland;

    (e) using any ship for illicit traffic in controlled drugs in circumstances which amount to the commission of an offence under section 19 of that Act.

(5) In this Article "corresponding law" has the same meaning as in the Misuse of Drugs Act 1971."

(16) In Article 55 after paragraph (6) insert –

"(6A) Proceedings for an offence are instituted –

    (a) when a summons or warrant is issued under Article 20 of the Magistrates' Courts (Northern Ireland) Order 1981 in respect of the offence;

    (b) when a person is charged with the offence after being taken into custody without a warrant;

    (c) when an indictment is preferred under section 2(2)(c), (e) or (f) of the Grand Jury (Abolition) Act (Northern Ireland) 1969.

(6B) Where the application of paragraph (6A) would result in there being more than one time for the institution of proceedings they must be taken to have been instituted at the earliest of those times."

(17) In Article 56(1) (extension of certain offences to the Crown), for "Articles 44, 45, 46, 47(2), 48 and" substitute "Article".

(18) In Schedule 2 (financial investigations) in paragraph 3A –

    (a) in sub-paragraph (1) for "any conduct to which Article 49 applies" substitute "his criminal conduct";

    (b) after that paragraph insert –

    "(1A) For the purposes of sub-paragraph (1) the question whether a person has benefited from his criminal conduct is to be decided in accordance with Part 4 of the Proceeds of Crime Act 2002."

Crime (Sentences) Act 1997 (c. 43)

32 (1) The Crime (Sentences) Act 1997 is amended as follows.

(2) In section 35 (fine defaulters) in subsection (1)(a) after "Drug Trafficking Act 1994" insert "or section 6 of the Proceeds of Crime Act 2002".

(3) In section 40 (fine defaulters) in subsection (1)(a) after "Drug Trafficking Act 1994" insert "or section 6 of the Proceeds of Crime Act 2002".

Crime and Punishment (Scotland) Act 1997 (c. 48)

33   The following provisions of the Crime and Punishment (Scotland) Act 1997 shall cease to have effect—
      (a)   section 15(3),
      (b)   in Schedule 1, paragraph 20.

Police (Northern Ireland) Act 1998 (c. 32)

34 (1) Section 27 of the Police (Northern Ireland) Act 1998 (members of the Police Service engaged on other police service) is amended as follows.

    (2) In subsection (1) after paragraph (c) insert—
          "(ca)   temporary service with the Assets Recovery Agency on which a member of the Police Service of Northern Ireland is engaged with the consent of the Chief Constable;".

    (3) In subsection (5)(b) after "(c)" insert "(ca)".

    (4) In subsection (7) for "or (c)" there is substituted "(c) or (ca)".

Crime and Disorder Act 1998 (c. 37)

35   In Schedule 8 to the Crime and Disorder Act 1998 paragraphs 115 and 116 shall cease to have effect.

Access to Justice Act 1999 (c. 22)

36 (1) Schedule 2 to the Access to Justice Act 1999 (services excluded from the Community Legal Service) is amended as follows.

    (2) In paragraph 2(2), after paragraph (d) insert "or
          (e)   under the Proceeds of Crime Act 2002 to the extent specified in paragraph 3,"
    and omit the "or" at the end of paragraph (c).

    (3) In paragraph 2(3) (magistrates courts), after "2001" insert—
          "(l)   for an order or direction under section 295, 297, 298, 301 or 302 of the Proceeds of Crime Act 2002,"
    and omit the "or" at the end of paragraph (j).

    (4) After paragraph 2 insert—
        "3   (1) These are the proceedings under the Proceeds of Crime Act 2002—
             (a)   an application under section 42(3) to vary or discharge a restraint order or an order under section 41(7);
             (b)   proceedings which relate to a direction under section 54(3) or 56(3) as to the distribution of funds in the hands of a receiver;
             (c)   an application under section 62 relating to action taken or proposed to be taken by a receiver;
             (d)   an application under section 63 to vary or discharge an order under any of sections 48 to 53 for the appointment of or conferring powers on a receiver;

    (e)   an application under section 72 or 73 for the payment of compensation;

    (f)   proceedings which relate to an order under section 298 for the forfeiture of cash;

    (g)   an application under section 351(3), 362(3), 369(3) or 375(2) to vary or discharge certain orders made under Part 8.

(2)   But sub-paragraph (1) does not authorise the funding of the provision of services to a defendant (within the meaning of Part 1 of that Act) in relation to —

    (a)   proceedings mentioned in paragraph (b);

    (b)   an application under section 73 for the payment of compensation if the confiscation order was varied under section 29."

Powers of Criminal Courts (Sentencing) Act 2000 (c. 6)

37   (1)   The Powers of Criminal Courts (Sentencing) Act 2000 is amended as follows.

    (2)   In section 110(5) (minimum sentence for third drug trafficking offence) for the definition of "drug trafficking offence" there is substituted —

    ""drug trafficking offence" means an offence which is specified in —

    (a)   paragraph 1 of Schedule 2 to the Proceeds of Crime Act 2002 (drug trafficking offences), or

    (b)   so far as it relates to that paragraph, paragraph 10 of that Schedule."

    (3)   In section 133 (review of compensation orders) in subsection (3)(c) after "Criminal Justice Act 1988" insert ", or Part 2 of the Proceeds of Crime Act 2002,".

Financial Services and Markets Act 2000 (c. 8)

38   In Schedule 1 to the Financial Services and Markets Act 2000 (provisions relating to the Financial Services Authority) after paragraph 19 insert —

    "19A   For the purposes of this Act anything done by an accredited financial investigator within the meaning of the Proceeds of Crime Act 2002 who is —

    (a)   a member of the staff of the Authority, or

    (b)   a person appointed by the Authority under section 97, 167 or 168 to conduct an investigation,

    must be treated as done in the exercise or discharge of a function of the Authority."

Terrorism Act 2000 (c. 11)

39   (1)   Schedule 8 to the Terrorism Act 2000 (detention) is amended as follows.

    (2)   In paragraph 8 (authorisation of delay in exercise of detained person's rights) for sub-paragraph (5) substitute —

    "(5)   An officer may also give an authorisation under sub-paragraph (1) if he has reasonable grounds for believing that —

    (a)   the detained person has benefited from his criminal conduct, and

        (b)   the recovery of the value of the property constituting the benefit will be hindered by —

           (i)   informing the named person of the detained person's detention (in the case of an authorisation under sub-paragraph (1)(a)), or

           (ii)   the exercise of the right under paragraph 7 (in the case of an authorisation under sub-paragraph (1)(b)).

  (5A)   For the purposes of sub-paragraph (5) the question whether a person has benefited from his criminal conduct is to be decided in accordance with Part 2 of the Proceeds of Crime Act 2002."

(3) In paragraph 17(3) (grounds for authorising delay or requiring presence of senior officer), in paragraph (d) for "Part VI of the Criminal Justice Act 1988, Part I of the Proceeds of Crime (Scotland) Act 1995" substitute "Part 2 or 3 of the Proceeds of Crime Act 2002".

(4) For paragraph 17(4) (further grounds for authorising delay in exercise of detained person's rights) substitute —

  "(4)   This sub-paragraph applies where an officer mentioned in paragraph 16(4) or (7) has reasonable grounds for believing that —

        (a)   the detained person has benefited from his criminal conduct, and

        (b)   the recovery of the value of the property constituting the benefit will be hindered by —

           (i)   informing the named person of the detained person's detention (in the case of an authorisation under paragraph 16(4)), or

           (ii)   the exercise of the entitlement under paragraph 16(6) (in the case of an authorisation under paragraph 16(7)).

  (4A)   For the purposes of sub-paragraph (4) the question whether a person has benefited from his criminal conduct is to be decided in accordance with Part 3 of the Proceeds of Crime Act 2002."

(5) In paragraph 34 (authorisation for withholding information from detained person) for sub-paragraph (3) substitute —

  "(3)   A judicial authority may also make an order under sub-paragraph (1) in relation to specified information if satisfied that there are reasonable grounds for believing that —

        (a)   the detained person has benefited from his criminal conduct, and

        (b)   the recovery of the value of the property constituting the benefit would be hindered if the information were disclosed.

  (3A)   For the purposes of sub-paragraph (3) the question whether a person has benefited from his criminal conduct is to be decided in accordance with Part 2 or 3 of the Proceeds of Crime Act 2002."

Criminal Justice and Police Act 2001 (c. 16)

40   (1) The Criminal Justice and Police Act 2001 is amended as follows.

(2) In section 55 (obligation to return excluded and special procedure material) in subsection (5) (powers in relation to which section does not apply as regards special procedure material) omit "and" after paragraph (b), and after paragraph (c) insert —

"and

    (d)   section 352(4) of the Proceeds of Crime Act 2002,".

(3) In section 60 (cases where duty to secure seized property arises) in subsection (4) (powers in relation to which duty does not arise as regards special procedure material) omit "or" after paragraph (b), and after paragraph (c) insert —

"or

    (d)   section 352(4) of the Proceeds of Crime Act 2002,".

(4) In section 64 (meaning of appropriate judicial authority) in subsection (3) after paragraph (a) omit "and" and insert —

"(aa)   the power of seizure conferred by section 352(4) of the Proceeds of Crime Act 2002, if the power is exercisable for the purposes of a civil recovery investigation (within the meaning of Part 8 of that Act);".

(5) In section 65 (meaning of "legal privilege") —

    (a)   in subsection (1)(b) for the words "33 of the Criminal Law (Consolidation) (Scotland) Act 1995 (c. 39)" substitute "412 of the Proceeds of Crime Act 2002";

    (b)   after subsection (3) insert —

        "(3A)   In relation to property which has been seized in exercise, or purported exercise, of —

            (a)   the power of seizure conferred by section 352(4) of the Proceeds of Crime Act 2002, or

            (b)   so much of any power of seizure conferred by section 50 as is exercisable by reference to that power,

        references in this Part to an item subject to legal privilege shall be read as references to privileged material within the meaning of section 354(2) of that Act."

(6) In Part 1 of Schedule 1 (powers of seizure to which section 50 applies) at the end add —

"Proceeds of Crime Act 2002 (c. 00)

73A   The power of seizure conferred by section 352(4) of the Proceeds of Crime Act 2002 (seizure of material likely to be of substantial value to certain investigations)."

(7) In Part 3 of Schedule 1 (powers of seizure to which section 55 applies) at the end add —

"Proceeds of Crime Act 2002 (c. 00)

110   The power of seizure conferred by section 352(4) of the Proceeds of Crime Act 2002 (seizure of material likely to be of substantial value to certain investigations)."

SCHEDULE 12

REPEALS AND REVOCATIONS

Short title and chapter	Extent of repeal or revocation
Misuse of Drugs Act 1971 (c. 38)	In section 21 the words "or section 49 of the Drug Trafficking Act 1994".
	In section 23(3A) the words "or section 49 of the Drug Trafficking Act 1994".
Criminal Appeal (Northern Ireland) Act 1980 (c. 47)	In section 30(3) the word "and" after paragraph (b).
Police and Criminal Evidence Act 1984 (c. 60)	In section 65 — (a) the definitions of "drug trafficking" and "drug trafficking offence"; (b) the words from "references in this Part" to "in accordance with the Drug Trafficking Act 1994".
Criminal Justice Act 1988 (c. 33)	Sections 71 to 102. In section 151(4) the word "and" after paragraph (a). In section 172 — (a) in subsection (2) the words from "section 76(3)" to "extending to Scotland"; (b) in subsection (4) the words from "sections 90" to "section 93E". Schedule 4.
Housing Act 1988 (c. 50)	In Schedule 17, paragraphs 83 and 84.
Extradition Act 1989 (c. 33)	In section 22(4)(h) the word "and" after sub-paragraph (ii).
Police and Criminal Evidence (Northern Ireland) Order 1989 (S.I. 1989/1341 (N.I. 12))	In Article 53 — (a) the definitions of "drug trafficking" and "drug trafficking offence"; (b) the words from "References in this Part" to "Order 1996".
Criminal Justice (International Co-operation) Act 1990 (c. 5)	In section 13(6) the words "the Drug Trafficking Act 1994 or". Section 14. In Schedule 4, paragraph 1.
Criminal Justice (Confiscation) (Northern Ireland) Order 1990 (S.I. 1990/2588 (N.I. 17))	In Article 37 — (a) paragraph (2); (b) in paragraphs (3) and (4) sub-paragraph (b) and the word "and" before it; (c) paragraph (5).
Criminal Justice Act 1993 (c. 36)	Section 21(3)(e) to (g). Sections 27 to 35. In Schedule 4, paragraph 3. In Schedule 5, paragraph 14.
Criminal Justice and Public Order Act 1994 (c. 33)	In Schedule 9, paragraph 36.

Short title and chapter	Extent of repeal or revocation
Drug Trafficking Act 1994 (c. 37)	Sections 1 to 54. In sections 55(4)(a) and 56(3)(a) and (4)(a) the words "or has benefited from". In section 59, subsections (1) to (10) and in subsection (11) the words "An order under subsection (1) above, and". In section 60(6), in the definition of "specified offence", in paragraph (a) the words "Part III or" and paragraph (c) and the word "or" immediately preceding it. In section 60(6), the words from "and references to the institution of proceedings" to the end. Section 60(7) and (8). Section 61(2) to (4). Sections 62, 63(1), (2) and (3)(a) and 64. In section 68(2), paragraphs (a) to (c) and in paragraph (g) the words "1, 41, 62" and "64". In section 68(3), paragraph (a) and in paragraph (d) the word "64". In Schedule 1, paragraphs 3, 4(a), 8, 21 and 26.
Proceeds of Crime Act 1995 (c. 11)	Sections 1 to 13. Section 15(1) to (3). Section 16(2), (5) and (6). Schedule 1.
Criminal Law (Consolidation) (Scotland) Act 1995 (c. 39)	Part V.
Criminal Procedure (Consequential Provisions) (Scotland) Act 1995 (c. 40)	In Schedule 3, paragraph 4(2). In Schedule 4, paragraphs 69 and 94.
Private International Law (Miscellaneous Provisions) Act 1995 (c. 42)	Section 4(3).
Proceeds of Crime (Scotland) Act 1995 (c. 43)	Part I, except section 2(7). In section 28, subsections (1)(a) and (2) and in subsection (5) the words "(including a restraint order made under and within the meaning of the 1994 Act)". Section 29. In section 31, subsection (2), in subsection (4) the words "or (2)". Sections 35 to 39. In section 40, subsections (1)(a), (2) and (4). In section 42, subsections (1)(a) and (b). In section 43, in subsection (1) the words "confiscation order", subsection (2). Section 45(1)(a). Section 47. In section 49, in subsection (1) the definitions of "the 1988 Act", "the 1994 Act" and "confiscation order" and subsection (4).

Short title and chapter	Extent of repeal or revocation
Proceeds of Crime (Scotland) Act 1995 (c. 43) — *cont.*	In Schedule 1, in paragraph 1, in sub-paragraph (1)(b) the words "or a confiscation order", in sub-paragraph (2)(a) the words "subject to paragraph (b) below", sub-paragraph (2)(b), in sub-paragraph (3)(a)(i) the words "or confiscation order".
	In Schedule 1, in paragraph 2, in sub-paragraph (1)(a) the words ", and if appointed (or empowered) under paragraph 1(1)(b) above where a confiscation order has been made", paragraph 4, in paragraph 5(1) the words "Part I of", in paragraph 8(2) the words from ", unless in a case where a confiscation order has been" to "4(4)(b) above,".
	In Schedule 1, in paragraph 10(1) the words "or the recipient of a gift caught by Part I of this Act or an implicative gift", paragraphs 10(2) and (3), in paragraph 12(1)(a) the words "paragraph (a) or (b) of section 4(1) or".
	In Schedule 2, in paragraph 1(2) the words "and 35 to 38", in paragraph 2(1) the words "realisable or", in paragraph 2(2) the words "and 35 to 38", paragraph 2(5), in paragraph 3(2) the words "and 35 to 38", paragraphs 3(4) and (5), in paragraph 4(2) the words "and 35 to 38", paragraph 6(2)(a).
Proceeds of Crime (Northern Ireland) Order 1996 (S.I. 1996/1299 (N.I. 9))	Parts II and III.
	In Article 2 in paragraph (2) from the definition of "charging order" to the definition of "external confiscation order" and from the definition of "modifications" to the definition of "restraint order" and paragraphs (3) to (10) and (12).
	Article 3.
	In Article 49, in paragraph (1) sub-paragraph (c) and the word "and" immediately preceding it, in paragraph (1A) sub-paragraph (c) and the word "and" immediately preceding it, paragraph (4) and in paragraph (5) the definitions of "customs officer" and "relevant property".
	In Article 52 in paragraph (2) sub-paragraph (b) and the word "and" immediately preceding it, and paragraph (3).
	In Article 54 paragraphs (1) to (10) and (13) and in paragraph (11) the words "An order under paragraph (1) and,".
	In Article 55, in paragraph (6) in the definition of "specified offence" in paragraph (a) the words "Part III or" and paragraph (c) and the word "or" immediately preceding it, and paragraph (7).
	Article 56(2) to (4).

Short title and chapter	Extent of repeal or revocation
Proceeds of Crime (Northern Ireland) Order 1996 (S.I. 1996/1299 (N.I. 9)) — *cont.*	In Schedule 2— (a) in paragraph 1(3) "3 or"; (b) paragraph 3; (c) in paragraphs 4(2), 5(1) and 6(1) "3". In Schedule 3, paragraphs 1 to 3 and 18.
Justices of the Peace Act 1997 (c. 25)	In Schedule 5, paragraphs 23 and 36.
Crime and Punishment (Scotland) Act 1997 (c. 48)	Section 15(3). In Schedule 1, paragraph 20.
Crime and Disorder Act 1998 (c. 37)	Section 83. In Schedule 1, paragraphs 115 and 116. In Schedule 8, paragraph 114. In Schedule 9, paragraph 8.
Access to Justice Act 1999 (c. 22)	In Schedule 2— (a) in paragraph 2(2) the word "or" at the end of paragraph (c); (b) in paragraph 2(3) the word "or" at the end of paragraph (j). In Schedule 13, paragraphs 139 and 172.
Powers of Criminal Courts (Sentencing) Act 2000 (c. 6)	In Schedule 9, paragraphs 105 to 113 and 163 to 173.
Terrorism Act 2000 (c. 11)	In Schedule 15, paragraphs 6, 10 and 11(2).
Criminal Justice and Police Act 2001 (c. 16)	In section 55(5) paragraph (a) and the word "and" after paragraph (b). In section 60(4) paragraph (a) and the word "or" after paragraph (b). In section 64(3) the word "and" after paragraph (a). In Schedule 1, paragraphs 47 and 105.
Financial Investigations (Northern Ireland) Order 2001 (S.I. 2001/1866 (N.I. 1))	Articles 3(2)(b) and 4(1)(a) and (c), (2), (3) and (5).
Land Registration Act 2002 (c. 9)	In Schedule 11, paragraphs 22 and 32.
This Act	Section 248(2)(a) and (4).

© Crown copyright 2002

Printed in the UK by The Stationery Office Limited
under the authority and superintendence of Carol Tullo, Controller of
Her Majesty's Stationery Office and Queen's Printer of Acts of Parliament

Short title and chapter	Extent of repeal or revocation
Proceeds of Crime (Northern Ireland) Order 1996 (S.I. 1996/1299 (N.I. 9)) — cont.	In Schedule 2— (a) in paragraph 1(3) "3.0?", (b) paragraph 3, (c) in paragraphs 4(2), 5(1) and 6(1) "32". In Schedule 3, paragraphs 1 to 3 and 18. In Schedule 5, paragraphs 29 and 36.
Justices of the Peace Act 1997 (c. 25)	
Crime and Punishment (Scotland) Act 1997 (c. 48)	Section 15(3). In Schedule 1 paragraph 20.
Crime and Disorder Act 1998 (c. 37)	Section 83. In Schedule 7, paragraphs 115 and 116. In Schedule 8, paragraph 174. In Schedule 9, paragraph 8.
Access to Justice Act 1999 (c. 22)	In Schedule 2— (a) in paragraph 2(2) the word "or" at the end of paragraph (c); (b) in paragraph 2(3) the word "or" at the end of paragraph (f). In Schedule 13, paragraphs 1-8 and 172.
Powers of Criminal Courts (Sentencing) Act 2000 (c. 6)	In Schedule 9, paragraphs 105 to 119 and 162 to 173.
Terrorism Act 2000 (c. 11)	In Schedule 15, paragraphs 6, 10 and 11(2).
Criminal Justice and Police Act 2001 (c. 16)	In section 55(3) paragraph (a) and the word "and" after paragraph (b). In section 60(6) paragraph (a) and the word "or" after paragraph (b). In section 64(3) the word "and" after paragraph (a). In Schedule 1, paragraphs 47 and 105.
Financial Investigations (Northern Ireland) Order 2001 (S.I. 2001/1866 (N.I. 1))	Articles 3(2)(b) and 3(4)(a) and (c), (2), (3) and (5).
Land Registration Act 2002 (c. 9)	In Schedule 11, paragraphs 29 and 32.
This Act	Section 248(2)(a) and (3).

© Crown copyright 2002

Printed in the UK by The Stationery Office Limited
under the authority and superintendence of Carol Tullo, Controller of
Her Majesty's Stationery Office and Queen's Printer of Acts of Parliament.